CAREY'S
R A D O

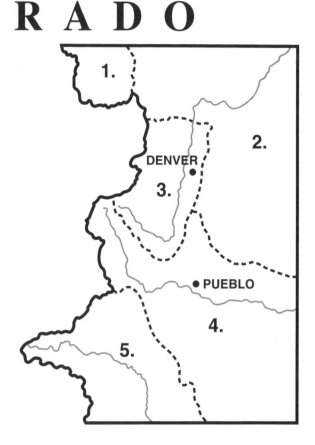

1. **NORTH PLATTE RIVER / LARAMIE RIVER**

2. **CACHE LA POUDRE / ROCKY MOUNTAIN NATIONAL PARK / NORTHEAST COLORADO**

3. **SOUTH PLATTE / FRONT RANGE**

4. **ARKANSAS RIVER /SOUTHEAST COLORADO**

5. **RIO GRANDE RIVER**

KIP CAREY'S

OFFICIAL
COLORADO
FISHING
GUIDE

KIP CAREY
PUBLICATIONS
LITTLETON, COLORADO

KIP CAREY'S OFFICIAL COLORADO FISHING GUIDE

ORIGINATED AS TIM KELLEY'S FISHING GUIDE IN 1954

NINETEENTH EDITION

KIP CAREY
Editor and Publisher

JILL CAREY
SUZZETTE RUMMELL
Associate Editors

DENNIS AGREN
DANA AGREN
Technical Assistance
www.dlaconsulting.com

ISBN 0-970736-20-7
Copyright © Kip Carey Publications 2001
6732 West Coal Mine Ave. #230
Littleton, Colorado 80123
www.fishingcolowyo.com

DEDICATION

This book is dedicated to all the special people who have helped make this book possible. For my children, Zac, Caleb, and Mollie, who have shown so much excitement for this book. For my mother who believes in me and tells me, "all things are possible". And for my father who taught me how to catch brookies when I was five with bait holder spinners on Willow Creek. My sister, Suzzette for never doubting the possibilities, and who has always stuck up for me and protected me. And special thanks to Kevin (although he did out fish me one time on the Eagle River). My sister Sandi and my brother Steve, thank you for your support.

My special dedication goes to my loving wife, Jill. I could not accomplish anything in life without her. I cherish her support, her insight, and her sense of humor. Enduring my late hours, my countless time sitting at the computer and who knows how many minutes on the phone, proves that I am blessed she is my wife.

ACKNOWLEDGEMENTS

Thanks to God's grace, and the church family of Rejoice Christian Fellowship for their continual prayers for this project. I wish to acknowledge the following for without whose help this book would not be. To Dennis and Dana Agren, who provided technical support when it was most needed. And to Dan Bankson, who proves that fishing friends are friends for life.

I wish to acknowledge Tim Kelley and the countless people who have worked on the completion of the previous eighteen editions of this guide.

Table of Contents

PREFACE 1
COLD WATER FISH OF COLORADO 2
WARM WATER FISH OF COLORADO 11
COLORADO'S RECORD FISH 21
GOLD MEDAL WATERS 22
WILD TROUT WATERS 24
NOTES TO READERS 26

NORTH PLATTERIVER/ LARAMIE RIVER
NORTH PLATTE RIVER INTRODUCTION 31
    LOWER NORTH PLATTE (GOLD MEDAL) 32
    CANADIAN RIVER 33
    MICHIGAN RIVER 34
    ILLINOIS RIVER 35
    NORTH FORK NORTH PLATTE RIVER 35
    LAKE JOHN 37
    DELANEY BUTTE LAKES 37
    SEYMOUR LAKE 39
    LITTLE GRIZZELY DRAINAGE 39
    BIG CREEK 42
LARIMIE RIVER INTRODUCTION 44
    CHAMBERS LAKE 44
    RAHAW WILDERNESS 45
    RAHAW LAKES 47
    CAMP LAKES AREA 48
    HOHNHOLZ STATE WILDLIFE AREA 50

CACHE LA POUDRE/ ROCKY MOUNTAIN
NATIONAL PARK/ NORTHEAST COLORADO
CACHE LA POUDRE INTRODUCTION 53
    HORSETOOTHE RESERVOIR 55
    WATSON LAKE 55
    LOWER CACHE LA POUDRE RIVER 56
    NORTH FORK CACHE LA POUDRE 56
    RED FEATHERS LAKES AREA 57
    SOUTH FORK CACHE LA POUDRE RIVER 60
    CACHE LA POUDRE RIVER 62
    LONG DRAW RESERVOIR 63
    JOE WRIGHT RESERVOIR 63
    POUDRE HEADWATERS 64
ROCKY MOUNTAIN NATIONAL
  PARK INTRODUCTION 65
    RMNP PROTECTED WATERS 66
    NORTH ST. VRAIN CREEK DRAINAGE 67
    BIG THOMPSON RIVER 68
    FALL AND ROARING RIVERS 70
    WESTERN SIDE OF PARK 71
NORTHEAST COLORADO INTRODUCTION 72
    CARTER LAKE 74
    LONETREE LAKE 74
    BOYD LAKE 74
    FORT COLLINS AREA 75
    JACKSON RESERVOIR 77
    NORTH STERLING RESERVOIR 77
    JUMBO RESERVOIR 78
    BONNY RESERVOIR 78

SOUTH PLATTE/FRONT RANGE

SOUTH PLATTE INTRODUCTION 81
    JEFFERSON LAKE 81
    TARRYALL RESERVOIR 83
    MIDDLE FORK SOUTH PLATTE 85
    SOUTH FORK SOUTH PLATTE 85
    ANTERO RESERVOIR 86
    SPINNEY MOUNTAIN RESERVOIR 86
    ELEVENMILE RESERVOIR 88
    CHEESEMAN RESERVOIR 91
    WATERTON CANYON 94
    STRONTIA SPRINGS RESERVOIR 95
    NORTH FORK 95
    GENEVA CREEK 97
    CHATFIELD RESERVOIR 101
    BEAR CREEK RESERVOIR 102
    CHERRY CREEK RESERVOIR 102
    QUINCY RESERVOIR 103
    AURORA RESERVOIR 103
    FRONT RANGE SUBURBS 104
    BOULDER AREA 105
    LONGMONT AREA 105
FRONT RANGE INTRODUCTION 106
    CLEAR CREEK 106
    FALL RIVER 107
    GEORGETOWN LAKE 109
    SOUTH FORK CLEAR CREEK 109
    BEAR CREEK 109
    SOUTH BOULDER CREEK 110
    GROSS RESERVOIR 111
    MIDDLE BOULDER CREEK 112
    SOUTH FORK MIDDLE BOULDER CREEK 113
    NORTH BOULDER CREEK 114
    SOUTH ST. VRAIN CREEK 115
    BRAINARD LAKE 115
    MIDDLE ST. VRAIN CREEK 116
    LAKE ESTES 117

ARKANSAS RIVER INTRODUCTION 119
    LEADVILLE AREA 119
    TURQUOISE LAKE 120
    TWIN LAKES RESERVOIR 123
    CLEAR CREEK 124
    COTTONWOOD LAKE 126
    CHALK CREEK 128
    SOUTH FORK ARKANSAS RIVER 130
    SANGRE DE CRISTOS AREA 132
    DEWEESE RESERVOIR 133
    COLONY LAKES 135
    PIKES PEAK REGION 135
    WET MOUNTAINS 137
    BRUSH HOLLOW RESERVOIR 138
    PUEBLO RESERVOIR 139
SOUTHEAST COLORADO INTRODUCTION 140
    PUEBLO AREA 140
    HENERY RESERVOIR 141
    HOLBROOK RESERVOIR 141
    JOHN MARTIN RESERVOIR 144

NEE GRONDA, NEE NOSHE,
    NEE SKAH RESERVOIRS 145
HUERFANO RIVER 146
LATHOP STATE PARK 148
NORTH FORK PURGATORIE RIVER 149
TRINADAD RESERVOIR 149

RIO GRANDE RIVER
RIO GRANDE RIVER INTRODUCTION 151
UPPER RIO GRANDE RIVER 153
UTE CREEK 155
CONTIENTAL RESERVOIR 157
SOUTHERN TRIBUTARIES 160
CREEDE AREA 161
DEL NORTE AREA 167
SAN LUIS VALLEY 168
LA GARITA CREEK 172
ALAMOSA RIVER 172
SMITH RESERVOIR 174
CONEJOS RIVER 175
SOUTH FORK CONEJOS RIVER 178

UPPER COLORADO RIVER/BLUE RIVER
UPPER COLORADO RIVER INTRODUCTION 181
SHADOW MOUNTAIN LAKE 182
GRAND LAKE 182
LAKE GRANBY 183
FRASER RIVER 187
BYERS CANYON 189
WILLIAMS FORK RIVER 189
GORE CANYON 191
DERBY CREEKS 192
DEEP CREEK 196
BLUE RIVER INTRODUCTION 197
UPPER BLUE RIVER 197
DILLION RESERVOIR 199
TENMILE CREEK 200
SNAKE RIVER 201
LOWER BLUE RIVER
    AND EAGLES NEST WILDERNESS 202
GREEN MOUNTAIN RESERVOIR 204
GORE RANGE LAKES 205

EAGLE RIVER/ ROARING FORK RIVER
EAGLE RIVER INTRODUCTION 207
GYPSUM CREEK DRAINAGE 209
BRUSH CREEK DRAINAGE 209
LAKE CREEK DRAINAGE 210
VAIL AREA 211
CROSS CREEK DRAINAGE 215
GOLD PARK AND HOMESTAKE CREEK 216
UPPER EAGLE RIVER 218
ROARING FORK RIVER INTRODUCTION 219
ROARING FORK RIVER 219
CRYSTAL RIVER 220
FRYINGPAN RIVER 224
RUEDI RESERVOIR 225
SOUTH FORK FRYINGPAN RIVER 228
MAROON BELLS/SNOWMASS
    WILDERNESS AREA 228

ASPEN AREA 230
UPPER ROARING FORK AREA 231

YAMPA RIVER/WHITE RIVER
YAMPA RIVER INTRODUCTION 233
STILLWATER RESERVOIR 234
UPPER YAMPA RIVER 234
MANDALL LAKES 235
YAMCOLO RESERVOIR 235
CHAPMAN RESERVOIR 236
STAGECOACH RESERVOIR 238
ELK RIVER 240
STEAMBOAT LAKE 243
ELKHEAD RESERVOIR 245
WILLIAMS FORK RIVER 246
LITTLE SNAKE RIVER DRAINAGE 248
WHITE RIVER INTRODUCTION 250
RIO BLANCO LAKE 253
LAKE AVERY 254
MARVINE CREEK DRAINAGE 254
TRAPPERS LAKE 258
SOUTH FORK WHITE RIVER 261

LOWER COLORADO RIVER/GUNNISON RIVER
LOWER COLORADO INTRODUCTION 263
PLATEAU CREEK DRAINAGE 264
VEGA RESERVOIR 264
GRAND MESA AREA 264
MESA LAKES 266
BULL CREEK RESERVOIRS 266
ISLAND LAKE AREA 268
BATTLEMENT LAKES 268
CARP LAKE 268
WARD LAKE 269
EGGLESTON LAKE 269
PARK RESERVOIR AREA 270
LEON LAKE 270
COTTONWOOD LAKES AREA 272
CANYON CREEK 273
ELK CREEK 274
RIFLE CREEK 275
GUNNISON RIVER INTRODUCTION 276
PURDY MESA RESERVOIR 276
UNCOMPAHGRE RIVER 276
NORTH FORK GUNNISON RIVER 279
SMITH FORK GUNNISON RIVER 280
BLACK CANYON OF THE
     GUNNISON RIVER 282
CRYSTAL RESERVOIR 283
MORROW POINT RESERVOIR 283
CIMARRON RIVER 284
BLUE MESA RESERVOIR 285
NORTH OF BLUE MESA RESERVOIR 287
SOUTH OF BLUE MESA RESERVOIR 288
LAKE SAN CRISTOBAL 289
CEBOLLA CREEK DRAINAGE 291
POWDERHORN CREEK DRAINAGE 293
OHIO CREEK DRAINAGE 293
COCHETOPA CREEK DRAINAGE 295
TOMICHI CREEK 296

QUARTZ CREEK DRAINAGE 297
TAYLOR RIVER 298
TAYLOR RESERVOIR 302
TEXAS CREEK 302
CRESTED BUTTE AREA 306

SOUTHWEST COLORADO
SOUTHWEST COLORADO INTRODUCTION 309
SAN JUAN RIVER 310
NAVAJO RIVER 313
NAVAJO RESERVOIR 313
PIEDRA RIVER 314
LOS PINOS RIVER 316
BIG EMERALD LAKE 317
VALLECITO RESERVOIR 317
ANIMAS RIVER 321
LA PLATA/MANCOS RIVERS 324
DOLORES RIVER 326
WEST FORK DOLORES RIVER 329
SAN MIGUEL RIVER 329
MCPHEE RESERVOIR 333

INDEX 334

PREFACE

It is hard to believe today but once long ago there was a fishing season in Colorado. Yes, fishing was prohibited until the second week in May each year in Colorado. All things change, when I was a youngster the rules changed and fishing became available year round. My father still kept with the time-honored tradition and we would wait with anticipation for that second week in May when the fishing season would officially begin for us. May 16th was our day, my father and I would leave early in the morning for North Park with hopes of finding some open water to fish. Anyone reading this who has been to North Park in early May knows what we found plenty of …remaining and unmelted snow from the winter, and plenty of it. Deep snow banks and high runoff water, in all but a few cases, did not stop us from fighting streamside brush in search of spring brook and brown trout. It was not just the fishing and the beautiful outdoors in Colorado; it was time spent together making memories. Eating wintergreen Lifesavers while shivering in the early morning cold waiting for the fish to start feeding. Eating lunch while sitting on edge of the stream recounting the marvelous fish caught so far. To the disappointment of realizing that it was getting dark and that our fishing day would soon be coming to a close, only to be encouraged knowing there was dinner waiting for us in one of the many small towns on the way home. Knowing that if we were lucky enough on the way home the malt shop in Tabernash would be open for a cherry malt to top the day off.

Growing up in Denver I have had ample opportunities to fish the best Colorado has to offer. I have spent many days on the water in North Park, South Park, the Buena Vista area, and the Eagle and Colorado River valleys. Colorado has so much to offer, I hope reading the pages of this book will give you an idea on where to find your special fishing spots, so get your fishing pole, a kid or a friend and go make some memories of your own. God bless and good fishing.

RECOGNIZING COLORADO'S COLD WATER FISH

RAINBOW TROUT

The rainbow is a native of West Coast streams and was introduced in Colorado in the 1880's. The rainbow is the most popular trout in Colorado, and millions are stocked around the state each year. Rainbows are heavily spotted on the middle and upper body fins and tail. A classic rainbow has a dark back, is heavily spotted, has a silverish side and a light or white belly. They are distinguished by a rose or reddish band running down their sides. Rainbow are an enjoyable fish to catch, they strike hard, usually make a swift run and many times leap out of the water. Brightly colored fly patterns and lures motivate rainbows. Rainbows also feed off the bottom especially in the early mornings and early evenings. Rainbow seek deeper, warmer, swift waters, although rainbows are found in some the very high cold mountain lakes. Larger rainbows are found in lower warmer bodies of water. Rainbows usually seek small headwater streams in the spring to spawn. They will scour into the gravel of a streambed where they deposit 200 to 9,000 eggs. Rainbow can live up to 11 years but most only make it to five years old in Colorado. A **cuttbow** is a cross between a rainbow and a cutthroat. McConaughy, Snake River and Emerald Lake rainbow derive their names from where they were originally transported.

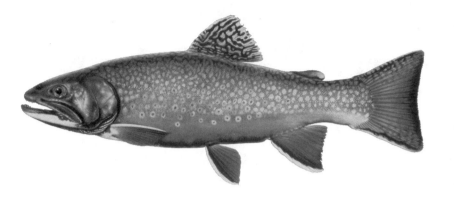

BROOK TROUT

Brook trout, or "brookies", are originally native to the eastern United States. They are now found in almost every part of the country, adapting to even the smallest of streams. Although they are spread throughout Colorado in great numbers, being prolific reproducers, they do reach not reach large sizes in but a few of the states waters. Brookies seldom reach over a half-pound. They differ from other trout mainly in the structure of a tooth bearing bone in the center of the roof of the mouth. Brook trout do not generally put up a great fight when hooked, they usually fight deep and rarely break water. Brook are very greedy and are undoubtedly the easiest of the trout species to lure to bait or a fly. Brook trout are readily distinguished by sides spattered with red and white spots on a background of darker color. It is identified by the pure white leading edge of the lower fins and the mottled "worm track" pattern on the back. Brook trout bellies are a muted orange, during spawning the males bellies turns to a brilliant bright orange. Scales on the brook are numerous, small and deeply embedded, giving the skin a soft, fine textured appearance. They generally like spring-fed lakes and the gravelly bottom of cold-water streams with a moderate current. They are most active in 48-degree water, and cannot survive in water over 68 degrees. Look for the brook near the bottom of eddies, pools, under banks and logs, and behind rocks. In October or November, brook seek cold spring-fed tributaries with gravel bottoms to spawn. The female usually travels upstream leaving nests of 100 to 5,000 eggs in the gravel bottom along the way. Brookies live about 4 years and average 7 to 10 inches.

CUTTHROAT TROUT

The cutthroat trout, also known as native, is the only trout indigenous to the central Rocky Mountains. Three types of cutthroat are native to Colorado, the greenback cutthroat, the Colorado River cutthroat and the Rio Grande cutthroat. Other cutthroat subspecies stocked in Colorado waters are Snake River cutthroat and Yellowstone Cutthroat. In Colorado, with the exception of the endangered greenback cutthroat, pure strains of cutthroat are rare today because hatcheries have interbred the species. The dash of red found between the gills and the body gives the cutthroat its name. Sometimes it is necessary to separate the folds about the gills on the bottom side of the fish to see this feature. Cutthroats often are heavily spotted on a background of lighter color. There may be a reddish wash along the length of the body during spawning season. Cutthroat seem slimier than other trout because their scales are small. Cutthroat-rainbow hybrids are common, identified by having some measure of both the red slash on the throat and the rainbow stripe down the side. Found mostly in the upper stretches of cold, clear streams and mountain lakes, the cutthroat seems to do best in waters not subject to heavy silt. The range of the cutthroat has been greatly reduced throughout the West because most major streams carry a substantial silt load at some time during the year. Competition from other species has helped reduce their numbers as well. Cutthroat head for the bottom when hooked and usually fight hardest when brought in close. Flies and spinning gear are commonly used to catch them. Spawning occurs in spring from April to June, preferring clear headwater streams. They have no success reproducing in lakes without an entering stream.

BROWN TROUT

The brown trout is originally from Europe, the brown trout was introduced into the United States in 1883 and found its way to the Colorado Rockies soon after. Two species were introduced, the Loch Leven, which came from Scotland, and the German brown. These have become hybridized to the point that it is accepted that only this mixed form exists in Colorado. Against a golden-brown background, the brown trout has many dark spots and scattered reddish-orange specks surrounded by faint halos. Despite this, browns lack the vivid coloration of other trout. Their tail usually lacks spots and has a straight back edge from top to bottom. Browns lower fins are a pale yellow to a whitish color. Due to its hardy nature and adaptability browns often survive and flourish in streams in which other trout cannot. They are the more tolerant of high water temperatures and muddy stream conditions of all the trout species. As well, browns seem to thrive in larger bodies of slower water with deep, quiet pools. Unless they are feeding in shallow riffles, browns usually hide in heavy cover, under cut banks or deep pools. Brown trout have earned a reputation for being difficult to catch, particularly in lakes. Anglers tend to catch larger browns at night. The brown, the most predatory of trout, is ordinarily a bottom feeder. It is a shy and wary fish, and, if mature, probably "educated." Seldom does a brown rise a second time for a fly. They are also the least spectacular of the trout to catch because they do not often break water; dart and resist like other trout. When hooked, browns react stubbornly and with little finesse. During spawning, which occurs in the fall, browns prefer headwater streams from 10 to 30 feet wide. Depending on egg size, a female produces 200 to 600 eggs. **Tiger trout** are a cross between a female brown and a male brook trout.

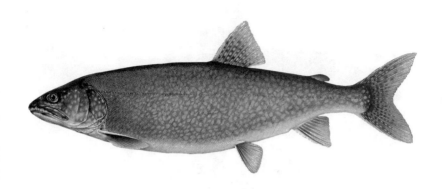

MACKINAW
(LAKE TROUT)

The mackinaw, or lake trout, is found in deeper cold water lakes. It is the largest of all trout, reaching 60 pounds. The "mack" is an excellent food fish, although oilier than other trout. It is so closely related to brook trout that the two have been successfully crossed, resulting in a fish called a splake. A long, slender fish, the mackinaw can be readily identified by its deeply forked tail. Its color varies from gray to almost black with light gray spots. Pelvic and pectoral fins are bordered in light gray. The head is long and flattened with a large, toothy mouth. These fish's eyes are set closer to the top of the head than other trout. Mackinaws spend a great part of the year in deep waters, but there is a period in spring and again during fall spawning season when they move to shallower waters. Small fish make up most of the mature mackinaw's diet, but some mackinaws continue to eat insects throughout their lives. Because it is a cold-water fish, it is slow growing. Mature 6-year-old mackinaws may average 17 inches and 1.5 pounds. Catching the mackinaw requires special planning and equipment. Successful techniques vary, but for deep-water fishing try salmon eggs and sucker meat. Trolling gear usually is regarded as essential. Patience and knowledge of lake temperature stratification and currents help. Mackinaws spawn at age 3 in shallow waters. In October or early November they leave 1500 to 2500 eggs in gravel beds and rocky areas. They tend to be very mobile during this time.

MOUNTAIN WHITEFISH

The mountain whitefish is a native of Colorado found mainly in the Yampa and White rivers. They have been introduced in the Colorado River and the Cache la Poudre drainage. Its weak mouth makes it a difficult fish to hook and land. Although slightly more bony than trout, whitefish are good to eat. Many anglers smoke them. Whitefish are not a very colorful fish, best described as dirty white in color with shadings of silver and a white belly. A patch of a light olive or muted brown my color their sides. The white, soft-fleshed fish cannot be mistaken for trout, but it is sometimes mistaken for a grayling. Whitefish do not have spots on their top dorsal fins, whereas grayling do. The fish's mouth and jaws are very small, requiring the use of very small hook sizes. It can reach 18 inches and 4 pounds. The whitefish lives in fast, clear waters, preferring large rivers with deep pools, riffles, and gravel bottoms. Whitefish largely feed on the bottom at dusk and during the night. Its main diet consists of insects, particularly caddis flies and other larvae. When fishing, try bait or flies, but take care when setting the hook, otherwise it will pull out. Whitefish also make good winter sport for ice anglers. Whitefish spawn in the fall, moving only a short distance from pools and riffles to scour out nests and lay eggs.

GRAYLING

Grayling are a rare gamefish prized for their beauty. The grayling is a favorite of anglers who knows the species. Rising eagerly to the fly, it is not as easily hooked as trout, due partially to its smaller mouth and quick movements. Part of the trout family native to the West Coast they are taken on flies and likely to jump when hooked. It will often dart repeatedly after a fly only to return swiftly to deep water without taking it. Fish using dry or wet flies, nymphs, small spinning lures, and natural bait especially salmon eggs. Grayling are found in a few Colorado waters. In Colorado, they are rarely stocked by the Division of Wildlife, although plans to increase their numbers have been implemented. The grayling can be distinguished by its large, sail-like dorsal fin, patterned with pink and black stripes, and green, orange or pink spots. The males sail like dorsal fin is larger than the females. Its body is grayish to silver with purplish dark spots. Grayling may reach 20 inches and 4 pounds, but most in Colorado do not exceed 1.5 pounds. Usually found in schools, grayling like cool clear lakes and streams with gravelly bottoms. Their principal food is aquatic insects, making fly fishing the most productive way to take them. Grayling will take spinners, bait or other lures. To spawn, grayling migrate to tributary streams from March to June. The female lays about 6,000 eggs. The maximum life span for grayling is about 7 years. They are very slow growing and late to mature.

GOLDEN TROUT

Golden trout are native to the Kerr River in California, and their state fish. The exact date of introduction into Colorado is unknown but is believed to be in the mid 1950's. Golden trout in Colorado are found only in very high, very remote mountain lakes. Because of the limitations on food sources at such high altitudes golden trout in Colorado do not flourish. Golden trout have an olive green back and spots on the upper fin and tail only. They have an orange belly, yellow on their lower sides, and a reddish stripe along the middle of their sides. They are most recognized by the 10 round marks that run down their sides, called parr marks. The tips of their orange lower fins are white. Golden trout feed on small insects, notably caddisflies and midges. The hardest part of catching golden trout in Colorado is getting to them because of their remoteness.

SPLAKE

Splake are a hybrid between a mackinaw and a brook trout. Splake look very similar to brook trout in appearance except they do not have the red spots on their sides surrounded by blue halos. Splake may also exhibit more of the light color spotting on their sides, which is common to mackinaw. Splake grow quicker than mackinaw but do not grow as large.

KOKANEE SALMON

The kokanee salmon is the landlocked cousin of the pacific sockeye salmon. It was introduced to Colorado waters in the early 1950s. Since it inhabits many of the same waters as trout, it is often taken by trout anglers. The kokanee has a few black spots on a rich metallic blue back. Its sides and belly are silvery. During its immature years, it has a weak jaw, and its scales can be removed easily. By the end of its third summer, its jaw becomes stronger. As maturity is reached by mid-fall, the kokanee goes through numerous physical changes as it prepares to spawn. The male kokanee becomes brick red, develops a hump in front of its dorsal fin, a pronounced hook in the lower jaw. The female's color changes to a reddish gray. The number of kokanee inhabiting a given body of water determines their size more so than the food supply. Studies in Colorado show that the kokanee feeds near the surface from dawn to dusk. It drops down about 60 feet or more as night sets in. It feeds mostly on plankton. Kokanee will take flies, but trolling and bait land the bulk of the catch. During the spawning season, mid-September through December, kokanee begin to school and to swim up tributaries to spawn. Snagging is a very popular way to take this fish from October to January. As they look for spawning places they can easily be taken on egg flies. After spawning, kokanee die. Some of the better waters for kokanee include Blue Mesa, Cheesman, Granby, Eleven Mile, Green Mountain and Horsetooth reservoirs, Boyd, Carter and the Grand lake area.

Photo Courtesy of Morrison Angler

Kokanee Salmon - East River

RECOGNIZING COLORADO'S WARM WATER FISH

BLUEGILL

The bluegill, introduced to Colorado in the 1920s, is found in many reservoirs and low elevation streams. This scrappy little fish, also known as bream, fights deep, swimming at right angles to a rod. Pound for pound, it may well be the most sporting of freshwater fish, especially on light tackle. Known for both tenacity and an appetite limited to anything handy, bluegills are best caught in the morning or evening using light terminal tackle ranging from a cork and worm on a hook to delicate dry flies. When one bluegill is located, others are usually near by. As summer heat becomes extreme, bluegills move into deeper water and shady weed beds. Bluegill vary in coloration, but are distinguished from other sunfish relatives by the 6 to 8 vertical bars on its sides, long black earflap that has no trim and a black spot on the posterior of the dorsal fin. The maximum length is usually 12 inches weighing about one pound. Bluegill primarily feed on insects, but, when available, fish eggs or smaller fish are also a part of its diet. They tend to live and feed in shallower waters, close to shore. They are rather easy to catch and take wet or dry flies, worms, grasshoppers or other live baits. Spawning season for bluegill is from late spring through August. Closely related and very similar in looks and characteristics are **green sunfish**, **hybrid bluegill**, **Sacramento** and the brightly colored **pumpkinseed.**

CRAPPIE

Crappie were introduced to Western waters in the 1880's and now is abundant in low elevation Colorado waters. It is tolerant of warm, muddy waters. White crappies have silvery-olive sides shading into olive green on its back with eight to nine dark, vertical side bands. It usually has six distinguishing dorsal fin spines. Black crappie look very similar to white crappie except they have black spots or blotches on their sides, and more spines in their fins. White crappies are more prevalent than the closely related black crappie. In large reservoirs, crappie reach 9 to 12 inches at the mature age of 4. Crappies are attracted to submerged brushy, weedy, rocky areas. Dams of most reservoirs are favorite areas of concentration. In deep water, crappie seeks irregular bottom areas, rock ledges or other types of cover where they feed on smaller fish, competing directly with black bass. During summer, crappies are usually found in depths of 15 to 25 feet. Small jigs cast around submerged brush piles is an effective way to catch them. Flies or poppers fished at dusk are also reliable. Trolling or drifting with minnows in the spring is a favorite technique for catching crappie. A bobber with a small live minnow hung 5 to 8 feet below the surface is a popular method. A pork-rind hanging a foot or so below the surface often produces as well. Crappie spawn in spring, generally in water 3 to 8 feet deep. They prefer spawning sites near brush piles, stumps or rock outcroppings. John Martin, Pueblo and Brush Hollow reservoirs are good choices for crappie anglers.

YELLOW PERCH

Yellow perch, sometimes call ring perch, have adapted well to Colorado's lower elevation fluctuating reservoirs. It is most at home in a lake environment, but can be found in some slow moving streams. Yellow perch tend to overproduce and large fish are usually not caught. Perch rarely exceed more than 12 inches or weigh more than one pound. Young perch prefer shallows while adults prefer deeper waters. They are a favorite food of larger walleyes. Yellow perch have a white belly and golden-yellow to olive-green sides with 6 to 8 evenly spaced dark stripes. Spawning males have bright reddish-orange lower fins. They live in large schools, spending the entire day in deep waters, moving to shore to feed in the late afternoon or evening. Yellow perch are not picky eaters and will eat anything that moves. Foods include aquatic insects, clams, snails and even its own young. Small flies and spinners or natural bait fished a foot or two off the bottom are time-proven techniques. During summer, worms are often the most productive bait. If possible, fish shaded areas giving a worm some action. Large perch are often taken by trolling lures slowly near the bottom. Winter ice fishing can produce good catches, often with larger fish. When ice fishing, seek out the deepest areas of the lake. But, since the fish continue to move during winter it may be necessary to drill several holes before finding a school. A small minnow fished near the bottom is the best bet. Yellow perch spawn in spring at age three. Eggs are laid in gobs attached by ribbons to bottom vegetation. In reservoirs without rooted vegetation, eggs are laid on the bottom, drifting with water motion.

SMALL AND LARGEMOUTH BASS

The large mouth bass was the first fish introduced into Colorado in the late 1800s. The largemouth bass is the largest member of the sunfish family. It gets its name from its upper jawbone, which extends under and behind the eye. The smallmouth bass, introduced into Colorado in 1951, differs from the largemouth in that its upper jaw extends to a point under the middle of the eye. The largemouth has a lustrous yellow-green body laced with dark horizontal bars. The average Colorado largemouth is 12 to 18 inches long and weighs about 3 to 4 pounds, larger ones can weigh over 10 pounds. The smallmouth bass is a golden-bronze or copper color with dark vertical bars and weighs 1 to 2 pounds. Bass are most often found in shallow, weedy lakes with soft bottoms and sparse vegetation. Young bass feed mainly on plankton; but, as it matures, its diet changes to fish, crayfish, frogs, tadpoles and larger insects. Spring is one of the best seasons for bass fishing. Work the shorelines and shallows that have shade. Try to lure them from beneath fallen trees, lily pads and boat docks. Smallmouth are attracted to rocky areas. Bass will strike throughout the day, but early morning and evening fishing is better. Bait casting and spinning are the most widely used methods for catching bass. A wide assortment of artificial lures can be used. Although bass stay deep in the summer, they lurk around submerged objects and can be caught by fishing deep with live minnows, crayfish or frogs. Most bass anglers prefer to work the shores, but many bass are taken from boats by casting toward the shore and retrieving towards the boat. Bass build nests for spawning in late May or early June. Other bass stocked in Colorado include **white**, **striped**, **rock**, and **spotted bass**.

WALLEYE

The walleye is the largest member of the North American perch family. Walleye are primarily only found in very large reservoirs. The walleye varies in color depending on where it is found, but it is usually has a light colored belly which blends into an olive green on the sides and back. The back is crossed with 6-7 narrow dark bands. Markings on the tail and dorsal fin differentiate the walleye from its close relative, the sauger. Walleye dorsal fins have no defined rows or spots, and its tail has a silver or milky colored white tip. Distinctive characteristics include well-developed canine teeth and large eyes with milky white corneas, thus their name. Their eyes are extremely sensitive to light, so they seeks out cool, dimly lit waters during the day. At night it will prowl the shallows in search of food. Walleye can vary in length depending on the character of the water. Mature fish (about 2 years old) are usually more than 12 inches long. Walleye can obtain weights over 10 pounds. Walleye are schooling fish that stay near the bottom in both deep and shallow waters. It forages for food around sandy bars and rocky reefs and often frequents the waters off dams, particularly where lots of small fish are found. Walleyes are primarily fish eaters but also eat crayfish, frogs and snails. Trolling for walleye with artificial lures or lures combined with live and cut bait produce well. Casting with lures and live bait off sandbars and rocky reefs also gets results. Use deep and medium running lures about 6 to 18 inches off the bottom. Shortly after ice-out in early spring, walleye find a shallow, gravelly area or rocky reef to spawn. Both male and female walleye move around at this time and may be taken near the spawning areas.

NORTHERN PIKE

The northern pike is a fierce-looking predator that eats other fish up to one-half its own size and may grow 15 inches in one year. Stocking this aggressive predator since 1956 in several plains and mountain reservoirs has possibly made Colorado second only to Minnesota for big-pike fishing in the lower 48 states. Pike were originally stocked in mountain reservoirs to control heavy populations of suckers. This management tact appears to have backfired with the discovery that pike prefer small trout and kokanee salmon. Pike feed only during daylight hours. The northern pike has a long-tapered body and pointed nose lined with needle-sharp teeth. It has light-green sides marked with white or pale yellow spots and a white or yellow belly. A mature pike weighs 5 to 20 pounds or more; pike are one of the fastest growing freshwater fish. Northern pike are a popular because of their size and the hard fight they put up when hooked. Pike seek shallow (1-5 ft) water with abundant vegetation during most of the year; however, they move into deeper waters during extremely warm or cold weather. The pike is attracted to weedy or grassy areas. The best time to hook a northern is right after the ice recedes from shorelines in reservoirs - usually early June. Trollers working rocky points and edges of weed beds take pike on big spoons and plugs. Weedless hooks and snag-resistant gear is preferred. A steel leader is also a must to combat the mouth full of sharp teeth. Northern pike spawn immediately after the ice leaves the reservoir. Short, dense vegetation is preferred for egg laying.

TIGER MUSKIE

The tiger muskie is a cross between the northern pike and muskellunge, and incorporates the most desirable of its parents' characteristics. Like muskellunge, tiger muskies can potentially grow to be huge fish. They have the savage nature of the northern, making it easier to entice to a lure. Tigers go after bait with the intensity of a pike, and go airborne, fighting like the muskie. Introduced into Colorado in 1983, they have also found a home in the same reservoirs as wipers. Tigers resemble muskies more than pike. The northern generally has horizontal rows of dots along its lengthy body. The tiger and muskie have vertical markings but the tiger's are more distinctive, giving it a tiger-like striping. The general color is olive-green with yellowish-white mottling. As a hybrid, it is sterile and does not spawn. Fishing techniques that work for pike also work for tigers. Sharp teeth necessitate the need for fish with a steel leader. This fish prefers water 15 feet deep or less, with underwater vegetation and many weeds. Tigers use the same weed patches, pockets and brush piles pike and largemouth bass prefer. Large lures, spoons and spinner baits get their attention. The Colorado Division of Wildlife imposes a statewide 30-inch minimum on tigers, which equates to an 8 to 12-pound fish.

CATFISH

The channel catfish, a native of eastern Colorado, is stocked in warm-water rivers and reservoirs in other parts of the state. Night fishing provides the best sport. A variety of bottom bait - night crawlers, minnows, crayfish, chicken innards and flavored dough balls - all work well. Many anglers will let this wary, flavorful fish run several seconds on an open bail before setting the hook. The channel catfish has a forked tail and is greenish-colored with small irregular dark spots. It has a gray or dusky-brown spine. Channel catfish over 50 pounds have been caught, but few weigh over 20 pounds. Most channel cats weigh less than 5 pounds. Channel cats are attracted to muddy bottoms; however, they also frequent areas containing heavy vegetation. The crayfish is the choice item on the channel catfish diet, but it also feeds on minnows. Generally, channel catfish forage at night. Anglers who expect to take them on a regular basis must fish well into the night. In reservoirs, the channel cat tends to concentrate in midsections of deep, narrow bays. Its highly developed sense of smell draws it to rotting chicken innards, a variety of cheeses or licorice-flavored dough balls. Most eastern Colorado, impoundments contain good populations of channel cats. Other varieties of catfish found in Colorado include **blue catfish** and several species of **bullhead catfish**.

WIPER

The wiper, a cross between a white bass and striped bass, was created by the game and fish departments of Tennessee and South Carolina. The first offspring were introduced to Cherokee Lake in Tennessee, then introduced to Colorado in 1982. The wiper's attraction is that it grows larger and more rapidly than a white bass. It is easier to harvest and is better table fare than the striped bass. They've earned a reputation as determined fighters. The wiper is similar in marking to the striped bass. It is a silvery-white fish with distinctive spotted lateral lines. A darker gray tail, spine and fins are indicative of the species. Six to seven pounds are common for mature fish. Basically sterile, wipers go through a ceremonial spawning in spring, when they seek moving water. Their primary diet consists of gizzard shad and other small fish. Find shad, and wipers should be nearby. Anglers often seek surface activity, where gizzard shad are breaking the surface, attempting to escape schooled wipers beneath them. Wipers are more of an open-water fish, not dependent on structure. Jigs, spoons and shad-imitation baits cast into a school of shad get the best results. Trolling through these schools is often productive. In spring and fall, wipers are found in shallower water, deep water in summer.

SAUGER

Saugers are closely related to walleye and are found only in large bodies of water. Sauger will not survive in smaller bodies of water, no one is quite sure why. Sauger are savage fighters, mature fish average 1 to 2 pounds. This fish plies open waters looking for smaller fish to eat, almost only feeding at night. The sauger closely resembles the walleye in appearance but has a white belly that turns into an olive green color mixed with a muted yellow on its sides and back. Three to four darker patches run over the fishes back and down its sides. Saugers upper fins have rows of dark spots; the tail may have some spots present. The white belly runs all the way down to the tip of the tail, but does not form a white tip, as does the walleye. Sauger eyes are sensitive and glassy in appearance, and are found in deeper water during daylight hours. A **saugeye** is a cross between a sauger and walleye.

COLORADO RECORD FISH

SPECIES	YEAR	LOCATION	WT (LBS.-OZ.)	LENGTH (INCHES)
TROUT				
RAINBOW	1972	SOUTH PLATTE RIVER	18-5.25	32
BROOK	1947	MIDDLE CATARACT LAKE	7-10	N/A
BROWN	1988	ROARING JUDY PONDS	30-8	36.4
CUTTHROAT	1964	TWIN LAKES	16-0	N/A
MACKINAW	1998	BLUE MESA	38-6.5	39.5
SPLAKE	1976	ISLAND LAKE	18-15	32
TIGER	1999	PRIVATE POND, YAMPA	3-5	20
GOLDEN	1979	KELLY LAKE	3-12	22.5
GRAYLING	1974	ZIMMERMAN LAKE	1-7	15
WHITEFISH	1982	ROARING FORK RIVER	5-2	18.75
KOKANEE	1986	SPINNEY MTN. RES.	6-13	27.5
SUNFISH				
BLUEGILL	1988	HOLLENBECK RES.	2-4	11.5
GREEN	1997	BIG THOMPSON POND	1-5	11.2
HYBRID	1986	GRAVEL PIT, LARIMER CO	1-8.5	1035
CRAPPIE				
BLACK	1990	PRIVATE POND, LA PLATA	3-4	17
WHITE	1975	NORTHGLENN LAKE	4-3	17
BASS				
SMALLMOUTH	1993	NAVAJO RESERVOIR	5-12	21
LARGEMOUTH	1997	ECHO CANYON RES.	11-6	22.5
WIPER	1996	NEE NOSHE RESERVOIR	23-15	34
PERCH				
SACRAMENTO	1974	BANNER LAKES	1-14	13.25
YELLOW	1993	GRAVEL PIT, LARIMER CO.	2-5	12.5
WALLEYE	1907	STANLEY LAKE	18-13	34
SAUGER	1980	CF& I RES. #3	3-1	20.5
SAUGEYE	1999	JOHN MARTIN RESERVOIR	7-9	26.25
PIKE				
NORTHERN	1996	WILLIAMS FORK RES.	30-6	43.5
TIGER MUSKIE	1994	QUINCY RESERVOIR	40-2	53
CATFISH				
CHANNEL	1994	HERTHA RESERVOIR	33-9	38.25
BLUE	1976	POND, LINCOLN CO.	20-4	32.75
BULLHEAD	1993	POND, DELTA CO.	5-1	23

COLORADO'S GOLD MEDAL WATERS

Fisheries designated as Gold Medal Waters categorize Colorado's finest trout streams. The Colorado Division of Wildlife manages Gold Medal Waters to maximize opportunities for catching large trout. Each watershed must have the highest quality aquatic habitat, a high percentage of fish 14 inches or longer and the greatest potential for trophy trout fishing and angling success to qualify as "Gold Medal." They also include some of the states most scenic and relaxing places. Of the 6,000 miles of trout streams in the state, only 161 miles are designated Gold Medal.

Animas River from Lightner Creek to the Purple Cliffs. Browns are most common (12-17 inches) in this portion of the Animas River.

Blue River downstream from Dillon Reservoir to the confluence with the Colorado River (34 miles) south of Kremmling, paralleling Hwy 9. Rainbows (10-14 inches) and browns (10-17 inches) are common fare on the Blue.

Colorado River from Windy Gap to the confluence with Troublesome Creek, about 3 miles east of Kremmling. US 40 parallels this portion of the Colorado. Both browns and rainbows (16-21 inches) are taken in the Colorado.

Fryingpan River from Reudi Reservoir Dam downstream to the confluence with the Roaring Fork River, which occurs near Basalt on Hwy 82 (14 miles). A catch-and-release four miles below Reudi Reservoir has rainbows in the 12- to 15-pound range. Browns and rainbows (12-17 inches) are found in the remaining ten miles of Frying Pan's Gold Medal Water.

Gore Creek from Red Sandstone Creek downstream 4 miles to its confluence with the Eagle River near Vail on Interstate 70. Browns are the most highly prized of Gore Creek's four species.

Gunnison River from the upstream boundary of the Black Canyon of the Gunnison National Monument to its confluence with the North Fork of the Gunnison River, lower section is most accessible from Hwy 92 east of Delta, and the upper section from US 50 east of Montrose. Rainbows and browns (16-25 inches) are common in the Gunnison.

North Delaney Butte Lake is approximately 10 miles west of Walden. North Delaney Butte Lake is an extremely productive lake that grows trophy browns.

North Platte River from the Routt National Forest boundary downstream to the Colorado/Wyoming state line, about 5.3 miles, is Gold Medal Water. Brown trout predominate, but rainbows are also caught. It is reached via Hwy 125 north of Walden.

Rio Grande River from the Farmer's Union Canal upstream 22.5 miles to the upper boundary of the Coller State Wildlife area. Paralleled most of the way by US 160 west of Del Norte. Browns (14-18 inches) and smaller brook, rainbow and cutthroat are possible.

Roaring Fork River from the confluence with the Crystal River downstream to the confluence with the Colorado River, and parallels Hwy 82 from Carbondale to Glenwood Springs (12 miles). The browns and rainbows (12-18 inches) mix with mountain whitefish (2-3 pounds) through this stretch.

The **South Platte River** has 4 areas that are designated Gold Medal Waters. The first is the Middle Fork downstream from US 285 and the South Fork downstream from the outlet of Antero to the inlet of Spinney Mountain Reservoir. The second is from the outlet of Spinney Mountain downstream to the inlet of Elevenmile Reservoir. These portions are best served by US 24 and Hwy 9 near Hartsel. The third Gold Medal area runs from Cheesman Dam downstream to the Wigwam Club, and the last from the lower boundary of the Wigwam Club to Scraggy View picnic ground. This area is accessible from Hwy 67 near Deckers. Together, they form 45 miles of Gold Medal Waters. Huge browns, rainbows and cutthroats (5-12 pounds) are found in the stretches near Spinney Mountain. The 3-mile section below Cheesman Dam has more than 700 pounds of fish per surface acre, primarily rainbows (15-22 inches).

Spinney Mountain Reservoir, about 2000 acres when full, has exceptional fishing for cutthroat, brown and rainbow, as well as kokanee salmon and northern pike. Access is the same as for the Gold Medal section of the South Platte.

The Colorado Division of Wildlife manages its Gold Medal Waters by using a variety of techniques that maintain and upgrade populations of large trout. Stocking is used in some waters, while others support a mostly naturally reproducing population. The Division has acquired public access leases in many of its Gold Medal locations and works closely with federal agencies and private landowners to improve public access. Permission is necessary to enter Gold Medal waters on all private property. If public access is not clearly indicated, please ask first.

Central to the Gold Medal program are special regulations that ensure populations of bigger fish. Bag and possession limits vary, check each listing for further details. Fishing is by artificial flies and lures only. Reducing the harvest and the hooking mortality rates allows the trout to grow to larger than average sizes and perhaps be caught several times. Trout are delicate out of their natural element, so try to minimize the time spent in handling them out of the water. Avoid squeezing their stomachs or gill areas when you intend to release them. Place them in the water and allow the fish to swim away; don't toss them back in.

COLORADO'S WILD TROUT WATER

Selected trout lakes and streams are managed by the Division of Wildlife for the production of wild trout and are, therefore, not stocked with hatchery fish. Wild trout waters total nearly 150 miles of streams and 566 surface acres of lakes in Colorado. These trout, raised entirely within the natural environment, afford an opportunity for anglers to experience the challenge of catching wild trout. Fishing is by artificial flies and lures only, the bag and possession limits vary, check each listing for further details. Many are catch and release. These waters are subject to change, and new waters may be added, check the latest copy of the Colorado fishing regulations for further information. Permission is necessary to fish wild trout waters on private property. Many of these wild trout waters are also Gold Medal waters as well. The following list describes waters that have received this special designation.

Blue River from Green Mountain Reservoir Dam downstream (2.5 miles).

Cache la Poudre River from Black Hollow creek upstream to and including Big Bend Campground (5.7 miles). From Pingee Park Road bridge upstream to the west boundary of Hombre Ranch just below Rustic (5.2 miles).

Cascade Creek six miles east of Cumbres Pass from its headwaters to the confluence with Rio De Los Pinos (2.5 miles) alongside the Cumbres and Toltec Railroad.

Cochetopa Creek within the Cochetopa (Coleman) State Wildlife Area, 38 miles southeast of Gunnison on Hwy 114 (4.5 miles).

Colorado River from the upper end of Gore Canyon downstream to the town of State Bridge (16 miles).

Conejos River from the Menkhaven Ranch downstream to the Aspen Glade (Forest Service) campground (4 miles).

East River (Gunnison County) from Roaring Judy Fish Hatchery downstream for one mile.

Emerald Lake located in the Weminuche Wilderness area (279 acres) on the Lake Creek tributary of the Los Pinos River.

Fraser River from one mile below the town of Tabernash downstream to one mile above the town of Granby (5 miles).

Gunnison River from the upper boundary of the Black Canyon of the Gunnison National Monument downstream to the confluence with the North Fork of the Gunnison (26 miles).

Lake Fork of the Conejos from the headwaters to the natural dam at the outlet of Rock Lake (3 miles).

Laramie River within the Hohnholz Lakes State Wildlife Area (2.5 miles) along Hwy 10 just south of the Wyoming border.

Los Pinos Creek within the Cochetopa (Coleman) State Wildlife Area (2 miles); 10 miles west of North Pass on Hwy 114.

Middle Fork South Platte River within the Tomahawk State Wildlife Area (3 miles).

North Platte River from the Routt National Forest boundary downstream to the Colorado/Wyoming State lines (5.3 miles).

North St. Vrain Creek from the confluence with Horse Creek downstream to Button Rock Reservoir (8.5 miles).

Osier Creek seven miles east of Cumbres Pass from the headwaters to the confluence with Rio De Los Pinos, same vicinity as Cascade Creek (2 miles).

Roaring Fork River from the Hallum Lake in the town of Aspen downstream to Woody Creek Bridge (7 miles).

South Platte River from the confluence with Beaver Creek downstream to the South Platte Arm gauging station, 0.2 mile above Cheesman Lake (9 miles). And from Cheesman Reservoir Dam downstream to the Wigwam Club (3 miles).

Tarryall Creek from the confluence with the South Platte River upstream to the Pike National Forest boundary (3 miles).

Trappers Lake located in the White River National Forest, Flat Tops Wilderness Area (200 acres), 40 miles east of Meeker.

Photo Courtesy of the Morrison Angler

Catch and release

NOTES TO THE READERS

I hope everyone finds this guide useful and practical. The following information should be helpful in answering questions about the guide.

MAPS - While there are reference maps in the Guide, you are encouraged to augment them with maps appropriate for your planned activity. A highway map is adequate if you intend to stay on the main roads, but a national forest map is recommended if you plan to venture off the blacktop. Make sure you have the current edition (available at www.parks.state.co.us or 303-866-3437). Many roads have been closed, new ones constructed and use restrictions have been imposed in numerous areas. If your plans involve hiking into the backcountry, a USGS topographic (topo) map is recommended. The 7.5-minute map shows the most detail, but the 15-minute county map series is adequate and requires fewer maps to cover a large area (available at www.mapmart.com or 303-759-5050). Be advised of changes, mostly roads, may have been made since the map was printed. Many roads have been closed and routes of others have changed. Best to use the USFS maps for roads. Several quality retail maps are available at Colorado sporting goods stores, bait shops, and area bookstores. With your copy of Kip Carey's Official Colorado Fishing Guide and the right maps, you're ready to enjoy Colorado's fishing to the fullest.

TIM KELLEY - Tim Kelley, teacher and fisherman, founder of the Colorado Fishing Guide, passed away in September of 1982, in Scottsdale Arizona. He was 75. This edition is the 19th edition of the classic Tim Kelley Fishing Guide, which he started producing every few years beginning in 1954. Tim Kelley's vision was to chronicle in detail all of the fishing waters in Colorado. The resulting guides have been a valuable resource to countless fishermen over the past 46 years, and with this new edition that tradition continues today. In 1999, I was able to obtain the rights to this great resource, with the hope to continue the work started by Tim Kelley so that you may enjoy fishing Colorado as much as I do.

HOW TO CATCH FISH - I can not pretend to be able to teach you how to catch fish in Colorado with a few words in the pages of this book. Even if an entire chapter was devoted to the subject it would still not prepare a person adequately enough. This guide is a "where" to fish guide, many specific books on "how" to fish exist. I will say however, if you want to catch fish in Colorado there is a wealth of information available, probably right around the corner. Area fishing and sporting goods stores are a great place to start, fishing is their business, and they are a wealth of information. Colorado has numerous quality guide services which offer fishing trips which include instruction. Possibly the best way to increase your abilities is to go fishing with someone who knows how to catch fish, who knows, you just might make a friend for life.

DISCLAIMER - The information in this book is a result of information gained from area fishing and sporting goods stores, the Colorado Division of Wildlife, the US Forest Service, guides and guide services, and fishermen from around the state. Every attempt has been made to present accurate information, however situations change often. Lakes once stocked no longer are, or now they are stocked with brown instead of rainbow. Roads once opened are now closed, and public access on leased land once available is now closed. If you find the directions, descriptions, or conditions are different than what is listed in this guide, please go to my web page at www.fishingcolowyo.com and let me know what you have found.

WHERE ARE THE FISH? - Many of the streams and lakes in this guide list several types of fish present for a particular location. A word of note: chances are at different times of the year an angler might not encounter all species listed. For instance, during my numerous trips to Fourmile Creek near Buena Vista in the fall I have found the catch to consist entirely of brown running up from the Arkansas River. During spring and summer this little stream is strictly fishing for brook only. Remember, brown run in the fall and rainbow and cutthroat spawn in the spring, which has a definite effect on what species of trout the angler may encounter. Lakes are no different, at Cataract Lake above Green Mountain Reservoir in early spring I have tied into some very large brown, only to come back during the summer to find nothing but small brook. All of the above is true for warm water species also, many times what you catch is just what is feeding.

TERMS AND DEFINITIONS - Throughout this guide references are made about the following terms, and here is what they mean:

- **National Forests** - About 35 percent of Colorado is designated as public land. Managed by the Department of Agriculture, National Forests in Colorado offer nearly all of the available public fishing opportunities. Colorado's National Forests are Arapaho, Grand Mesa, Gunnison, Pike, Rio Grande, Roosevelt, Routt, San Isabel, San Juan, Uncompahgre, and White River National Forests. National Forest lands and Wilderness land may overlap. Keep in mind private property does restrict access in some locations. Colorado State maintains and manages Colorado State Forest in the North Platte drainage near Rand.

- **National Parks** - Black Canyon of the Gunnison River National Park and Rocky Mountain National Park offer outstanding fishing opportunities and are managed by the National Park Service. In addition two Recreational Areas; Arapaho National Recreational Area, near Grand Lake (managed by the U.S. Forest Service) and Curecanti National Recreational Area near Gunnison are areas set aside because of their recreational features.

- **Wilderness Areas** - In 1964, Congress passed the Wilderness Act which stated that the United States must retain pristine portions of national forests, designating them as ,wilderness areas. These areas, managed by the UFSF, lie in defined boundaries and must remain undisturbed. Wilderness areas are to retain their primitive status, which precludes timber cutting, road building, and any new mining activities. All Wilderness access is by foot or horse only. No motorized or mechanical modes of transportation are allowed. Colorado's Wilderness areas are: Big Blue, Byer's Peak, Cache la Poudre, Collegiate Peaks, Comanche, Eagles Nest, Flat Tops, Fossil Ridge, Holly Cross, Hunter, Fryingpan, Indian Peaks, La Garita, Lizard Head, Lost Creek, Maroon Bells-Snowmass, Mt. Evans, Mt. Massive, Mt. Sneffels, Mt. Zerkel, Neota, Never Summer, Platte River, Raggeds, Rawah, Sangre de Cristo, Sarvice Creek, South San Jaun, Vasquez Peak, Werninuche, and West Elk Wilderness Areas.

- **Colorado State Parks** - Colorado State Parks are part of the Colorado Department of Natural Resources and are developed and managed for recreational activities, including fishing. A daily or seasonal parks pass is required, Colorado State Parks which offer fishing are: Arkansas Headwaters, Barbour Ponds, Barr Lake, Bonny Reservoir, Boyd Lake, Chatfield Reservoir, Cherry Creek Reservoir, Colorado River (Corn Lake), Crawford Reservoir, Elevenmile Reservoir, Elkhead Reservoir, Golden Gate Canyon, Harvey Gap Reservoir, Highline Lake, Jackson Lake, Lathrop (Martin and Horseshoe lakes), Mancos (Jackson Gulch Reservoir), Navajo Reservoir, North Sterling Reservoir, Paonia Reservoir, Pearl Lake State Park, Pueblo Reservoir, Ridgway Reservoir, Rifle Gap Reservoir, San Luis Reservoir, Spinney Mountain Reservoir, Stagecoach Reservoir, Steamboat Lake, Sylvan Lake, Trinidad Reservoir, and Vega Reservoir.

- **USFS** - United States Forest Service - In 1905 the U.S. Forest Service was created to manage public lands in America's National Forests. The Forest Service is a Federal Agency part of the Department of Agriculture. Responsibilities include; construction and maintenance of Forest Service trails and roads, operation of campgrounds, wildlife habitat management, and the protection and management of all resources on National Forest lands.

- **BLM** - Bureau of Land Management - Created in the mid-1940's, the BLM is part of the Department of the Interior. The BLM is responsible for balancing the use of public land for recreation, mining, livestock grazing, and wildlife habitat on about 8.3 million acres in Colorado, including around 1,500 miles of fishable waters.

- **DOW** - Division of Wildlife - the Colorado Division of Wildlife is the agency responsible for regulating fishing activities, issuing fishing licenses and enforcing regulations. Dow currently manages over 235 State Wildlife Areas (SWA), stocks and maintains fish in Colorado waters, and works hard to protect threatened and endangered fish species such as the greenback cutthroat trout, humpback chub, Bony tail, Colorado squawfish, razorback sucker and several types of darters on the eastern plains.

PRIVATE PROPERTY - Private property is just that - PRIVATE. No matter how good the fishing appears to be, the property is owned by someone. Colorado has so much quality public waters to fish, please respect others rights and do not trespass.

- **SR, CR, FR, FT** - State Road, County Road, Forest Road and Forest Trail.

CONTACTING KIP CAREY

The best way to contact me is through my website at
www.fishingcolowyo.com
or
U.S. Mail-Kip Carey's Official Colorado Fishing Guide
6732 West Coal Mine Ave, # 230
Littleton, Colorado 80123

NORTH PLATTE RIVER/
LARAMIE RIVER

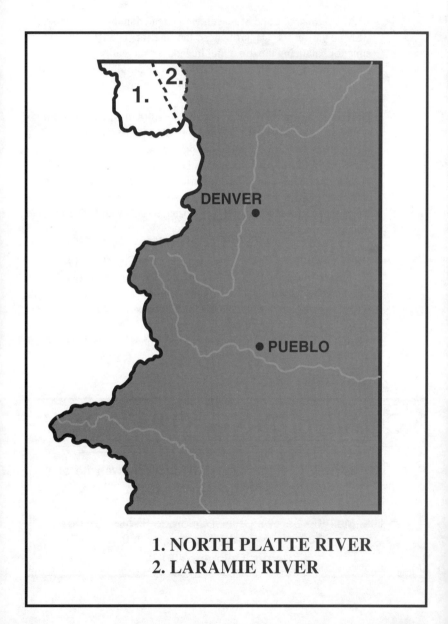

1. NORTH PLATTE RIVER
2. LARAMIE RIVER

NORTH PLATTE RIVER

The North Platte River rises in the Sierra Madre and Park Range Mountains on the west side of North Park in Northwest Central Colorado. This 50-square-mile open region is primarily in Jackson County, with Walden the principal community. North Park is a mixture of private and public land, 8,000 feet or more above sea level, and takes its name from the open basin of its topography. It is northwest of Rocky Mountain National Park and readily reached via Hwy 14 west from Fort Collins over Cameron Pass; Hwy 125 north from Granby over Willow Creek Pass; Hwy 14 north from U.S. 40 east of Steamboat Springs at Muddy Pass; and from Wyoming via Hwy 230 from Laramie or from Hwy 130 and 230 from Saratoga.

The Colorado State Forest and Rawah Wilderness Area in Roosevelt National Forest lie on the east, Arapaho National Forest on the south, Routt National Forest and the Mt. Zirkel Wilderness area on the west and Medicine Bow National Forest across the Colorado/Wyoming state line to the north. This public land surrounds primarily private ranch lands and some Bureau of Land Management sections at the lower elevations of North Park. The Colorado Division of Wildlife manages 17 wildlife and/or leased fishing areas within this region. There are four state recreation areas in addition to the Arapaho National Wildlife Refuge and the North Sand Hills Natural Area.

Perhaps the North Park's outstanding characteristic is the unusual abundance of water and wetlands resulting from melting snow off the adjacent peaks and from its own U-shape, which catches precipitation funneling in from the north. The result is a multitude of lakes and clear-flowing streams with rainbow, cutthroat and brown trout. Beaver ponds teem with brook trout. With all of this water, the summer mosquito population is significant. The open terrain of the valley floor includes sagebrush expanses, irrigated hay meadows and patches of marsh and bog—even alkaline ponds. Numerous irrigation ditches confine access to established roads.

North Park features the headwaters of the North Platte River at the confluence of Little Grizzly and Grizzly creeks, the Illinois and Michigan rivers and other tributaries, not all of which are good fisheries. Superb angling usually can be found at the Delaney Butte lakes, Lake John and a host of other lakes and ponds, primarily on the west side of the basin. Little Gem Lake in the northwest corner of the area in Routt National Forest gives rise to the delightful Encampment River, which like its more accessible counterparts, flows north. These are all southwestern tributaries of the vast

Missouri River system.

Jackson County has a rich heritage as an Indian summer hunting and fishing area, with a later history of ranching, mining, railroading and logging. The variety of game and non-game wildlife is surprising for an area where winter snows often arrive in early fall and linger into mid-spring. Rocky Mountain bighorn sheep, mule deer, elk, antelope, black bear and moose share habitats with bobcat, beaver and other creatures. In the Arapaho National Wildlife Refuge, more than 154 species of birds have been listed, as well as 32 mammals and 13 other vertebrates.

In March of 1978, a Shiras moose reintroduction program began with a dozen animals released on the upper Illinois River in southeastern Jackson County. In the southeastern portion of the valley, an expanding moose population often provides spectacular viewing.

Numerous shore birds, including snipe, snowy egret, grebe, killdeer, heron and bittern, mingle with many species of ducks, coots, mergansers and Canadian geese. Mourning doves are everywhere from spring to fall, the sagebrush is home to the sage grouse, and the blue grouse is found at higher elevations. Hawks, owls and both bald and golden eagles are found in North Park.

Timber cutting on all sides of North Park has created a network of logging roads for access to national forest lands and some adjacent BLM lands.

North Park is within the Central Flyway, and ducks can be found on many

Photo Courtesy of Kevin Rummell

Early season fishing trip in North Park

of the waters in the valley. Some of the preferred waters include Lake John, Delaney Buttes Reservoirs, Walden Reservoir, Cowdrey Lakes, Mac-Farlane Reservoir and, in particular, Arapaho National Wildlife Refuge.

LOWER PLATTE RIVER

The lower 5.3 miles of the **North Platte River** upstream from the Wyoming state line has been designated Gold Medal water. The predominant fish species in the North Platte is brown trout, with rainbow trout also offering sport. The best fishing occurs in late summer and fall following spring run-off, which has a tendency to dirty the waters in this drainage. This section of the river is just north of the confluence of the North Platte and Canadian rivers along Hwy 125. Fishing by artificial flies and lures only from the southern boundary of the Routt National Forest downstream to the Wyoming State line. A 2-trout limit applies. Fishing access is by hiking and wading in the shallower portions. On the Brownlee, Manville, Verner State Wildlife Areas, fishing is by artificial flies and lures only, two fish limit.

Moving upstream from the Wyoming line, the northeast corner of North Park has several sandy-bottomed streams which flow down out of the mountains. They offer fishing for mostly small trout and then only in the higher reaches. From Kings Canyon on Hwy 127, a road winds up into the forest, along **Pinkham Creek**, which has small brook, as does **Camp Creek** and its adjacent beaver ponds to the north. These roads may not be negotiated in passenger cars.

East of Walden, the most significant tributary is the **Canadian River**. Access to this mostly mediocre fishery is reached from Hwy 125 north of Walden 3 miles via CR 10 or from Walden itself on CR 12. The river and its tributaries are best fished in the higher terrain of the Colorado State Forest where small brook and cutthroat are found in the deeper beaver ponds and larger streams.

The most productive fisheries are **Kelly Creek** and **Clear Creek**, north of Hwy 14 at Michigan Hill, 12 miles southeast of Walden. The road, 30R (keep to the left), crosses the Canadian, then Kelly and Clear creeks after about 5 miles of 4wd. At the headwaters of Clear Creek is **Clear Lake** (10,580 ft; 10 ac), good for cutthroat. Artificial flies and lures only with a two trout limit. **Kelly Lake** (10,800 ft; 25 ac) is 2 miles south and also offers cutthroat. Golden trout were stocked in Kelly in 1988. Fishing by artificial flies and lures only with a 2-trout limit. These lakes are up against 12,000-foot peaks and are accessible only on foot or horseback, but it can be worth the 10-mile climb.

Ruby Jewel Lake (11,240 ft; 4 ac), at the headwater of the South Fork of the Canadian River, is a hike of 3 miles of steep trail from Jewel Lake Road and the state forest road. It has cutthroat to 14 inches but is not rated as a good fishery. Fishing is by artificial flies and lures only.

North of Gould 2.5 miles on Hwy 14, a road goes east to the **North Fork Michigan River** and **North Michigan Creek Reservoir** (8,920 ft; 130 ac), and on to the headwaters of the Canadian River. It crosses several small streams that flow west out of the Medicine Bow Mountains. Fishing in the reservoir is by artificial flies and lures only. From Gould, CR 21 goes south to provide access to Aspen and Pine Campgrounds and to the **South Fork of the Michigan River**, **Porcupine Creek** and **Silver Creek**. Silver and Porcupine creeks are in Routt National Forest. The South Fork holds cutthroat, rainbow, brown and brook and is heavily fished. The lower reaches along Hwy 14 are on private land and posted, but fishing is usually good in the forest. The tributary streams offer small trout. These waters are in the Colorado State Forest, with headquarters near Ranger Lakes along Hwy 14. You must stop to check on parks pass requirements, maps and other information. A parks pass is needed for access into Ruby Jewel, Kelley, and Clear Lakes.

Lily Lake (9,560 ft; 3 ac) is shown on most maps about 3 miles south of Pine Campground on USFS road 740; it has no fish.

On Hwy 14, 5 miles from the summit of Cameron Pass and 3 miles east of Gould, are the **Ranger Lakes** (lower 9,250 ft; 6 ac, upper 9,265 ft; 11 ac) on the south side of the highway. They are stocked with rainbow. The Michigan River along the highway offers brook, brown and rainbow trout to 8 inches.

A mile and a half west of Cameron Pass summit, a trail winds south around the east side of the 12,485-foot Nokhu Crags to **Snow Lake**, (11,900 ft; 17 ac). It is rated fair for rainbow and cutthroat averaging 12 inches. There is a parking area just off the highway and signs mark the site. Fishing is by artificial flies and lures only with a two fish limit.

Down the pass summit 2.5 miles, a trail at timberline leads from a parking area beside the highway south 2 miles to **Lower Lake Agnes** (10,600 ft; 20 ac). Fishing action is usually slow on this lake but the patient angler is rewarded with larger-than-normal catches. Rainbows average 17 inches and an occasional brown is caught

about the same size. Cutthroat are usually less than 12 inches. Artificial flies and lures with a two fish limit.

Farther upstream, **Upper Lake Agnes** (11,200 ft; 4.2 ac) may yield Pikes Peak cutthroat for those willing to climb to it. It has also been stocked with mackinaw. This is no country to be in when thunderstorms are imminent. Mineralization of the rock seems to attract lightning. Ice frequently lingers on the high lakes until July. Fishing with artificial flies and lures only with a two fish limit.

The **Michigan River** is a major tributary to the North Platte River, joining it north of Walden. **Cowdrey Lake**, (7,940 ft; 80 ac) State Wildlife Area, also known as Carlstrom Reservoir, is accessible from Hwy 125 about 1 mile south of Cowdrey and is well marked. A boat is needed to fish, but none is locally available; motors are allowed at wakeless speed only. Once a good fishery for rainbow and brown, Cowdrey has been recovering from a kill-off to reduce rough fish. Camping is allowed on this state wildlife area.

The **Brownlee State Wildlife Area**, when combined with the **Diamond J** and the **Murphy State Wildlife Areas**, offers 16 miles of trout fishing along the Michigan and Illinois rivers. The properties are east and west of Hwy 125 immediately north of Walden, as well as on both sides of the Michigan River east of Walden via CR 12E and from the road that leads to the Walden-Jackson County Airport from Hwy 125 about 0.5 mile north of Walden. Camping is permitted immediately north of Walden. From Gould to Walden, the

0

Michigan flows through private lands.

The **Illinois River** merges with the **Michigan River** just northwest of Walden. The **Illinois River** has some very good fishing in the Arapaho National Wildlife Refuge south of Walden. It is closed to fishing from June 1 to August 1 to permit migratory waterfowl to nest and raise their young. Antelope, sage grouse, deer, elk and other animals and some 150 species of bird frequent the refuge and its irrigated meadows. The refuge is primarily east of Hwy 125, although some tracts are west of the highway.

The Illinois originates more than 20 miles to the south above Rand. The river provides good pools, quiet water, riffles and other tempting stretches with rainbow and nice-sized brown. Ponds in the area freeze solid in winter and offer no fishing. The best fishing is in spring and early fall.

Willow Creek enters the Illinois near Rand, and is on private land to the forest boundary. Small, brushy and ponded in the forest. Good for small brook and rainbow. Access from Hwy 125 north of Willow Creek Pass. Take USFS road 106. Other streams in the area only offer poor fishing.

Seven miles from the pass summit and 2 miles southeast of the hamlet of Rand, CR 21 leads off to the northeast. It soon forks to provide access to the headwaters of the **Illinois River** in Routt National Forest. It is 3 miles across private land to the public land. The Illinois River is best fished for brown trout in the Arapaho National Wildlife Refuge. Fishing is for small brook in the upper portion of the river

and in **Jack Creek**, both of which wind steeply back into the Never Summer Mountains bordering Rocky Mountain National Park.

Owl Mountain State Wildlife Area southeast of Walden offers camping. Drive on Hwy 14 southeast from Walden 13 miles, then south on CR 25 for 6 miles.

NORTH FORK OF THE NORTH PLATTE

The **North Fork of the North Platte River** rises in Routt National Forest northwest of Walden and winds south through private property on the west side of Sheep Mountain before looping north again south of Lake John to enter the North Platte 6 miles due west of Walden.

The North Fork is about 20 feet wide with many deep holes, riffles and quiet water. While much of it is posted, the Colorado Division of Wildlife has obtained easements to some 6 miles of the stream for public fishing at the **Richards State Wildlife Area.** Get there by following Hwy 14 to CR 12W west-northwest from Walden for about 14 miles. Fishing is with artificial flies and lures only. Two fish limit.

In the vicinity of Lake John, **Irving, Oddfellows, Manville, and Peterson State Wildlife Areas** provide fishing on the **North Fork** and **Roaring Fork Creek**. These have naturally reproducing rainbow and stocked brown. No camping allowed. Fishing is by artificial flies and lures only. Two fish limit.

Near the confluence of the North Fork and the main North Platte,

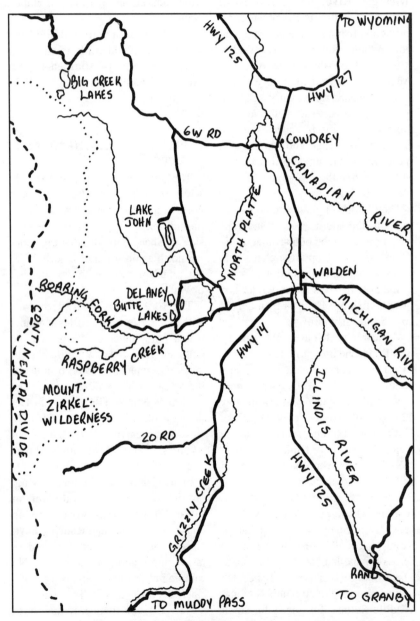

WALDEN/NORTH PLATTE RIVER

Brownlee State Wildlife Area No. 2 runs along the **North Platte River.** Reached by driving west 0.5 mile from Walden on Hwy 14 to CR 12W, then west 5.3 miles to CR 18, and 0.5 mile more to the wildlife area. The **Verner State Wildlife Area** is 0.75 mile west. Two miles of trout fishing are available. Artificial flies and lures with a two fish limit.

Lake John (8,050 ft; 556 ac) and **Lake John State Wildlife Area** offers fishing, boating and picnicking. Fishing usually is exceptional in the 565-acre lake. The lake also provides good fishing for brown, Snake River cutthroat, some brook and good-size rainbow, most often with the use of boats, canoes and belly boats. The bag and possession limit for trout is 4 fish. It is a very popular ice-fishing destination. Access from Walden is well marked by traveling west on CR 12W, then north on CR 7 about 7 miles to the south entrance turnoff.

In the national forest, **Lone Pine**, **Bear**, **Ute**, **Hill**, **Shafer**, **Goose** and **Forester** creeks are principal tributaries of the North Fork. Except for Lone Pine Creek, access is mostly by foot or horseback via USFS trail 1126 that parallels the wilderness boundary USFS road 640 from CR 16 leads up Lone Pine to the trailhead. Lone Pine has lots of brookies and some larger browns in the beaver ponds.

The streams have brook and cutthroat trout, though fishing is often difficult because of the brush and timber. There are many small ponds, some of which have brook in the 6- to 7-inch range. **Goose Creek** and the beaver ponds are stocked with rainbow.

Lakes in the Mt. Zirkel Wilderness in this area include **Lake Katherine** (9,860 ft; 22 ac), **Bighorn Lake** (10,000 ft; 17 ac) at the headwaters of Lone Pine Creek. Reportedly, Bighorn has large cutts and rainbows as well as mackinaws. Katherine has good fishing for cutthroat to 3 pounds and some smaller mackinaw. Both lakes are about three miles south of TR 1129.

Other lakes in the headwaters of North Fork tributaries include **Ute Lake** (9,750 ft; 6 ac) requiring a 5 mile hike, **Twin Lake** (9,800 ft; 37 ac) requiring an 8 mile hike up Lake Creek. **Peggy Lake** (11,165 ft; 10 ac) and **Blue Lake** (10,000 ft. 6 ac) require 9 and 11 mile hikes up Hill Creek. These lakes are in high, rugged country, often at or above timberline and are tough to reach. Trails 1174 and 1178 off trail 1126 provide access. The lakes offer brook and cutthroat, with some mackinaw in the larger, deeper water. The **Bear Lakes** (10,000 ft; 20 and 13 ac) on Bear Creek have some brown as well as cutthroat, but fishing is usually poor.

DELANEY BUTTE LAKES

Delaney Butte Lakes (8,100 ft; 163, 150, and 67 ac) have ample feed and good water that nourish many large trout, mostly brown and cutthroat. The average fish is 10 to 14 inches, with many larger ones taken. It is a year-round fishery, very popular and tightly managed with size and limit restrictions. Because it is difficult to fish from shore, boats and belly boats are widely used.

North Delaney Butte Lake is designated a Gold Medal fishery. Regulations are fishing by artificial flies or lures only. Two trout limit. All brown trout between 14 and 20 inches must be returned to the water immediately. **East Delaney Butte Lake** offers fishing for16- to 18-inch brown and good brook, especially in the spring and fall. Fishing by artificial flies or lures only. Two trout limit. **South Delaney Butte Lake** is fair fishing for larger rainbow, brown, and cutthroat trout. Regulations are fishing by artificial flies and lures. Two trout limit.

Boat-ramp areas, picnic and camping grounds in this treeless region fill up early, particularly on weekends in spring and summer. Ice fishing is popu-lar. Access is well marked via Hwy 14 and county roads 18 and 12 W.

Traveling southwest on Hwy 14 from Hwy 125 just south of Walden gets you to the main stem of **Grizzly Creek** near the Peterson State Wildlife Area. Grizzly enters and is joined by **Buffalo Creek** from the southeast. Both Buffalo Creek and its headwaters are also reached by taking county roads 11A, 11 and 28 east from Hwy 14 toward the town of Rand. There are numerous irrigation reservoirs on this private land, and permission to fish is absolutely necessary. USFS road 715 provides access to Buffalo Creek and its principal tributary **Grassy Run Creek** in the national forest. Fishing is good for rainbow and brook.

Zac and Caleb taking home dinner near Rand

Photo Courtesy of C. Carey

County roads 11A and 11 also lead to **Seymour Lake** (8,360 ft; 35 ac) State Wildlife Area. The reservoir offers boat and shore fishing for rainbow. Camping is permitted. Some larger fish have been taken, but most are around 12 inches.

Farther south on CR 11 in the national forest, the road passes near numerous ponds and lakes, most of which offer good to excellent angling for small brook. **Bundy Lake** (10,000 ft; 2 ac) with rainbow, **Willow Lake** (9,100 ft; 4 ac) with some brown, **Kathleen Lake** (9,200; 2.5 ac) with cutthroat, **Kidney** (9,050; 4 ac) with rainbow, **Slack Weiss Reservoir** (8,920 ft; 8 ac) with rainbow, **Two Ledge Reservoir** (9,780 ft; 6 ac) with rainbow, **Flat Lake** (9,300 ft; 5.5 ac) with rainbow and **Disappointment Lake** (9350 ft; 1.5 ac) with rainbow. Two Ledge fishing regulations are artificial flies and lures only with a 2-trout limit. Other nearby lakes include **Deep**, **Finger**, **Beaver**, **Long**, **Alder**, **Round** and **Cliff**. Undeveloped campsites available. All have rainbow; Deep and Alder also have brown.

Arapaho Creek joins Grizzly Creek from the east at Spicer. The lower reaches of the creek and its tributaries are closed to the public. The headwaters in the national forest provide stream and lake fishing and are most easily reached from Hwy 14 about 5.5 miles north of Spicer, then turning east on CR 11A for a mile, then south on CR 11. This slender, brushy, ponded stream is good for small, wild brook. There are three forks at the headwaters, with **Middle** and **West Fork of Arapaho Creek** the best.

SOUTHERN AND WESTERN SIDES

Hwy 14 from Walden winds up the southwest corner of North Park toward Muddy Pass on U.S. 40 about 25 miles east of Steamboat Springs. At the summit, **Muddy Pass Lake** (8,800 ft; 10.5 ac) is an unimposing puddle, but it is stocked with rainbow to 10 inches. **Grizzly Creek,** its tributaries and associated ponds provide better fishing. For the next 10 miles the brushy steam meanders near the highway. The streams are on private land offer catchable rainbow, brown and brook, if permission to fish is received.

LITTLE GRIZZLY CREEK

Little Grizzly Creek rises from a host of lakes and streams in Routt National Forest south of the Mount Zirkel Wilderness and flows northeast to join Grizzly Creek about 10 miles southwest of Walden. Access to the headwaters and beyond to Steamboat Springs over the Continental Divide at Buffalo Pass is via CR 24 (or 26 from Coalmont). CR 24 is improved gravel east of the pass, not as good on the west side but still suitable for 2WD vehicles. It provides access to upper Grizzly Creek and Hidden Lakes, National Forest campgrounds, the headwater of Colorado Creek and the drainage south of Little Grizzly. It also provides access to USFS road 615 that leads north to the drainages of Chedsey, Newcomb and Whale creeks.

The lower reaches of the Little Grizzly are on private land and are posted.

Peterson State Wildlife Area is 8 miles southwest of Walden along Hwy 14. It offers trout fishing on **Grizzly** and **Little Grizzly** creeks and the **North Platte River**. **Pole Mountain Reservoir**, prominent in the valley 1.5 miles west of Coalmont, is on private land. Even if permission is obtained fishing success is marginal.

Farther up Little Grizzly Creek, fishing is for good-size brown, rainbow and brook and is rated fair in the national forest. About a mile west of the Grizzly Campground on USFS road 615, Little Grizzly is joined by the north-flowing **Sawmill Creek**. **Sawmill Lake**, (8,700 ft; 15 ac) at the headwater of the creek, is rated poor.

Crosby Creek feeds into the Little Grizzly from the south. USFS road 20 goes south from the campground another 5 miles to Hidden Lakes Campground, and on for another 4 miles to the ponds of **Colorado Creek**. Several small streams flow down from the Continental Divide to the west. Three miles south of Hidden Lakes Campground, the Percy Lake Trail winds upward 1.5 miles to **Percy Lake** (10,035 ft; 17 ac) and a few yards farther, **Round Lake** (10,060 ft; 16 ac). Both have good brook trout angling. Don't neglect the creek in this area. It lies south of the trail and has good brook. A mile further south is **Lost Lake** (10,330; 15 ac), which is fair to good for 8-15 inch brook and rainbow.

Stambaugh Reservoir (8,800 ft; 10 ac) is stocked with rainbow. It is about 300 yards east of the road and just north of Hidden Lakes Campground. It is rated good for 12-inch rainbow with some up to 2 pounds due to good feed conditions. Lots of down timber in the water.

Hidden Lakes (8,900 ft; 11 and 4 ac) at the campground have poor fishing for stocked rainbow and for Snake River cutthroat in the larger lake.

North of Grizzly Creek Campground and the ranger station at the forest boundary, USFS road 615 continues for 4 miles and provides access to an area with several forest lakes, most of which have rainbow and tend to be sporadic, moody producers of good fish. The lakes are part of the headwaters of **Chedsey**, **Newcomb** and **Whale** creeks, which merge east of the forest boundary into Chedsey Creek. **Chedsey Creek** is prime trout fishing and, as with the other two creeks, offers rainbow, cutthroat and brook. USFS road 625 is a 4WD road that goes up the north side of Chedsey Creek from the point where USFS road 615 crosses the stream.

Teal Lake (8,800 ft; 16 ac) and **Tiago Lake** (8,850 ft; 8 ac) are in timber beside USFS road 615 and are readily fished from shore and boat (no ramps) for stocked rainbow to 12 inches. **Burns Reservoir** (8,600 ft; 9 ac) also has rainbow and some brook. It can readily be reached by a short walk east from the road about a mile north of the campground.

Lakes in the area west of the Grizzly Campground and south of the wildernesson the east side of Buffalo Pass, include **Summit** (10,000 ft; 7 ac) **Jonah** (10,164 ft; 9 ac), **Whale** (10,050 ft; 11 ac) **Martha** (10,303 ft; 10 ac), **Shoestring** (10,000 ft; 7 ac) **Albert**

(10,177 ft; 11 ac), **Victoria** (10, 040 ft; 4 ac), **and Round Mountain** (9,880 ft; 10 ac) are all in the Mt. Zirkel Wilderness. Look for cutthroat, rainbow and brook. The beaver ponds in the area can be great fun, although the trout may be small. These lakes are right up against the Continental Divide within a 5-mile walk from Buffalo Pass in negotiable terrain. Steeper country is to the north.

Grizzly Creek and the Roaring Fork combine about 9 miles west of Walden to create the North Platte River. **Manville State Wildlife Area** west of Walden features trout fishing along 4.4 miles of the **Roaring Fork River** and 3 miles of the **North Platte River**. Restricted to artificial flies and lures only. Two fish limit. Access from Walden is CR 12W to CR 18. Turn south on CR 5 and watch for signs. The Roaring Fork provides fair fishing for brown, rainbow, and occasional brook. Lower reaches are on private land, but higher portions are in Routt National Forest and fed by alpine lakes in the wilderness. Fishing on the North Platte River inside Manville is prohibited.

Beaver Creek, the first of the tributaries of the Roaring Fork, enters the Fork from the southwest. **Aqua Fria Lake** (10,000 ft; 28 ac) on **Beaver Creek** is squeezed between steep ridges and can be reached by trail from the end of USFS road 615 at Newcomb Creek. Hike north 3 miles on a relatively flat segment of the Grizzly Helena Trail, then 3.5 miles west up an abandoned 4WD road. The trail climbs 1200 feet to the lake. Aqua Fria was previously stocked with mackinaw but

area anglers' report fair fishing for brook. The creek has cutthroat.

On the southwest side of the **Roaring Fork** of North Platte drainage, **Norris Creek** and **Raspberry Creek** combine. Fishing by artificial flies and lures only. Two fish limit. Both are reached by CR 5 running southwest from Manville SWA to CR 22 and USFS trail 1130.

Irvine State Wildlife Area offers 6 miles of trout fishing along Raspberry Creek and Roaring Fork River. Camping is prohibited. The area is southwest of Delaney Butte SWA and adjacent to the **Odd Fellows State Wildlife Area** to the north. Odd Fellows provides access to Roaring Fork Creek. Fishing by artificial flies and lures only. Two fish limit.

Roxy Ann Lake, (10,200 ft; 65 ac) above Red Canyon is part of the headwaters of the Roaring Fork. It is probably most easily reached from the USFS trail 1130 to the west that runs along the Continental Divide. Requires a tough 8-mile hike. Fair for rainbow, cutthroat and a hermit golden trout or two.

Spike Lake (10,400; 4 ac), one mile above Roxy Ann to the northwest, has cutthroat and an occasional golden. It is quite shallow. Several other small streams in the area lend themselves to investigation, but, often as not, prove to be difficult to fish for small brook or cutthroat. There are numerous beaver ponds, especially in the Roaring Fork headwaters.

USFS trail 1130 from Livingston Park climbs 1700 ft. in 7.5 miles to **Upper Slide Lake** (10,500 ft; 8 ac) and

Photo Courtesy of Kevin Rummell

Cutthroat near Buffalo Pass

Slide Lake (10,400 ft; 27 ac) with rainbow and cutthroat. The Upper Lake is rated good, especially with dry flies. The lower lake is fair. Downstream from Slide Lake on **Norris Creek** are the **Rainbow Lakes** (9,800 ft; 127 ac total). All are rated fair for rainbow and cutthroat to 16 inches.

About 0.5-mile north of Rainbow Lakes, beyond the ridge in the next drainage, is **Ceanothuse Lake** (9,440 ft; 10 ac). It is most easily reached by hiking up Norris Creek from USFS trail 1126 that crosses the upper end of Livingston Park. The lake is rated good for cutthroat and rainbow to 12 inches with a few larger fish taken.

BIG CREEK

North from Walden 9 miles on Hwy 125, CR 6W goes northwest from the village of Cowdrey about 16 miles to the hamlet of Pearl. Four miles southwest is the Big Creek Lakes Campground. This is a jumping-off place for trips into the northeastern portion of the Mt. Zirkel Wilderness. At the wilderness boundary, 2 miles west of South Big Creek Lake, is Big Creek Falls, a good hike of nearly 4 miles from the campground.

Big Creek Lakes are on the **South Fork of Big Creek**. The creek is good fishing for rainbow, brown and brook. It offers 5 miles of good fishing in the forest below the north, or **Lower Big Creek Lake** (8,997 ft; 350 ac), which has brown, mackinaw, splake, hybrid tiger muskie and rainbow. Bag and possession for mackinaw and slake is 1 fish. All mackinaw and splake 22-34 inches must be returned to the water immediately. A campground is at the lower lake. At **Upper Big Creek Lake** (9,010 ft; 101 ac) fishing is for brown, mackinaw, splake, brook and rainbow.

Lake Eileen (10,240 ft; 4 ac) and **Seven Lakes** (10,640 ft; 14 ac total) are reached by USFS trail 1125, the Big Creek Trail. Eileen is 6 miles up the trail; Seven Lakes are 7 miles. Eileen has cutthroat, while six of the Seven Lakes are too shallow to support fish. The one lake that has fair fishing for cutthroat to 12 inches is **Seven Lakes #1**. Three miles farther west is **Gem Lake** (10,160 ft; 7 ac) rated excellent for brook. Gem is reached by the Big Creek Trail (USFS 1125) to USFS trail 1152. This is a steep hike over a 10,490-foot ridge into the headwaters of Encampment River. A less steep hike, though longer, is by way of the Stump Park Trail (USFS 1127) for five miles up Beaver Creek, which can be reached by USFS road 689 about 1.5 miles northwest of the Big Creek Campground. This **Beaver Creek** has many beaver ponds. The fishing is fair for brook to 9 inches. **Davis Creek** and **Line Creek** are just north of Beaver Creek and most readily reached via USFS road 80 west from Pearl. They

have brook trout.

This country has been logged, and from a map one cannot ascertain if the country is in timber, meadow or cut over with regeneration of trees. Local inquiry about 4WD roads still open is recommended.

ENCAMPMENT RIVER

The **Encampment River** is another beautiful stream with good fishing for brook and cutthroat; occasionally, a brown may be taken. These trout are wild and wary. More than 15 miles of river and 7 miles of the **West Fork of the Encampment River** over 10,787-foot Black Mountain to the west provide a superb challenge to the firm-footed angler whom is willing to walk.

There are two lakes at the headwater of the West Fork, **West Fork Lake** (9,400 ft; 20 ac) and **Manzanares Lake** (9,240 ft; 4 ac), that offer fine brook and cutthroat fishing. Access is west from Pearl on USFS road 80 about 18 miles to Hog Park, then 0.75 miles to the confluence of the two streams coming out of the lakes. **The South Fork of Hog Park Creek** is to the west 1.5 miles, or reached by 4WD trail 3 miles to the southwest of Hog Park. The stream provides lively cutthroat and brook to 12 inches in some stretches. Hog Park is also accessible from Encampment, WY.

LARAMIE RIVER

The **Laramie River** is ideal for early-season fly-fishing and remains a top-notch fishery much of the year. It is primarily brown trout water, though tributary streams and lakes in the drainage teem with rainbow, cutthroat and brook trout as well.

The Laramie Road that goes north from Hwy 14 east of Chambers Lake parallels most of its 27 miles in Colorado. About half the river is in the Roosevelt National Forest, and the rest flows through private ranchlands, where fishing for pay is permitted on several large ranches. While some of the lakes and tributary streams are stocked, fish in the river are wild.

Upper reaches of the river, from Chambers Lake to Glendevey, are rated fair for rainbow averaging 11 inches and brown averaging 12 inches. The river in this area is mostly brushy with some beaver ponds and a few brook trout, but difficult to fish. The Laramie is open to public access for an 8-mile stretch from Chambers Lake north to Lily Pond Lake.

Below Glendevey, the river meanders through private hay meadows. Though almost all private, it offers some of the finest brown trout fishing in the state. Most fish are about 13 inches, but many larger fish are taken. Ranches that permit fishing for pay strongly encourage release of fish. Only two sections of the river below

Lily Pond Lake are open to the public. One is a 0.25-mile stretch at the picnic grounds south of the Glendevey intersection. The other is Hohnholz State Wildlife Area. (See details on the latter area further on in this section.)

CHAMBERS LAKE

The Laramie River heads at **Chambers Lake** (9,164 ft; 350 ac when full), a crater lake with a maximum depth of 91 feet, which is used as a diversion basin to send water down the Cache la Poudre River for irrigation. Chambers' water level fluctuates greatly. Hwy 14, 52 miles west of US 287 at Fort Collins, skips past Chambers' southeast shore. From Hwy 14, the Laramie Road heads north along Chambers' flat east shore. Trolling and bait fishing from the banks give best results for rainbow averaging 8 to 10 inches, kokanee to 10 inches and occasional brown, and cutthroat. There are a few lake trout. Flies are often successfully used at the mouth of **Fall**, **Joe Wright** and **Trap** creeks, which enter the lake's southern and eastern shores. All three tributaries have been stocked with rainbows. Chambers is rated fair, with best results in October when the water is low. No boats are available to rent, but boats and motors are allowed at wakeless speeds only. A boat ramp is available. A campground on Chambers' southern end has trails up western drainage's to the Rawah Wilderness Area and alpine lakes. (See Poudre River section for details on Joe Wright and Trap creeks and other waters south of Chambers Lake.)

Laramie Lake (9,300 ft; 15 ac) is about 1-mile northeast of Chambers Lake by trail. Rated poor for rainbow to 1 pound with occasional lunkers; rainbows are stocked. Fish are there, but hard to catch. Laramie Lake has a maximum depth of 21 feet.

Lost Lake (9,290 ft; 25.7 ac) lies between Chambers Lake and Laramie Lake about 1 mile north of Hwy 14 on Laramie Road. It is shallow and often winterkills. Good for stocked rainbow to 12 inches and an occasional brown.

Two miles beyond Laramie Lake by trail are Twin lakes. **Twin Lake East** (9,450 ft; 21 ac) is 24 feet deep. It has been stocked with rainbow, as is the case with **Twin Lake West** (9,450 ft; 15 ac), 0.5 mile northwest.

RAWAH WILDERNESS AREA

On the west side of Chambers Lake, **Fall Creek** carries water from several alpine lakes in the Rawah Wilderness Area. Fall Creek is rated poor for small fish all through its 3-mile length, but at its headwater, Blue and Hang Lakes offer challenging fishing for cutthroat. Access to the lakes is by a 5-mile pack trail that climbs 1600 feet from the campground on Chambers' southern shore. **Blue Lake** (10,720 ft; 16 ac) is fair for cutthroat and rainbow to 14 inches and some smaller brook. **Hang Lake** (11,160 ft; 4 ac) is 0.75 mile above Blue to the southwest by a marked trail. Good for large cutthroat,

though they are difficult to entice. Northwest from Blue Lake for 2 miles, the trail loses 660 feet in elevation before intersecting the West Branch Trail (USFS 960).

West Branch Creek, downstream from Chambers Lake about 5 miles, meets the Laramie River at Tunnel Campground on the Laramie Road. A trail from the campground follows the West Branch into the Rawah Wilderness and forks with the river. The northwestern trail (USFS 961) follows the **North Fork of the West Branch** for good brook fishing to its headwater lakes. The southwestern trail stays with the West Branch to its tributary lakes.

At the head of the North Fork, **Bench Lake** (10,950 ft; 6 ac) is about 8 miles from Tunnel Campground. Two miles after the fork, the trail makes several switchbacks. Bench is very good for 10- to 12-inch brook. **Rock Hole Lake** (11,200 ft; 6 ac) is difficult to find, it lies over the ridge south of Bench Lake. There is no direct trail to the lake, but it can be reached by bushwhacking from Bench Lake or by taking the trail (USFS 962) that breaks south from the North Fork Trail about 2.5 miles after the fork. This same trail leads to the **Twin Crater Lakes** (11,045 ft; 7 and 17 ac). They are good for 10- to 12-inch cutthroat.

West Branch Creek reaches high into the Rawah Wilderness Area to **Carey Lake** (11,044 ft; 5.7 ac), **Island Lake** (10,900 ft; 15 ac) and **Timber Lake** (10,900 ft; 10 ac). They are about 8 miles southwest of Tunnel Campground. The trail forks just before reaching Carey Lake and goes south to

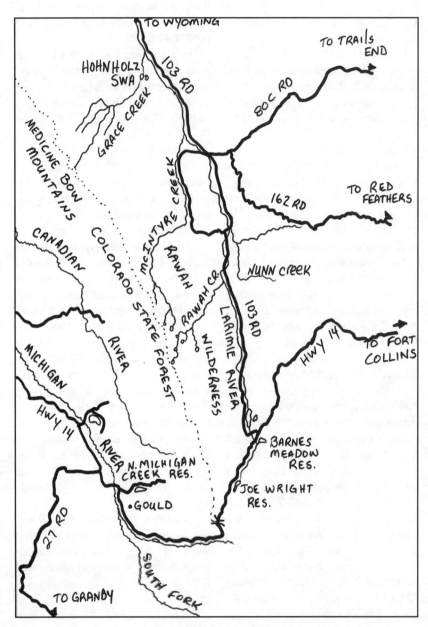

LARAMIE RIVER

Blue Lake and Hang Lake in the Fall Creek drainage. This trail leads all the way to Chambers Lake and is a shorter route to the headwaters of West Branch Creek. The lakes at the West Branch headwaters are about 0.5 mile apart. Carey Lake is fair for brook and cutthroat to 12 inches, and Timber Lake is good for rainbow and cutthroat to 10 inches. Island is stocked with small cutthroat.

The West Branch lakes, along with the lakes at the headwaters of Rawah Wilderness Creek, are located in the Rawah Wilderness Area. The Rawah is steep, mountainous country dotted with more than 35 bodies of water. The Rawah Wilderness is very popular, and the fishing pressure is heavy. Many of its waters are stocked.

Rawah Creek feeds into the Laramie River from the southwest about 7 miles downstream from Tunnel Campground. At its headwaters in the Rawah Wilderness are several alpine lakes. An 8-mile trail from Rawah Ranch, 1 mile south of the Laramie-Rawah confluence, roughly follows the Rawah to its headwaters. Follow the trail to the headwaters for good, small brook fishing. The lower reaches are fair to good for small rainbow. At the headwaters of the Rawah, the stream forks, as does the trail. Take the trail to the right (heading west) about 0.75 mile to **Little Rainbow Lake** (10,838 ft; 6 ac), a shallow lake, which is rated fair for small brook and rainbow. Little Rainbow is also accessible from McIntyre Lake to the north. A pack-trail from Glendevey heading south to the headwaters of the McIntyre Creek

goes along the east shore of McIntyre Lake to Little Rainbow Lake and on to the Rawah Lakes.

The **Rawah Lakes** lie east of Little Rainbow at the headwaters of Rawah Creek. These lakes are known by several names, but on the USGS map they are numbered. **Lake No. 1** (10,700 ft; 8 ac) is a shallow, heavily fished lake on the trail. It is rated good for small brook. Good campsites. South of Lake No.1, less than 0.5 mile by trail, is **Lake No. 2** (10,750 ft; 8 ac), which also is shallow, but rated very good for small brook and an occasional rainbow. **Lake No. 3** (10,850 ft; 22ac) is a deep 25-acre lake about 0.75 mile up creek from No. 2. It has brook and rainbow up to 13 inches that are difficult to catch. Good fly lake. Easiest fishing is with spinning gear. Rated fair to good most of the summer. Good campsites. **Lake No. 4** (11,400 ft; 31 ac) lies farthest south and is set far from the main trail. The trail to the lake is not well marked. Follow trail from other Rawah Lakes to the ridge top, and then hike west along the ridge. Trail is steep in places. Lake No. 4 is a deep lake with sheer sides and is difficult to fish. Cutthroat 11 to 17 inches.

Over the ridge to the east from Rawah Lakes is the **Upper Sandbar Lake** (10,690 ft; 9 ac). Hike 0.25 mile south of Rawah Lake No. 2 to trail junction, turn east. Follow trail about 0.5 mile to **Middle Sandbar Lake** (10,600 ft; 1 ac) and **Lower Sandbar Lake** (10,600 ft; 4 ac). The Sandbar Lakes are very shallow and rated good for brook 9 to 10 inches. They are heavily fished; waders are helpful.

Photo Courtesy of Suzzette Rummell

Colorado Wildlife

Follow the trail from the Rawah Lakes beyond Upper Sandbar Lake to **Big Rainbow Lake** (10,720 ft; 6 ac). This lake suffers winterkill; fishing is doubtful, but there are a few brook and rainbow.

CAMP LAKES

To the southeast of Big Rainbow Lake, **Upper Camp Lake** (10,720 ft; 41 ac) can be reached from Big Rainbow by following the ridge. Upper Camp is good for brook, cutthroat and a few rainbows averaging 11 inches. It is easy to fish, but waders are desirable. Downstream of Upper Camp Lake is **Lower Camp Lake** (10,510 ft; 13 ac). Lower Camp Lake can be reached from Lower Sandbar Trail or from a horse trail (USFS 968) that follows the ridges from Tunnel Campground on the Laramie River Road. It is rated very good for brook to 14 inches. Good fly lake; heavily fished. Good campsites.

Several tributaries flow into the

Laramie below Rawah Creek. From the west, these include **Drink**, **Stub** and **Link** creeks and from the east, **Nunn** (6.1 miles public) and **Deadman Creeks**. Most of the streams are small, brushy, fast and wadable, and offer good brook fishing; the latter two also have brown. The lower portions of Nunn and Deadman creeks are on private property. The headwaters on public land are accessible from the Four Corners-Red Feather road. It crosses Deadman Creek in Deadman Park. A 7-mile 4WD road that intersects the main road 0.5-mile east of Deadman Creek provides access to the Nunn Creek headwaters.

Farther downstream, **McIntyre Creek** enters the Laramie River from the southwest about 4 miles, north of Four Corners. At Four Corners, a road going west parallels the stream south to Glendevey and then loops back to the Laramie River Road south of Four Corners (about 7 miles). West of Glendevey about 0.5 mile is the Hooligan Roost Campground. A trail from the campground follows the stream about 5 miles to headwaters. Rawah Creek Trail or a pack trail (USFS 963) heading south of the Browns Park Campground outside of Glendevey can reach the lakes at the headwaters.

McIntyre Lake (10,200 ft; 14 ac) is shallow and rated fair for brook from 9-to 11-inches; an occasional large brown is taken. Easy to fish; good campsites. To the west, **Sugar Bowl Lake** (10,790 ft; 8 ac) is a moderately deep lake and tends to be overpopulated with small brook; needs some fishing. Good for small brook and some mackinaw. **Iceberg Lake** (11,100 ft; 6 ac) lies farther west. It has cutthroat.

Nice Rainbow

There is no trail. Best access is by hiking up the farthest west fork of McIntyre Creek. **Upper Twin Lake** (10,600 ft; 9 ac) is fairly deep and has rainbow trout. Upper and Lower Twin are on the middle fork in the lake area. Both are good for small brook with a few larger browns taken occasionally. **Lower Twin Lake** (10,500 ft; 5 ac) is very shallow and lies 0.5 mile north of Upper Twin Lake. These lakes do not get much fishing pressure. Good for small brook and some brown.

The northern portion of the Rawah Wilderness is drained by the northeast flowing **LaGarde Creek**. Its headwaters are in Shipman Park, a high mountain valley just east of Ute Pass. The South Fork of LaGarde is rated poor for very small brook. The **North Fork of LaGarde** offers fair fishing for brook in the 6- to 9-inch range. The lower portion of the creek is swift and offers minimal fishing opportunity. Shipman Park is accessible by trails from trailheads at Hooligan Roost Campground and at the south end of the landing strip 6 miles north of Glendevey. The park is also accessible from the Ridge Trail, which has a trailhead at the headwater of Grace Creek's South Fork.

HOHNHOLZ STATE WILDLIFE AREA

The 22-mile stretch of the **Laramie River** between the Wyoming State line and the picnic area just south of the Glendevey intersection flows through private ranch land. It is some of the finest brown-trout water in the state, but public access is quite limited. The river typically clears up early in the summer and provides excellent fly-fishing while other streams are still in runoff.

Public access to the **Laramie River** is restricted to a 1-mile stretch at **Hohnholz State Wildlife Area**, which is located 7.5 miles north of the Four Corners intersection or, if coming from the north, 5.5 miles from the Wyoming line.

The river in this stretch has been designated wild trout water. Fishing regulations include the use of artificial lures and flies only, with a bag and possession limit of 2 trout. The river here is rated good for brown in the 12- to 15-inch range, but an occasional fish to 18 inches is caught. The northern limit of the public easement can be recognized by the trailer on the west side of the river. The public area south from the camping site extends to the upper end of the beaver pond. Camping is permitted at the river, but sites are not improved.

An improved gravel road crosses the river at the campsite and provides access to the **Hohnholz Lakes**. The three lakes offer excellent feeding conditions, as they are full of shrimp. One mile beyond the bridge is **Hohnholz Lake No. 1** (7,900 ft; 8 ac). It is about 10 feet deep and stocked with catchable rainbow. It is rated good. **Hohnholz Lake No. 2** (7,900 ft; 37 ac), a mile further west, is rated excellent for rainbow averaging 11 inches. Cutthroats have also been stocked.

The western and largest lake is **Hohnholz Lake No. 3** (7,900 ft; 40 ac). It is about 30 feet deep and contains the largest fish. Fishing on Lake No. 3 is with artificial flies and lures only, with a bag limit of 4 trout. Brown trout offer good action in the 12- to 14-inch range, with many up to 3 pounds. Snake River cutthroats have also been stocked in Lake No. 3. Only hand-paddled boats are allowed on the lakes.

Access to forest lands west from the Hohnholz Lakes nearly to the Continental Divide and north to Mountain Home, Wyo., is by USFS road 200. It is usable by passenger cars except during spring run-off and after extended wet periods. The road follows a serpentine route northwest across several drainages. Timber harvesting in the area has enhanced deer and elk habitat and provided a number of 4WD roads.

West 3.5 miles from Hohnholz Lake 3, a 4WD road branches to the **Grace Creek** drainage. The headwaters of Grace Creek offer excellent elk and deer hunting but poor fishing.

Three miles beyond the Grace Creek turnoff, USFS road 200 crosses **Stuck Creek**. It offers fair fishing for small brown.

Pole Creek, the next drainage northwest, offers excellent fishing for brook averaging 7 inches from beaver ponds. Easiest access to the ponded portion of stream is by USFS road 203 for 3 miles north from Old Roach townsite (at the junction with USFS road 200), then an unmaintained 4WD road east for l mile. The turnoff for this road is not marked, and it is easy to miss. It might be more appropriately considered a hiking trail. Ponds are both upstream and down. There are also some beaver ponds on Stuck Creek east of USFS road 203.

Fish Creek, the stream west of Pole Creek, offers excellent fishing for brook averaging 10 inches, but the best fishing is in less accessible areas. USFS road 202, a 4WD road, crosses Fish Creek a mile north of USFS road 200. Best fishing is the 1.5 miles downstream to where USFS road 202 again crosses the creek. There are several small beaver ponds in this area.

West of Fish Creek is **Johnson Creek**. It offers fair fishing for brook averaging 8 inches and brown averaging 10 inches.

Boswell Creek and **Beaver Creek East**, are rated good fishing for brook averaging 9 inches. Both have been stocked with fingerling cutthroat. The area west of USFS road 200 begins a mile west of the west fork of Johnson Creek and parallels the road for 4 miles to Roach. Three 4WD roads provide access to the stream from USFS road 200.

On the east side of the Laramie River, the upper reaches of **Sand Creek** stretch into Colorado from its confluence with the Laramie River east of Woods Landing, Wyo. Sand Creek offers 25.2 miles of water with small brushy ponds that are difficult to work. Best access is by turning east at Four Corners on the Laramie River Road to Sand Creek Pass. Road roughly parallels the stream from the pass north. Sand Creek is heavily fished in the early season; rated fair for small brook and brown to 10 inches. The creek has several beaver ponds near Sand Creek Pass that are stocked with brown.

CACHE LA POUDRE RIVER
ROCKY MOUNTAIN NATIONAL PARK
NORTHEAST COLORADO

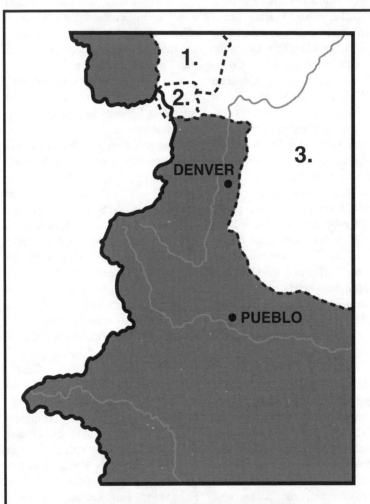

1. CACHE LA POUDRE RIVER
2. ROCKY MOUNTAIN NATIONAL PARK
3. NORTHEASTERN COLORADO

CACHE LA POUDRE RIVER

The **Cache la Poudre River** rises in the northwest section of Rocky Mountain National Park and flows northerly out of the park before looping east toward the city of Fort Collins. Highway 14, the Cameron Pass road, parallels the river for most of its 47 miles. In its reaches above the confluence with the South Platte River to the mouth of Poudre Canyon, fishing is generally not worth the effort as most of the river runs through private land. It's waters warm to lethal temperatures during the dog days of late summer, preventing the river from sustaining a viable fishery. However, isolated pockets of fish do exist.

The Cache la Poudre is the only Front Range stream without a major dam and reservoir constructed on it, although some of its water is diverted for irrigation. Portions of the stream are private and closed to public fishing. Where Hwy 14 follows the stream, there are many cabins, stores, cafes, and tackle/bait shops.

The river offers diverse fish-holding water, tempting anglers to pursue its rainbow, brown and brook trout. The upper reaches of the river above the Poudre Rearing Unit may have a few cutthroat and whitefish. It's a fine fly fishing stream.

The Poudre area encompasses the upper Cache la Poudre River drainage west of I-25 and north of Estes Park.

This is somewhat deceptive country. On first glance it seems to be mainly open ridges, grassy parks with scattered Ponderosa pine and little undergrowth. It's open terrain with light vegetation, especially at lower elevations. Once the 6000-foot level is passed, fairly open stands of lodgepole pine, spruce and aspen occur with increasing regularity. The deceptiveness lies in the abrupt canyons and steep hillsides farther up Poudre River tributaries.

The Poudre area is also referred to as the Poudre-Red Feather area, so named for the Red Feather Lakes near the center of the area. Plateau areas around the lakes provide fairly easy walking for people willing to stray from roads and trails. The entire area is comparatively easy to navigate compared to more mountainous areas of the state.

The area is a popular one. It has good accessibility for residents of Fort Collins, Greeley and other towns in the vicinity of Hwy 287 northwest out of Fort Collins, and west on Hwy 14 up the Cache la Poudre River, or a bit farther north and then west on the Red Feather Lakes Road.

Roosevelt National Forest boundaries encompass the majority of public lands in this area, although there is a fair amount of BLM land in the northwestern portion of the drainage. Because of the checkerboard pattern of private and public lands in the Poudre area, using a USFS map of the Roosevelt National Forest is a must. The map shows the types of vehicle roads and trails, which help in getting around.

Two wilderness areas along the western and southwestern borders of the drainage offer remoteness. The Rawah Wilderness Area to the west is actually at the headwaters of the Laramie River, an area located between the Poudre and North Park. The Comanche Peak Wilderness Area shares its southern border with Rocky Mountain National Park. Both of these wilderness areas are shown in detail on the Roosevelt National Forest map.

The Laramie River valley, just to the west of the Poudre area, has similar vegetation and topography. It is a comparatively small drainage running north, into Wyoming, but is accessible on the same roads from the Fort Collins and Poudre-Red Feather areas and also by Cherokee Park road and Boulder Ridge road from the northeast. While some public lands are available, there are large blocks of private land along the valley bottom from the Rawah trailhead downstream to within a several miles of the Wyoming border. Occasional BLM lands adjoin the main county road.

The Roosevelt National Forest map includes the Laramie River. Both the Rawah and the Link McIntyre trailheads provide foot or horse access into the Rawah Wilderness. The West Branch and Lost Lake trailheads near Chambers Lake at the extreme southern end also serve as access to Rawah. Zimmerman Lake trailhead, to the northeast of Cameron Pass, provides access into the small Neota Wilderness Area, sandwiched between the Rawah and Comanche Peak areas.

Suzzette and Kip heading for the high country

Photo Courtesy of Kevin Rummell

Fishing regulations on the Poudre River are as follows: Section 1- from the Pingree Park Road bridge upstream to the west boundary of the Hombre Ranch (just below Rustic); and Section 2- from Black Hollow Creek upstream to and including Big Bend campground. Classified as Wild Trout water. Fishing is by artificial flies and lures only. The limit for trout is 2 fish 16 inches or longer. From the Rocky Mountain National Park boundary downstream to the confluence with Joe Wright Creek fishing is by artificial flies and lures only, catch and release.

HORSETOOTH RESERVOIR

West of Fort Collins, **Horsetooth Reservoir** (5,430 ft; 1800 ac) is part of the Colorado-Big Thompson reclamation project. About 7 miles long, Horsetooth averages about 0.75 mile wide when full and has many deep coves. Access is a few miles south of Fort Collins at Cunningham Corner on US 287. Sign indicates 4 miles to dam and another 2 miles to the boat dock. Reservoir is rated good for 12-inch rainbow.

In 1989, the DOW began stocking some McConaughy rainbow in Horsetooth. They feel the more predatory nature of this variety will allow it to attain greater size. Kokanee are stocked but apparently have a very low survival rate. They are rarely caught. Mackinaws are stocked but the reservoir is rated poor for this species. Those caught are in the 25- to 30-pound range, but the catch is limited to only 2 or 3 a year. Most success is from the Spring Creek Dam on the south end of

the reservoir in April or May.

Horsetooth is rated good for small-mouth bass. An occasional largemouth is taken. Most bass are in the 2.5- to 3-pound range with some to 4 pounds. Bass under 15 inches must be released. Walleye under 18 inches must be released, and there is a 5 fish limit. Fishing is prohibited in the inlet area as posted from March 15 through May 31.

Perch and wipers are also present in Horsetooth Reservoir. Occasionally the ice on Horsetooth will freeze solid enough to permit ice fishing. Boats are available at the Horsetooth concession on the southwest shore; motors are allowed. Geese nest on rocky ridges around lake in the spring and should not be disturbed.

Just to the east of the reservoir on CR 23 is **Dixon Reservoir** (5,430 ft; 50 ac). Fishing is for Small- and largemouth bass, yellow perch, and sunfish. All bass must be 15 inches or longer.

WATSON LAKE

Near the mouth of Poudre Canyon, **Watson Lake** (5,120 ft; 49 ac) is 10 to 12 feet deep. Take US 287 north from Fort Collins to Bellevue Junction. Follow road west about 1 mile until the road crosses the Poudre. Take the first road to the right. Watson is rated fair to good for 8- to 10-inch rainbow, brown and small brook. An occasional walleye and perch are also caught. It is easy to fish; no boats are allowed. Camping is prohibited except at designated sites. Live bait and ice fishing also are prohibited. The west side is closed to the public.

POUDRE CANYON

The **Cache la Poudre River** is Colorado's first river to be designated as a Wild and Scenic River. Primary access to the Cache la Poudre River is Colo. 14 (a scenic byway to Walden) west from Hwy 287. The intersection, formerly known as Ted's Place, is 10 miles northwest of Fort Collins.

Fishing below the confluence of the **North Fork of the Cache la Poudre**, which is 7 miles from Hwy 287, is poor to non-existent. Severe siltation in the North Fork frequently turns the river brown downstream. Below the irrigation diversion dam at the mouth of the canyon, the river is dry or nearly dry several months of the year, rendering it worthless as a fishery.

Downstream, the river flows through Fort Collins and Greeley before joining the South Platte. Fish rarely survive in this portion of the river due to periodic low water levels.

Upstream from the North Fork confluence for 26 miles to the Pingree Park Bridge, the Cache la Poudre River offers good fishing for stocked rainbow and wild brown in the 10- to 12-inch range. Larger fish are rarely caught. Fishing is by artificial flies and lures only. The limit for trout is 2 fish 16 inches or longer. In this stretch, the river is commonly swift, dropping 1400 feet over the 26 miles, with large boulders and deep holes in the streambed. Most of the water is open to the public with numerous developed roadside camping and picnic grounds.

Owned by the city of Greeley, **Seaman Reservoir** (5,748 ft; 150 ac), at the confluence of the North Fork and

the Cache la Poudre River, is closed to the public.

NORTH FORK

Portions of the **North Fork Cache la Poudre River** upstream from Seaman Reservoir are on National Forest but access is not permitted through surrounding private land. It is a narrow, fast mountain stream rated poor for small rainbow and brook with some stretches rated fair. While a long, rugged hike through National Forest can reach it, it's not worth the effort.

Rabbit Creek enters the North Fork just 5 miles northwest of Livermore on US 287. The **Middle Fork of Rabbit Creek** has cutthroat at its headwaters on National Forest lands west of the Cherokee Park SWA lower unit. Primary accesses are by Cherokee Park Road (80 C) or the Red Feather Road. Both run west from Hwy 287 into the Cherokee Park lower unit where other roads and trails criss-cross the area. Consult a map.

Above **Halligan Reservoir**, (closed to the public) from Bull Creek upstream to Divide Creek is catch-and-release, artificial lures. The stretch offers good fishing for brown to 18 inches and rainbow to 16 inches. Easiest access to this area is by Cherokee Park road which intersects Hwy 287 four miles north of Livermore.

Upstream of Phantom Canyon, **Panhandle Creek** enters the North Fork from a southwesterly direction reached by way of USFS roads 169 and 188, the latter being 4WD. **Creedmore Lakes** (8,300 ft; all three less than 10 ac) lie about 12 miles north of Red

Feather Lakes. Only one lake, where the campground is located, has fish, and it is rated good for 10- to 16-inch brown and smaller brook. It is accessible from Red Feather village. Follow 73 C from the north end of town to CR180. It parallels Columbine Creek for a short stretch, then follows North Lone Pine Creek to a left turn marked by the sign "Creedmore Lakes". **Panhandle Reservoir** is private.

Above the confluence of Panhandle and the North Fork, **George** and **Cornelius** creeks are catch-and-release waters with artificial lures and flies only. Both are reached by USFS road 188 off USFS road 169. In Cornelius, all cutthroat must be returned to the water immediately, while all fish must be returned to George. Cutthroat in these two streams are the threatened greenback variety. These streams are accessible from Cherokee Park Road to USFS road 182, a 4WD road.

Some tributaries near North Fork headwaters are open to the public. These include **Sheep** and **Beaver creeks**. Sheep Creek has 10.6 miles of stream leading from **Eaton Reservoir** (8,545 ft; 86 ac) which contains brook trout. The reservoir is closed to the public. Beaver Creek flows for 5.6 miles. Sheep and Beaver can be accessed via the Cherokee Park Road. These small streams with beaver ponds are rated good for small brook and some brown.

RED FEATHER LAKES AREA

Southeast of North Fork of the Poudre headwaters, **Red Feather Lakes** (8,365 ft) is a popular recreation area. Primary access is via Hwy 287 for 24 miles north from Fort Collins to Livermore (also known as The Forks), then west on the Red Feather Lakes Road for 27 miles. The Red Feather area can also be reached by USFS road 162 from the community of Rustic in the Poudre Canyon. This road passes the site of Manhattan, a gold mining camp established in 1886 on the southern slope of Prohibition Mountain. All structures have been removed from the townsite that had 300 residents at its peak in 1898.

The largest of the lakes in the Red Feather group, **Dowdy Lake**, (8,133 ft; 115 ac) is the only lake where motors are allowed. This 25-foot-deep lake is rated good for stocked rainbow averaging 12 to 13 inches. It also has brook, brown and Snake River cutthroat. Trout to 5 pounds are taken. On the west and south sides of the lake are several campgrounds with facilities for trailers.

Parvin Lake (8,130 ft; 63 ac) is fenced as a Wildlife Commission research area. Fishing is by flies and lures only. All fishing is prohibited November 1 through April 30. During the balance of the year, fishing is prohibited between the hours of 10 pm and 4 am. Bag, possession and size limits are posted at the check station. No boating or inflatables. Fishing in the inlet is prohibited

From parking area to lake is about a 100-yard walk. There is no shoreline parking or overnight fishing. Rated good with flies for rainbow and brown averaging 11 inches.

There is a creel clerk on duty much

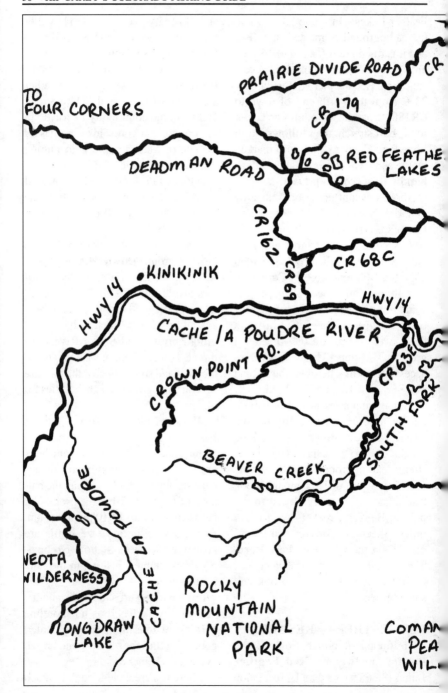

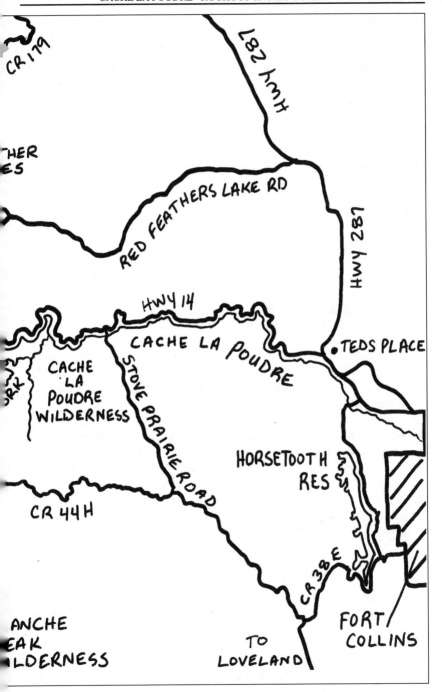

of the time that will explain the experimental work with Colorado cutthroat, rainbow, brook and brown trout. Having some fins clipped marks them. Information sought includes comparable rates of growth, catchability and other factors to be considered in managing fishing statewide.

The next lake to the west is **West (Twin) Lake** (8,200 ft; 25 ac). It is a temperamental lake, but rated good for 11-inch rainbow and brown. Campground on south shore; boats without motors are allowed.

Other lakes in the Red Feather group are private. They include **Lake Ramona**, **Hiawatha Lake**, **Shagwa Lake**, **Letitia Lake**, **Snake Lake**, **Lake Nokomis** and **Lake Erie**.

Lone Pine Creek in the Red Feather area offers good fishing for rainbow and brown averaging 8 inches with some over 10 inches. From its headwaters in the Bald Mountain area the **South Fork of Lone Pine** generally follows the Red Feather road east through Parvin Lake. This fork flows mostly through private land but is open at its headwaters, in a 1-mile section below Parvin Lake and in National forest land immediately before merging with the North Fork. Fishing in Lone Pine Creek is prohibited from the confluence of the lake upstream to the Red Feather Lake road, CR 74E, as posted. The **North Fork of Lone Pine Creek**, from headwaters west of Red Feather, swings north of the town before flowing east through private land and then dumping into the North Fork of Cache la Poudre. Private property is interspersed with public throughout

this area. Refer to a reliable ownership map or check locally to avoid trespassing.

Three miles south from the Red Feather Lake road on USFS road 162 then west 0.5-mile is **Bellaire Lake** (8,600 ft; 11 ac). It offers good fishing for 9- to 11-inch rainbow. It is a put-and-take lake with a campground at its south end.

Elkhorn Creek, 0.5-mile farther south, is rated fair for brook and brown. The lower end, before flowing into the Poudre, is posted. A 5-mile stretch in the upper end is open.

SOUTH FORK CACHE LA POUDRE

The **South Fork of the Cache la Poudre** enters the Poudre about 1 mile west of Narrows Campground, just east of Indian Meadows. Fishing is prohibited from the Rocky Mountain National Park boundary downstream for 1 mile. Pingree Park Road at Egger (USFS 63E), about 5 miles west of Narrows Campground on Hwy 14, heads south about 8 miles and then parallels the South Fork for a few miles. The lower portion of the South fork is accessible only by hiking into the Cache la Poudre Wilderness area. There are no developed trails to this part of the river that offers good fishing for 12-inch brown.

Two miles beyond the Crown Point turnoff (FR139), a 4WD road (Flowers Road) west skirts the edge of Comanche Peak Wilderness area and leads to the headwaters of **Little Beaver Creek**, rated poor fishing for small brown. The road leads to the Beaver

Fishing Beaver Ponds

Photo Courtesy of Kevin Rummell

Park Trailhead. From there, a foot trail accesses the Little Beaver Creek. No OHV's are permitted on this route.

The main road (FR63E) briefly leaves the South fork to follow **Pennock Creek**, which offers fair fishing for 10-inch brown, before rejoining it at the Tom Bennett Campground. After another 1.5 miles, the main road joins the South Fork, where it offers fair fishing for 8- to 10-inch brown.

A road (44 H) intersecting from the east crosses 9143-foot Pennock Pass then follows **Buckhorn Creek**, which offers fair fishing for small brook. It is brushy and difficult to fish. The road ends at Stove Prairie Road.

A mile beyond Tom Bennett Campground is Colorado State University's Pingree Park campus. The South fork is closed to fishing from Pingree Park upstream to its headwaters in Rocky Mountain National Park as this is critical habitat of the threatened greenback cutthroat.

A 4WD road (USFS 147) from Tom Bennett Campground goes southwest to **Fall Creek**, rated fair for small brown. The road leads to private land and is closed to the public. A trailhead has been established for foot access only. A 3-mile trail from the end of the road leads to **Emmaline Lake** (11,000 ft; 5.7 ac) and **Cirque Lake** (11,000 ft; 2.8 ac) above timberline. Emmaline, with a depth of 23 feet, has cutthroat, while 13-foot-deep Cirque has very few, if any, fish. A south fork in the trail, near the trailhead, leads into the park to Mummy Pass and beyond to Mirror Lake.

USFS road 145 from Bennett Campground goes past Sky Ranch to **Beaver Creek**. There is no public access to and beyond Sky Ranch except by foot trail from the trail before Sky Ranch. This is private property with no public access. This 7-mile stream is 6 to 8 feet wide with several ponds. It is rated good for small brook and cutthroat.

Two and one half miles past Sky Ranch on FDR 145 is **Comanche Reservoir** (9,400 ft; 20 ac) Rated fair for brook.

Downstream from Comanche, the road passes the privately owned **Hourglass Reservoir** (9,200 ft; 20 ac). At Comanche Reservoir, a foot trail leads to Beaver Creek's headwater lakes, including **Browns Lake** (10,520 ft; 18.5 ac), **Timberline Lake** (10,500 ft; 4 ac) and **Comanche Lake** (10,500 ft; 8 ac). Browns is reached by hiking north from the fork in Beaver Creek; Comanche, by hiking south. The last part of the 4-mile hike to Browns is steep but easy. Browns is 52 feet deep and is rated good for brook that averages 12 inches. Timberline, less than a quarter mile short of Browns, is a shallow lake with small brook.

These areas are within Comanche Peak Wilderness and have travel, camp and fire restrictions. Please check with the local Ranger District for information.

The main **Cache la Poudre River** upstream from the Pingree Park Road Bridge for 17 miles to the upper end of Big Bend Campground is wild trout water. This stretch, except a segment of private land that extends from just east of Rustic to the Black Hollow Creek inlet, is restricted to flies and lures only. Limit is 2 fish 16 inches and over. The river here is rated good for brown.

Five miles from Hwy 14 at Egger, Crown Point Road, USFS 139, forks west from USFS 131, the Pingree Park Road. Crown Point Road goes west 18 miles to the Zimmerman and Crown Point trailheads and headwaters of **Sheep Creek**. The East and West fork, as well as the main stream, are catch and release waters restricted to flies and lures only due to the reintroduction of threatened greenback cutthroat. Sheep Creek has numerous beaver ponds near the confluence of its East and West forks. **Black Hollow Creek**, drainage to the east of Sheep Creek, has the same restrictions.

At Kinikinik, **Roaring Fork Creek** enters the Poudre from the north. The 5-mile-long stream is 5 to 8 feet wide and is rated fair for small brown, rainbow and cutthroat. It is open to the public and accessible by pack trail from Kinikinik.

Upstream from Kinikinik to the confluence of Joe Wright Creek, the river is either on private property or, on the upper end, swift and rated only fair for browns.

LONG DRAW RESERVOIR

Long Draw Reservoir (10,100 ft; 242 ac), west of the Poudre on **La Poudre Pass Creek**, is set in bighorn sheep country just outside the park. This reservoir fluctuates greatly but has a maximum depth of 70 feet. Fishing is rated poor; however, a few large cutthroat are taken. The Pikes Peak cutthroat is stocked. Access to Long Draw Reservoir is by turning south from Hwy 14 on the Long Draw Road (USFS 156), which is just opposite the Blue Lake Trail parking lot. Turn right just after Trap Lake. La Poudre Pass Creek, also known as **Long Draw Creek**, and the reservoir are fishing with artificial flies and lures only, and have a two fish limit. The road is blocked a mile beyond the reservoir. The old Poudre Pass 4WD road is closed.

Trap Creek, a 6-mile-long southern tributary of Chambers Lake, is paralleled by the Long Draw Road. It has a few cutthroat. **Trap Lake** (9,960 ft; 13 ac) is a shallow, 6-foot-deep, put-and-take lake that is fair for rainbow, brook and cutthroat. At Trap Lake, follow east fork in road to **Peterson Lake** (9,400 ft; 41 ac), which offers difficult fishing for stocked Pikes Peak cutthroat to 14 inches, some larger. This

12-foot-deep lake is a part of the city of Greeley's water supply. Boats are not allowed. The trail at the end of the road, just beyond the lake, leads to the Poudre River.

Corral Creek intersects the Long Draw Road about 1 mile before the reservoir. Corral, which provides 6 miles of stream fishing, is a small brushy stream with small cutthroat. It enters the Poudre from the west. Fishing by artificial flies and lures only. All cutthroat are catch and release.

Joe Wright Creek enters the Poudre from the southwest. Its headwaters are at Cameron Pass on Hwy 14. It is closed between January 1 and July 31, and fishing is with artificial lures and flies, when you can fish, with a bag limit of 2 trout 16 inches or longer. **Zimmerman Lake** (10,495 ft; 11 ac) near its headwaters, produced the state-record grayling. The 1 pound, 7-ounce grayling, caught in 1974, was 15 inches long. Fishing by artificial flies and lures only. All cutthroat must be returned to the water immediately. Fishing is prohibited in the inlet area as posted January 1 through July 31. Zimmerman is a glacial lake reached by trail, which junctures with Hwy 14 at the west end of Joe Wright Reservoir; 1- mile to Zimmerman. At the outlet of the lake, a small fall cascades down the mountainside. It can be seen from Hwy 14. This 18-foot-deep lake is rated good for 8- to 12-inch grayling and some cutthroat. It has strong natural reproduction for grayling.

Joe Wright Reservoir (10,184 ft; 163 ac when full) is on Hwy 14 just 3 miles upstream from Chambers Lake.

This elongated body of water is home to Emerald Lake rainbow, a unique strain transplanted from the Weminuche Wilderness Area, northeast of Durango. Fishing is restricted to artificial lures and flies, with a limit of 2 trout 16 inches or longer, while grayling of any size may be kept. There are plenty of fish, with some reaching 17 inches. Only electric motors may be used on boats. Joe Wright Creek enters the south end of Chambers Lake (see Laramie River section) and picks up again off its eastern shore.

Just off Hwy 14, near Chambers' eastern shore, **Barnes Meadow Reservoir** (9,153 ft; 113 ac when full) is stocked with fingerling rainbow and Pikes Peak cutthroat. This 40-foot-deep lake is rated fair for 11-inch cutthroat.

POUDRE RIVER HEADWATERS

Headwaters of the Poudre River in Rocky Mountain National Park (RMNP) can be reached by following a pack trail south along the Poudre River from Big South Campground on Hwy 14 near Chambers Lake. The Big South Trail follows the river more than 20 miles to its headwaters on US 34 (Trail Ridge Road) in the park. This section of river, restricted to flies and lures, offers some of the Poudre's finest fishing. It averages 20 feet to 30 feet wide with all types of water. Two miles up the trail a small tributary, **May Creek**, is closed to fishing.

A road leaving Hwy 14 where the bridge crosses Joe Wright Creek also reaches the high branches of the Poudre. Sign on Hwy 14 reads "Long Draw Reservoir." Then take left fork in road to Peterson Lake. The Big South Bridge is out near Peterson Reservoir and restricts access to RMNP and along Big South. The last 0.5-mile of this road is rated 4WD. From the end of the road either follow the trail upstream about a mile or bushwhack directly down the steep hillside to the river. The headwaters of the Poudre are good for cutthroat, brown and a few rainbow averaging 10 inches, though larger fish are taken.

At the Poudre's headwaters, **Poudre Lake** (10,700 ft; 14 ac) at Milner Pass just off the Trail Ridge Road in the park offers plenty of feed for brook trout.

Downstream 7 to 10 miles, follow the pack trail to where **Chapin, Hague** and **Cascade Creek** feed into the Poudre. These tributaries offer good brook fishing in the lower reaches. Obey park regulations when fishing in the park. There is not a park-fishing permit, but a Colorado fishing license is required.

At the headwaters of Cascade Creek, **Mirror Lake** (11,000 ft; 19 ac) lies inside the park boundary of RMNP. It can be reached from the trail at the headwaters of the South Fork Cache la Poudre or by a trail that forks from the Poudre River near Hague Creek. Another access is via a trail from the Long Draw Road down Corral Creek to Poudre Pass Creek then down it to the fork in the trail. Cascade Creek enters the Poudre 0.5 mile downstream, the trail to Mirror Lake 0.5 mile upstream. Mirror is fair for small brook, though some to 14 inches have been taken. It's a long trip in, so plan to stay overnight.

Photo Courtesy of Suzzette Rummell

"Badger Boy"

ROCKY MOUNTAIN NATIONAL PARK (RMNP)

Few fishing settings have the spectacular alpine backdrop of Rocky Mountain National Park, refuge of the rare greenback cutthroat and the most genetically pure strains of the Colorado River cutthroat. Only a few of the millions of annual visitors ever wet a line, and then with only sporadic success, even in waters with good trout populations. It's temperamental angling, but there are brown, brook, rainbow, Colorado River and Yellowstone cutthroats and hybrids thereof to tempt any fisherman. The setting of high altitude, heavy snowfall, short summers, as exemplified in the name of the Never Summer Mountain Range, doesn't lend itself to big fish. However, there are exceptions.

Rocky Mountain National Park spans the Continental Divide in north Central Colorado, about 80 miles northwest of Denver. While no major fishing waters are among the exceptionally rugged 13,000- and 14,000-foot peaks, there are some sections of streams and remote lakes that will challenge any angler willing to hike to reach them. Repopulating park streams with the indigenous greenback cutthroat has been successful and many streams are open to catch and release fishing.

Supplemental stocking of native cutthroat trout is done only to restore native species to waters previously altered. Populations of rainbow, brook and brown are reproducing naturally since they were introduced in streams years ago. Fishermen need only a Colorado fishing license. Except for children 12 years and under, fishing is with flies and artificial lures only. Fishing regulations, restrictions, and closed waters periodically change. When entering the park check for current information. Except for Bear Lake, hand-powered boats are allowed on all lakes.

Access to Rocky Mountain National Park from the east is by US 36 from the Boulder-Lyons area or by US 34 west from Loveland to Estes Park, gateway to the park. From the west, the park is reached by US 34 just west of Granby and through Grand Lake. The road is paved all the way through the park. From Deer Ridge Junction on the East Side of the park to the Grand Lake entrance at Rocky Mountain National Park, the highway is called Trail Ridge Road. Even though Trail Ridge Road closes in October after the first heavy snows, the park is open year round. Trail Ridge Road, with a maximum elevation of 12,183 feet, traverses the tundra and crosses the Continental Divide providing breathtaking views along the way.

Deer and bighorn sheep can be seen throughout the summer months, but the best viewing time for elk is in the early fall (normally mid- September to October), when the bull elk are in the rut and bulging. Open Meadows on the eastern side of the park are the best spots to hear and see this annual spectacle. Rangers at the entrances to the park can provide details on when and where one might have the best opportunities to view elk.

The alpine topography of the park provides excellent background for photographs. Due to familiarity with humans, animals have the tendency to lose their natural fear. Visitors should never get too close to a wild animal. Even a peaceful-appearing mule deer doe or fawn can cause injury to the less than careful human. Keeping a respectful distance is better for the animal and the human.

Hiking and camping are popular activities within the park, and many photographers get their better pictures away from the heavily traveled roads and trails. Check with Park Service personnel for information about camping, hiking and fishing regulations.

Blue grouse, ptarmigan and band-tailed pigeon are but a few of the birds one might encounter in the park. Also present are several varieties of squirrel, chipmunk, pika and marmot. Wildflowers are everywhere in the summer. In all respects, it is a great place to visit.

PROTECTED WATERS

To protect endangered greenback cutthroat, these waters are closed to fishing: **Bear Lake** (including inlet and outlet streams as posted); **Bench Lake; Hunters Creek** above Wild Basin Ranger Station; **Lake Nanita** outlet for 100 yards on **North Inlet Creek; Ptarmigan Creek; South Fork of the Poudre River** above Paingree Park;

and **West Creek** above West Creek Falls.

From April 1 to July 31 **Hidden Valley Creek** and the beaver ponds on **Hidden Valley Creek** are open for brook trout fishing with barbless hooks only. All greenback cutthroats caught are to be returned to the water immediately. Many of the lakes and streams in the park have special restrictions; read descriptions for each for further information. Other lakes and streams in the park are open to fishing year-round. Ice fishing in the deeper lakes— **Black Lake**, (for 9-inch brookies) and the **Glacier Gorge** lakes area—can be very productive.

NORTH ST. VRAIN CREEK

Some of the more likely fishing waters in the park's southeast corner are accessible by trail from the community of Allenspark on Colo. Hwy 7.

North St. Vrain Creek, flowing out of the park north of Allenspark, is fair fishing for brook and brown to 10 inches and for rainbow and cutthroat, mostly small. Access is via the Wild Basin Ranger Station. **Sandbeach Lake** (10,300 ft; 17 ac) is 4.2 miles west of the park boundary. The trail to the lake is rough and steep. Sandbeach is deep when full, with a sloping, sandy shoreline. It is fair for rainbow and cutthroat from 6 to 14 inches. Both of these waters are catch and release. **Hunters Creek** is closed to fishing above the ranger station.

Thunder Lake (10,600 ft; 17 ac) is 6.8 miles west of Wild Basin Ranger Station on the well-maintained Thunder Lake Trail. Fishing is only fair, but

there is some good-size cutthroat. **Box Lake** (10,700 ft; 6 ac) is about 1.5 miles south of Thunder, cross-country (no trail); it is deep and at timberline. Can be fair for brook to 12 inches. A half-mile farther south is **Eagle Lake** (10,800 ft; 12 ac), which probably is barren.

To the southeast are **Ouzel Lake** and **Ouzel Creek,** which are catch and release areas. These are greenback cutthroat waters. **Bluebird Lake**, above Ouzel Lake, is barren. South and east is **Cony Creek**, (catch and release only), a pretty stream with good fishing for rainbow and cutthroat as it drains the southeastern part of the park. Near its headwaters is **Pear Reservoir** (10,582 ft; 7 ac). Rated fair for catch and release cutthroat.

West of Pear Reservoir are the **Hutcheson Lakes** (10,200 ft; 0.5 to 3 ac). They and the creek are good for catch and release cutthroat. To the west, **Cony Lake** (11,440 ft; 2 ac) is barren. Access as far as Pear Reservoir is on the Finch Lake-Pear Reservoir Trail, which heads out of both Allenspark and the Wild Basin Ranger Station on Hwy 7. It is about a 10-mile hike. From Wild Basin Ranger Station, it is about 7 miles by walking up North St. Vrain Creek and, at the Calypso Cascades sign, south up Cony Creek. Beyond the cascades, the trail is poor and the going rough. Pretty country.

North of Allenspark about 7 miles, a well-marked road leads west to Longs Peak Ranger Station, the trailhead and campground. Southwest of the station is **Peacock Pool** (11,360 ft; 4 ac) and **Chasm Lake** (11,800 ft;

19 ac), both on **Roaring Fork of Cabin Creek**. Take the Longs Peak Trail to a fork in the trail about 2.5 miles below the boulder field. A sign indicates the Chasm Lake Trail to the west, directly toward the diamond (east face) of Longs Peak. It is 0.75 mile to Peacock, which has brook and cutthroat to 9 inches. Another 1.5 miles, mostly westerly, is Chasm, very deep and rocky, and hard to fish for cutthroat. There are some large ones, though very temperamental. Chasm is about 4.2 miles from the campground. Roaring Fork has some cutthroat and brook. Pools are best, but access often is difficult.

BIG THOMPSON RIVER

Farther north, the **Big Thompson River** flows northeastward out of the park into the town of Estes Park and Lake Estes. Its lower reaches provide meadow fishing, although, from a mile west of the Moraine Park Bridge, it is brushy. Fishing is fair for 10-inch brown, rainbow and some brook. Access to it and several high lakes is from the Beaver Meadows entrance, west of Estes.

Going west into the park, turn south at the first junction to Moraine Park. After a mile, turn west onto the dirt road along the Big Thompson River to Fern Lake trailhead parking area and picnic ground. Three miles up **Spruce Creek** is **Spruce Lake** (9,640 ft; 4 ac), and a mile further is **Loomis Lake** (10,200 ft; 3 ac). Both lakes are catch and release. **Fern Lake** (9,550 ft; 10 ac) is 2.5 miles up **Fern Creek** and **Odessa Lake** (10,100 ft; 11 ac) is one

mile further. Both of these lakes are open to catch-and-release fishing. To the northwest, Forest Canyon on the Big Thompson is open to catch-and-release fishing above lost falls.

Rock Lake and **Little Rock Lake** (10,300 ft; 1 ac), **Arrowhead Lake** (11,200 ft; 43 ac) and **Donut Lake** (11,520 ft; 5 ac) have cutthroat. Access via Forest Canyon is extremely difficult; inquiry is advised. High lakes like these provide unpredictable fishing.

Going back to the Bear Lake Road south of Moraine Park and the Big Thompson River, several lakes are fishable; many of them heavily fished. A mile west and south of Bear Lake is **Dream Lake** (9,840 ft; 6 ac) which has poor fishing for cutthroat. A mile past Dream Lake is **Emerald Lake** (10,200 ft; 7 ac) with cutthroat; and to the south, **Lake Haiyaha** (10,200 ft; 6 ac), a deep lake, also provides cutthroat fishing. Both, however, are rated poor.

From the Glacier Gorge parking area on the Bear Lake road, several lakes are accessible up a steep, well-marked trail to the southwest. A mile above Alberta Falls, **Brook Creek** joins **Glacier Creek** from the southwest. Glacier has mostly brook, some cutthroat and possibly brown trout. Up Brook Creek 3.5 miles from the trailhead is **The Loch** (10,200 ft; 15 ac), **Lake of Glass** (10,900 ft; 5 ac) and **Sky Pond** (11,000 ft; 11 ac) are 0.5 mile apart and 2 miles farther up Loch Trail. All are rated poor. The Loch Trail stream and Sky Pond have 8- to 9-inch brook. The others are rated fair for brook and cutthroat. Loch Lake has some rainbow and is rated fair.

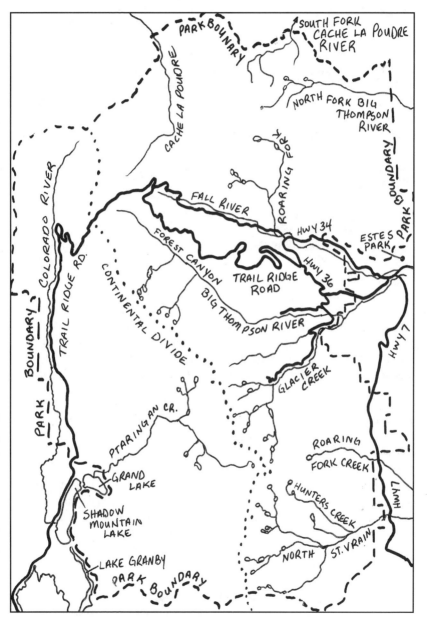

ROCKY MOUNTAIN NATIONAL PARK

Five miles south up Glacier Creek is **Black Lake** (11,000 ft; 9 ac), with fair fishing for brook and cutthroat. It is a tough, rocky trail for horse and man. Downstream, the creek between Black and **Mills Lake** (10,000 ft; 16 ac) is poor, though the fish are there. Mills has rainbow, and its companion, **Jewel Lake** (10,230 ft; 3 ac), has cutthroat. Both lakes are less than a mile upstream from Glacier Falls. Glacier Creek has good populations of cutthroat and some rainbow.

About halfway between Jewel and Black lakes up the ridge west of Glacier Creek are **Lake Solitude** and **Shelf Lake**, both are barren.

Sprague Lake (8,720 ft; 3 ac) is a shallow roadside lake midway between Glacier Junction and Moraine Park. It is good for brook to 10 inches.

FALL RIVER/ROARING RIVER

From Estes Park west, Hwy 34 parallels **Fall River** for 6 miles until the highway crosses the stream at Horseshoe Park and proceeds up Trail Ridge Road. Fishing is rated fair for cutthroat. **Lawn Lake** (10,987 ft; 20 ac) near the head of **Roaring River**, was good fishing and heavily fished until the Lawn Lake Dam broke, reducing the size of the man-made reservoir from its original 40 acres. The flood washed-out the downstream river and streams. Although smaller, Lawn Lake is still a good catch and release fishery.

Fishing on the upper reaches of Fall River and the Roaring River are poor, lower sections are fair for catch and release fishing.

Above Lawn Lake, a mile by trail, are **Crystal Lake** (11,480 ft; 25 ac) and **Little Crystal Lake** (11,560 ft; 4 ac). Crystal is poor to good for cutthroat, catch and release only. Little Crystal is barren.

Moving downstream, a mile above the Fall River-Roaring River confluence on the old Lawn Lake Trail, and above Horseshoe Falls, the Ypsilon Lake Trail crosses Roaring River and heads northwest to **Ypsilon Lake** (10,520 ft; 7 ac) and **Chiquita Lake** (11,360 ft; 4 ac). This is a rough 3-mile hike for only fair fishing for good populations of cutthroat in Ypsilon. Chiquita is virtually barren. Due north of Ypsilon Lake are three **Fay Lakes** (11,000 ft; 1 to 5 ac). It is a 1.5-mile hike for cutthroat, no trail. The lower lake is best.

In the northeast corner of the park, the **North Fork of Big Thompson River** flows east from the 13,000-foot peaks of the Mummy Range. The North Fork is catch and release above Lost Falls. There are several high lakes including **Lost Lake** (10,500 ft; 9 ac) and **Lake Husted** (11,000 ft; 1 ac). Lost is fair for brook and cutthroat; Husted, a mile west of Lost and above timberline, has many brook trout. Both lakes are catch and release.

Inside the park, the North Fork is fast, with beaver ponds, and supports some brook and cutthroat. Access is by the Dunraven Road, 1.75 miles northeast of Glen Haven, which follows the stream. From the parking area at the end of Dunraven Road, it is 2.5 miles to the park boundary and another 4.5 miles to Lost Lake. West of Glen Haven, **West Creek** above West Falls is closed to fishing.

The principal fishing on the north and northwest sides of the park is in the **Cache la Poudre River** and its tributaries. The river originates at brook trout-filled **Poudre Lake** (10,700 ft; 14 ac) at Milner Pass on Trail Ridge Road (Hwy 34). The river can be seen in the canyon north of the road. Park the car along the road and hike down to the stream for good fishing for small brook, especially late in the season. It is a rough hike back up to the road. Poudre River Trail runs along the West Side of the river. Tributary streams—**Chapin Creek**, **Hague Creek**, **Willow Creek** and **Cascade Creek**—are all good brook trout streams for a mile or so up from the river. Hague has some cutthroat. (See Cache la Poudre chapter for more details.)

WESTERN SIDE OF PARK

On the far west side of the park, the **North Fork of Colorado River** flows south more than 13 miles in the park and 5 miles on private land before entering Shadow Mountain Reservoir. It is a medium-size, often-brushy stream with rainbow, brown and lots of brook, particularly above Lulu City trailhead at the northern end of the river. There are many beaver ponds. Several small streams enter the river from the west, but generally yield poor fishing for small fish. Moving south, **Lake of the Clouds** (11,400 ft; 3 ac), above timberline at the headwaters of Hitchens Gulch on **Big Dutch Creek**, has cutthroat. It is a 6.5-mile hike northwest from the western foot of Milner Pass.

Farther south, **Timber Creek** and **Timber Lake** (10,900 ft; 10 ac) on the east side of the river are open to catch and release fishing for Colorado River cutthroat. **Julian Lake** (11,080 ft; 6 ac), at the headwaters of **Onahu Creek,** is barren. The creek has some brook to 10 inches. It is reached by a difficult walk from the signed trailhead above Green Mountain Ranch on Hwy 34, 6 miles north of Grand Lake.

Fishing in **Tonahutu Creek**, also reached from Green Mountain Trail, is best in the meadows. It is reached by walking east 2 miles up the Green Mountain Trail from the trailhead on Hwy 34, 5 miles north of Grand Lake. Fishing is good for small brook and, higher up above Granite Falls, for cutthroat to 10 inches. It is a great open-meadow fishing stream for children.

The last 5 miles of the Colorado River above Shadow Mountain Reservoir are on private property. The area tends to be brushy except where improvements have been made.

Several small streams flow out of the park from the east and into Grand Lake, Shadow Mountain Lake or the Colorado River downstream from Shadow Mountain Lake. Foremost of these is **North Inlet Creek**, which flows through the town of Grand Lake and into the lake. North Inlet has brook in the 3 miles below Cascade Falls and cutthroat above the falls. It is heavily fished; fishing is fair.

Three miles above the falls, the trail forks. The west fork goes 9 miles to **Lake Nokoni** (10,800 ft; 25 ac) and another mile to **Lake Nanita** (10,800 ft; 34 ac). These are deep lakes that are home to what is thought to be the most genetically pure strain of native Colorado River cutthroat. A recovery program for this species is based upon the collection of eggs from fish in the spawning areas of Lake Nanita. It is for this reason the outlet stream is closed to fishing for 100 yards downstream from the lake.

Flowing into North Inlet from the east about 5 miles from Grand Lake is **Ptarmigan Creek.** It drains **Ptarmigan, Snowdrift** and **Bench Lakes,** of which only the latter has fish. It is about a mile by steep trail from North Inlet. Bench Lake, and Ptarmigan Creek above War Dance Falls, is closed to fishing due to the Colorado River cutthroat recovery program.

East Inlet Creek flows into the southeast shore of Grand Lake. The lower 5.5 miles below Lone Pine Lake have brook trout. **Lone Pine Lake**

(9,840 ft; 13 ac) is shallow, usually loaded with small brook and heavily fished. Upstream 1.5 miles is long, narrow **Lake Verna** (10,200 ft; 33 ac). It too has plenty of brook. **Spirit Lake** (10,240 ft; 8 ac) and **Fourth Lake** (10,400 ft; 7 ac) both have brook and are a short walk upstream from Spirit. **Fifth Lake** (11,020 ft; 7ac) at timberline offers catch and release fishing for cutthroat to 12 inches.

Paradise Creek, which flows from the south into East Inlet between the falls and Lone Pine Lake, offers good fishing for cutthroat, especially in the upper reaches, but it takes very strenuous effort to get there. At the headwaters of the first sizable tributary to Paradise Creek, an arduous 7 miles from East Inlet, is **Lake Adams** (11,200 ft; 5 ac) with cutthroat. Paradise Creek, as well as, Lake Adams is catch and release.

NORTHEAST COLORADO

After leaving the Denver Metro area, the South Platte River runs north to Greeley before angling toward Colorado's northeastern prairie and eventually, Nebraska. From Ft. Morgan to the Nebraska State line I-76 closely parallels the South Platte River. While the river does not offer much in the way of fishing, it does provide water for several outstanding reservoirs. While the eastern plains contain hundreds of small ponds and lakes they are beyond the scope of this book, only the major and most popular are covered.

Northeastern Colorado is home to warm water fishing; the primary species are walleye, largemouth bass, crappie, wiper, tiger muskies, and channel catfish. This area of the state, although wind blown at times, offers some of the best wiper and tiger muskie fishing. Bluegill and other sunfish, as well as stocked rainbow are also available. Some of the states best known waters, Boyd Lake, North Sterling Reservoir, Jumbo Reservoir, Bonny Reservoir, are situated near the northern corner of Colorado.

Photo Courtesy of Suzzette Rummell

Kevin with Cutthroat

BERTHOUD AREA

West of Berthoud on Hwy 56 is **Carter Lake Reservoir** (1158 ac). Carter has stocked rainbow, mostly in the 9- to 12-inch range, and kokanee. Largemouth bass are in the 12- to 14-inch class with medium size walleye caught. Bass must be 15 inches or longer. Snagging for kokanee is permitted from October 1 through December 31. Best access to Carter is by driving 7 miles west from the town of Berthoud on Hwy 56.

LOVELAND AREA

In the Loveland area there is good fishing in several lakes and reservoirs. Southwest of Loveland is **Boedecker Reservoir** (380 ac), which has walleye, yellow perch, crappie, largemouth bass, channel catfish, bluegill, carp and bullhead. Walleye, while not plentiful, average 2 pounds. Boats are allowed, but not available to rent. Camping is prohibited. Boedecker Reservoir low is reached by taking US 34 west from Loveland. Turn south at Ft. Namaqua, about 0.5 mile outside of town. Drive 1-mile south, then 0.5-mile west.

Lon Hagler Reservoir (200 ac) is located about 1 mile south on County Road 21-S and 1 mile north of Lonetree Reservoir. Lon Hagler is stocked with rainbow, channel catfish, muskie, crappie and largemouth bass. Best fishing is along west shore. Boat ramp and campsites are available. Bass must be 15 inches or longer. Fishing is prohibited in the Lon Hagler inlet structure as posted. Lon Hagler is a very popular ice-fishing lake. Use fee permit is required.

Lonetree Reservoir (502 ac) is a good lake for channel catfish, crappie and wiper, and also has bass, crappie and perch. Lonetree is regarded as a good ice-fishing lake. Restrictions: bass must be 15 inches or longer; wipers have a 10 fish limit, must be 15 inches or longer; and walleye have a 5 fish limit, must be 15 inches or longer. Access to Lonetree is gained by turning off US 287 about 3 miles south of Loveland on County Road 14-W and then south on Lonetree Drive. Camping is prohibited.

The city of Loveland surrounds **Lake Loveland** (500 ac). It is good fishing for walleye, bass, crappie, channel catfish and a few rainbow. A boat permit from the city is required.

Northeast of Loveland less than 0.5 mile, **Boyd Lake** (1674 ac), **Horseshoe Lake** (900 ac), and **Equalizer Reservoir** (60 ac) offer warm-water fishing with an occasional rainbow taken. Boyd is especially popular and offers good fishing for stocked rainbow, walleye to 8 pounds, pike, channel catfish and white bass. There is a boat marina and ramp on Boyd, and a use fee permit is required. Fishing is prohibited on the south inlet area of Boyd as posted. All small- and largemouth bass and walleye must be 15 inches in length or longer. The bag and possession limit for walleye is 5 fish. Horseshoe Lake has good fishing for walleye, channel catfish, bluegill hybrid, crappie and large- and smallmouth bass. Access to these reservoirs is by driving 2 miles east from Loveland on US 34; or about 1 mile west and north of the US 34 and I-25 junction.

In the same area, adjacent to I-25 on the west side, **Big Thompson Ponds** (40 ac) have channel catfish, large-mouth bass and bluegill hybrid, as well as crappie and wipers. Boats or any other floating devices are prohibited. Camping is permitted. All large- and smallmouth bass must be 15 inches in length or longer. **Windsor Lake** only has carp.

On the east side of I-25 and Hwy 392 is Frank State Wildlife Area. **North and South Frank Easement Ponds** (20 ac total) offer fishing for Small- and largemouth bass, bluegill, and crappie. All bass must be 15 inches or longer.

FORT COLLINS AREA

In the Fort Collins area, **Wellington Reservoir** (100 ac) offers fishing for walleye, yellow perch, crappie, channel catfish, stocked rainbow, tiger muskie, carp and bullhead. Take Hwy 1 north from Fort Collins about 5 miles to reach the reservoir.

Riverbend Ponds are just south of Hwy 14 between the east side of Fort Collins and I-25. There's a dirt road near the state highway patrol building, but it's not marked for access. All small and largemouth bass must be 15 inches in length or longer.

Simpson Ponds (15 ac total) are 2 miles west of I-25 at Exit 402. At CR 9E, turn north 0.5 miles to the ponds. **North Shields Pond** (10 ac) is just north of Cache la Poudre River along Shields Street in north Fort Collins. **Prospect Ponds** (12 ac) are on the south side of Prospect Street just west

of the river. Turn onto Sharp Point Drive, then go 0.5 mile south. These ponds are gravel pits obtained by the Division of Wildlife for warm-water fishing. They have bass, yellow perch, bluegill, catfish and crappie. On ponds #2 and #3, all small- and largemouth bass must be 15 inches or longer.

Alongside that portion of the Cache la Poudre River that lies between US 287 and Colo. 28, just west of LaPorte, is **Watson Lake** (40 ac). It has stocked rainbow and some brook. Nearby **Horse Paster Ponds** are restricted to youth fishing only. **Douglas Reservoir** (565 ac) located off County Road 60 and La Vina Dr. offers fair fishing for rainbow trout, walleye, wiper, crappie, channel catfish, yellow perch, and largemouth bass. The limit for trout is 4 fish. Boats are allowed. **Black Hollow Reservoir** is closed.

Seeley Lake (125 ac) is a small lake with boat ramp and a stable fish population consisting of bass, crappie, yellow perch, bluegill and catfish. The lake is 9 miles east of the town of Windsor on Hwy 392, then south 1 mile. No facilities other than toilets and trash cans. Rainbow are also occasionally stocked, usually in early spring and fall. **Riverside Reservoir** is closed to public access.

NORTHEAST

Glenmere Lake (4 ac) is a small lake in the City of Greeley. Glenmere has bass, bluegill, crappie and rainbow. Shore fishing only.

Milton Reservoir is privately owned and not open to the public. It is in the area northeast of the town of

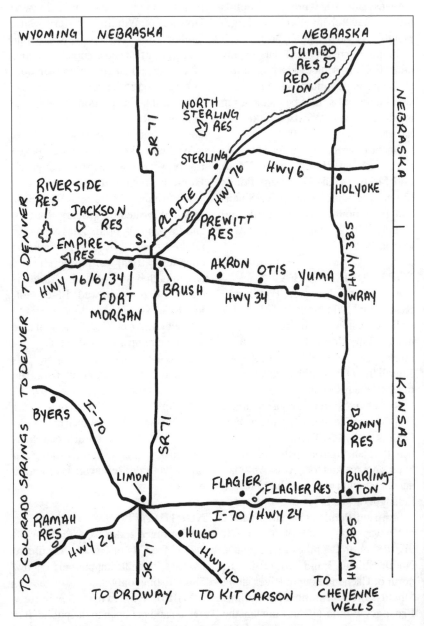

NORTHEAST

Plattesville. **Empire Reservoir** and **Muir's Spring Ponds** are closed to public access.

Banner Lakes (6 to 23 ac) are a collection of frog ponds a mile or so downstream from Horse Creek Reservoir. At the town of Hudson, on I-76, take Hwy 52 four miles east. Sunfish, bass, crappie and catfish are prime fish species available. Fishing is allowed from shoreline only. Toilets and trash cans, as well as a parking area are available. A good place for kids.

East of Greeley about 30 miles, in the northwest corner of Morgan County, **Jackson Reservoir** (2260 ac) and State Park is one of the better fisheries for walleye. Stocking consists of walleye, white bass, wipers, yellow perch, crappie, channel catfish and rainbow trout. Restrictions include; all walleye and wiper must be 15 inches or longer; the limit for wiper is 10 fish, walleye have a 5 fish limit. A use fee permit is required. Ice fishing shelters must be portable. Fishing is prohibited from November 1 through the last day of the regular waterfowl season, except that fishing is permitted from the dam through November 30 and ice fishing is permitted in designated areas only. The Jackson Lake outlet ditch, immediately below the dam, is closed to all public access and fishing in an area around the rotary screen structure as posted. Fishing access is negotiated, check for current status at (970) 645-2551.

Several miles northeast of Fort Morgan, **Prewitt Reservoir** (2230 ac) lies on the Logan-Washington county line. Take US 6 about 30 miles northeast of Brush to Hillrose, then turn south to the reservoir. Access roads are marked. South side is barren of trees, but north side has many tall cottonwoods. Boat ramp, toilets and trash cans on grounds, but other camping facilities are not available. The reservoir is stocked with walleye, crappie, channel catfish and wiper, and has yellow perch. Wiper and walleyes must be over 15 inches. The limit for wiper is 10 fish, and 5 fish for walleye. This is a good ice-fishing reservoir for the fat yellow perch. Use fee permit is required.

From October 1 through November 31 fishing is restricted to the banks of the reservoir. Ice fishing and fishing from boats is prohibited. From November 1 through November 30 fishing is restricted to the dam only. Ice fishing and fishing from boats is prohibited. From December 1 through the last day of the migratory waterfowl season fishing is prohibited.

NORTH STERLING RESERVOIR

One of the best warm-water fishery in the state is **North Sterling Reservoir** (2880 ac). The reservoir is stocked with crappie, smallmouth bass, channel catfish, tiger muskie, wiper and yellow perch. Wiper and walleyes must be over 15 inches. The limit for wiper is 10 fish, and 5 fish for walleye. The reservoir has about 44 miles of jagged shoreline, of which about 7 miles are accessible by vehicle. There are 4 boat ramps and a marina. Boat fishing is prohibited from November 1 through the last day of the waterfowl season. Use fee permit is required.

East and a bit north of North Sterling Reservoir near the Nebraska state line, **Jumbo Reservoir** (1580 ac) is 32 miles northeast of the town of Sterling and about 20 miles west of the town of Julesburg. The reservoir is stocked with walleye, wiper and channel catfish, and has largemouth bass, bullhead, carp, crappie and yellow perch. Crappie must be 10 inches or longer. Boat ramps, toilets and drinking water is available. This reservoir is on the Sedgwick-Logan county line off I-76, north on Hwy 138 and 1 mile east. The reservoir is in the Red Lion State Wildlife Area. A use fee permit is required. From October 1 through October 31 fishing is restricted to the banks of the reservoir. Ice fishing and fishing from boats is prohibited. From November 1 through November 30 fishing is restricted to the south dams only. Ice fishing and fishing from boats is prohibited. From December 1 through the last day of the migratory waterfowl season fishing is prohibited. Fishing is prohibited within 50 feet of the outlet structure.

The **Red Lion Management Pond**, or **Jumbo Annex**, (60 ac) is immediately below the dam on the south side of Jumbo Reservoir. It is stocked with largemouth bass, bluegill hybrid, channel catfish and yellow perch. Bass must be 15 inches or longer, and crappie must be10 inches or longer. When the wind is blowing on Jumbo, this might be the perfect place to spend a few hours.

From Julesburg, US 385 runs south toward the town of Wray. Northeast of Wray, 3 miles northeast of the junction of US 385 and US 34, is **Stalker Lake** (26 ac), which does not appear on most maps. To get to Stalker Lake from Wray go two miles west on Hwy 37 to County Road FF for one and a half miles to access road. Stalker is stocked with largemouth bass, bluegill hybrid, channel catfish, tiger muskie and rainbow trout. Bass must be 15 inches or longer. The lake has picnic tables, toilets and trashcans. Only craft propelled by hand, wind or electric motor is allowed on this 26-acre pond. Camping is prohibited.

REPUBLICAN DRAINAGE RESERVOIRS

South of Wray about 30 miles on US 385, **Bonny Reservoir** (1900 ac) is on the east side of the highway. Bonny averages 30 to 50 feet deep. Bonny is in the South Republican State Wildlife Area, in the southeastern corner of Yuma County, and offers boating, water skiing and swimming, as well as fishing and hunting in season. A Parks Pass is required. White-tailed deer are numerous, and the wildlife area also has the Rio Grande subspecies of wild turkey.

Fishing from the dam is prohibited from March 15 through April 15 between the hours of 1/2 hour before sunset to 1/2 hour after sunrise.

Bonny is stocked with channel catfish, walleye, largemouth bass and large wiper. Bullhead, carp, yellow perch, bluegill, white bass and a few northern pike are also available. Walleye, crappie and channel catfish are all found in lunker sizes, and the wipers and largemouth are close to them. All bass must be 15 inches or longer. From I-70, at Burlington, the lake is 20 miles north on US 385. Bonny has good boat ramps on the north and south sides, as well as several very good campground areas, with drinking water, trailer dump station, showers, rest rooms and picnic tables.

The **Hale Ponds** (15 ac) are east of Bonny Reservoir about 6 miles. From the reservoir take road east to hamlet of Hale, then north 0.5 mile, then east about 5 miles to pond area. Ponds are formed in an old oxbow portion of the South Fork of the Republican River, which also flows through the area. The Hale Ponds are stocked with largemouth bass, channel catfish and bluegill hybrid, and also have yellow perch, crappie, white bass, carp and bullhead. At times, rainbow trout have been stocked in the spring months. Toilets, trash cans and picnic tables are available, but there is no overnight camping. Fishing from shoreline area only; no boats. Many trees, poison ivy, sand, mosquitoes and deer flies are on hand to greet you if you stray away from the ponds.

Chief Creek and **North Fork Republican River** are spring-fed streams flowing from 10 to 15 miles southeast of the town of Wray to the Nebraska State line. Rainbow and brown are stocked in public areas of the streams, which are marked with state signs. Take Hwy 34 to the town of Wray and any county road north and south on either the east or west side of town to fishing areas.

Traveling south from Bonny Reservoir on US 385, turn west at the town of Burlington (20 miles south) onto Hwy 24, paralleling I-70. Drive about 32 miles west to the town of Seibert. About 6 miles west of Seibert, **Flagler Reservoir** (160 ac) is in the Flagler Reservoir State Recreation Area. It is a water-less wonder on the plains. When constructed it was to have 160 surface acres of water, but after the rains came so did evaporation, which limits this lake to approximately 40 to 50 acres. It has been bone dry at times. Presently, Flagler is being stocked with bluegill hybrid, channel catfish and tiger muskie. Largemouth bass and bullheads are also available, as are yellow perch, some walleye, carp and a few northern pike. Boat ramp, toilets and trash cans comprise the facilities.

SOUTH PARK
FRONT RANGE

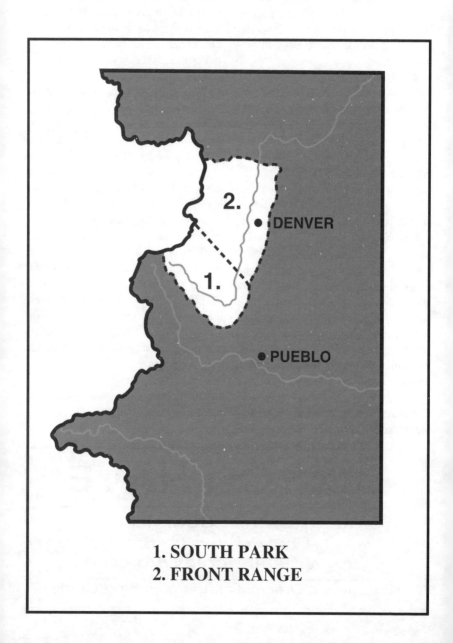

1. SOUTH PARK
2. FRONT RANGE

SOUTH PLATTE RIVER/ SOUTH PARK

South Park is a huge intermountain valley with Pikes Peak to the east and the Continental Divide on the west. Gold lured fortune-seekers to this buffalo-hunting ground of the Ute in the early 1860s. Miners poured into camps called Fairplay, Alma, and Como, as well as others, such as Sacramento and Horseshoe, now inhabited by ghosts.

Today, outdoor enthusiasts pour into this valley, coming west on US 24 from Colorado Springs and southwest on US 285 from Denver. They camp at places with names such as Elevenmile, Tarryall, Jefferson Creek and Lake George. Attractions now are the headwaters of the South Platte River, a profusion of lakes and reservoirs, and the abundant wildlife scattered on the valley floor and mountain slopes.

The **South Platte River** provides some of the best fishing in the state. Several sections of the river, as well as Spinney Mountain Reservoir, are designated Gold Medal waters by the state. Honored sections of the river are the Middle Fork downstream from US 285; the South Fork downstream from the outlet of Antero Reservoir to the inlet of Spinney Mountain Reservoir; the South Platte from the outlet of Spinney Mountain Reservoir downstream to the inlet of Elevenmile Reservoir and from Cheeseman Reservoir downstream to the confluence with the North Fork.

The river, above and below Spinney, and including Spinney Mountain Reservoir also are Gold Medal sections. Cutthroat, cutt-bows, rainbows and brown trout that reach trophy proportions can still be found during spring and fall spawning runs out of Spinney Mountain and Elevenmile Reservoir. Because of its proximity to Denver and Colorado Springs, the area receives heavy fishing pressure. Even with tight fishing regulations, the number of big fish caught has steadily declined during the last decade.

JEFFERSON LAKE

A little north and west of Kenosha Pass, Jefferson Lake (10,687 ft; 125 ac) is situated at the headwaters of Jefferson Creek. It is a very popular fishery, with brook, mackinaw and rainbow, and heavily stocked and fished. Boats are allowed. Water level is low in the late fall, exposing a sandy area on the northeast side from which fly fishing for brook or rainbow can be good both morning and evening.

County Roads 35, 37, and 54 reach the lake, north from US 285 in the village of Jefferson. Two miles north of the village, CR 37 branches off and leads to Jefferson Lake. A mile farther west, CR 54 leads to upper Michigan Creek, with several miles of stream and beaver pond fishing. **Teter State Wildlife Area** offers some fishing on the

South Platte River Rainbow

lower portion of Michigan Creek.

At the headwaters of Michigan Creek is **Lower Michigan Lake** (11,222 ft; 4 ac). Fair for small cutthroat. Rough road to lake.

TARRYALL CREEK

Tarryall Creek is formed by **Michigan**, **Jefferson** and **Snyder** creeks. Snyder Creek is entirely on private land. All three of these small streams contain small brook, and range from open land to willow/brush fishing. At the headwaters above Como, north of US 285 east of Fairplay, the creek has several beaver ponds, much of it posted. Access to Tarryall Creek is from Boreas Pass Road to the North Tarryall Road paralleling the stream. Tarryall Creek, joined by Jefferson and Michigan creeks, flows out of the northwest through almost all private property to Tarryall Reservoir.

Tarryall Reservoir (9,500 ft; 175 ac) is a state recreation area that has camping, a boat ramp and a picnic ground. Fishing is for kokanee, rainbow, and brown, with 2- to 3-pound fish a possibility. It is heavily fished from boats and is open for ice fishing. No public access from the dam, spillway and outlet structures.

Below the reservoir **Tarryall Creek** runs parallel to CR 77 for 14 miles. Tarryall Creek from the confluence with the South Platte River upstream to the Pike National Forest boundary is classified as Wild Trout Water (about 2 miles). Tarryall Creek enters the South Platte from the north between Lake George and Cheeseman Reservoir.

MIDDLE FORK OF THE SOUTH PLATTE

The headwaters of the Middle Fork of the South Platte River arise in the northern flanks of 14,000 foot Mt. Democrat and Mt Lincoln. It Flows through Fairplay and southwest into Spinney Mountain Reservoir after joining the South Fork about three miles east of Hartsel.

The headwaters of the Middle Fork may be reached by driving north on Hwy 9 and CR 4. **Montgomery Reservoir** (10,820 ft; 80 ac) is reached by CR 4. Montgomery is stocked with rainbows to 10 inches and fingerling cutthroat. Best in spring and autumn. Algae bloom in summer hampers angling; draw-down prevents ice fishing, which is prohibited. Fishing is prohibited on the south side of the reservoir

and from the west face of the dam as posted. Fishing is prohibited from December 1 through May 31. On a very rough 4WD road 3.5 miles west of Montgomery are the **Wheeler Lakes** (12,180 and 12,500 ft; 28 and 4 ac). The lower lake offers fair fishing for cutthroat and brookies to 10 inches.

In the vicinity of Alma, **Alma State Wildlife Area** provides fishing on the Middle Fork. Located about 2 miles north of town, fishing is for small rainbow, brown, and cutthroat. Restrooms and campsites are available.

At Alma, 6 miles north of Fairplay, **Buckskin Creek** joins the river. Six miles up the creek via CR 8 are **Kite Lake** (12,000 ft; 6 ac) and **Lake Emma** (12,620 ft; 9 ac). Kite is uphill to the north and right on CR 416, on an easy trail much used by mountain climbers. There is a USFS campground at Kite. Rated good for 12-inch rainbow.

Lake Emma is out of view to the west about a mile up a steep, rocky trail. Emma contains rainbow and some small cutthroat to ten inches, with some up to 15" reported. The creek itself is only fair for small brook, rainbow and cutthroat.

Two miles south of Alma, well-named **Mosquito Creek** is fair for small cutthroat and some rainbow. Near the headwaters, **Oliver Twist Lake** (12,250 ft; 6 ac) is reached by taking the Mosquito Pass Road (about 4.3 miles west from Hwy 9) to FR 438. Take the north fork (the rougher 4wd, less traveled road) about 2 miles more to just below the north London Mine. The lake is about a half-mile northwest.

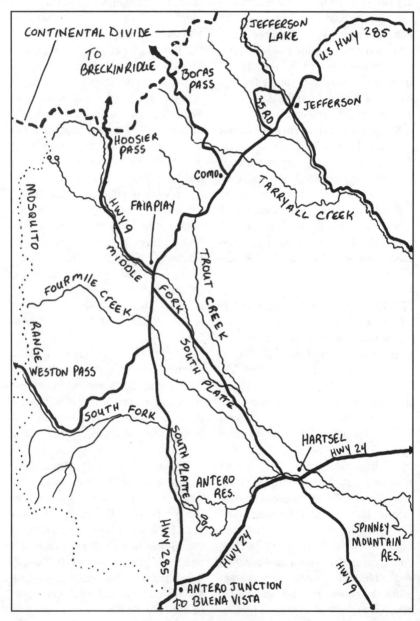

SOUTH PLATTE EAST

Beyond Oliver Twist, a 4-wheel-drive-only road continues north about 2 miles to **Cooney Lake** (12,600 ft; 8 ac). There is a bad marsh that may not be negotiable. Fishing at Cooney Lake is fair for cutthroat 10 to 12 inches. There is heavy 4WD and trail-bike activity in this area, since Mosquito Pass provides 4WD access to Leadville when snowdrifts have melted.

From Alma, along Hwy 9, the Middle Fork bisects private property for 6 miles down to Fairplay. West of Hwy 9, **Salt**, **Sacramento**, and **Beaver Creek** across Hwy 9 to the east, are small, clear streams with small brook and rainbow. No public fishing available in **Pennsylvania Creek** as it is a private subdivision. Old mining roads make these creeks easily accessible, but most areas are private property and posted. Willows, bogs and some ponds are in the lower reaches.

The **Middle Fork of the South Platte River**, from US 285 downstream to the confluence with the South Fork, has been given Gold Medal status. The stream parallels Hwy 9 and is surrounded by a considerable amount of private land. It is heavily posted in some areas.

From the Highway 9 bridge (4.9 north of Garo) downstream, including Buffalo Peaks and Tomahawk State Wildlife Area, to the confluence with the South Fork South Platte, fishing is by artificial flies or artificial lures only. All trout caught between 12 and 20 inches in length must be returned to the water immediately. The bag and possession limit for trout is two fish, of which no more than one can be greater than 20 inches in length.

Just above Hartsel, **Trout Creek** joins the Middle Fork. At the juncture is the Tomahawk State Wildlife Area. This area is 5 miles west and north on Hwy 9 to a cattle guard and sign on east side of Hwy 9. There is a parking area 0.25-mile from highway. Trout Creek downstream to the Middle Fork, and including the Middle Fork, are posted for fishing only with flies and lures. No camping or fires are allowed.

SOUTH FORK SOUTH PLATTE RIVER

The **South Fork of the South Platte River** begins southwest of Fairplay at Weston Pass. It flows southeasterly, in and out of Antero Reservoir, and merges with the Middle Fork near Hartsel.

At the top of Weston pass, **Ruby Lake** (11,850 ft; 2 ac) is a rock-rimmed pond with small rainbow and cutthroat. From the headwaters, the South Fork flows southeasterly for 15 miles to U.S. 285. About six miles of the 15 miles are on National Forest land.

West of U.S. 285, the tributary creeks of the South Fork—**Rich**, **Rough and Tumbling**, **Lynch** and **Willow**—are small, creeks with some small rainbow trout, but mostly small brook. Rich and Rough and Tumbling are stocked cutthroat. To reach the headwaters, take County Roads 5 to Weston Pass.

Twelvemile Creek flows into the South Fork of the South Platte River above Antero Reservoir. Take U.S. 285 about 4.5 miles south of Fairplay to County Road 5. After about 1.6 miles on CR 5, turn right onto the Breakneck

Pass Road, a dirt road (4-wheel-drive recommended) that goes off to the west and ends within a mile of the lower **Twelvemile Lakes** (Upper 11,580 ft; 3 ac, Lower 11,180 ft; 8 ac). Campsites are dotted along the creek, and there are some beaver ponds for small brook and cutthroat.

The South Fork flows mostly through private lands outside of the national forest enroute to Antero reservoir. **Knight-Imler State Wildlife Area** does offer 2.5 miles of fishing on the river directly above Antero Reservoir. Located 11 miles south of Fairplay on U.S. 285. The public is welcomed on this lease for only 25 feet on each side of the stream itself, as posted.

ANTERO RESERVOIR

From its appearance, **Antero Reservoir** (8,000 ft; 1000 ac when full) gives no clue that it is one of the easiest to reach and one of the best fisheries in Colorado. On the high, windswept South Park, which is void of trees or shrubs, Antero is a basin containing rainbow, brown and brook. Northern pike were stocked several years ago, but they did not take. Best fishing is from boats. Shoreline is shallow, so waders are essential. It is a good spincaster's lake when the wind isn't blowing. Brown and rainbow up to ten pounds have been taken. The limit on trout is 4 fish. As part of 63 Ranch State Wildlife Area, it has a campground, boat ramps and picnic area. The wildlife area also provides limited fishing on the South Fork of the Platte directly above the reservoir.

Ice fishing is often excellent, but all shelters must be portable. Antero is reached via U.S. 24 or U.S. 285 on several access roads. It is six miles west of Hartsel and 20 miles south of Fairplay.

Badger Basin State Wildlife Area, from the Highway 9 bridge 1 mile west of Hartsel downstream to the confluence with the Middle Fork South Platte (Gold Medal), fishing by artificial flies or artificial lures only. All trout caught between 12 and 20 inches in length must be returned to the water immediately. The bag and possession limit for trout is two fish, of which no more than one can be greater than 20 inches in length.

Fourmile Creek, a tributary of the South Fork, is six to eight feet wide and is fair for small brook. To reach Fourmile Creek, County Road 18 turns west of U.S. 285 a mile south of Fairplay and crosses private land for three miles before entering the Pike National Forest. There is some posted land and two USFS campgrounds. Two small ponds are located at Fourmile Creek's headwaters, known as Horseshoe Basin. The creek from the national forest boundary to Badger Basin State Wildlife Area at Hartsel is private. Inside the wildlife area is restricted to artificial flies and lures only. All trout 12 to 20 inches must be returned to the water immediately. The limit for trout is 2 fish, only one of which can be over 20 inches.

SPINNEY MOUNTAIN RESERVOIR

Spinney Mountain Reservoir (8,700 ft; 2500 ac) has enjoyed long-

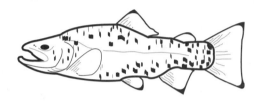
term Gold Medal success for its outstanding fishing. Accessible to both boat and shore fishermen, it is extremely productive, with fast growing Snake River cutthroat, rainbow and brown. Each year large fish are taken from shore and by boats.

Spinney is part of the water system for the city of Aurora. Constructed in the late 1970s and early '80s, it was opened to the public in 1983. All fishing on Spinney Mountain is with artificial flies and lures only, and the bag, possession and size limit for trout is one fish 20 inches or longer. Fishing is prohibited from 1/2 hour after sunset until 1/2 hour before sunrise, and no ice fishing is allowed. There is a boat ramp located on the north shore, but the lake has no marina.

Access is 6 miles south from US 24 and 9 miles east of Hartsel on CR 59, then 1 mile south to the lake.

From the confluence of the Middle and South Forks downstream to Spinney Reservoir (Gold Metal water), fishing is with artificial flies and lures only; catch-and-release for trout between 12 and 20 inches; trout limit is two fish only one of which can be longer than 20 inches. These regulations extend up the Middle Fork to the Hwy 9 bridge, and up the South Fork to the lower boundary of the Denver Water Department's property line. Fishing is prohibited in the Homestake Conveyance Channel (Spinney Mountain Reservoir inlet ditch).

Between Spinney Mountain and Elevenmile reservoirs the South Platte

River is classified Gold Medal. Fishing in this stretch is catch-and-release with artificial flies and lures only. Best fishing is in the spring when rainbows and Snake River cutthroat, in the 2- to 5-pound class, move into the stream from Elevenmile and in the fall when the browns, some even larger than the rainbows, make their spawning run. The meandering river here is considered to some to be perfect for the fly fisher — almost no brush along the river, short grass and flat ground behind. Accessed from CR 247.

ELEVENMILE RESERVOIR

Elevenmile Reservoir (8,600 ft; 3000 ac) is a state recreation area that offers camping, boating and some of the best lake fishing in the state of Colorado. CR 90, then CR 92 southeast from the town of Lake George or by CR 23 from US 24 just west of Wilkerson Pass can reach the reservoir.

Elevenmile, which is heavily fished from shore and boats, is rated excellent for brown, rainbow, and northern pike. There are also a few mackinaw. Brown and rainbow are large and 2- to 6 pound fish are commonly caught. In fact, the reservoir is a better producer of large fish than it is of smaller trout, except for the stocked rainbow that are taken by shore anglers.

The northern pike are in the trophy-size range, and some anglers prefer to hook them rather than the trout. While no longer stocked, the population is quite healthy. Boat ramps and campgrounds are on both north and south shores. Ice fishing is often excellent, with some of the largest trout of the year taken during winter. Only portable shelters may be used.

The bag, possession and size limit for trout is eight fish and shall not include more than two trout 16 inches in length or longer. Snagging of kokanee salmon is permitted from October 1 through December 31 from the east (lake) side of the inlet buoy line. Elevenmile is owned by the Denver Water Department, in drought years, it is drawn down substantially.

From Elevenmile, CR96 follows the river down Elevenmile Canyon to Lake George. There are six campgrounds and four picnic grounds in this 9-mile stretch, plus numerous parking areas, however, camping in this part of Pike National Forest is permitted only in developed campgrounds. Fishing is rated fair in this section of the river for rainbow and brown. From immediately below the Cove Campground downstream to the bridge at Springer Gulch (Elevenmile Canyon), fishing is with artificial flies and artificial lures only. The bag, possession and size limit for trout is two fish, 16 inches in length or longer.

Lake George, located south of US 24 at the town of the same name, is private, as is the land over which the South Platte flows downstream from the lake for 5 miles, except for a 1-mile section at Happy Meadows campground. Below the private property to Cheeseman Reservoir the South Platte meanders through a steep, isolated canyon, commonly called Wildcat Canyon, which is criss-crossed by a myriad of foot trails, ATV/motorbike trails and 4WD roads. The canyon offers good

fishing for brown and rainbow trout to 14 inches and, occasionally, a larger one. Numerous pocket water stretches interspersed with huge boulders connected by fine riffles and small runs characterize these canyon waters. Fishing pressure is less in this section of the river than elsewhere. While use is high by four-wheelers and hikers, most do not fish.

There are five routes to the river from USFS 360, which goes northeast from Lake George, but all require a hike of at least 3 miles or use of an off-street vehicle. Easiest access to one of the least intensively used sections of the river is by USFS 210, which meets CR 77 4 miles north of US 24. From the parking area at the end of the road, it's about a mile hike to the river down **Platte Spring Creek**. It's an easy walk down a good trail except for the last quarter-mile. In that short horizontal distance, the trail descends 800 feet on loose gravel. There's no trail up or down the stream. There is a lot of climbing up and around massive boulders. Hiking boots are more appropriate than waders in this stretch.

Another trail from the parking area (trail 619) leads 3 miles northeast to the confluence of Tarryall Creek and the South Platte.

CHEESEMAN RESERVOIR

Cheeseman Reservoir (6,842 ft; 915 ac) offers good fishing for brown and rainbow. Access from Hwy 285 is via County Road 126, after about 20 miles turn onto County Road 211 to lake. The reservoir contains rainbow, brown, brook, northern pike, sucker, kokanee and small yellow perch. Shore fishing only; no boats. Fishing is prohibited from January 1 through April 30. Fishing is also prohibited from 1/2 hour after sunset until 1/2 hour before sunrise and on the dam and around the reservoir as posted. Kokanee salmon may be snagged between September 1 and December 31, but ice fishing is prohibited.

The reservoir is owned by the Denver Water Department and was closed to fishing until 1982. The Colorado DOW manages the campground.

Goose Creek flows into Cheesman from the west. Primary access is via Hwy 126 to USFS roads 211 and 558 to USFS trail 612. Fishing is for rainbow, brown, but mostly brook trout. Excellent kokanee salmon fishing from September to December in Goose Creek inlet to Cheesman Reservoir. Good camping at Molly Gulch and Goose Creek campgrounds. Excellent access to scenic brook trout fishing in Lost Creek Wilderness Area via USFS road 558.

Hankins Gulch, a tributary of Goose Creek, offers fishing for brook trout. Primary access is via Hwy 126 to USFS roads 211 and 558. Proceed to parking lot on USFS road 558 to USFS trail 630.

Above Deckers, **Wigwam Creek** flows into the South Platte at the lower end of Cheesman Canyon at the private Wigwam Club property. Above the club public fishing is for rainbow and brown. Excellent brook trout fishing the further up you go. It might be worth the demanding hike. A parking lot just west of the junction of Hwy 126 and

USFS road 211 is a good place to start. Downhill access from the west via Lost Creek Wilderness area accesses from US 285 south of Kenosha Pass. Drive east to the end of USFS road 127, park at the campground, then follow USFS trail 609 along Lost Creek for 2.5 miles to small tributary of Lost Creek, and hike northeast to its headwater.

A 3-mile stretch below **Cheesman Dam** the South Platte River is Gold Medal water. The hike is well worth the outstanding fishing. For access take the Gill Trail from the junction of CR 126 and USFS road 211, just east of the Wigwam Picnic grounds.

The South Platte River from Cheesman Dam downstream to the upper Wigwam property line is fishing by artificial flies or artificial lures only. All fish caught must be returned to the water immediately.

With more than 700 pounds of fish per surface acre and rainbow trout averaging from 15 to 22 inches, the South Platte River is rated among the most productive streams in the world. As its trout are shy and selective, persistent, cautious anglers may find success presenting small dry flies and frequently changing patterns. Water level does fluctuate. The Wigwam Club property below the mouth of the canyon is private, posted and patrolled for trespassers.

In the **Cheesman Canyon** stretch above the town of Deckers, 34 miles southwest of Denver, the South Platte is considered world-class fishing. Beyond Cheesman Reservoir, the river flows northeast through Jefferson, Douglas, Teller and Park counties.

Plans for Two Forks Dam and Reservoir to be built at the confluence of the South Platte and the North Fork of the South Platte were halted by an Environmental Protection Agency veto. There are four USFS picnic areas from the confluence en route to Deckers, and numerous vehicle turnouts. This area is heavily used on weekends.

From the lower boundary line of Wigwam Club at the mouth of Cheesman Canyon to Scraggy View picnic ground, fishing is classified as Gold Medal water, artificial flies and lures only. Catch and release on all fish. Rainbow and brown average 14 to 19 inches with some brook trout. Early morning hours in spring and autumn are good fishing times.

At Deckers, the South Platte is up to 100 feet wide. Downstream, alternating sections of fast water, boulder strewn pocket water and deep holes offer prime fish habitat. At the resort and community of Deckers, the river is joined from the south by **Horse Creek**. It is best in spring and fall when trout swim up from the South Platte, but mostly has small rainbow and brook.

West Creek, which flows northerly into Horse Creek, is paralleled for 10 miles of its length by Hwy 67 from Woodland Park (12 miles south). It has small brown and rainbow. Headed south, along Hwy 67, **Trout Creek** is a small tributary rated fair for brown and rainbow. **Long Hollow Gulch** is another tributary. Primary access is via Hwy 67 to USFS road 300 (Rampart Range Road) and USFS road 348. Hike in from headwaters. No trail, use of

Photo Courtesy of the Morrison Angler

Todd and Andrea of the Morrison Angler on the Gill Trail near Cheeseman

topographic map advised. This stream has rainbow and brown trout. The secluded lower section is worth the hike but has an undefined trail. Continuing south on Hwy 67 and on CR 350, **Rainbow Falls**, is a series of privately owned ponds. **Manitou Lake** (7,700 ft; 10 ac) is 6 miles south of the village of Westcreek. The lake is stocked with rainbow, and an occasional brook trout is caught.

A mile south of the confluence of the north and south forks, **Spring Creek** enters the South Platte from the west near Eagle Rock. Fair for rainbow, brown and brook. **Pine Creek** enters the South Platte from the east at Twin Cedars. Fishing for rainbow and brown, with good fishing in the beaver ponds.

Just across the Rampart Range is **Jackson Creek** with primary access via US 105 to USFS road 502 or USFS road 300 (Rampart Range Road) from

the north or south. Jackson Creek has brook trout and generally gets heavy use on weekends. **North Fork Jackson Creek** has brook and greenback cutthroat trout. Observe closure regulations that protect threatened greenback cutthroat trout recovery efforts. Fishing is allowed downstream of this closure. Fishing is prohibited from the headwaters downstream 1.25 miles (including **Zinn Ponds** and connecting streams as posted). Jackson Creek flows into **Plum Creek**, which offers very poor fishing opportunities.

WATERTON CANYON

Waterton Canyon, also known as **South Platte River Canyon**, offers good fishing for rainbow and brown. The canyon is also home to a variety of wildlife. A herd of approximately 20 bighorn sheep is year-round residents. It is also the beginning of the 470-mile long Colorado Trail, a popular hiking trail. East entrance to the canyon is reached by driving south to the end of Wadsworth Blvd. (Hwy 121) from Denver to Kassler. An alternate route is via Hwy C-470 west from US 85 (South Santa Fe Dr.), about 3 miles south of Littleton. From the south, the area is reached by taking Titan Rd. west from US 85 about 5.7 miles north of Sedalia.

An old narrow-gauge railroad grade at Lasser provides walking access for 6 miles up the canyon to Strontia Springs Dam. Fishing is rated good for rainbow and brown to 12 inches. Heavy fishing pressure in the lower canyon because of easy access. Three rest areas provide restrooms and benches. A drinking fountain is located at the 3-mile marker. From there the walk becomes slightly more difficult. The upper end of the canyon is reached by going north from Deckers on Hwy 67 to the confluence with the North Fork. Rough hike down river 1-mile to Strontia Reservoir.

Water levels in **Strontia Springs Reservoir** (6,000 ft; 83 ac) may fluctuate greatly. There is limited habitat for trout in steep bank sections. Poor fishing is the rule as sheer-walled sections and frequent drawdown of the reservoir severely limits natural food-production. To offset the detrimental effects of unnatural flow regimens, catchable rainbow trout are periodically stocked. The limit for trout is 2 fish.

From Strontia Springs Dam downstream to 300 yards upstream from the Denver Water Board's Diversion structure, fishing is by artificial flies or lures. The trout limit is 2 fish, 16 inches or longer.

Bear Creek, a small stream crossed by the Colorado Trail, enters Strontia Springs Reservoir from the east, 2.5 miles downstream from the confluence of the North Fork and the South Platte. Fair for small rainbow and brown. Fishes best near the reservoir.

Once through Waterton Canyon, where the river leaves the mountains and enters Chatfield Reservoir, it assumes a more restful flow as it moves across a metropolitan area of well over 2 million residents. As the South Platte flows across the northeastern plains into Nebraska, it becomes better known for waterfowl hunting than fishing.

NORTH FORK SOUTH PLATTE

The **North Fork of the South Platte** begins on the east side of Kenosha Pass, 22 miles east of Fairplay, where US 285 crosses into South Park. The river flows east before merging with the South Platte just above Strontia Springs Reservoir.

This area is accessible via Hwy 126 south from US 285 at Pine Junction or by Hwy 67 either southwest from US 85 at Sedalia or northwest from US 24, west of Colorado Springs, at Woodland Park. Good roads, such as CR 543, make much of the 19.5 miles of river above the confluence of the South Platte River and the North Fork of the South Platte easily accessible. Rainbow and brown trout provide year-round fishing, particularly in upper sections.

Much of the North Fork's character depends on water releases from the Roberts Tunnel, owned by the Denver Water Board, that brings water from Dillon Reservoir on the Blue River. This 23-mile long tunnel, located 0.5 mile above Grant on US 285, can contribute a trickle of water or heavy stream flows five times in excess of the natural North Fork flow at this point.

As a result, the river has been rebuilt upstream from its confluence with the South Platte at the site of South Platte village, enabling it to accommodate the additional water. In the stretch that parallels US 285, the river can be deceptively swift, deep and powerful, especially after the first 2 weeks of May when the Denver Water Department begins running water through the Roberts Tunnel. Much of the river in this area is on private property and posted.

Reconstruction of the river included many measures to promote fishing. Boulders, small dams, riffles, gravel areas for spawning and willow plantings to minimize erosion were among the measures taken in both fast and quiet water sections. Fishing is for brook, brown and rainbow in the lower reaches.

From its confluence with the South Platte, you can travel northwest along CR 96. The North Fork has alternating sections of public and private water in this section. Country Road 96 ends at Hwy 126. A left turn on Hwy 126 brings you to CR 543.

Buffalo Creek is small and brushy with rainbow, cutthroat, brown and brook. It flows from the west into the North Fork at the community of Buffalo Creek. At its headwaters to the southwest is **Wellington Lake** (8,015 ft; 480 ac), a popular weekend camping and fishing fee area.

Rolling Creek flows into Buffalo Creek on the northwest side of Wellington Lake. Access is via US 285 to USFS road 543 southeast of Bailey and from Hwy 126 to USFS road 543 southwest of the town of Buffalo Creek. Fishing is for brook trout. Heading northwest on Hwy 126 to US 285, **Elk Creek**, which intersects US 285 at Shaffer's Crossing, is poor for brook and is private.

A right turn onto Hwy 126 from CR 96 takes you to the town of Pine. At Pine the North Fork exits a canyon at the site of Pine Valley Ranch, previously a private resort but now owned by Jefferson County Open Space. The ranch is open to the public. The river is heavily fished. The limit for trout is 4.

In the canyon upstream from Pine Valley Ranch, some signed public water exists above and below the abandoned privately owned town of Crossons, reached by driving southeast from the town of Bailey on the EOS Mill road, bearing left onto USFS road 532 and left on USFS road 139. A short walk down the road from the gate at the Forest Service parking area takes you to the Crossons property. Fair for small browns and slightly larger rainbows.

A short hike upstream along the river on an old narrow gauge railroad grade takes you to the confluence with **Deer Creek**.

Turning off US 285 at Crow Hill onto CR 100 may also access Deer Creek. Deer Creek flows south off the slopes of Mt. Evans, and is substantially developed with cabins and summer homes. The road goes 9 miles to the upper reaches to Deer Creek and Meridan campgrounds, where trails head up into the forest. Fair for brook trout.

Craig Creek flows from the Lost Creek Wilderness Area into the North Fork at Estabrook. Access west of Bailey via US 285 and USFS roads 109 and 111 to USFS trails 606, 607 and 608 and from South Park via US 285 to USFS roads 127 and 134 to USFS trails 606 and 607. Excellent fishing for nice-sized brook trout in a spectacular high-elevation meadow setting (Craig Park and Meadows area) makes this a difficult hike well worth the effort. Be prepared for any weather condition. An overnight backpack trip is recommended. Observe Forest Service rules for this wilderness area.

From Bailey upstream along US 285 to Grant, the North Fork races through mostly private land that is posted, developed for resorts or mountain ranches. There is limited public access along this stretch.

About halfway between Bailey and Grant is **Ben Tyler Gulch.** Access west of Bailey via US 285 to USFS trail 606. Parking available adjacent to highway. Fair for brook trout. Continue to follow USFS trail 606 to Craig Creek headwaters.

GENEVA CREEK

Geneva Creek, which enters the North Fork from the north at Grant, is stocked with rainbow and cutthroat. Some brown and brook are present in the 4.5 miles north along CR 118 from the North Fork of the South Platte to the falls. The stream is alternately public and posted private land. Upstream of Scott Gomer Creek fish do not survive due to heavy metal pollution and acidic water from mining activities. There are four USFS campgrounds in the valley (Whiteside, Geneva, Burning Bear and Duck Creek) that offer pretty scenery but poor stream fishing, despite stocking efforts. **Threemile Creek** (entering Geneva from the northeast) offers some brook and brown trout to 8 inches.

A good trail flanking **Scott Gomer Creek** starts at the confluence with Geneva Creek. Scott Gomer Creek is virtually barren because of acid poisoning from a precious metal mine. Sandwiched between the 14,000-foot peaks of Mt. Evans and Mt. Bierstadt is **Frozen Lake** (12,960 ft; 7 ac). Hike 3.5 miles from Burning Bear Campground, take Lake Fork Trail, pass two trails going east, and continue 1 mile north on Scott Gomer. Follow the creek north where the trail heads west. Hike 2 miles upstream to Frozen Lake. Rugged terrain, use of topo map advised. Fishing is for temperamental cutthroat.

Another 2.5 miles up the east trail reaches **Abyss Lake** (12,640 ft; 20 ac). Abyss Lake has rainbow, some up to 18 inches, and cutthroat, but the lake is considered temperamental.

Farther north up Geneva Creek **Burning Bear Creek** is nearly fished-out but has some hardy brook trout. Access **Bruno Gulch** via I-70 or US 285 to USFS road 118 and USFS trail 600, south of Guanella Pass. Fishing is for brook and greenback cutthroat trout.

Farther north, Geneva Creek is barren above the falls due to natural conditions. **Kirby Gulch** is reached via CR 118 onto USFS road 119 to USFS trail 600. Fishing for brook trout.

Access **Duck Creek** via I-70 or US 285 to USFS road 118, south of Guanella Pass. Good for brook trout. Numerous USFS campgrounds in area. Can be crowded on weekends. Due to dense streamside vegetation, spinning or bait fishing is effective in this stream. **Duck Lake** (11,100 ft; 42 ac), up Duck Creek on the south side of Guanella Pass, is closed to the public.

To the northwest above Duck Lake are the two **Square Tops Lakes** (12,240 ft; lower 2 ac, upper 4 ac).

TO GEORGETOWN

MOUNT EVANS WILDERNESS

GUANELLA PASS

GENEVA CREEK

• HARRIS P

GRANT

U.S. HYW 285

NORTH FORK SOUTH PLATTE

• BA

FR 127

LOST CREEK WILDERNESS

77 RD

TARRYALL CREEK

TARRYALL RES.

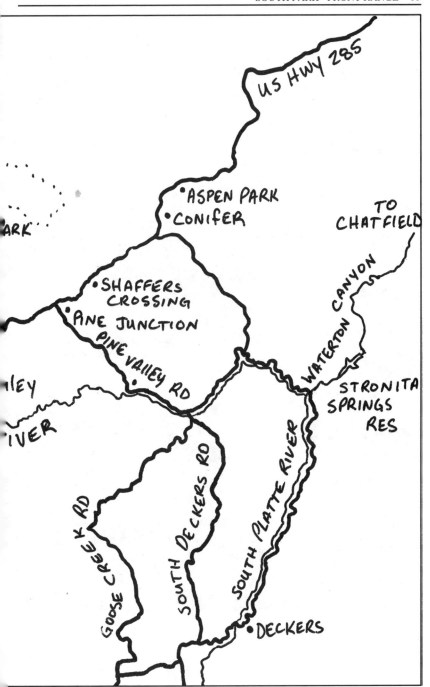

Todd Andersen of the Morrison Angler - Cheeseman Canyon

They are good for cutthroat and can be most easily reached by a good trail from the top of Guanella Pass, about a 2-mile hike west from the pass. Guanella Pass and Clear Lake campgrounds are nearby on the south fork of Clear Creek. Non-motorized boats only.

West of Square Top Lakes is **Shelf Lake** (12,000 ft; 9 ac) at the headwaters of Geneva Creek. Rated good for cutthroat and brook. It can be reached by CR 119 to USFS road 634 up the valley. Rough road. Park vehicle at ruins of old mill (now only a large mound of dirt), and hike 3 miles on good trail. The last 0.25-mile is a fairly steep switchback.

From the town of Grant to the headwaters of the North Fork, along US 285, fishing is poor for small brook. Tributaries of the upper reaches on the North Fork, **Beaver Creek, Handcart Gulch** and **Kenosha Creek**, are small, defended by clusters of willows and dotted with small ponds.

At the headwaters of the North Fork, **Gibson Lake** (11,500 ft; 4 ac) offers fishing for good size brook. The lake is reached from the east foot of Kenosha Pass by driving north on the Hall Valley Road (CR 120) toward Webster Pass. Travel 9 miles and leave vehicle near old mining road at Handcart Gulch. Hike 3 miles northeast on old Missouri Mine Road, where it deteriorates, then take trail west up Lake Fork Creek. It's a 3,000-foot elevation rise to the base of Whale Peak at the Continental Divide. There is camping at the Hall Valley or Gibson Lake campgrounds. The area is popular with 4WD enthusiasts.

FRONT RANGE WATER

As it leaves Waterton Canyon, the South Platte River courses through Denver on its route to Nebraska, filling several reservoirs on its way. The river itself provides little, if any, trout fishing once it passes through Chatfield Reservoir, but there are catfish, carp and suckers. Some large catfish are taken in the river.

Chatfield Reservoir (5,426 ft; 1100 ac when full) is a state recreation area on the south side of the metropolitan Denver area. More than 2 million visitors annually visit the 5,600-acre park to enjoy a range of outdoor activity. It has become one of the best and most popular year-round fisheries.

The reservoir is stocked with largemouth bass, rainbow trout, channel catfish and walleye. It also has resident populations of crappie, perch and bluegill, as well as carp. Walleye limit is 4 fish, 18 inches or longer. Boat ramps are located on the south and north shores. A park pass is required. Camping is permitted in late spring, summer and early fall, and there are solar-heated shower and laundry facilities. Chatfield is reached by driving south of C470 on Wadsworth Blvd. (Hwy 121) or via Hwy 470 west from US 85 (South Santa Fe Drive), about 3 miles south of Littleton. From the south, the recreation area may be reached by taking Titan Road west from US 85 about 5.7 miles north of Sedalia. The reservoir is 2 miles west, 1.5 miles north. The area is open 24 hours. There is a pier near the marina for handicapped anglers. Ice fishing can be excellent.

There are five walk-in ponds south of Chatfield reservoir with warm water fishing for crappie, bluegill, bullhead, largemouth bass, yellow perch, sunfish and suckers. Channel catfish are also stocked.

Downstream from Chatfield Dam are the South Platte Park Ponds at South Santa Fe Drive and C-470 along the South Platte River. There are five ponds: 80 acres total; 27 feet maximum depth. A parks pass is required. No boats. Artificial fish habitat structures are located in some of the ponds and there is also a nature center. There are bluegill, yellow perch, sucker, rainbow trout and large and smallmouth bass. All bass taken must be 15 inches in length or longer.

Bear Creek Reservoir (5,700 ft; 1205 ac) has stocked rainbow, large- and smallmouth bass, bluegill, green sunfish, tiger muskie, yellow perch, bullheads and suckers. Power boats with motors to 10 hp are allowed at wakeless speeds. Boat ramp on north side of reservoir. There is a marina with boat rental near the boat ramp. Walk-in access is free, while a Lakewood parking pass has a fee. Fishing, including ice fishing, is only fair. Regulations on tiger muskie is one fish, 30 inches or longer. Hours are; 7 am to 8 pm from May through September, winter hours are 7 am to 6 pm.

The reservoir is reached by traveling north from West Hampden Avenue (US 285) to C470, turn north onto C470 and get off at the Morrison Road exit. Travel east on Morrison Road. The parking lot is on the right, a few hundred yards from the exit.

Walk-in access is from access road off Morrison Road 0.75 mile west of S. Kipling Street or south from a signed area about 1.75 miles farther west on Morrison Road.

Cherry Creek Reservoir (5,548 ft; 800 ac) is a state recreation area visited by more than 2 million people annually. The reservoir has good fishing for largemouth bass, walleye, northern pike, crappie, yellow perch, sunfish, bluegill, channel catfish, bullheads, suckers, carp, an stocked rainbow trout. In recent years, wipers and tiger muskie have also been stocked in the reservoir. Walleye have a 4 fish limit, 18 inches or longer.

There are boat ramps on the east and west sides. In good weather the water teems with sailboats and other watercraft. The reservoir is heavily stocked and fished. It is usually best after ice-out or late in the fall when cooler weather discourages the number of boaters. There is a handicapped accessible fishing pier. Ice fishing is popular and often excellent. The area closes at times when capacity is reached. A parks pass is required.

Cherry Creek Reservoir is accessible from the east by Hwy 83 (Parker Road). I-225 passes below the dam, and access via Parker Road and Yosemite Street is signed from the interstate. It is also reached by taking the Belleview Exit east from I-25 to Yosemite Street and then north. Parker Road from County Line Road (between Arapahoe and Douglas counties) just west of Cherry Creek, reaches the area from the south.

Quincy Reservoir (5,544 ft; 160 ac) has variable hours and is a fee area. Only artificial flies and lures are permitted. An Aurora park permit is required.

Fishing is rated good for larger trout, bass and tiger muskie. The reservoir is closed from November 1 through February 30. Ice fishing is forbidden. This is an exceptionally good metro area fishery. Special regulations; limit on trout is 2 fish, all bass must be 15 inches or longer, tiger muskies must be 40 inches or longer. Access is off East Quincy Avenue 3 miles east of Parker Road in the southeast metro area.

Popular for sailing and wind-surfing, **Aurora Reservoir** (820 ac; max depth 100 ft) is also known for its fishing, which attracts anglers of all ages. Go east on Quincy Avenue, 1 mile past Gun Club Road, and turn south on the access road. Owned and operated by the City of Aurora, the 2,000-acre park is open year-round from dawn to dusk. An Aurora entrance permit is required. Circling the reservoir is an 8-mile trail. Other facilities include a swimming beach and a marina area with boat launch. No gas-powered boats or equipment are allowed but electric motors can be used. Handicapped-accessible rest rooms are available. The reservoir has fishing for rainbow trout, largemouth bass, wiper, smelt, yellow perch, spot-tail shiner, crappie, catfish and walleye. Special regulations are; 2 trout limit, black bass must be 15 inches or longer. Walleye have a 5 fish limit, 15 inches or longer.

Like other Denver area recreation spots, **Standley Lake** (5,506 ft; 1210 ac) gets lots of attention from boaters, water skiers and fishermen. Operated by the City of Westminster, it is basically a water-skiing lake. Boating is allowed only with a Westminster boat permit. Reservoir can fluctuate significantly, putting boat ramps out of the water by 100 feet or more. Fishing is for stocked large and smallmouth bass, walleye, wiper, channel catfish, bluegill, carp, sunfish, yellow perch and brown and rainbow trout. There is no fishing from the dam. Hours for vehicular access are limited as posted. Walk-in fishing access anytime. Parking fee at 88th Avenue entrance. The only public access is by taking West 88th Avenue west from Wadsworth Blvd. to the Kipling Street parking area. Jefferson County Open Space owns most of the south shore, but fishing from it is difficult and usually poor.

FRONT RANGE SUBURBS

Denver and the surrounding Front

Range suburbs have many other ponds and lakes, which mostly offer only marginal to poor fishing and is beyond the scope of this book. Fishing is for crappie, sunfish, bass, bluegill, yellow perch, carp, goldfish, sucker, and catfish. The more popular and productive lakes are listed here.

Arvada Reservoir (Blunn) - Jefferson County: Between Highway 93 and Indiana on W. 66th Ave. 180 ac; max. depth 77 ft. City of Arvada permit required, which is available at Arvada City Hall. No ice fishing. Non-motorized boats only. Open dawn to dusk. Hard-surface foot trail. Fish present: rainbow and brown trout, walleye, large- and smallmouth bass, yellow perch, tiger muskie. Limit for trout is 2 fish.

Croke Reservoir (Carlson Reservoir) - Adams County, Northglenn: North of 104th Ave. off Huron Street (by Danahy Park). Parking off 104th. 16 ac; max. depth 20 ft. Open 5 am to 11 pm. No boats or tubing. North shore closed to fishing. Fish present: Largemouth bass, pumpkinseed, bluegill, green sunfish, black bullhead. Artificial flies and lures only, all bass must be 15 inches or longer.

Ketner Lake - Jefferson County, Westminster: Off W. 100th Ave. and Country Side Drive (by Kensington Park). 25 ac; max. depth 30-ft. Belly boats allowed for fishing. Ice fishing prohibited. Fish present: largemouth bass, crappie, bluegill, green sunfish, yellow perch and bullhead. Large mouth bass must be 15 inches or longer

Lake Arbor - Jefferson County, Arvada: Pomona Dr. and Lamar St.

north of W. 80th Ave. 37 ac; max. depth 19 ft. Non-motorized boats only. Open dawn to 11 pm. Handicapped fishing pier and restrooms. Hard-surface foot trail. Fish present: channel catfish, bullhead, large- and smallmouth bass, bluegill, green sunfish, sunfish, carp, crappie, and pumpkinseed. All bass and walleye must be 15 inches or longer.

Prospect Lakes - Jefferson County, Wheat Ridge: East of I-70 and south of W. 44th Ave. Parking for Prospect Lake and North Prospect Lake is available south of 44th on Robb Street, next to park headquarters. Parking for West Lake and Bass Lake is available south of 44th on Youngfield Street. Foot trail runs between all the lakes along Clear Creek. **Bass Lake** - 3 ac; max. depth 13 ft. **North Prospect** - 16 ac; max. depth 26 ft. **Prospect Lake** - 7 ac; max. depth 22 ft. **West Lake** - 46 ac; max. depth 15-ft. Open dawn to dusk except for Prospect Lake, which is open until 10 pm. West and Bass lakes, artificial flies and lures only. Large and small mouth bass must be 15 inches or longer in all lakes. No boats on Bass Lake. Non-motorized boats allowed on other lakes with a Wheat Ridge Parks Permit. Prospect Lake has a boat ramp and restrooms. Some steep banks. Good bass fishing. Fish present: Bass Lake: Largemouth bass, bluegill, crappie, green sunfish, sucker. Artificial lures and flies only. North Prospect (Tabor) and Prospect Lake: Largemouth bass, bluegill, channel catfish, crappie, green sunfish. West Lake: Largemouth bass, pumpkinseed, sucker, bluegill, bullhead, crappie, and green sunfish.

Ward Road Pond - Jefferson

County, Arvada: W. 48th Ave. and Ward Rd. 7 ac; max. depth 30 ft. Open 24 hours. No motorized boats. Belly boats allowed. Flies and lures only. Catch and release all fish. Restrooms. Fish present: bullhead, bluegill, crappie, green sunfish, largemouth bass, and pumpkinseed. Good bass fishing,

BOULDER AREA

The sixteen **Sawhill Ponds** (100 ac total.), 1 to 10 acres with a maximum depth of 16 feet, offer good fishing for crappie, bluegill, yellow perch, bullhead, channel catfish, largemouth bass and suckers. Some of the ponds have good size, scrappy bass in the 5 pound range. Fishing is by artificial flies or lures only on all ponds except ponds 1 and 1 A.

This popular area is west off 75th Street between Jay Road and Valmont Drive, Boulder. It is about 2 miles north of Arapaho Avenue. Open dawn to dusk; no boats are allowed.

The five ponds that make up the **Walden Ponds** area are located immediately north of Sawhill Ponds. On 7th street go .5 mile north of Valmont Road, cross the railroad tracks and turn west to the ponds. The ponds are known as **Picnic Pond** (northeast: 5.7 ac; max depth 7 ft), **Cottonwood March** (middle; 30.3 ac; max depth 8 ft) **Duck Pond** (south; 6 ac; max depth 5.6 ft), **Island Lake** (10 ac; max depth 12 ft) and **Bass Pond** (10 ac; max depth 12 ft). They are noted for small- and largemouth bass, crappie, bluegill, carp, bullhead and channel catfish. All small- and largemouth bass must be returned to the water immediately, ex-

cept in Picnic Pond. Fishing, is by artificial flies or lures only on all the ponds except Picnic. The ponds are open dawn to dusk with Picnic Pond restricted to handicapped and elderly by Boulder permit only. Permit available at the park and county annex at 2045 13th Street.

Boulder Reservoir (660 ac), built and operated by the city, is fair fishing for stocked walleye, rainbow, largemouth bass and channel catfish, it also has crappie, yellow perch and bullhead. Trolling usually gives good results. Boulder Reservoir is less than 0.5 mile from Hwy 119 northeast of Boulder on the Longmont Diagonal. Turn north at Jay Road intersection and continue to 15th Street, then east. Admission is charged. Fishing hours are 7 am until dark. Weekend and holiday boating is reserved for City of Boulder residents with boat permits. Public boat ramp and marina are available.

LONGMONT AREA

North on 1-25, and about 7 miles east of Longmont, are the three **Barbour Ponds** (80 ac total). They are good for crappie, channel catfish, carp and sunfish. Several of the ponds have good fishing for stocked rainbow (ponds #1, #2 and #3). The ponds are heavily fished, and a use permit is required. Only hand-propelled craft, sailboats and boats with electric motors are permitted.

Barr Lake (5,210 ft; 1660 ac) in Barr Lake State Park, northeast of Denver, is heavily stocked with largemouth bass, channel catfish, rainbow trout, tiger muskie, walleye and wiper. There are also smallmouth bass, crappie, yellow perch and suckers. It is open from 5 am to 10 pm. A state parks pass is required. It is a popular fishery, located just east of I-76 and west of Picadilly Road. The north boundary is Bromley Lane; southern, 128th Avenue. Park entrance, parking and boat ramp are off Picadilly Road. No motorboats permitted. Free walk-in access.

FRONT RANGE

Numerous streams flow east out of the Front Range of the Rockies as tributaries to the South Platte River. Numerous lakes are found at the headwaters of these steams tucked away near the high peaks just miles from Denver, Boulder, Longmont, and Fort Collins. Many of these lakes are over looked by the 2 million plus residents who live along the Front Range, some are not. Early spring or late fall is the best times to miss the crowds. The Colorado Division of Wildlife has done a great job stocking and maintaining in the rivers, stream, and lakes with catchable rainbow, brown, brook, cutthroat, and mackinaw. Harder to reach lakes still offer solitude from the crowds, not to mention great fishing opportunities.

CLEAR CREEK

Numerous streams flow east out of the Front Range from the Denver area north to the Cache la Poudre River at Fort Collins. **Clear Creek** is one of the streams close to a major metropolitan area where 1-pound stocked trout can be found. It rises near Loveland Pass, some 40 miles west of Denver, near the Eisenhower Tunnel on I-70. It follows

I-70 to 6.5 miles below Idaho Springs, where Hwy. 6 and 40 emerge from Clear Creek Canyon. I-70 turns south and the stream follows Hwy 6 until it emerges from the canyon at Golden. (The water from this stream has been immortalized by the Coors Brewing Company.) It offers fair fishing above Idaho Springs for stocked rainbows, brown, cutthroat, and brook. Below Idaho Springs Clear Creek is mostly channeled to its confluence with the South Platte River north of Denver. It fluctuates widely in water volume and degree of pollution, and is de-watered by domestic and industrial use. Rough fish, maybe some rainbow and browns in pools.

Golden Gate Canyon State Park (Ralston Creek) has fishing for stocked rainbow, brown and brook trout in small streams and ponds. The park is reached by taking the Golden Gate Canyon Road 0.5 mile north of Golden off Hwy 93 and winding 14 miles west. A state parks pass or day permit is required for this fee area. It also is accessible from the west via Hwy 119 north of Blackhawk.

Progressing up Clear Creek from Golden, **North Clear Creek** rises northwest of Central City in Arapaho National Forest, and flows southeasterly through Blackhawk to join Clear Creek in Clear Creek Canyon. Reaches below Apex on **Pine Creek** may have a few brooks, but it is mostly private land. Otherwise polluted and not large enough to support fish.

Central City maintains two city reservoirs; **Dorothy Lee Pond** (8,940; 2 ac) and **Chase Gulch Reservoir**

(8,595; 25 ac). Dorothy Lee Pond is located off County Road 2 and Chase Gulch Reservoir is off County Road 3. Both offer fishing for stocked rainbow and is open during daylight hours only.

At Idaho Springs, **Chicago Creek** bubbles into Clear Creek from the southwest. Hwy 103 loops up from Bergen Park off Hwy 74 to Echo Lake and parallels Chicago Creek to Idaho Springs. The creek rises in the Chicago Lakes in a deep valley beneath 13,307-foot-high Mt. Warren. **Upper Chicago Lake** (11,700 ft; 10 ac) and **Lower Chicago Lake** (11,400 ft; 26 ac) are in spectacular settings, but heavily fished for cutthroat. They are visited by campers, picnickers and hikers who walk in from Echo Lake on the Mt. Evans Road or up the creek on an old road past **Idaho Springs Reservoir** (10,600 ft; 16 ac). The reservoir has fishing for brook, cutthroat and suckers.

From Idaho Springs, drive south 12 miles on Hwy 103. **Echo Lake** (10,720 ft; 18 ac) is south of the highway just west of Mt. Evans Road. Fishing is for catchable-size stocked rainbow. No boats allowed. West Chicago Creek Campground is 8 miles west.

FALL RIVER

Fall River, with brook and cutthroat, flows into Clear Creek a mile west of Idaho Springs. Access to its upper reaches and several small lakes and reservoirs is from the I-70 interchange marked Fall River Road/St. Mary's Glacier, a mile west of Idaho Springs, or from the interstate service road. The lower most stretch has mining pollution. Lower portions of the road are paved through posted, fenced, private property.

Just below St. Mary's Glacier is **St. Mary's Lake** (10,710 ft; 7 ac), loaded with stunted brook trout. It is about 8.5 miles from the interstate. **Silver Creek** and **Lake Quivira**, are private and fished by area homeowners.

Through Arapaho National Forest, Fall River is only fair for small brook and rainbow. There is much posting, and fishing is difficult because of brush and streamside timber.

From the paved road, about 6.5 miles from the interstate, turn west on a good dirt road at the old mining town site of Alice, now a mountain subdivision. You can drive about 1.5 miles before the road becomes too rough and narrow to negotiate without 4WD. Road continues on to provide access to Ice, Ohman, Reynolds, Fall River Reservoir, Ice Lake, Stuart Lake, Loch Lomond and Lake Caroline, all high—above timberline—waters at 11,200 to more than 12,000 feet. Ohman has no fish. 4wd needed to reach many of them without having to walk.

Loch Lomond (11,200 ft; 29 ac) is a man-made lake reachable by 4WD from midsummer on. Deep, slow to melt snowdrifts can abruptly halt vehicle access. Loch Lomond is heavily fished for brook, brown and lake trout. **Lake Caroline** (11,889 ft; 8 ac), is about a half-mile to the south, around a rocky point. Fishing for brook and cutthroat is good, but temperamental. Other lakes are difficult, steep trail hikes from the waterfall at the west end of Loch Lomond in a basin between James Peak on the north and Mount

Bancroft on the south. **Ice Lake** (12,200 ft; 9 ac) has cutthroat, **Reynolds Lake** (11,200 ft; 6 ac) and **Steuart Lake** (11,400 ft; 7 ac) are fair for cutthroat.

About 5.5 miles up Fall River Road from I-70 at the foot of a steep switchback, a rough dirt road goes off to the west along the river to **Chinns Lake** (11,000 ft; 10 ac), stocked with rainbow and splake, **Sherwin Lake** (11,090 ft; 7 ac) with brook, rainbow, splake, and cutthroat, **Slater Lake** (11,460 ft; 3 ac) with cutthroat and **Fall River Reservoir** (10,880 ft; 24 ac) with rainbow and cutthroat. After about 2 miles at a prominent fork in the road, take the south fork to Chinns and Sherwin lakes. Regulations for Chinns and Sherwin: the bag, possession and size limit for splake is 2 fish, 16 inches or longer with artificial flies and lures only. All are heavily fished. Slater Lake is a short hike northeast from Sherwin Lake by easy trail along the stream. Camping sites.

At the headwaters of **Mill Creek**, which flows into Clear Creek at the truck stop and weigh station in the village of Dumont, west of Idaho Springs, are **Ethel Lake** (12,560 ft; 6 ac), **Byron Lake** (12,100 ft; 3 ac) and **Bill Moore Lake** (11,300 ft; 7 ac). Best access is from the town of Empire, going up North Empire Creek to the ridge top, then keeping north across relatively level land to the creek. Hike upstream 1.5 miles to Bill Moore Lake. There is also a winding 4WD-road loop about 3 miles along the ridge to Bill Moore Lake. Use a topographic map and take bearings from Breckenridge Peak

(12,889 ft) on the south and Witter Peak (12,884 ft) on the north. The lakes are in the valley between. Lake fishing for 12-inch cutthroat is fair. The creek is fair for small brook. The lakes also may be reached by taking a dirt road just south of the summit of Berthoud Pass (US 40) to where the dirt road ends at a radio relay shack; then walk cross country along the Continental Divide to the northeast for about 2 miles.

Cone Lake (11,600 ft; 3 ac) is off the above-mentioned dirt road and below it, about a mile east of US 40. It's a 2-mile hike with a steep descent and climb out. Good for 9- to 10-inch cutthroat.

From the confluence of the **West Fork** and **Clear Creek** at the junction of Hwy. 6, 40 and I-70, fishing for rainbow can be good as far as the east side of Idaho Springs. A paved service road provides best access. It's heavily fished, as the stream is stocked.

Bard Creek flows into the West Fork of Clear Creek from the west at the town of Empire; small, many ponds, brushy, and good for small brook, rainbow and greenback cutthroat. Fishing is catch and release with artificial flies and lures only. Road travels upstream about 1.5 miles, then 4WD for 2 more miles, then a trail the rest of the way.

The West Fork flows past the Henderson and Urad molybdenum mines, which are near the Jones Pass road about 1.5 miles west of Hwy 40. The stream is often brushy, in light timber and difficult to fish for small rainbow. Woods Lake is up Woods Creek from the juncture of the Jones Pass

Road and Hwy 40. A dirt road crosses West Fork about 0.25 mile from junction, goes up past Urad Mine to **Woods Lake** (10,700 ft; 31 ac). **Hassell Lake** (11,400 ft; 9 ac) is 1 mile beyond by a steep trail. Both are fair for brook. **Urad Reservoir** (10,560 ft; 30 ac) has stocked rainbows and brown and brook; no fish in section of creek in lower woods.

At Georgetown, Clear Creek is dammed. Shallow **Georgetown Lake** (8,442 ft; 46 acres) is stocked with brown and rainbow, and has some brook and cutthroat as well; many anglers and boats. In winter, good ice fishing, but watch out for iceboats, jeeps and ice skaters. Windy. Handicapped-accessible fishing pier.

SOUTH FORK CLEAR CREEK

The **South Fork of Clear Creek** enters at Georgetown. USFS road 381 (paved most of the way) goes upstream to Guanella Pass. **Green (Georgetown) Reservoir**, 3 miles south of Georgetown, is closed to the public. **Clear Lake Reservoir** (9,900 ft; 45 ac) has catchable-size, stocked rainbows and brook trout. **Lower Cabin Creek Reservoir** (Public Service Co. of Colorado) is a fluctuating body of water and dangerous; it's fenced off and closed to fishing. Above the reservoir, the South Fork is brushy, has several beaver ponds and attracts anglers for small brook and rainbow. Several campsites and one campground.

Above the campground a road goes off to the west to **Naylor Lake**, which is private and posted. Trails from Naylor Lake go west one mile to **Sil-**ver Dollar Lake** (11,950 ft; 18 ac) and **Murray Lake** (12,080 ft; 11 ac). Both are above timberline and can be good for 12-inch cutthroat. Temperamental. Murray Lake is 0.5-mile northwest of Silver Dollar.

From Bakerville west to headwaters, Clear Creek is brushy and hard to fish for small rainbow. From the cascades below Empire to Bakerville, highway construction and mining have altered the stream, but some stretches may have trout.

About 2 miles east of the Eisenhower Tunnel on the north side of the interstate is the trailhead to **Herman Lake** (12,000 ft; 7 ac). It no longer has fish.

Atop Loveland Pass is **Loveland Pass Lake** (11,800 ft; 1 ac), shallow and fair for stocked rainbow. The lake is just west of the summit of the pass, parking and lake are visible from the highway.

BEAR CREEK

Another interesting Front Range stream is Bear Creek, which flows down from 14,264-foot Mount Evans through the town of Morrison to Bear Creek Reservoir. Upstream on **Bear Creek** from Bear Creek Reservoir there is some fishing for wary wild browns and rainbows to 8 inches with a few larger. Supplementary stocking of catchable-size rainbows between Morrison and Kittredge. Land along the stream is administered by various agencies, Jeffco Open Space and city/county parks. Lair of the Bear Park above Idledale provides parking and picnic area. Above Kittredge to Evergreen Lake is primarily private.

At Evergreen, west on Hwy 74 from Morrison, is **Evergreen Lake** (7072 ft; 55 ac). In a pretty setting, it is stocked with brown, rainbow and tiger muskie. The lake can also be reached by taking the Evergreen Parkway exit from I-70 in the foothills west of Denver and going south through Bergen Park, past Hiwan to Evergreen.

Above the lake, **Upper Bear Creek**, is heavily developed and mostly posted to Mount Evans State Wildlife Area in Arapaho National Forest. Area is popular with hikers. **Vance Creek** is primarily accessed via Hwy 103 to USFS trails 41 and 46 from Echo Lake. Fishing is for brown and brook trout. Upstream, **Lost Creek** has brook trout.

Bear Track Lakes (11,100 ft; 1 and 2 ac) are poor for rainbow. Reached by hiking about 6 miles southwest from Camp Rock Campground. To reach **Roosevelt Lakes** (10,400 ft; 6 acres total) hike 1-mile southeast of Beartrack Lakes on USFS trail 78 or 4 miles on Tanglewood Creek Trail 636. Fishing is for cutthroat, brook and rainbow. **Summit Lake** (12,830 ft; 33 ac) and **Lincoln Lake** (11,620 ft; 13 ac) may be reached from the Bear Creek Trail by walking west from Camp Rock Campground. Campground is reached by driving up Bear Creek Road to its end. Summit Lake is adjacent to the Mt. Evans Road. Lincoln Lake is a steep descent of some 1200 vertical feet down and a mile from the Mt. Evans road. Great view to east. The road is the highest in the U.S. at 14,000 feet elevation. Summit has a few rainbow and cutthroat, Lincoln tends to be fished out, but some rainbow or cutthroat may be taken.

SOUTH BOULDER CREEK

South Boulder Creek flows from the Continental Divide west of Rollinsville in Gilpin County. It's a beautiful stream with brook, cutthroat, and 10- to 12-inch stocked rainbow. Primarily accessible between Pinecliffe and Gross Reservoir via State Highway 72 and a moderately difficult hike from Gross Reservoir. The stretch west of Rollinsville to the Moffat Tunnel is reached from Hwy 119 to USFS road 149. Between the Moffat Tunnel and its headwaters, access is primarily via Hwy 119 to USFS road 149 and USFS trail 900, west of Rollinsville. Brook and cutthroat.

Jenny Creek is accessed via Hwy 119 to USFS roads 149 and 503 and USFS trail 808, west of Rollinsville. Brook trout. **Jenny Lake** (10,920 ft; 5 ac) and **Yankee Doodle Lake** (10,710 ft; 6 ac) are northwest of South Boulder Creek and are most easily reached from East Portal by the narrow-gauge railroad grade road over Rollins Pass (also called Corona Pass). Yankee Doodle is lower and deeper; both are fair for rainbow and brook. Both are heavily fished, often with bait, and are about 11 miles from East Portal by road. Boats are allowed on Yankee Doodle.

The first creek coming in from the northwest of East Portal is **Arapaho Creek,** fair for small cutthroat, as is South Boulder Creek near there. The trail up the creek to **Forest Lakes** (10,680 ft; about 4 ac each) is beyond the creek about a third of a mile and cuts back and up about 2 miles to the lakes. There are several small ponds in the area. The lakes have brook trout. Fish are small in the two largest lakes. About 1.5 miles up a poorly defined trail from South Boulder Creek, a small stream comes in from the four **Arapaho Lakes** (10,165 ft; largest 10 ac). Good for cutthroat and small brook.

Over a ridge south of the Arapaho lakes are the four **Crater Lakes** (10,480 to 11,000 ft). They are 2.8 miles west of East Portal and upstream from the second stream coming into South Boulder Creek from the northwest. Ranging in size from 5 to 14 acres, all are fair for cutthroat, brown, some brook and rainbow.

At the headwaters of South Boulder Creek lie **Clayton Lake** (11,000 ft; 6 ac) and, upstream against the Continental Divide, the **Iceberg Lakes** (11,640 ft; 10 and 6 ac). Clayton is just south of Crater Lakes and all are fair for cutthroat up to 12 inches, except the south lake, which has no fish. To the south just off the main forest trail up South Boulder Creek about a mile from Clayton Lake is **Heart Lake** (11,320 ft; 17 ac), which is heavily fished for cutthroat. Just south of Heart Lake is **Rogers Pass Lake** (11,000 ft; 5.6 ac) with cutthroat. The headwaters are easily reached by driving west on Rollins Pass Road, a good gravel road to the Moffat Tunnel.

Downstream from the village of East Portal, the stream is channeled and mostly private property. At the western edge of the railroad village of Tolland, a 4WD road goes south up a steep hill. Nearly at the top, a fork goes southwest to Mammoth Gulch, Mammoth Reservoir, James Peak Lake and Little Echo Lake.

Mammoth Reservoir, with brook, cutthroat and rainbow, is private. The road goes another 2.5 miles to old mines and mill sites. From there a trail goes up a brushy stream to **Little Echo Lake** (11,184 ft; 14 ac) just off the trail to the north. It is deep with a brushy shoreline, but can be good for rainbow and lake trout. **James Peak Lake** (11,200 ft; 10 ac) is a few hundred yards west from Little Echo. It has cutthroat, but is above timberline and very temperamental.

Both of these lakes can also be reached over a 4WD road on the ridge just south of Mammoth Creek. It follows the old Ute Trail to within a mile of James Peak Lake. The lakes are easy to see from the road. The Ute Pass Road goes west from the top of the hill south of Tolland. Great view. The area is a maze of old roads and trails, and topographic maps are helpful.

GROSS RESERVOIR

East of Tolland, South Boulder Creek races past Rollinsville and Pinecliff through mostly private property and into its steep, rugged and narrow canyon to **Gross Reservoir** (7,287 ft; 440 ac). There is bank fishing only at this fluctuating reservoir operated by the Denver Water Department. Access from the south is from Hwy 72 in Coal Creek Canyon. A dirt road turns off to the north about 1.25 miles east of Wondervu and winds down to the east end of the reservoir.

From Boulder, the Flagstaff Mountain Road leads to the reservoir, about 12 miles southwest. Follow signs. Rainbow, kokanee salmon and tiger muskie are stocked in the reservoir; also has brook, lake trout and some brown. Fishing is best in the spring when the reservoir is full. Because no boats are allowed, it's hard to get the bigger fish, and most of the bank fishing is difficult. Some good-sized fish— 4 to 5 pounders and up. Open from 4 am to 9 pm. No camping; fires only in fire pits on the north side; ice fishing is at your own risk. Snagging for kokanee is permitted from September 1 through January 31 in the South Boulder Creek inlet area.

Downstream from the dam, angling for brook and brown can be excellent, but tough to get to in the narrow canyon. The portion above Eldorado Springs is posted; from there downstream to the juncture with Boulder Creek northwest of **Valmont Reservoir** east of Boulder, the stream is on private land. No fishing at Valmont.

MIDDLE BOULDER CREEK

Along Hwy 119 upstream from the city of Boulder is Boulder Canyon, shaped by **Middle Boulder Creek**. West of Nederland, Middle Boulder Creek rises along the Continental Divide between Arapaho Pass on the north and Rollins (Corona) Pass on the south. Immediately east of Nederland along Hwy 119 is **Barker Reservoir** (8,183 ft; 420 ac), a fluctuating reservoir that is one of the most heavily fished waters in the state. Largely a put-and-take fishery, it is heavily stocked

in summer with rainbow. Good fishing for rainbow and brown to 12 inches. Boating and ice fishing are prohibited.

Headwaters of Middle Boulder Creek are reached by driving west on the road to Eldora from Hwy 119 on the south edge of Nederland. After 1.5 miles, the road forks; follow the stream on north fork 1.5 miles to Eldora and another 2.5 miles to Hessie where the **North Fork of Middle Boulder Creek** enters from the north. There's a good road through private land to this point. Drive about 4 miles to the Fourth of July Campground, 20 acres with no designated campsites, a few picnic tables and fire rings. This area serves mostly as a trailhead for south entry into the Indian Peaks Wilderness, to the north of Arapaho Pass. The road is slow and rough. Stream is small, brushy and has rainbow, especially between the falls 2 miles up from Hessie and the campground. Road above the campground is closed. The area is heavily used with as many as 100 cars on a summer or autumn weekend.

Follow USFS trails 975 and 904 to **Diamond Lake** (10,920 ft; 14 ac) and, a mile farther west, **Upper Diamond Lake** (11,720 ft; 6 ac). Both are above timberline; good for rainbow, cutthroat and some lake trout. Heavily fished; campsites. Walk up North Fork of Middle Boulder Creek from the parking area about 0.25 mile, take the well-defined trail to the west that crosses the creek, and climb steeply. Upper Diamond Lake is in a cirque of rocks reachable by cross-country hike from the lower lake. The **Neva Lakes** (11,800 ft; 9 and 10 ac) at the base of

Colorado's true rock climbers

Mt. Neva have cutthroat. They are north of Diamond Lakes and are hard to reach and find. Upper lake is barren.

From the campground, the trail to **Lake Dorothy** (12,100 ft; 16 ac) is an old mining road for most of the 2.5 miles. The lake is above timberline and is usually iced over until July, but there is good fishing in late afternoon and early evening for cutthroat in late summer. The lake is heavily fished. **Banana Lake** (11,320 ft; 2 ac) is about a mile south of Lake Dorothy in high, rough country. It is fair for cutthroat and brown. It can be reached over a faint trail leading northwest 0.75 mile off the Diamond Lakes Trail, just west of the Fourth of July Campground.

Up the **South Fork of Middle Boulder Creek** from Hessie about a mile, USFS trail 813 from the south intercepts the main trail. A quarter-mile south through the woods is **Lost Lake** (9,740 ft; 8 ac), which can be good for small rainbow and brook.

Six miles upstream on USFS trail 901 up the South Fork is **King Lake** (11,431 ft; 11 ac). It is above timberline and is fair for cutthroat and rainbow. It also can be reached from the summit of Rollins Pass by going north on the Corona Trail and, after about 0.5 mile, dropping steeply down to the lake from the top of the divide.

North from the east side of King Lake about 1.75 miles on USFS trail 810 are **Betty Lake** (11,500 ft; 8 ac) and, 0.25 mile farther, **Bob Lake** (11,600 ft; 8 ac). Both are above timberline and fair for cutthroat. These two lakes are readily reached by walking along the top of the ridge north from Rollins Pass.

About a mile west of Hessie, a trail goes northwest up **Jasper Creek** to Jasper Lake, Devil's Thumb Lake, Storm Lake and Upper Storm Lake,

Woodland Lake and Skyscraper Reservoir. Jasper Creek is fair for brook trout.

A half-mile up Jasper Creek, a southwest trail leads about 2 miles to **Woodland Lake** (10,972 ft; 10 ac) with cutthroat and grayling. **Skyscraper Reservoir** (11,221 ft; 13 ac) with cutthroat is situated 0.25 mile farther.

Following Jasper Creek north, **Jasper (Reservoir) Lake** (10,814 ft; 21 ac) is fair to good for brown and cutthroat. Due west about 2 miles, **Devil's Thumb Lake** (11,260 ft; 12 ac) is easily reached by trail from the south end of Jasper Lake. Devil's Thumb Peak is just to the northwest; above-timberline fishing rated good for cutthroat.

Northwest from the north end of Jasper Lake is **Storm Lake** (11,660 ft; 7 ac), which is fair for cutthroat but takes a steep climb. It may winterkill and have no fish.

Glacier Lake (9100 ft; 24 ac) is on the east side of Hwy 72, six miles north of Nederland. It is a private, posted man-made lake. It drains into **Fourmile Creek,** which flows easterly through Fourmile Canyon to enter Boulder Creek just west of Boulder in Boulder Canyon. The stream offers little public fishing for small rainbow.

NORTH BOULDER CREEK

About 8 miles below Nederland, **North Boulder Creek** sweeps over Boulder Falls and merges with Middle Boulder Creek to form Boulder Creek, which cuts through beautifully sculpted rock to the City of Boulder, turning northeasterly to join St. Vrain Creek just east of I-25 in Weld County.

Boulder Creek joins **St. Vrain Creek** just above Barbour Ponds State Recreation Area. From there, the St. Vrain travels northeast, joining the South Platte about 7 miles farther downstream. Fish are sparse, as the river does not provide suitable habitat for sustaining a viable, self-sustaining population of fish. Public access is difficult to determine as much private property adjoins the river.

North of Nederland about 3 miles, North Boulder Creek is crossed by Hwy 72. Its headwaters are to the west and northwest along the Continental Divide on the east side of the Indian Peaks Wilderness. **Como Creek** is accessible from US 72 or USFS road 505, north of Nederland. Contains rare greenback cutthroat trout. Fishing is prohibited from the headwaters downstream to its confluence with North Boulder Creek. Observe strict regulations on threatened greenbacks.

Caribou Creek is accessed via Hwy. 119 and 72 to USFS roads 108 and 505, west of Nederland. Good fishing for larger brook trout in upper reaches. **Horseshoe Creek** is a tributary of Caribou Creek. Access is via Hwy. 119 and 72 to USFS roads 108 and 505, west of Nederland. Small brook trout.

About 8 miles north of Nederland, a dirt road to the west leads 6 miles to 10 beaver ponds called **Rainbow Lakes** (10,200 ft; 1 to 4 ac) and the Rainbow Lakes Campground. This is the takeoff point for the Arapaho Glacier hiking trail.

The upper reaches of North Boulder Creek are in a privately owned valley south of Niwot Ridge and north of the Caribou Mining District. There are several lakes and ponds, including the four **Green Lakes** (10,960 to 11,680 ft; 11 to 34 ac), the **Triple Lakes, Goose Lake, Island Lake, Silver Lake** and **Lake Albion,** all at 10,000- to 11,000-foot elevations and from 2 to 40 acres in size. These properties are posted and private. Downstream from Hwy 72, North Boulder Creek is on mostly private land.

Moving north, **Left Hand Creek** rises in a basin west of Hwy 72 and west of Ward that contains **Left Hand Park Reservoir** (10,600 ft; 100 ac when full). The reservoir is reached by the Brainard Lake Road. The reservoir fluctuates; it's often windy and difficult to fish for stocked splake. The creek is brushy and in peat bog; only fair for rainbow, brooks and browns. East of Hwy 72, Left Hand Creek is brushy and fast, and flows alternately in and out of national forest and posted land. Two miles above the confluence with Little James Creek (Jim Creek), Left Hand Creek is fair for small rainbow and some brook. The stream is dewatered for irrigation as it works its way east of Jamestown and out of the mountains. **James Creek** is poor fishing. County roads in the Gold Hill and Jamestown areas provide access. Left Hand Creek flows into the St. Vrain at Longmont.

SOUTH ST. VRAIN CREEK

From Nederland, north on Hwy 72, Brainard Lake Road goes west from Ward to **Brainard Lake** and several other lakes in the **South St. Vrain Creek** drainage. This is a good, heavily used road with several picnic areas and a campground at Brainard Lake. The creek is fair for small rainbow and some brook. Upstream from the bridge at the inlet of Brainard Lake to the creek headwaters, fishing is by artificial flies and lures only and there is a 2 trout limit.

Brainard Lake (10,350 ft; 15 ac) is a beautiful, shallow lake with rainbow, and brown. It is in a very popular area and is heavily fished. Brainard Lake is a fee area. En route to Brainard from Ward is **Red Rock Lake** (10,300 ft; 6 ac) on the south side of the road. It is basically a pond with grass and lily pads—hard to fish for 12-inch rainbow. **Moraine Lake** (10,150 ft; 2 ac) is another pond with good feed much like Red Rock Lake and, while it is difficult to fish (waders recommended), it produces some good rainbow despite its unimposing appearance. It is just south of Red Rock Lake, over a small hill.

Just upstream, 0.5 mile from Brainard Lake, is **Long Lake** (10,500 ft; 40 ac), with rainbow. Fishing is with artificial lures and flies only. The limit for trout is 2 fish. Fishing is prohibited upstream from the bridge at the inlet of Brainard Lake to Long Lake from May 1 through July 15. **Lake Isabelle** (10,868 ft; 30 ac) is 2.5 miles above Long Lake via a well-used trail. Lake Isabelle, like its companions, is heavily fished for rainbow. Again, it's fishing with artificial lures and flies only.

A short distance northwest of Brainard Lake is a parking area and a trailhead to the Mitchell Lakes 1.5

miles beyond. **Lower Mitchell Lake** (10,700 ft; 4 ac) and **Upper Mitchell Lake** (10,700 ft; 14 ac) have brook and cutthroat, and fishing can be good. Another 1.75 miles west up the stream is **Blue Lake** (11,320 ft; 16 ac), fair for cutthroat and cutthroat.

Past Ward, several lakes in the area are private and posted, including **Stapp Lakes** and **Beaver Reservoir.**

MIDDLE ST. VRAIN

South St. Vrain Creek flows northeast and converges with **Middle St. Vrain Creek** 2.5 miles east of Riverside. Middle St. Vrain Creek's scenic headwaters are popular, and have many small streams and lakes west of Hwy 72. Two campgrounds are Peaceful Valley and Camp Dick, each just west of the highway a few hundred yards on a good USFS road.

The Middle St. Vrain is a fast, full stream that parallels the road for more than 8 miles. It tends to be brushy and difficult to cross, but with good rainbow fishing. The trail up the Middle St. Vrain goes to Buchanan Pass. A trail about 6 miles up from Peaceful Valley Campground goes northwesterly a mile to **Red Deer Lake** (10,700 ft; 16 ac)— deep and easily fished for brook, rainbow and some cutthroat. **Pika Lake** (11,140 ft; 2 ac) is 1.8 miles by trail from the end of the road along Middle St. Vrain Creek. It has cutthroat, as do **Envy Lake** (10,990 ft; 2 ac) and **Gibraltar Lake** (11,200 ft 3 ac). Gibraltar is off the St. Vrain Glacier Trail 2 miles northwest from the old sawmill site along the creek. Envy is 2 miles cross-country and hard to find.

The streams receive substantial fishing pressure and are heavily stocked.

The St. Vrain is joined by **Coney Creek,** flowing in from the southwest. A trail leads upward three miles to **Lower Coney Lake** (10,600 ft; 9 ac) and another mile to **Upper Coney Lake** (10,940 ft; 10 ac), where there is good fishing for cutthroat from 12 to 14 inches. The upper lake is the deeper of the two.

Below the confluence of the Middle and South St. Vrain Creeks there is good fishing, although much of the stream is posted. Some good brown trout are taken in the 2 miles of the stream that flows through Lyons. Artificial flies and lures only. Access is along Hwy 7 south of Lyons.

North St. Vrain Creek rises in the southeastern portion of Rocky Mountain National Park and also is discussed in that chapter. Downstream from Hwy 7 and the park, the creek tends to be brushy and difficult to fish for brown and some rainbow. Several stretches are posted against fishing without permission. From its confluence with Horse Creek downstream to the inlet of Button Rock Reservoir there is a 2 trout, 12 inches or longer, limit and artificial flies and lures only regulations. **Button Rock Reservoir** (9,850 ft; 21 ac), formerly **Ralph Price Reservoir**, is owned by the City of Longmont. Fishing by artificial flies and lures only and limit for trout is 2 fish. Fishing is prohibited from Nov 1 through April 30 each year. Upstream from the reservoir to Horse Creek is wild trout water; fishing is with artificial flies and lures only. Bag and possession for trout is 2 fish. Catch-and-release fishing is encouraged. Access is from Hwy 36 about 5 miles northeast of Lyons where the highway leaves creek. Turn left across bridge onto dirt road.

BIG THOMPSON RIVER

The **Big Thompson River** rises in Rocky Mountain National Park and flows east through Estes Park and down Big Thompson Canyon to Loveland. Just outside the park and south of the river is **Mary's Lake** (8,050 ft; 42 ac), a fluctuating reservoir on the east end of the Alva B. Adams diversion tunnel of the U.S. Bureau of Reclamation's Big Thompson power and irrigation project. It is along Hwy 7, south of Estes Park about 2 miles, and is good for rainbow. It is heavily stocked as part of a put-and-take management regimen. Some big trout dwell at the intake of the lake, feeding on nutrients brought through the tunnel from Grand Lake.

Lake Estes (7,475 ft; 185 ac) at Estes Park is stocked with rainbow, and also has a few brown. Although most fish average 8 to 12 inches, some bigger ones are there. Boats and boating permits are available at the boathouse. Bait, flies and lures are allowed. Heavily fished.

Downstream from the Lake Estes Dam, fishing for rainbow and brown is good, especially in pools. The river is recovering well from the 1976 flood and fishing is better than was forecasted a decade ago. Lower sections are posted. Hwy 34 follows the river. From the bridge at Waltonia upstream 4.5 miles to the bridge at Noel's Draw (Common Point or Estes Park Gun Range Bridge) fishing is by artificial flies and lures and catch and release only.

At Drake, the **North Fork of the Big Thompson River** enters the main stream. The North Fork rises in northeast Rocky Mountain National Park. There are 6 miles of stream northwest of Glen Haven that are in the national forest and accessible by road, although some sections of the stream are on private land. Above that, access for a dozen miles is by trail. Stream is fast and tends to have 8- to 12-inch rainbow and some brown, especially in pools.

Access to North Fork is easy from paved county road that makes loop off Hwy 34 between Estes Park and Loveland.

ARKANSAS RIVER
SOUTHEASTERN COLORADO

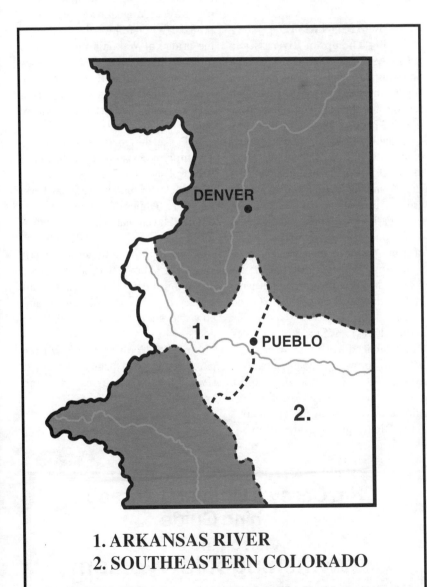

1. ARKANSAS RIVER
2. SOUTHEASTERN COLORADO

ARKANSAS RIVER

The Arkansas River is a favorite destination for fishermen and whitewater rafters. The Arkansas has long been known for large browns and fat rainbow, although it no longer has a state-designated Gold Medal section (a classification that was removed in 1987), fantastic fishing opportunities abound. The Arkansas River begins near Leadville as a small trickle of a stream, but before it reaches Colorado's eastern plains the river acquires characteristics that make it one of the most beautiful rivers in Colorado.

Owing to runoff from old mining sites near Leadville, the Arkansas above the small community of Granite provides only fair fishing. Brown trout there tend to be small. The nearby lakes and reservoirs, however, are unaffected by this problem and offer excellent fishing, as does the main river through its lower reaches after it is buffered with uncontaminated water from tributaries.

Some of the state's popular lakes — from Turquoise Lake and Twin Lakes near Leadville to Clear Creek Reservoir and Cottonwood Lake near Buena Vista — are located along the Arkansas, as is Pueblo Reservoir, Colorado's most-visited recreation area and a premier warm-water fishery.

In addition to these major lakes, more than 100 high lakes in the Collegiate and Sangre de Cristo ranges, once barren of fish owing to natural barriers in their outlet streams, now support healthy trout populations. Fingerlings, primarily cutthroat, are stocked periodically by the Colorado Division of Wildlife.

The upper reaches of the Arkansas are surrounded by some of Colorado's highest mountains, portions of three national forests, wilderness areas, and countless high lakes and streams.

The journey of the Arkansas River that takes eastern-slope Colorado waters to the Gulf of Mexico begins on the south side of 11,316-foot Fremont Pass at Climax. With the Mosquito Range of mountains on the east and towering peaks of the Collegiate Range to the west, US 24 parallels the Arkansas as it flows south-southeast through Leadville, Buena Vista and Salida. After bumping into the northern flank of the Sangre de Cristo Range, the river turns more easterly before slicing through Royal Gorge and then going through the towns of Cañon City and Pueblo before flowing across the eastern plains to Kansas.

LEADVILLE AREA

The **East Fork of the Arkansas** comes down from Fremont Pass beside Hwy 91. A small brushy stream, it lies above the problem areas with stream pollution and, consequently, holds fair numbers of brook and brown trout.

About 4.5 miles south of the pass, a dirt road leaves the highway going northwest 2.5 miles up a rough 4WD road to **Buckeye Lake** (11,900 ft; 2 ac) where there is fair fishing for cutthroat.

Two miles northwest of Leadville, the East Fork merges with **Tennessee Creek** to form the Arkansas River. US 24 parallels Tennessee Creek in its assent to Tennessee Pass. The creek flows mostly across private land and through a number of private lakes; among them are **Diamond Lake, Home Lake, Rainbow Lake, Island Lake, Morton Lake** and **Sylvan Lakes**. About 6 miles west of US 24, high up in the wilderness area, are a number of lakes that offer good fishing for cutthroat and a few brook. Northeast of Homestake Park is **Slide Lake** (11,725 ft; 35 ac) on the edge of the wilderness area. At the head of **West Tennessee Creek** are the **West Tennessee Lakes** (11,800 ft; 3 ac, 20 ac). **Deckers Lake** (11,350 ft; 14 ac) is a difficult-to-reach lake on a bench 400 feet above the Colorado Trail in Longs Gulch.

TURQUOISE LAKE

Ringed with USFS campgrounds, **Turquoise Lake** (9,869 ft; 1650 ac) is popular both in summer and winter. Turquoise is stocked each year with Snake River cutthroat and rainbow, and also offers brown and mackinaw trout. The limit for mackinaw (lake) trout is 2 fish. Reached by a 4.5-mile paved road from Leadville or from a marked turnoff south of Leadville on US 24, Turquoise is heavily fished from the bank and from boats, as well as through the ice in winter.

Above Turquoise Lake, **Lake Fork Creek**, its tributaries and the high lakes in the Holy Cross Wilderness are stocked with greenback cutthroat. This threatened species is being reintroduced around the state through a joint effort of the Colorado Division of Wildlife, US Fish and Wildlife Service, the US Forest Service and other agencies. A log barrier a short way up Lake Fork Creek above Turquoise Lake inlet prevents any of the lake's fish from moving upstream. The creek is restricted to catch-and-release fishing with artificial lures and flies only.

Lake Fork Creek feeds into the reservoir from **Timberline Lake** (10,950 ft; 26 ac), 2.5 miles upstream, which

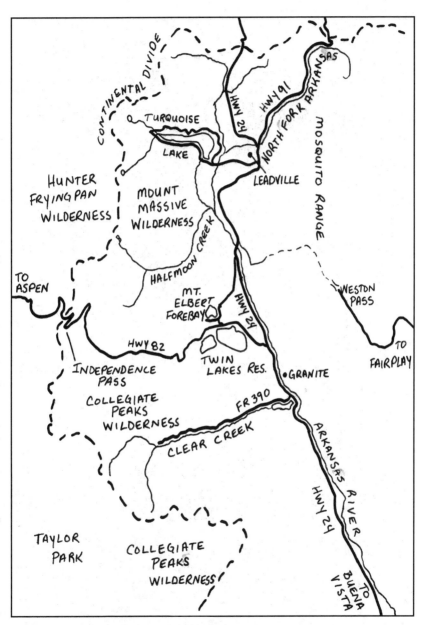

ARKANSAS RIVER (UPPER)

has cutthroat and is surrounded by timber. It is in the Holy Cross Wilderness, but take the 4-wheel drive road form Turquoise Lake's west end to within a mile of Timberline. Restricted to Flies and lures only, 2 trout limit.

It is a tough cross-country hike through timber and swamp for 2 miles to the southwest of Timberline to **Virginia Lake** (11,500 ft. 7ac). Up against the Continental Divide, the lake has cutthroat and lots of mosquitoes. It also can be reached by easy walk across 1.5 miles of tundra from Hagerman Pass and then down 800 vertical feet to the lake. Restricted to Flies and lures only, limit on trout is 2 fish.

Also just inside the wilderness a mile north of Turquoise, are **Galena Lake** (11,050 ft; 2ac), a shallow pond, and **Bear Lake** (11,000ft; 12 ac), both with

cutthroat. A 5-mile-long 4-wheel drive road leads to within a half-mile of Bear Lake. The road is off the north side of the Turquoise Lake loop and often is barricaded. **St. Kevin Lake** (11,850 ft; 5 ac) is up the ridge to the northwest of Bear. Follow along the old road to the end and keep on the ridge, up a mile from Bear. St. Kevin has cutthroat.

Along the south side of the reservoir, the old Colorado Midland Railroad grade (USFS 105, the Hagerman Pass Road) rises a bumpy 6 miles to the trailheads to several lakes. **Hagerman Lake** (11,365 ft; 5 ac), **Windsor Lake** (11,650 ft; 50 ac), **Notch Lake** (11,950 ft; 5 ac), **Three Lakes** (11,955 ft; 3 ac), **Rainbow Lake** (12,020 ft; 10 ac) and **Native Lake** (11,250 ft; 5 ac). All these lakes plus **Swamp Lakes** (10,800 ft; 6 ac) and others in the **Rock Creek** drain-

Collegiate Peaks

Photo Courtesy of Kevin Rummell

age have had the greenback cutthroat introduced into them and are under strict catch-and-release/artificial flies and lures regulations.

Below Turquoise dam, **Lake Fork Creek** continues, first on national forest land and then on private land to join the Arkansas River about 4 miles southwest of Leadville. Fishing is fair for brook, cutthroat and rainbow.

Beautiful, clear **Halfmoon Creek** holds stocked rainbow and cutthroat. The main stream and the North Fork offer the best fishing; **South Halfmoon Creek** is very steep. Access is by gravel USFS road 110 past Halfmoon and Elbert Creek campgrounds. Turn west from US 24 toward the federal fish hatchery on a paved road, then south after 0.75 mile.

Emerald Lake (10,000 ft; 10 ac), located between the two campgrounds, is stocked with catchable rainbows. **North Halfmoon Lakes** (12,000 ft; 3 ac, 6 ac) may be reached by hiking up **North Halfmoon Creek** from the trailhead. The lakes offer fair fishing for cutthroat.

Crystal Lake (9,350 ft; 10 ac) on the west side of US 24, 3.5 miles south of Leadville, holds rainbow to 14 inches. Fishing is with artificial lures and flies only. Boats are not allowed.

Cache Creek, west of Granite, is mostly on private land. East of US 24, **Union Creek** and **Big Union Creek** parallel the Western Pass Road (USFS 425). Both are occasionally stocked with rainbow above the national forest boundary.

TWIN LAKES RESERVOIR

Twin Lakes Reservoir (9,700 ft; 1700 ac) is skirted by Hwy 82 on its way to Independence Pass. A dam has made the two lakes into one, and the fishing is for brown, rainbow, mackinaw and kokanee salmon, with rainbow the most prevalent. Mackinaws have been taken in the 30-pound range; the limit is 1 fish, those between 22 inches and 34 inches must be returned to the water immediately. Ice fishing is quite popular. To the north **Mount Elbert Foresbay** (9,500 ft; 200 ac) offers good fishing for stocked rainbow, cutthroat, and mackinaw. The restrictions on mackinaw are the same as those at Twin Lakes.

Lake Creek is stocked with rainbow near the Twin Peaks and Parry Park Forest Service campgrounds along Hwy 82. Fishing is rated poor due to heavy fishing pressure.

The **South Fork of Lake Creek** is almost barren owing to poisonous mine runoff.

Good cutthroat fishing can be found at **Blue Lake** (12,495 ft; 13 ac) by hiking north off Hwy 82 on a trail that continues up the creek as the highway turns away to make a steep switchback. Follow the trail a mile to a little stream flowing from the west. Follow the stream up in elevation 1,600 feet to the lake.

Willis Gulch is a small, brushy creek that joins Lake Creek at the west end of Twin Lakes. At the headwaters of the West Fork is **Willis Lake** (11,800 ft; 22 ac), with cutthroat. It is a steep 5-mile hike from the lakeside trail. From the trailhead, keep to the west as you go up the larger stream. You can try for rainbow and brown in the creek's lower portions, but it's difficult fishing.

At the head of the next drainage to the west is **Crystal Lake** (12,475 ft; 8 ac). It is 4 miles and 3,000 feet higher than the point where Crystal Lake Creek dumps into Lake Creek across from Monitor Rock.

From Leadville down to Granite the Arkansas River is still a small stream that offers angling for small brook and some rainbow. Fishing is confined mostly to the nearby lakes as the river flows mostly through private property.

CLEAR CREEK

Clear Creek Reservoir (8,875 ft; 150 ac) is just west of US 24, 13 miles north of Buena Vista on CR 120. An irrigation reservoir, its level can drop considerably by late summer. Camping is permitted at the reservoir, although facilities are minimal. It is heavily stocked with rainbow, cutthroat, brown, and kokanee salmon for the heavy fishing pressure it receives.

CR 120 passes the reservoir and goes up **Clear Creek**, which offers fishing for brown in the first quarter mile above the reservoir where it flows through state land. Small rainbow and brook are also caught and, higher up, some cutthroat.

The **North Fork of Clear Creek** is reached by trail from the end of the road near Winfield. It has fair angling for brook and small cutthroat. **Alan Lake** (12,100 ft; 2 ac) is 3.5 miles by trail up the North Fork, at the headwaters of a small tributary stream coming in from the northwest. There's no clear trail, and it's a steep hike for small cutthroat.

South Fork of Clear Creek offers more brook and small cutthroat fishing (and some beaver ponds) along a rough road for 3 miles to the wilderness boundary. The creek offers good fishing for brook in the meadows above Banker Mine. **Ann Lake** (11,800 ft; 18 ac) is 3 miles up a well-defined trail from the end of the road. It has cutthroat. **Harrison Flats Lake** (12,155 ft; 10 ac) has cutthroat.

To the northeast, **Cloyses Lake** is private. The lake is on **Lake Fork Creek**, from where a steep 4-wheel drive road provides access into the wilderness. The creek has brook and cutthroat in the upper portions.

Two miles south of Clear Creek Reservoir on US 24 is the trailhead for USFS 1467 that goes west along **Pine Creek**, a good stream for brook trout at lower elevations and cutthroat higher up in the Collegiate Peaks Wilderness. A well-defined trail goes 11 miles to **Silver King Lake** (12,600 ft; 16 ac) where there is temperamental fishing for cutthroat and a few grayling. The trail up Pine Creek intersects the Colorado Trail about 4 miles up, just inside the wilderness boundary. **Rainbow Lake** (11,650 ft; 5 ac) is about 2 miles to the south and also has cutthroat.

From the town of Granite down to Buena Vista the size of the **Arkansas River** increases as a result of the many tributaries flowing out of the surrounding high moutains. This stretch of river contains fair sized rainbow with a few brook present. Two easements, Granite Fishing Easement above Clear

Sawatch Range looking west

Photo Courtesy of the Morrison Angler

Creek and the Arkansas confluence and Clear Creek Fishing Easement below, offer fishing for rainbow to 12 inches in length.

Between Buena Vista and Northrop the **Arkansas River** gains some size and so do the fish. Railroad Bridge and Buena Vista Fishing Easements provide access to the river at Buena Vista, Johnson Village and Champion Fishing Easements directly below the town offer fishing for rainbow to 14 inches. Special restrictions from the hwy. 24 overpass downstream to the lower boundary of the Hayden Ranch; fishing by artificial flies and lures only, limit for trout is 1 fish 12 inches or shorter. Nearer to Northrop, Ruby Mountain provides accesses the river as it prepares to enter Browns Canyon,

which was designated as Gold Medal until the late 1980's. Browns Canyon is difficult to access as a result of being surrounded by private land, the fishing may be difficult as well, but there are some large fish in the canyon. Get permission before crossing private land.

BUENA VISTA AREA

Trout Creek gives its name to Trout Creek Pass, where US 285-24 leaves the South Platte drainage in South Park and enters the Arkansas basin east of Buena Vista. It flows parallel to the highway. Trout Creek is fed by springs that keep flows and temperature fairly constant. It holds small brook and maybe a small brown, but is brushy and fishing is difficult.

On the east side of the Arkansas, **Fourmile Creek** and **Sevenmile Creek** have some brook, brown and cutthroat, but are hampered by erratic water flows. Beaver ponds at the head of Fourmile Creek may be reached by taking CR 371 on the east side of the railroad track north of Buena Vista for 2 miles, then following CR 375 for 8 miles.

Cottonwood Creek, west of Buena Vista along CR 306, has brook and some brown and, near the campgrounds, is stocked with rainbow. **Cottonwood Lake** (9,500 ft; 43 ac) on south **Cottonwood Creek** is a popular fishing area and is also stocked with rainbow. Fishing is good on the creek above and below the lake for brook and brown.

Middle Cottonwood Creek is a steep, fast flowing stream with fair fishing for brown, brook and some cutthroat, and is stocked occasionally with rainbow as well. It parallels Cottonwood Pass Road (CR 306). **Rainbow Lake**, beside the road, is private.

In the Collegiate Peaks Wilderness north of Middle Cottonwood Creek is **Hartenstein Lake** (11,430 ft; 16 ac). The first mile of the 3-mile hike is along an old road following **Denny Creek,** which offers limited fishing for small brook. Keep to the west on a good trail. There is fair to good fishing for good-size cutthroat and brook. A sign 12 miles west of Buena Vista indicates access a half-mile above Collegiate

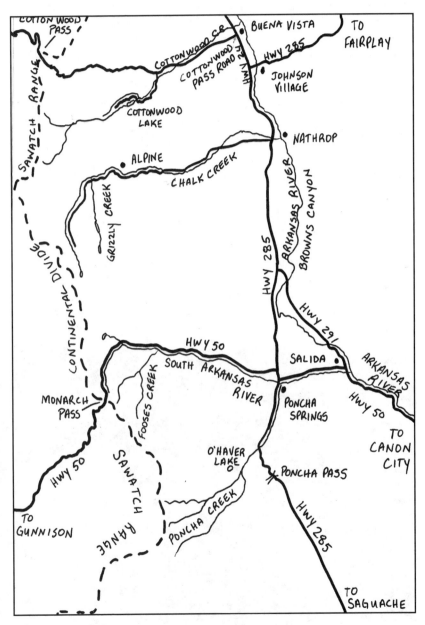

ARKANSAS RIVER (SALIDA)

Peaks Campground.

South off Middle Cottonwood up **Ptarmigan Creek** 4 miles is **Ptarmigan Lake** (12,147 ft; 28 ac). Access is from the highway 2 miles west of Denny Creek along an old logging road and then a trail. The lake offers cutthroat fishing.

North Cottonwood Creek offers only poor to fair fishing for brook, but a trail along it provides access to three high country lakes. Road access from Buena Vista is by CR 365 to the wilderness trailhead. The right fork in the trail (TR 1449), 1.5 miles into the wilderness, leads 4 miles up **Horn Fork Creek** to **Bear Lake** (12,377 ft; 18 ac) and has cutthroat. **Anglemeyer Lake** (11,338 ft; 1 ac) has small cutthroat. There's no trail, and the lake is hard to find. About 1 mile from the trail fork going toward Bear Lake, go 0.25-mile

uphill through timber to the west. A small stream flows out of the lake and joins Horn Fork Creek just above **Kroenke Creek** confluence. **Kroenke Lake** (11,500 ft; 14 ac), 3 miles up the left fork in the trail, has cutthroat.

MT. PRINCETON AREA

Hwy 162 leads west from Nathrop along **Chalk Creek** toward Mt. Princeton Hot Springs, the well-known ghost town of St. Elmo and a passel of high lakes with cutthroat. The road goes some 20 miles along old railroad and mining road rights-of-way. Private land is interspersed with national forest land, and some sections are posted and cannot be fished. Chalk Creek is heavily fished and is stocked with rainbow and cutthroat upstream to St. Elmo. Along side the road is **Chalk Lake** (8,800 ft; 3 ac), which is fair for

Fishing near Buena Vista

stocked rainbow. There are five USFS campgrounds: Bootleg, Chalk Lake, Cascade, Mount Princeton, and Iron City.

Just east of the hamlet of Alpine, **Baldwin Creek** flows in from the south from **Baldwin Lake** (12,100 ft; 21 ac). The road to Baldwin Lake is extremely rough, and walking the last portion is recommended. It offers generally good fishing for cutthroat. The creek has brook trout. **Alpine Lake** at Alpine is private.

Grizzly Lake (11,200 ft; 14 ac) is reached by turning up CR 296 just before St. Elmo. On the left side of the road, a USFS sign marks the beginning of a rough 2.5-mile road up **Grizzly Creek** to the lake. The shallow lake is rated good for brook to 13 inches. **Rosedale Lake** (12,100 ft; 3 ac) is two miles south of Grizzly Lake by a faint trail up a ridge to the west at the head of the drainage. It has cutthroat.

The **North Fork of Chalk Creek** comes in at St. Elmo. Rated only fair for small brook, CR 267 follows the stream as it climbs to Tincup Pass. CR 295 continues up **Middle Fork** of **Chalk Creek**; after 3 miles, a 4-wd USFS-road 297 turns left to **Lower Pomeroy Lake** (12,038 ft; 36 ac) and, 0.5 mile farther up, to **Upper Pomeroy Lake** (12,300 ft; 38 ac). Both have cutthroat and are deep enough that they seldom winterkill.

Lower Hancock Lake (11,615 ft; 53 ac) and **Upper Hancock Lake** (11,675 ft; 7 ac) lies 1.5 miles beyond the old town of Hancock. Lower Hancock Lake is known for large cutthroat, while the upper lake has smaller fish.

A trail from the lakes goes over Chalk Pass to the Middle Fork of the South Arkansas River. **Tunnel Lake**, 4 miles west of CR 245 on trail 1451, winterkills.

Browns Creek is accessible by CR 272 that goes west from US 285, 12 miles north of Poncha Springs. Going west 4 miles until road forks, then south 2 miles to trail that follows the creek west to its headwaters. Stream is rated fair for small brook and brown.

Below Browns Canyon the **Arkansas River** widens out and calms down again. Above Salida are several fishing easements. Heila Junction, Stone Bridge, Smyth and Big Bend fishing easements, provide access to prime fishing waters. Rainbow are the most prevalent and are in the 12 to 20 inch range. In Big Bend Fishing easement from the Highway 291 bridge downstream to CR 166 bridge fishing is by artificial flies and lures only, and a limit of 2 trout 16 inches or longer.

From Salida to Cotapaxi the Arkansas River is the start of "brown country". The river is full of deep water, long riffles and large fish. Look for brown to 18 inches, some larger. From the Stockyard Bridge below salida downstream to Badger Creek (7.5 miles) the river is restricted to artificial flies and lures only. The limit on trout is 2 fish 16 inches or longer. A mix of public and private properties lines the river, and easements are clearly marked. Carrochia, Treat/ Ogden, Rincon, and Vallie Bridge fishing easements offer fine fishing for large trout. Please respect private property.

From Cotopaxi to Texas Creek the river is home to large browns in deep holes. The river goes through some steep sections followed by smooth waters. Fishing can be excellent in the section of the river, but is limited by private properties.

MONARCH PASS

The South Fork of Arkansas River flows east from Monarch Pass to join the main stem at Salida. US 50 generally follows the stream for 25 miles. It is stocked with rainbow between Maysville and Monarch Park Campground and also has some brown and brook. Fishing can be good; the banks are often brushy.

To the west of US 50 are a collection of timberline lakes that can be reached by marked trails from Garfield. **Boss Lake Reservoir** (10,820 ft; 23 ac) has rainbow and cutthroat, but is not regularly stocked. To reach Boss Lake turn right off US 50, 1.5 miles west of Garfield on USFS road 235 (4WD). A trail from the inlet of Boss Lake leads 1.25 miles west to **Hunt Lake** (11,500 ft; 5 ac) stocked with small cutthroat. The two **Waterdog Lakes** (11,475 ft; 4 ac, 6 ac) are an easy hike of about 1.5 miles. The trail leaves US 50 just below the turnoff to Monarch Park Campground. Brook trout are the principal catch. **Grass Lake** (11,500 ft; 2 ac) is reached by hiking 1 mile through the forest up the small stream that crosses US 50 opposite the Monarch quarry. It holds small brook and cutthroat.

The **Middle Fork of South Arkansas River** flows in from the north at Garfield and is paralleled by USFS road 230. It has cutthroat and brook. The **North Fork of South Arkansas** is paralleled by USFS road 240, which leads to **North Fork Reservoir** (11,440 ft; 20 ac) after 10 miles. It has cutthroat, rainbow and some grayling and is usually ice-free by late June. A small stream that flows into the west edge of the reservoir leads .75 miles west to **Island Lake** (11,750 ft; 8 ac). A trail continues northwest from the reservoir for a mile to **Billings Lake** (11,740 ft; 4 ac). Island Lake and Billings Lake are barren. A small road that turns left at the Shavano townsite reaches **Hunkydory Lake** (12,000 ft; 4 ac). At the end of the road, walk up a steep rocky slope, then angle right to pick up the outlet creek. It holds small cutthroat.

Fooses Creek, a tributary of the South Arkansas, is paralleled by rough USFS road 225 between Garfield and Maysville. It has rainbow and brook trout.

Green Creek has a good population of brown as well as brook that tend to be in the higher stretches. It is reached by USFS road 221. From US 50, USFS road 221 leads up the creek in the direction of the Cinderella South Mine. Where the road turns south away from the creek, trail 1412 continues upstream.

Pass Creek and **Pass Creek Lake** (11,300 ft; 5 ac) are heavily visited. They are reached by turning south on CR 210 from US 50, 2 miles west of Poncha Springs. A narrow dirt road (USFS 212) forks to the right then dead-ends at an old mine on national

forest land. Pass Creek Lake is 4 miles up a trail and offers good fishing for small- to medium-sized cutthroat and small grayling. Pass Creek is a small stream with small brook trout. **Little Cochetopa Creek** has similar fishing; it is reached by taking CR 210 and continuing left at the first fork and following the Forest Service signs.

US 285 south of Poncha Springs on the way to Poncha Pass parallels **Poncha Creek** for 5 miles. Marshall Pass Road (USFS 200) follows the creek to its headwaters. The creek has brown and stocked rainbow on its lower stretches, brook and cutthroat at higher elevations. There is a parking lot for anglers at the Shirley townsite, 2 miles up from the highway turnoff. From there, USFS 200, a tightly winding gravel road, climbs 1.5 miles to

O'Haver Lake (9,600 ft; 15 ac) and campground. The lake is heavily stocked with rainbow and heavily fished, but offers the advantage of being ice-free earlier in the spring than many higher lakes. **Silver Creek**, which is brushy, joins Poncha Creek nearby, and holds some large beaver ponds with, primarily, brook. The **Silver Creek Lakes** and stretches of the stream are on private property. **Starvation Creek**, also a tributary of Poncha, has small brook trout.

Between O'Haver Lake and 10,842-foot Marshall Pass, the road crosses **Gray Creek**, with cutthroat, and **Ouray Creek**, with brook and cutthroat.

SANGRE DE CRISTO MOUNTAINS

Southwest of the Arkansas River and US 50, the Sangre de Cristo (Blood of Christ) Mountains extend for 150 spectacular miles into New Mexico. At its higher elevations, the San Isabel National Forest, southeast of Salida, forms a ragged ribbon of public land, no more than 6 miles across, that stretches from the crest of 13,000- and 14,000-foot peaks. Two islands of the San Isabel National Forest are east of the main range—one is the Wet Mountains and the other is south of LaVeta.

The rugged Sangres have good populations of elk, mule deer and bighorn sheep, although reaching them can be quite difficult, because the terrain is almost impossible to negotiate. Public access to the region's fishing and hunting is almost entirely from the eastern side of the Sangre de Cristos.

For the most part, streams flowing out of the Sangre de Cristos plunge through very rugged country. They have fast, clear water and many have marvelous beaver-pond angling, as well as a lot of brush and willows. The trails to and along the streams are steep. The Rainbow Trail runs along the range from north to south at about the 9000- to 10,000-foot level. Signs at its intersections with most westerly upstream trails keep the hiker aware of his location. Campsites at higher elevations are limited because of the steep terrain. Some 48 high-country lakes are stocked with cutthroat trout either annually or every other year, usually by helicopter.

The lower elevations, with pinon pine and juniper, also are classified as rugged and scenic country, rich in Indian and Spanish history. They offer some of the state's best elk, deer, wild turkey, mountain lion, black bear and small-game country, as well as fishing for trout and bass. The Spanish Peaks—cones of extinct volcanoes that rise to 12,683 feet and 13,626 feet at the eastern and western summits, respectively—contribute to the mystique of the region south of US 160.

SANGRE DE CRISTOS

About 14 miles south of the Arkansas on Hwy 69, a good road (198) turns west from the highway to Lake Creek and Lake Creek Campground, where there is a 4WD road to **Balman Reservoir** (9,400 ft; 5 ac), which is stocked with rainbow and some grayling. This is a popular area. To the west, about 3 miles, is **Rainbow Lake** (10,400 ft; 20 ac). It is an irrigation reservoir, which is sometimes stocked. Inquire locally for current information. Two miles farther on is Cloverdale Mine and a 2-mile trail leading to **Silver Lake** (12,000 ft; 5 ac), which has poor fishing for cutthroat.

Upper Brush Creek Lake (11,635 ft; 44 ac) and **Lower Brush Creek Lake** (11,500 ft; 45 ac) are favorite cutthroat and brook trout waters. Anglers may also find a few rainbows in the upper lake. For a change, the 4.5-mile hike to these lakes is relatively gentle compared with the steep terrain elsewhere in the Sangre de Cristos. To reach these lakes, turn off Hwy 69 at the Brush Lake Road just south of Hillside. Continue south on improved road

Near Cripple Creek

Photo Courtesy of Kevin Rummell

for 2.6 miles. Then take the dirt road south, then west, to Brush Creek trailhead at forest boundary and its juncture with Rainbow Trail. Signs in the area are helpful. **South Branch Creek** from where it joins **Brush Creek** is about a half-mile below Lower Brush Creek Lake. Brush Creek itself has rainbow and brook, but, as the name suggests, it's often difficult-to-impossible fishing.

Banjo Lake (12,320 ft; 2 ac) is at the headwaters of **Middle Brush Creek** under 11,621-foot Electric Peak. It also is stocked with cutthroat. A four-mile hike south of Brush Creek Lakes reaches Banjo Lake. This is well above timberline. The creek has some brook. Fishing is only fair. **South Brush Creek** is rated poor.

The three **Lakes of the Clouds** (11,200 ft; 9 to 11 ac) are stocked with cutthroat. The 4-mile trail is now closed to vehicles. Access is off the Brush Creek Loop Road to Rainbow Trail.

DEWEESE RESERVOIR

East of Hwy 69 about 4 miles north of Westcliffe is **DeWeese Reservoir** (7,665 ft; 240 ac) owned by the DeWeese-Dye Ditch & Reservoir Co. The reservoir was refilled in 1988 after concern about the safety of the 100-year-old dam was resolved, at least for the time being. DOW leases a portion of the shoreline for unimproved campsites. The water is heavily stocked and heavily fished for rainbows. Easy access is north from the center of town on the reservoir road, just east of Hwy 69. DOW enforces fishing and wildlife regulations, private landowners are in charge of boating and camping. The southwest shore is private.

Grape Creek (called **Swift Creek** west of the reservoir) is best below the dam, where it is stocked with rainbow. It is in a deep canyon, a lot of it on BLM land. Because of a relatively consistent flow of water from the reservoir, fishing is usually good for brown trout. Farther downstream on Grape Creek there is some fishing for brown in Temple Canyon Park. It is reached by taking South First Street out of Cañon City. There's no camping.

West of Westcliffe 8 miles on Hermit Lake Road (USFS 160) is the **Middle Taylor Creek State Wildlife Area**. It has campsites and brown and brook trout fishing in **Middle Taylor Creek**. A few browns lurk in beaver ponds.

The road continues west to provide access to a host of high-country lakes and streams. **Hermit Lake** (11,300 ft; 20 ac), a few yards from the end of the road, has mostly brook and cutthroat and some brown. It is rated fair. Uphill to the northwest less than a mile by following the trailside stream is **Horseshoe Lake** (12,000 ft; 10 ac), with cutthroat. **Eureka Lake** (12,000 ft; 10 ac) is just southwest of Hermit Lake and is reached by a switchback trail over a ridge. It has cutthroat averaging 9 inches. North of Hermit Lake Road are several small streams, including **Gibson Creek** and **North Taylor Creek**, with some fishing.

NEAR WESTCLIFFE

To the south are **Venable Creek**, the **Venable Lakes** (12,000 ft; 6 ac and 9

ac) and several beaver ponds, all with cutthroat. The lake offers good fishing for fish to 12 inches. A 7-mile trail leads up from Alvarado Campground to the lakes. The campground is easily reached by driving southwest from Westcliffe on well-marked and maintained roads. There are trail signs. The trail goes over the crest of the mountains via Venable Pass into the Rio Grande National Forest and the North Crestone Creek Campground. **Goodwin Creek** and **Goodwin Lake** (11,600 ft; 7 ac) are also reached by trail out of the Alvarado Campground to the northwest via the Rainbow Trail. It is rated good for 9-inch cutthroat. **Comanche Lake** (11,680 ft; 20 ac), with cutthroat, is most readily reached by trail up **Alvarado Creek** and skirting the southeast and south sides of Spring Mountain (12,701 ft). This is a steep, demanding hike in precipitous and dangerous terrain above timberline; one should be properly equipped and prepared for it.

Cottonwood Creek, **Hennequin Creek** and **Dry Creek** have some fishing, but the best bet is to hike up Dry Creek to the **Dry Lakes** (12,000 ft; 14 ac total), which have cutthroat. Access is via the Horn Ranch Road for the Dry Lakes and also for **Horn Creek** and **North Horn Lake** (11,800 ft; 3 ac) and **South Horn Lake** (11,680 ft; 24 ac). The shallow North Lake has poor fishing. The larger south lake has cutthroat. **Macey Lakes** (Lower 11,491 ft; 5 ac, North 11,861 ft; 10ac, South 11,650 ft; 8 ac) are at the headwaters of **Macey Creek** in this spectacular country. The three lakes are between 11,500 and

11,900 feet and have cutthroat. Below the falls, at about 11,300 feet, some brook and rainbow may be found in the creek.

COLONY LAKES

The spectacular 14,000-foot Crestone Peaks—ultimate technical mountain-climbing challenges in Colorado—are the backdrop for fishing the **North Colony Lakes**, a series of ponds on **North Colony Creek,** between 11,500 and 12,000 feet, and **South Colony Creek**. The lakes offer good fishing for cutthroat and rainbow. A road goes within a mile of South Colony Lakes Trail. This is a popular area, these waters are heavily stocked and fished. South Colony Creek is stocked with small cutthroat.

About 4.3 miles south of Westcliffe on Hwy 69, Colfax Lane (CR 119) continues due south as the highway bends easterly. Eleven miles south of Hwy 69 the road ends at the trail to Music Pass, a 4WD road that climbs only a couple of miles from the valley road. To the north are several small streams and the Colony Creeks. By going west over Music Pass (11,520 ft), **Upper Sand Creek Lake** (11,745 ft; 42 ac) and **Lower Sand Creek Lake** (11,450 ft; 62 ac) are reached only on foot or horseback, but nonetheless heavily fished for cutthroat. **Sand Creek** has cutthroat and brook trout.

Fishing farther south in streams intersected by the Rainbow Trail is very limited, mostly in beaver ponds, as the national forest narrows until the headwaters of the Huerfano River are reached just north of US 160 at LaVeta

Pass.

ARKANSAS RIVER

Between Texas Creek and Parkdale the **Arkansas River** flows through the Lower Arkansas River Canyon. The canyon lends itself well to white water rafting; fishing is better nearer to Parkdale. Stream improvements, some done inadvertently to help the white water rafters, have improved the fishing for brown to 15 inches and some Snake River cutthroat in the canyon. Below Texas Creek the Arkansas' quality is reduced due to an increase in silt in the river. Pinnacle Rock near Texas Creek, as well as, Five Points and Spike Buck Fishing Easements nearer to Parkdale provide public access to the river.

At Parkdale, where the Arkansas crosses under US 50 and leaves the highway for Royal Gorge, anglers may park about 200 yards south of the highway at a pullout on CR 3, then walk across BLM land to the river and fish the upper end of the Royal Gorge. There is no river access from the Royal Gorge Rim.

PIKES PEAK AREA

High above the Arkansas River to the north is Pikes Peak. Several small streams including **Beaver Creek, Fountain Creek, Fourmile Creek, Cottonwood Creek, and Badger Creek,** drain the higher elevations. These creeks offer very poor fishing opportunities. The Pike's Peak region does not have an abundance of fishing waters, though there are a few worth noting. Pike National Forest provides much of the public land available throughout the area. This vast area is limited primarily to lake and reservoir fishing.

Skaguay Reservoir (84 ac) is a small lake near the town of Victor. Fishing is for stocked rainbow and for brook and lake trout. Access is from Victor on Hwy 67. Signed county road leads to lake. There is a public boat ramp. Part of Beaver Creek State wildlife area. Access to **Beaver Creek** is provided but offers only poor fishing for rainbow and brook.

Rosemont Reservoir (20 ac), 25 miles east of Victor on Gold Camp Rd, offers fishing for rainbow, brook, brown, and cutthroat. Artificial flies and lures only. Fishing prohibited from 9 p.m. to 5 a.m. Ice fishing is not allowed.

Rampart Reservoir (500 ac) is located east of Hwy 67 north of Woodland Park, near the Teller-Douglas county line. This reservoir has stocked rainbow, mackinaw and cutthroat. Walk-in access; no boats. Ice fishing is prohibited. Limit for lake trout (mackinaw) is two fish.

Adjacent to Rampart Reservoir, **Nicholls Reservoir** (20 ac) is also a walk-in lake (trail 709). It's located off Hwy 67 about 8 miles north of Woodland Park. The majority of the fish are 10-inch stocked rainbow, but there are also a few brook.

Prospect Lake (85 ac) is located in the city park at the southeast edge of Colorado Springs, this 85-acre lake provides daylight fishing. Toilets and trash cans are available; boating is discouraged. Go south on Union St. to the lake, where rainbow and brown trout, walleye, channel catfish and black bass can be taken.

Located within the City of Colorado Springs, **Quail Lake** (17 ac) is stocked with catchable rainbow trout in early spring. It also has crappie, largemouth bass, hybrid bluegill and channel catfish. Access is from Cheyenne Mountain Blvd. in the southwestern part of the city.

PALMER LAKE

Palmer Lake (13 ac) has catchable rainbow. The Colorado Division of Wildlife leases this lake, owned by the county. Anglers can catch yellow perch, channel catfish, 10-inch rainbows, hybrid bluegill and a few brook trout. Palmer Lake is located in the town of Palmer Lake, north of Colorado Springs and west of I-25.

Green Mountain Falls (3.5 ac), just west of Colorado Springs on US 24, is a city lake that is open for public fishing, primarily for stocked rainbow. It is fed by Fountain Creek and may have a few brook and brown.

Constructed and stocked by the Colorado Division of Wildlife, **Ramah Reservoir** (170 ac) has crappie, black and largemouth bass, northern pike, bluegill and channel catfish. Rainbow trout might be stocked during spring months. Take US 24 east from Colorado Springs to town of Ramah; reservoir is 1 mile west. Facilities include campground, toilet, trash cans and a boat ramp. Subject to extreme drawdowns during the summer. A very nice place to fish during the spring months, with the panoramic view of Pike's Peak to the west.

PIKES PEAK NORTH SLOPE RECREATION AREA

On the north side of Pikes Peak, accessible from the Pike's Peak Road, are **Crystal Creek Reservoir** (120 ac), **South Catamount Reservoir** (93 ac) **and North Catamount Reservoir** (185 ac).

Fishing from the bank only, no boats. All areas require a Colorado fishing license. This is a fee area. The bag and possession limit for trout is four fish, no more than one of which can be a lake trout. Fishing in North Catamount Reservoir is fishing by artificial flies and lures only.

The three reservoirs, tributaries and streams that feed the reservoirs are part of the drinking water collection system for Colorado Springs and surrounding communities.

Due to steep grades, motor homes are not permitted at North and South Catamount reservoirs.

Currently, recreational activities such as swimming, camping, horseback riding, boating and mountain biking are prohibited.

The road to the reservoirs passes **Severy Creek**, where fishing is prohibited above the forest service boundary.

WET MOUNTAINS AREA

From the town of Florence, west of Pueblo, Hwy 67 leads south to the town of Wetmore and the adjacent Wet Mountains, most of which are in the San Isabel National Forest. The area receives abundant precipitation and is heavily forested; hence, it is a refuge from the dry heat and summer sun of the rolling uplands and plains to the east. The ranching valley and communities of Westcliffe and Silver Cliff are scenic country.

From Wetmore, Hwy 96 goes south and west paralleling **Hardscrabble Creek**, a fast-descending mountain brook with stocked rainbow and brook. **South Hardscrabble Creek,** with stocked rainbow, is paralleled by USFS road 387, then 306, which provides access to 4 miles of public fishing. It may also be reached by continuing west on Hwy 96 for 4 climbing, twisting miles to the intersection with Hwy 165 at McKenzie Junction and then turning south to the intersection with USFS road 306 after 5.5 miles.

Some 6 miles farther south on Hwy 165 is **Ophir Creek**. It is adjacent to USFS road 360, called the Ophir Creek Road or Burns Meadow Road, and ascends to the top of the Wet Mountains. Ophir Creek is partly on private land, and has rainbow and brook trout, though fishing in the brush is difficult. The USFS Ophir Campground lies just up the USFS road from the state highway. The best fishing is upstream from the campground. Don't neglect the beaver ponds for some lively fishing for brook.

The Greenhorn Mountain Road is a dead-end gravel road that follows the main ridge of the mountains south to **Blue Lakes** (11,280 ft; 2 ac each), which are about 20 miles south of the Ophir Creek Road. The lakes have been deepened and stocked with rainbow. The road, which continues on a mile or so, ends at Greenhorn Mountain

(12,347 ft).

Hwy 165 continues south from the Ophir Creek intersection to **Lake Isabel** (8,475 ft; 20 ac) and the hamlet of San Isabel. A scenic timberline lake, it has a campground beginning about 1/2 mile above the lake. Portions of the lake are shallow. The lake and campgrounds are heavily used. There are stocked rainbow and some brown. Boats without motors are allowed.

The **St. Charles River,** which flows through Lake Isabel, is stocked and heavily fished for brook and rainbow above the lake and for brown downstream from it. Fishing can be very good. About 1.5 miles south of Lake Isabel is **Little St. Charles Creek**, with brook and rainbow. USFS 318, about 0.5 mile south of Lake Isabel, provides access.

EAST OF THE SANGRE DE CRISTOS

West of Walsenburg, from the northeast slopes of Mt. Blanca, the **Huerfano River** begins its northeasterly course to join the Arkansas River near Boone, east of Pueblo. The Huerfano, along with other southern tributaries of the Arkansas, such as the **Apishapa River** and **Purgatory River**, is fishable mainly in the clear waters of its upper end in the Sangre de Cristo Mountains. Drawn down by irrigation water withdrawals, these streams when they reach the valley floors tend to become slow, shallow, muddy and warm, even before they reach I-25. The Ute Indian word apishapa means "stinking water," which describes that river's water qual-

ity and near-stagnate state during the summer on the plains. The best fishing tends to be in the spring and early summer in these streams. Fishing from the headwaters of the Huerfano downstream to the U. S. Forest Service boundary is by artificial flies or lures only. It is stocked with catchable rainbows and small cutthroats.

BRUSH HOLLOW RESERVOIR

North of the Arkansas River, 3.5 miles northwest of Penrose is **Brush Hollow Reservoir** (5,600 ft; 186 ac), an irrigation reservoir whose shoreline is leased by the Colorado DOW as a day-use area. No camping. Brush Hollow offers fishing for bass, crappie, walleye, bluegill hybrid, channel catfish, gizzard shad, and is stocked in the spring and fall with rainbow. Catfish specialists favor the shallower upper end; crappie anglers, the dam face. There is a gravel boat ramp on the northeast side of the lake. To reach it, turn west from Hwy 115 onto CR 123, which is marked for Brush Hollow Reservoir. Continue west 1 mile, then turn north on CR 127 for slightly more than 1 mile to the signed state wildlife entrance. A dirt road leads west and south to the lake's edge. To reach the west side and the dam, continue on CR 123 another 1.5 miles to a signed turnoff to the state wildlife area. All smallmouth, largemouth, and spotted bass that are kept must be 15 inches in length or longer. Brush Hollow's location in an area of huge boulders, rock outcrops and piñon-Juniper tree cover make it one of the most picturesque warm-water lakes in the state.

CAÑON CITY/FLORENCE AREA

Arkansas River fishing in the upper end of the Pueblo Reservoir SWA is rated poor for an occasional brown trout. The river is highly silted. Upstream to the town of Florence, the river flows through private land and is not accessible.

Fishing improves by Florence where public access is available at bridge crossings on Hwy 67 and Hwy 115. This section of the river is rated fair with most success in the fall for brown trout.

Public access to the Arkansas River within Cañon City is primarily on the south bank. The Riverwalk, a hiking and bicycling trail, follows the south bank between 9th St. and MacKenzie Ave. for about 2.5 miles. Both streets intersect US 50 (Royal Gorge Blvd.). Fishing pressure is surprisingly light in this part of the river. It is rated good for12-inch rainbow, and 11- to 16-inch brown and occasional cutthroat.

Above Cañon City, Tunnel Drive provides access to the River at the lower end of the Royal Gorge. Tunnel Drive turns south from US 50 at the bottom of Eightmile Hill where the highway drops into Cañon City from the west. The access road runs beside the state correctional facility's farm. A right turn at the sign for Tunnel Drive takes you to portions of the river in the Gorge.

PUEBLO RESERVOIR

Pueblo Reservoir (4,900 ft; 3000 ac) is in the Pueblo State Recreation Area. When the reservoir is near ca-

Nymph fishing for Rainbow

Photo Courtesy of the Morrison Angler

pacity, its upstream end spreads into the Pueblo Reservoir State Wildlife Area. The reservoir is the most popular warm-water fishery in the state. It is rated good for walleye, largemouth, smallmouth and spotted bass, crappie, wiper, bluegill, northern pike, rainbow, perch, catfish and it has some brown trout. Along with fishing, water-skiing and swimming are popular summer sports on the reservoir. Camping facilities include showers, electricity and a laundry.

All bass under 15 inches must be returned to the water immediately. From March 15 through April 15, fishing is prohibited from the dam and within 50 feet of it between the hours of 4 pm and 9 am. The bag, possession and size limit for walleye is 4 fish, 18 inches or longer.

North access to the recreation area is by turning west on US 50 just north of Pueblo. From US 50, turn south on McCullough Blvd. to the reservoir. The route is well marked, as is a park entrance from the south on Hwy 96.

SOUTHEASTERN COLORADO

After flowing through Pueblo Reservoir, the Arkansas River widens and slows and is joined by several other rivers on its way to Kansas. Catfish angling can be very good in stretches of the Arkansas, but the majority of the fishing opportunities in southeastern Colorado occur in the many reservoirs, some of which are filled by the Arkansas.

Colorado's southeast has become "wiper country" in recent years, as the sterile hybrid between white and striped bass has found these reservoirs to its liking. Growing to over 20 pounds, these aggressive fighters have become popular with anglers who appreciate the challenge of fooling large fish with lure or fly.

Tiger muskies are another recently introduced fish that provides large fish action. A sterile cross between northern pike and muskellunge; the potential for 30-pound tigers has almost been realized. Notwithstanding their potential, biologists say that tiger muskies have not done well in lower elevations despite much stocking. They seem to do better on Front Range waters. Lathrop State Park and Horseshoe Lake are outstanding fishing for tiger muskie. Largemouth bass, crappie, walleye, channel catfish, bluegill, sunfish, bullhead and carp can all be taken in these reservoirs.

PUEBLO AREA

Runyon/Fountain Lakes (20 ac) is a State Wildlife Area between the Arkansas River and the baseball park in southeast Central Pueblo. It is readily seen from I-25. This former sandpit is now a good fishing spot for catchable trout, largemouth bass and channel catfish. There are plans to stock walleye, crappie and hybrid bluegill. Boats and ice fishing are not permitted on Runyon.

St. Charles Reservoir is off the St. Charles River on the prairie southeast of Pueblo. Mostly dry, it may retain a small, shallow pool at times, with enough water to maintain fish populations. It is closed to public use.

Anticline Lake (5 ac) is due east of Pueblo Reservoir and is stocked with 10-inch rainbow trout, 3-inch crappie and 8-inch channel catfish.

LINCOLN COUNTY

Kinney Lake (7 ac) is in the Hugo State Wildlife Area. It is reached by driving 19 miles southeast of Limon to Hugo on U.S. 40, and then about 4 miles south on Hwy 109 to sign, then east to lake. It is stocked with largemouth bass, bluegill hybrid and channel catfish. Kinney also has crappie, carp, and bullhead and is annually stocked with rainbow in March and April. Toilets and trash cans available. Most fishing is from shoreline, although wakeless boats are permitted.

The **Clingingsmith Ponds** (20 ac), also located in the Hugo State Wildlife Area, are 2.5 miles south of Kinney Lake in the middle of the prairie. There are 19 ponds, four of which contain permanent fish populations of stocked largemouth bass, bluegill hybrid and channel catfish. Carp and bullhead may also be found.

Continue 35 miles south from the town of Hugo on Hwy 109. About 1.5 miles southeast of the town of Karval is the Karval State Fishing Area. **Karval Reservoir** (8 ac) is rated good fishing in the spring, and fair in the summer, for stocked largemouth bass, bluegill hybrid, channel catfish and rainbow. The lake also has rock bass and crappie. Wakeless boats are allowed. Toilets and trash cans are available.

CROWLEY COUNTY

Henry Reservoir (1120 ac) is about 3 miles northeast of Ordway. This State Wildlife Area is a great crappie producer when water levels remain high for several succeeding years. The water level of the reservoir fluctuates and the best fishing is obviously during wet cycles. Currently, the reservoir is being stocked with channel catfish (excellent), walleye and wiper. Crappie,

bluegill, largemouth bass, bullhead and carp may also be found. Campsites and boat ramp are available at this 6-foot-deep reservoir, but there is very little shade.

Meredith Reservoir (3220 ac) is about 15 feet deep with a mucky bottom and a sandy shoreline fringed with tamarisk and willow. This State Wildlife Area is located about 4 miles directly south of Lake Henry on the south side of Hwy 96 near Sugar City. Several county roads head to the reservoir. A boat ramp and sanitary facilities are available. Local anglers fish at night when the wind is not as likely to blow. Meredith is stocked occasionally with channel catfish, walleye, wiper and saugeye. Bluegill, carp and bullhead are also caught. The lake is used extensively by skiers and windsurfers.

Ordway Water Supply Pond or **Ordway Reservoir** (28 ac), State Wildlife Area is on Hwy 71 two miles north of its junction with Hwy 96. A prime put-and-take pond that is stocked with rainbow (catchable in March and April), sunfish, crappie, largemouth bass, hybrid bluegill and channel catfish.

Olney Reservoir (6 ac) is stocked with largemouth bass, bluegill hybrid and channel catfish. There are no facilities; primitive campsites. State Wildlife Area located northwest of the city of Olney Springs, west of Ordway.

OTERO COUNTY

About 7 miles south of Lake Meredith is **Holbrook Reservoir** (670 ac) and State Wildlife Area. Drive south on Hwy 71 to the intersection of U.S.

50, then east 2 miles through Rocky Ford and another 5miles farther to Swink. At Swink turn north, and drive about 4 miles to the Holbrook Reservoir. Holbrook has an open, sandy shoreline with cottonwood and tamarisk. It offers fair fishing for stocked largemouth bass, rainbows, channel catfish, saugeye, tiger muskie, walleye and wiper. Other fish present are crappie, bluegill, yellow perch, green sunfish, bullhead and carp. Toilets, trash cans and a boat ramp, but not much else in way of facilities. Water level fluctuates severely from spring to fall, so do your fishing in spring and early summer.

Timpas Creek meanders from a southeasterly course to a confluence with the Arkansas River west of the town of Swink. There are many spring-fed pools with a resident population of fat sunfish and bullhead plus some very nice channel catfish. To reach the area, go 2 miles northeast out of Swink, crossing the Arkansas River bridge, then west 1 mile and south 1 mile to the 141-acre area, through which the creek flows. No facilities or boating.

American Crystal Sugar Pond is no longer open to the public or stocked with fish. **Dye Reservoir**, like Lake Henry, is an irrigation storage reservoir that seldom contains water. It has been a dry lake for several years.

Rocky Ford Ponds, once known as **Ryan Ponds** or **Bird Farm Ponds**, are good for children, with many little sunfish, bass and bullhead. Stocked with bass, catfish, crappie, and hybrid bluegill. It's northeast of the town of Rocky Ford across the river bridge on Hwy

266 and 0.5 mile east. Trash cans, toilets and some picnic tables are available.

Northeast of Holbrook Reservoir, and about 7 miles northeast of the town of Cheraw on Hwy 109, is **Horse Creek Reservoir**, known for some odd reason, as **Timber Lake** (2636 ac). There may have been a tree near it in the distant past, but now there is not much else beside tamarisk. It is a typical desolate, prairie, irrigation pond with a terrible water-level fluctuation problem, which adversely influences the stability of the fish population. However, during wet weather cycles, higher water levels are maintained and large crappie, bullhead and channel catfish are taken.

BENT COUNTY

About 9 miles northeast of Horse Creek Reservoir and due north of Las Animas about 14 miles is **Adobe Creek Reservoir** or **Blue Lake** (1200 ac) with a depth of 35 feet. It is also located on barren prairie. During wet weather cycles, all 5,000 surface acres of the lake fill two basins, and fish populations explode. In dry cycles, the lake retreats into the north basin and fishing becomes more difficult. Largemouth bass, saugeye, blue catfish, channel catfish, tiger muskie, walleye and wiper are being stocked in Adobe Creek. Anglers may also find crappie, bullhead, white bass, bluegill, and a few northern pike and carp. Facilities are limited to boat ramps and restrooms. There is no shade, no trees; bleak is the best description. However, it is probably the best crappie fishery

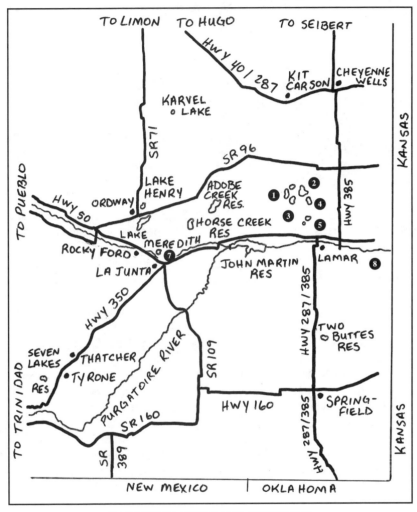

JOHN MARTIN RESERVOIR

1. Neesopah Reservoir
2. Neenoshe Reservoir
3. Neegronda Reservoir
4. Neeskah Reservoir
5. Thurston Reservoir
6. Woods Reservoir
7. Holbrook Reservoir
8. Arkansas Reservoir

Photo Courtesy of Kevin Rummell

Small mule deer

in Colorado. It is also an excellent channel catfish fishery for drift fishing in late summer. Fishing pressure is very light.

Seven Lakes Reservoir appears blue on many maps, but seldom has any water. Not enough water in these basins to keep a minnow alive.

Just east of the town of Las Animas, **John Martin Reservoir** (1700 ac when full), on the Arkansas River, offers 3 boat ramps and fishing for most warm-water species. At the present time, saugeye, largemouth and smallmouth bass, blue catfish, channel catfish, striped bass, walleye and wiper are being stocked in John Martin. Also available to anglers are crappie (probably the largest in the state), bluegill, bullhead, a few yellow perch and carp. This big lake produces big fish. Shoreline fishing among many rocky cliffs is good, with snakes for companions. Still, this is a small price to pay for the super fishing at the reservoir. All smallmouth and largemouth bass must be 15

inches in length or longer.

John Martin signs are along U.S. 50. At the town of Hasty, head south on paved road 2 miles to the reservoir area. Wild and wooly winds are fairly common in this region, so be prepared for them. On the reservoir, boaters can find a windless haven at Rule Creek inlet or among the rocky canyons on the north side.

Hasty Lake (53 ac) and **Stilling Basin** (22 ac) are at the eastern edge of John Martin Reservoir. Hasty Lake is 3 miles south of the town of Hasty by paved road. It is about 10 feet deep and has grassy shores. Fishing is limited to shoreline and boats at wakeless speeds. It is stocked with largemouth bass, bluegill hybrid, channel catfish, saugeye, walleye, wiper and rainbow trout. One might also expect to find crappie, carp and bullhead. Stilling Basin is adjacent to Hasty Lake, right below John Martin Dam; large fish include walleye, white bass, wiper and channel catfish. Also check out some of the deep-water pools in the river downstream from the Basin.

Merit Reservoir is no longer stocked and does not have public fishing any longer. However, **Kirkpatrick Pond** is stocked with 6-inch largemouth bass, 3-inch bluegill hybrid, and 8-inch channel catfish.

Setchfield Lake or **Muddy Creek Reservoir** is a washed-out reservoir located 16 miles south of Las Animas on Hwy 101, 1 mile west and 5 miles south on county road. Muddy Creek, which flows through the area, contains many spring-fed, deep potholes and pools, which contain permanent populations of sunfish and black bullhead. When seeking a little adventure, this is a good area to check out.

PROWERS COUNTY

Clay Creek meanders south to northeast through the town of Lamar. The creek, from U.S. 287 south of Lamar, is full of spring-fed potholes and pools. Sunfish and bullhead are available in the pools, and, when there is high water in the Arkansas River, channel catfish run up the creek for several miles. There is some fishing opportunity in this area. There are a lot of beaver dams on the lower stretch before the confluence with the Arkansas River.

Mike Higbee State Wildlife Area on the Arkansas River is 4 miles east of Lamar on U.S. 50. Camping permitted, but no facilities available. Bullhead, channel catfish and sunfish are found in the one pond that has water.

Thurston Reservoir (173 ac) is located 9 miles north of Lamar on Hwy 149, then a mile east on county road. It is a state wildlife area. Thurston Reservoir is stocked with tiger muskie, wiper, and channel catfish. The cattails that ringed the lake have been mostly cleared. There is a boat ramp. A few largemouth bass might be found.

KIOWA COUNTY

Drive east beyond John Martin and Hasty Lake to the intersection of U.S. 287, turn north about 13 miles to the Great Plains Reservoirs, sometimes known as the Eads Lakes. These include **Nee So Pah** (Sweetwater), **Nee Gronda** (Big Water), **Nee Noshe** and **Nee Skah Reservoirs**, all within a 5-mile radius. They are part of the Queens State Wildlife Area. Nee So Pah is closed. Nee Noshe is the largest at 3,696 acres, and Nee Gronda is close behind at 3,490 acres. Nee Grande has had the best fish population of all these lakes with a 40-foot water depth and the largest wiper population in Colorado. The variety of fish is basically the same in the various reservoirs. Walleye, saugeye, wiper, white bass, largemouth bass, a few northern pike, channel catfish, blue catfish, crappie, bluegill, bullhead and carp can be found. Wipers are up to 21 pounds. These are popular lakes. Wind can be very disturbing at times. Facilities include restrooms and a boat ramp. Night fishing during the summer can provide some monster catfish.

Three miles south of the Eads Lakes are the **Lower** and **Upper Queens Reservoirs** (1930 ac). These lakes may dry up or almost dry up in low water years. Wind is also a problem for Queens. Trotlines and jug fishing are permitted.

BACA COUNTY

About 30 miles south of Lamar on US 287, **Two Buttes Reservoir** (1700 ac) and State Wildlife Area is east of the highway. The reservoir has an open, rocky shoreline, and reaches depths of 50 feet. There are two boat ramps. It has relatively poor fishing for largemouth bass, crappie, bullhead, white bass and walleye. The water level here fluctuates. The reservoir catches occasional late summer floods in its narrow watershed. Sometimes a 9- to 14-foot rise from high water floods hundreds of acres of smartweed (persicaria amphibia). The DOW stocks warmwater species and/or trout and excellent growth occurs for 3-4 years until the lake goes dry again. Bass will reach 2-3 pounds. It has a trailer dump station, restrooms, drinking water and a rifle range.

Burchfield Lake (10 ac) is a marshy pond 7 miles east of the town of Walsh. Originally constructed as a fishing lake, it has become a swamp because of leakage, and fish are no longer stocked.

Farther south of Two Buttes, in the arid country southwest of Springfield, **Comanche Ponds** (10 ac), on the Colorado-Oklahoma state line, no longer has fish. There are some good private ponds in the area that may be fished by landowner permission.

Turks Pond State Wildlife Area is southeast of the town of Two Buttes. It is a 30-acre lake kept full by DOW for flooding wildlife crops. Excellent fishing for largemouth bass, hybrid bluegill and channel catfish. No motors are permitted, but there is a boat ramp, parking area, and covered picnic area. Just west of Pritchett is **Boyd Rose Pond** (1 ac), is stocked with channel catfish, largemouth bass, and bluegill hybrid. **Mayhem Pond** (2 ac), also west of Pritchett, and is stocked with small bluegill hybrid and largemouth bass.

HUERFANO RIVER

North of U.S. 160 at LaVeta Pass between Walsenburg and Alamosa on the northeast slope of Mt. Blanca (14,345 ft) is the **Huerfano River**. The major public land area on the river is the 544-acre Huerfano State Wildlife Area, 12 miles west of Gardner. It is a popular base camp for big-game hunters. The river has stocked brown and rainbow. Artificial flies and lures only, limit on trout is two. Upstream, the river runs through private land to the national forest, but there are stretches open to public fishing. Above Sharpsdale at the headwaters of the Huerfano is **Cascade Creek.** Fishing in the creek is prohibited above the USFS boundary. At Singing River Ranch, the river road branches, and USFS road 409 goes south to **Strawberry Creek**, which offers catch-and-release fishing for greenback cutthroat.

Cutthroat are stocked in **Lost Lake** (12,240 ft; 5 ac), which has a tendency to winterkill, and the **Lilly Lakes** (12,350 to 12,630 ft; 4 and 8 ac). They are reached from USFS road 408 at Singing River Ranch as it goes to the west 5 miles upslope. It is 4WD country and local inquiry is advised. Chances are you'll walk 2 or more miles to the lakes. This is high, well-above timberline country in precipitous terrain. There is no road to Lost Lake, located a mile north of the lower Lilly Lake.

Much of the land in the upper Huerfano area is private or leased BLM land. The only way to get around is on foot or horseback. West of I-25 just before the confluence with the Cacharas River, **North and South Apache Creek** tumbles out of the Wet Mountains to meet the Huerfano. Fishing in the National Forest is prohibited.

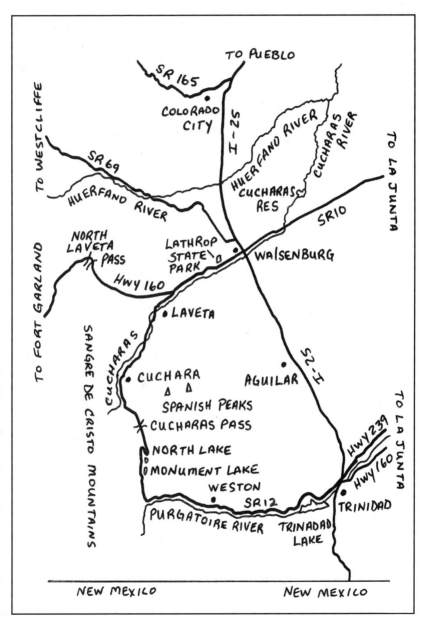

WALSENBURG

Photo Courtesy of Kip Carey

Lunch Break for Zac

LATHROP STATE PARK

Martin Lake (6,500 ft; 180 ac) and **Horseshoe Reservoir** (100 ac) are dominant features of **Lathrop State Park**, 1.5 miles west of Walsenburg along Hwy 160. The lakes, which are 12 to 15 feet deep, have bass, crappie, channel catfish and rainbow. Horseshoe also has sauger and tiger muskie. Martin also has wiper, walleye and gizzard shad. Boats are permitted on both lakes. There are camping facilities with showers, tables, laundry and a dump station for RVs. Ice fishing is marginal. All largemouth and spotted bass possessed must be 15 inches in length or longer.

Cucharas Reservoir, east of Walsenburg and I-25, is private and not open to public fishing.

SOUTH OF U.S. 160

Eight miles west of Lathrop State Park on U.S. 160, Hwy 12 turns south toward the Spanish Peaks (12,683 ft east; 13,626 ft west) and the towns of LaVeta and Cuchara before it swings east to Trinidad and I- 25. At the east edge of LaVeta on the Bear Creek Road is Wahatoya State Wildlife Area featuring **Lake Wahatoya** (7,000 ft; 28 ac) and **Lake Daigre** (pronounced dagger) (15 ac). Wahatoya holds Snake River cutthroat and some brown, while Daigre has rainbow and cutthroat. Artificial flies and lures only are permitted, and ice fishing is prohibited on both lakes.

South of LaVeta, Hwy 12 follows the **Cucharas River**, which is fishable but almost totally on private land. At the junction with **Cucharas Creek** and the **South Fork Cucharas River**, south of the town of Cuchara, USFS road 413 leaves Hwy 12 and goes west along the creek. The creek is stocked with brook, rainbow and cutthroat. The road continues to the Blue Lake and Bear Lake campgrounds and to **Blue Lake** (10,380 ft; 5 ac) and **Bear Lake** (10,440 ft; 8 ac). Both have rainbow and brook. A foot trail leads south from Blue Lake Campground 1.5 miles to **Wolf Lake** (10,080 ft; 2 ac). It has been stocked with rainbow and cutthroat trout in recent years.

STATE WILDLIFE AREA

Seven miles south of Cuchara Pass is **North Lake** (8,523 ft; 98 ac), and a mile farther south, **Monument Lake** (8,490 ft; 100 ac) both owned by the city of Trinidad. North Lake, managed by the DOW, has rainbow, cutthroat, brook trout and kokanee salmon. It can be fished from hand-propelled or electric-motor-powered boats. There is no camping. Fishing is by artificial flies and lures only. A concessionaire who charges an entry fee manages Monument Lake, which has rainbow, brown and kokanee salmon. Just south of North Lake, the **North Fork of the Purgatorie River** may be reached by taking USFS road 411 west from Hwy 12. The first 2.5 miles are through private land to the forest boundary. The river has rainbow, brook and cutthroat. Purgatorie, or Potato Patch, Campground is 4 miles upstream.

From their juncture, the **South Fork Purgatorie River** and the **Purgatorie River** itself flows mostly through private lands downstream. The picturesque and historic Stonewall and Picketwire valleys flank the river

TRINIDAD RESERVOIR

One of the better bass fishing lakes in the region is **Trinidad Lake** (6,230 ft; 800 ac when full), is just southwest of the city of Trinidad. Managed by the Colorado Division of Parks. An entry fee is charged for both warm- and cold-water fishing. Brown trout in the 11-inch-and-up range are frequently caught, and rainbows are usually plentiful. In addition, walleye, bass, wiper, crappie, gizzard shad and channel catfish are to be found. This somewhat unheralded lake is widely known in bass-angling circles, and bass-fishing tournaments have been held here. Largemouth bass weighing more than 7 pounds have been caught—and released to be caught again. All bass possessed must be 15 inches in length or longer.

There is a boat ramp on the north end of the lake. Tucked in the pinon-juniper stands of this sunny area are more than 60 campsites for RVs, tents and trailers. There are accommodations for handicapped persons, hot showers, a coin-operated laundry, electrical hookups and other facilities.

The angler will find a variety of fishing—underwater sandstone ledges, flooded grassy flats, fallen timber, islands and flooded groves of trees. To the east of Trinidad, the flood-prone Purgatorie River flows across private land, and fishing virtually disappears as the stream cuts its way into the soft soils in route to the Arkansas River

To the southeast of Trinidad is **Lake Dorothey** (7,600 ft; 4 ac), which is accessible by car by taking I-25 over Raton Pass into New Mexico. From Raton, New Mexico, follow New Mexico highways 72 and then 526, 12 miles east and north through Sugarite Canyon 5 miles. Restricted to artificial flies and lures only. The lake and all the drainages in the area have rainbow and cutthroat. Other reservoirs in the area do not have sufficient year-round water supplies to be attractive fisheries.

RIO GRANDE RIVER

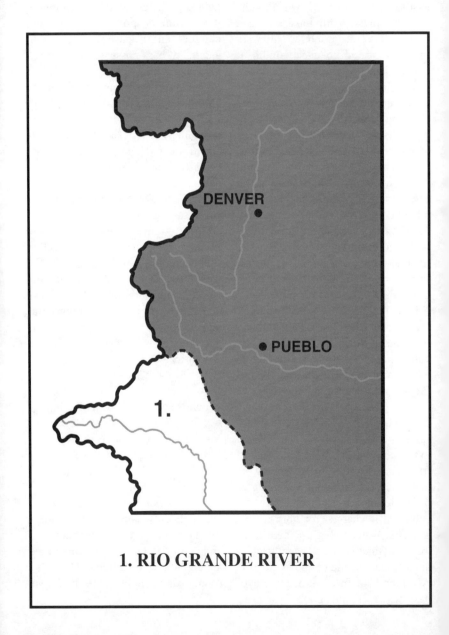

1. RIO GRANDE RIVER

RIO GRANDE RIVER

The Rio Grande runs out of a wilderness of 14,000-foot peaks, volcanic palisades, aspen and coniferous forests, cottonwood bottomlands, rustic cabins and old mine buildings. Some of the best fishing in Colorado and perhaps the entire Rockies can be found in these shimmering waters. The rainbow, brook, brown and native cutthroats abound in a beautiful land where places like Rio Grande, Conejos, Canyon Diablo, La Manga and Del Norte mix with the old west names of Shotgun Knob, Horse Thief Pasture, Wagon Wheel Gap and Deadman Creek. From Gold Medal Water, high lakes and countless tributaries, The Rio Grande basin offers a wealth of fishing opportunities.

With its headwaters in the Rio Grande National Forest west of Rio Grande Reservoir, the 1,900-mile-long Rio Grande River, America's second longest river, flows south of Creede and out of the San Juan Mountains on a southeasterly path that stretches for 100 miles in Colorado before entering New Mexico.

The river is one of great contrasts. In its upper reaches, sparkling water alternates with extensive, deep pools and tumbling riffles broken by massive boulders. Below Monte Vista, the river loses its sparkle and the Rio Grande becomes home to northern pike, including some very large ones.

From the Rio Grande headwaters east to the town of South Fork, the Rio Grande River flows through a mix of private land, national forest and the Coller State Wildlife Area. Most of its tributaries are on national forest land. The tributaries flow from the north out of the La Garita Mountains and La Garita Wilderness Area, and from the south out of the San Juan Mountains and Weminuche Wilderness.

Highway 149 from South Fork to Creede and on to Lake City is the "Silver Thread Scenic Byway." U.S. 160 roughly parallels the Rio Grande downstream from South Fork to Del Norte. At Del Norte, the Rio Grande rushes into the dry San Luis Valley, angles southeast through Monte Vista and, at Alamosa, swerves south. The Conejos River, a major tributary, is heavily stocked with rainbows and provides very good fishing in the Rio Grande National Forest and the South San Juan Wilderness before joining the Rio Grande in the San Luis Valley a few miles north of the New Mexico line.

Situated in the south-central portion of the state, the San Luis Valley is the largest and southernmost of the four high-elevation valleys that bisects Colorado. Bounded by the Rio Grande National Forest on the west, the San Luis Valley offers fishable waters other than the Rio Grande and its major tributaries, although none are as renowned.

Small mountain stream

The Rio Grande River from the upper boundary of the Rio Grande Campground 7 miles southwest of Creede downstream to the upper boundary of the Marshall Park Campground, and from the confluence with Willow Creek to the confluence with Goose Creek restrict fishing to artificial flies or artificial lures only. The bag, possession and size limit for brown trout is two fish, 12 inches in length or shorter. All rainbow trout caught must be returned to the water immediately.

From the Coller bridge downstream to the west fence of Masonic Park, and from Highway 149 bridge at South Fork downstream to the Rio Grande Canal diversion structure (Gold Medal water), fishing is also by artificial flies or artificial lures only. The bag, possession and size limit for brown trout is two fish, 16 inches in length or longer. All rainbow trout caught must be returned to the water immediately. From the west fence of Masonic Park to Farmers' Union Canal near Del Norte is Wild Trout Water. The stretch of the Rio Grande from just above the town of South Fork, downstream 2.5 miles to Del Norte has been designated Gold Medal trout waters.

Downstream from South Fork, the Rio Grande flows mostly through private land, but several sections have been leased for public fishing. A total of 7.68 miles of the river half way between South Fork and Del Norte are open to public fishing at **Del Norte State Wildlife Area**.

UPPER RIO GRANDE RIVER

US Hwy 149 from South Fork provides convenient access to the upper river and its headwater lakes and tributaries.

At the headwaters of the Rio Grande, about 27 miles west of Creede, **Rio Grande Reservoir (Farmer's Union Reservoir)** (9,541 ft; 1086 ac with minimum pool of 300 ac) is a 7-mile-long body of water directly affected by the irrigation needs of the San Luis Valley. Its southern shore is the Weminuche Wilderness Area's northern border. The stretch of river below the reservoir to Box Canyon has experienced significant improvements designed to improve fish habitat and fishing. The reservoir has brown, cutthroat and rainbow. Boating is good on the reservoir when there is plenty of water, but difficult when water level is low, because of mud flats between shore and water.

To reach Rio Grande Reservoir, travel 20 miles southwest of Creede on Hwy 149. Turn onto Forest Road 520 and proceed to the reservoir. Follow the western fork to Bristol View Ranger Station. From the ranger station, the road goes southwest past three campgrounds. At the eastern end of the reservoir is Thirtymile Campground. There are two other campgrounds on the reservoir as well—Reservoir and Lost Trail. Just past Reservoir Campground in Horse Thief Pasture is a primitive gravel boat ramp. It is a very steep and rough ramp, not suitable for launching boats with cars.

Several tributaries feed Rio Grande Reservoir, including the Rio Grande above the reservoir to the west. A rough 4WD road can reach the river, which

Colorado Aspens

Photo Courtesy of Kevin Rummell

averages 15 feet wide. It is open and offers fine fishing for cutthroat and rainbow to 10 inches. About 7 miles above the reservoir, to the west, the Rio Grande forks. The forks are Bear, Pole and Quartzite Creeks.

Quartzite Creek averages 6 to 8 feet wide and is rated good for cutthroat to 10 inches. The stream is about 5 miles long and is swift and open. A 4WD road that follows the Rio Grande beyond the reservoir branches north and follows Quartzite Creek for a short section, then runs over Stony Pass, just north of Quartzite Creek.

Bear Creek enters the Rio Grande River from the south about 8 miles above the reservoir. Its length can be paralleled in a 4WD vehicle. It averages four feet wide and is rated fair in the lower portions for small cutthroat. The upper stretch of the stream is fishless due to the acidity of the water from old mine drainage.

Pole Creek enters Bear Creek from the north near Bear Creek's confluence with the Rio Grande. With its tributaries, Pole Creek offers 20 miles of fishing in headwater streams 8 to 20 feet wide. An easy trail follows Pole Creek from the fork in the road at Bear and Quartzite creeks to Pole headwaters. Pole is open water with good fishing for cutthroat to 12 inches.

Where the Rio Grande feeds into the reservoir from the west, **Lost Trail Creek** also enters the reservoir from the north. A trail less than 0.5 mile west of Lost Trail Campground on the reservoir follows Lost Trail Creek and its tributaries. Access is by trail bike, horse or foot. The western water network in

the area offers more than 25 miles of streams averaging 8 feet wide. Regulations are fishing by artificial flies or artificial lures only. All cutthroat trout caught must be returned to the water immediately. Both **Lost Trail Creek** and **West Lost Trail Creek** are small with beaver dams, and are typical high country streams with brook and cutthroat. The upper reaches are accessible by 4WD from Carson ghost townsite. Inquire at Creede for directions.

UTE CREEK

Ute Creek enters Rio Grande Reservoir from the south near the west end of the reservoir. The Ute Creek trailhead is near the Lost Trail Campground at the west end of the reservoir. Ute Creek has three main forks, all beautiful wilderness streams. Their headwater lakes are probably the most popular lakes in the Weminuche Wilderness.

Ute Creek forks upstream about 6 miles south of the reservoir. **West Ute Creek** offers 5 miles of brushy fishing for small cutthroat, and is rated good. Where the creek forks, the trail also forks, with the western trail following West Ute Creek. At the headwaters of West Ute Creek and southwest of Rio Grande Reservoir, **West Ute Lake** (11,801 ft; 16 ac) is reached by a 7 mile marked trail from the West Ute Creek Trail. It is heavily fished but rated good for 10- to 16-inch cutthroat, and rainbow to 12 inches.

Upper West Ute Lake (12,000 ft; 4 ac) has bigger cutthroat averaging 14 to 18 inches. It lies less than 1.5 miles northwest of West Ute Lake.

At its headwaters, **Ute Lake** (11,847 ft; 32 ac) is the biggest and deepest of the lakes. It is 125 feet deep. The lake is 10 miles southwest of Rio Grande Reservoir by trail. It is stocked with cutthroat, and has the biggest fish of all the Ute headwater lakes. Pack in dinner, because fishing can be slow. But if the fish are biting, prepare to catch some large ones.

Just to the west of Ute Lake by trail are the **Twin Ute Lakes** (11,792 ft; 16 and 4.8 ac). The smaller lake has rainbow and the larger lake has brook 10 to 14 inches. An occasional cutthroat can be caught in either lake.

Northwest of Twin Lakes, less than 2 miles by trail, is **Middle Ute Lake** (11,949 ft; 11.5 ac). It is surrounded by willows and sometimes called **Willow Lake**. Fishing in this lake is cyclical; one year the catches will be small, but that indicates the following season will produce large catches. The lake occasionally winterkills. It is rated good for cutthroat 10 to 14 inches.

Weminuche Creek enters the Farmers' Union Reservoir from the south just four miles east of Ute Creek, and is regarded as a basic brook-trout stream. It, too, drains the high peaks of the Weminuche Wilderness and offers fishing from a trail paralleling the stream for about 5 miles. The trail leads over Weminuche Pass to the headwaters of the Los Pinos River, which flows south to the New Mexico border and the Navajo Reservoir.

To the east of Weminuche Creek about 2.5 miles, **Squaw Creek** enters the Rio Grande River from the south, just east of the Rio Grande Reservoir.

Squaw Creek stretches about 10 miles south to the Continental Divide in the San Juan Mountains in the Weminuche Wilderness. A trail follows the stream from Thirtymile Campground, near the mouth of the reservoir, to its headwaters. The upper stretches of the stream have brook and cutthroat. The lower stretches, near the reservoir, have brook and brown to 16 inches. At the headwaters of Squaw Creek, north of the Continental Divide, **Squaw Lake** (11,650 ft; 10 ac) has a naturally reproducing brook population.

Little Squaw Creek, about 1.5 miles east of Squaw Creek and 2 miles east of Rio Grande Reservoir, also enters the Rio Grande River from the south. It enters at River Hill Campground on the road leading to the reservoir. It is a cutthroat stream good for trout 10 to 14 inches. There is no trail to the lower portion of the stream, but the upper portion can be reached by the trail from Thirtymile Campground.

NORTHERN TRIBUTARIES

Crooked Creek flows from the northwest and enters the Rio Grande near Bristol View Guard Station at the junction of Forest Road 520 and 521. A road from Bristol View Ranger Station follows the creek about three miles to the foot of Crooked Canyon; 4WD vehicles are recommended. **House Creek** immediately to the south and **Regan Lake** (10,100 ft; 90 ac) have stocked brook and rainbow, some to 14 and 16 inches. Regan is reached by 4WD road and is a picturesque, natural lake. Surprisingly, these waters are heavily fished.

Just south of Crooked Creek and southeast of Regan Lake, **Road Canyon Reservoir** (9,725 ft; 100 ac) is located on the road leading to Rio Grande Reservoir. Road Canyon Reservoir has been a research site for years, including research with aerator pumps. The reservoir offers good fishing for brook up to 2 pounds, and rainbow up to 5 pounds. At the south end of Road Canyon Reservoir is Road Canyon Campground. From Creede, travel 20 miles west on Hwy 149 and then 7 miles west and south on USFS road 520 to reach the campground.

CLEAR CREEK AREA

Clear Creek enters the Rio Grande from the north just 3.5 miles southeast of Spring Creek Reservoir picnic ground on Hwy 149.

About 3.25 miles upstream from its confluence with the Rio Grande River, Clear Creek forks to become North Clear Creek and South Clear Creek. At the fork is Silver Thread Campground on Hwy 149, north of Spring Creek Reservoir Picnic Area.

North Clear Creek is crossed by Hwy 149. It flows from the northwest and the northern San Juan Mountains. North Clear is the larger of the two forks. North and South Clear Creek are stocked with 10-inch rainbows. At its headwaters is **Heart Lake** (11,600 ft; 30 ac). Heart is a shallow lake, but it usually does not winterkill and is stocked with rainbows. Reach Heart Lake by turning west off Hwy 149 at Silver Thread Campground. The road leads past Brown Lakes, then forks. Follow the northern road (FR 516) to Pearl and Castle Rock lakes. From there, travel is by 4WD for about 5 miles west. Heart has a naturally produced brook population, with some up to 15 inches; most average 10 to 12 inches.

Pearl and **Castle Rock Lakes**, just to the east of Heart Lake, are private lakes.

Downstream about 2.5 miles from Castle Rock Lake, **Continental Reservoir** (10,300 ft; 50 ac) is stocked with Snake River cutthroat, rainbow and brook. Continental Reservoir can be reached by vehicle by turning west off Hwy 149 on Forest Road 513 near the North Clear Creek Falls Campground. The road forks north to Rito Hondo Reservoir and has been improved and graveled.

Buck, **Deadman**, **Kitty** and **Ruby** creeks flow into North Clear Creek in the Continental Reservoir area. All of these streams are about 5 feet wide, have beaver ponds, and offer good fishing for 8-inch rainbow and cutthroat.

Rito Hondo Reservoir (10,240 ft; 40 ac) sits in a gently rolling, treeless area, just to the east of Continental Reservoir about 2 miles. It can be reached by the USFS road 513. Rito Hondo has been stocked with rainbow, but the bulk of the population is brook. An occasional lunker may be lured. No motor-propelled boats or rafts are permitted, but there is a boat ramp on its west shore.

Bennett Creek enters North Clear Creek from the north at North Clear Creek Falls Overlook Campground. **Big Spring Creek** flows from the north at Spring Creek Pass and is about 5

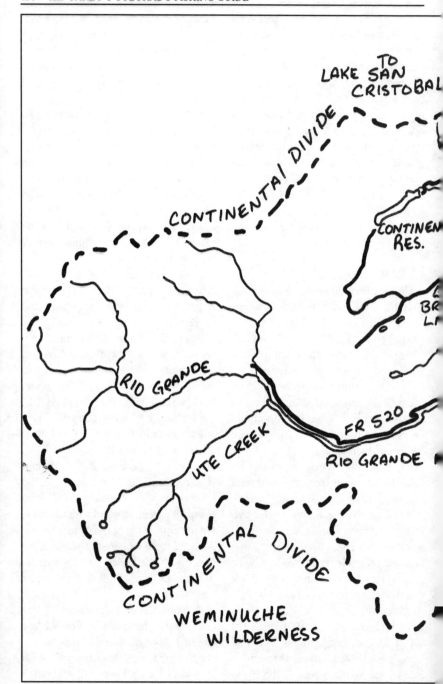

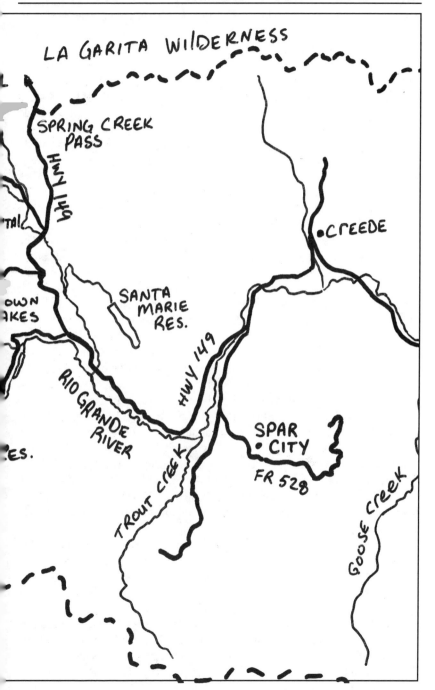

miles long and 5 feet wide with some beaver ponds. It is rated fair for small brook, cutthroat and rainbow. Fishing is by artificial flies and lures, all cutthroat must be returned to the water immediately. One of its main tributaries from the east is **Mesa Creek**. Mesa has no access and is a rugged stream to follow. It has some beaver ponds and is rated fair for small brook, cutthroat and rainbow.

North Clear Creek below the North Clear Falls Campground to its confluence with Clear Creek has cutthroat, brook and some rainbow. Portions of the stream flow through posted private property, and fishing is by permission only.

South Clear Creek feeds into Clear Creek from the west and is crossed by Hwy 149 at Silver Thread Campground. The upper reaches of South Clear Creek are private, including some of its headwater lakes lying less than 5 miles north of Rio Grande Reservoir. These lakes include **Lost Lakes** and **Hermit Lake**. Hermit Lake is a private fishing club for which the first U.S. Homestead Permit was issued for the purpose of commercial fishing.

Near Hwy 149 on South Clear Creek, **Brown Lakes** (9,840 ft; 180 total ac) have rainbow and brook from 8 to 15 inches. They may be reached by traveling 25 miles west of Creede on Hwy 149 and 2 miles northwest on USFS 515. Access to these lakes is gained by turning west at Silver Thread Campground. No camping is permitted at either lake. Both lakes are very shallow, the western lake being about nine feet deep and the eastern lake about 7 feet. These lakes sometimes winterkill. Brown Lakes are stocked with cutthroat, rainbow, brown and brook. Fishing is good for rainbow 12 to 14 inches.

SOUTHERN TRIBUTARIES

Texas Creek enters the Rio Grande from the south at about the same point that Clear Creek enters from the north, 18 miles southwest of Creede. Texas Creek stretches more than 10 miles south in the Weminuche Wilderness. Access to its headwaters is by hiking the Fern Creek Trail off Hwy 149 about 16 miles southwest of Creede. The stream is rated good for small brook and cutthroat in the upper meadows, and brown and rainbow in the lower stretches of the stream.

Fern Creek is a very small, fishless tributary of the Rio Grande about 2 miles east of Texas Creek. The Fern Creek Trail leads about 3 miles to the Fern Creek headwater lakes. The first lake by trail is **Little Ruby Lake** (11,250 ft; 3 ac). Little Ruby Lake is about 19 feet deep and occasionally winterkills. It is stocked with rainbow and brook, and is rated good. South of Little Ruby Lake, **Ruby Lake** (11,290 ft; 30 ac) is 55 feet deep. It is rated good for rainbow and brook from 10 to 14 inches.

Trout Creek is the next major tributary downstream to the east. It enters the Rio Grande from the south. It stretches more than 13 miles along the Weminuche Wilderness northeast boundary. Its **West** and **East Forks** are in the wilderness. Access to Trout Creek to where it enters the wilderness is over a rough Forest Road 523; from the wilderness boundary to its headwaters, travel is by foot or hoof only. Road access is about 6 miles southwest of Creede south to Spar City. Follow the road until it forks; stay with the western fork for access to Trout Creek. The creek averages 20 feet wide and is rated fair for cutthroat near the headwaters, and fair for 8- to 10-inch brown and rainbow in the lower reaches. At the headwaters of West Trout Creek, **Trout Lake** (11,685 ft; 24 ac) is in the Weminuche Wilderness. In the early 1900's, farmers and their draft horses dammed the east end of the lake for irrigation. The lake is still used for irrigation, but a conservation pool agreement maintains the lake at about an 18-foot depth. It has cutthroat 10 to 18 inches.

Middle Creek enters the Rio Grande from the south less than 0.25 mile east of Trout Creek. It reaches south about 10 miles, and access is by a rough road (FR 523) that reaches its headwaters. Take the Spar City road where it leaves Hwy 149 about 6 miles southwest of Creede. When the road forks, follow the west fork.

About 5 miles upstream from Middle Creek's confluence with the Rio Grande, **Love Lake** (10,000 ft; 5 ac) lies on Middle Creek. It is a 9-foot-deep lake accessible by car and rated good for small brook and rainbow with an occasional lunker brown taken. There are campsites on the lake. No motor-propelled boats or rafts are permitted.

Lime Creek enters the Rio Grande from the south about nine miles southwest of Creede. Take the Spar City road south from Hwy 149 west of Creede.

Lime Creek runs through Spar City. The stream contains small brook, but is rated poor for fishing.

South of Lime Creek, **Red Mountain Creek**, a major tributary of the Rio Grande, flows from the south, meeting the river just below Middle Creek. Follow the Spar City road; turn south just before reaching Spar City to the Ivy Creek Campground. A rough road follows Red Mountain Creek to its headwaters. Portions of the river are on private property. This stream is rated poor because a flood in the early 1970's damaged the canyon. Even though it has been restocked, it has never regained its reputation as a good fishing stream. **Ivy Creek** is a tributary of Red Mountain Creek entering from the east and flowing from the south. Its upper stretches are in the wilderness. It is about 6 feet wide, and rated fair to good for 8- to 10-inch cutthroat.

CREEDE AREA

Seepage Creek, **Ghost Lake** and **Seepage Lakes** are found up USFS Road 509 near Rio Grande Campground and about 8 miles southwest of Creede and exist as long as the water level in **Santa Marie Reservoir** (9,470 ft; 350 ac) is kept filled above the 8000-foot level. When the reservoir drops below this level, Seepage Creek and the lakes dry up. The lakes have a geological foundation that will not hold water if they are not receiving as much water as is flowing out. **Santa Marie Reservoir** is a private trout club. Seepage Lakes, Upper (9,100 ft; 30 ac when full), Lower (9,080 ft; 20 ac when full) and Ghost Lake (9,220 ft; 8 ac when

Photo Courtesy of Dana Agren

Tumbling mountain stream

full) have rainbow 8 to 16 inches. Inquire locally before planning to fish Seepage and Ghost lakes.

Miners Creek flows into the Rio Grande from the north, 3 miles west of Creede. It feeds from the northern San Juan Mountains. Access is by trail bike, foot or horse. The first 3 miles are accessible by a rough dirt road, the rest by trail. Turn north off Hwy 149 just west of Creede on Forest Road 507. The stream averages 6 feet wide, is open and has medium-swift waters rated fair for cutthroat in the upper headwater stretches, and fair to good for brook, rainbow and brown in the lower stretches.

Rat Creek is one of the main tributaries of Miners Creek entering from the northeast. It is a steep tumbling stream averaging four feet wide, with beaver ponds. Access is by driving northwest out of Creede on 4WD road (FR 505). The upper reaches of Rat Creek are good for brook. The lower stretches are on private land.

Deep Creek, about 8 miles long, enters the Rio Grande from the south, 2 miles due south of Creede. Access to the mouth of Deep Creek is by driving to the southeast corner of Creede airport. A trail from a parking area on the south side of the Rio Grande follows the stream from near the airport to the headwaters. The headwaters may also be reached by driving to Spar City and from there to the end of the Forest Road 528. Deep Creek averages 3 feet wide; it is open and swift, offering good fishing for small brook.

Entering the Rio Grande north of Creede is **Willow Creek**. It flows through Creede and meets the Rio Grande about 2 miles south. About a mile north of Creede, Willow Creek forks. **West Willow Creek** begins at San Luis Pass in Gunnison National Forest. Access is by car on a rough road north out of Creede. **East Willow Creek** also feeds from the Continental Divide, and access is easy by car; access to the upper half is by 4WD only. Fishing is good in the forks for brook. Willow Creek just south of the forks and through Creede has no fish. In the 1890's, zinc dumps precluded any fish life. The habitat is poor and the channel often changes direction, making it an undesirable stretch of river to rehabilitate.

BELLOWS CREEK

Bellows Creek lies east of Creede about 5.5 miles, and enters the Rio Grande from the north. For 5 miles upstream from the confluence with the Rio Grande, it is closed, private land. Bellows forks at this point, and **West Bellows Creek** offer 8 miles of excellent fishing in a 10-foot-wide stream for brook and brown to 12 inches. The water is open but not swift. Some beaver ponds. West Bellows headwaters are in the Wheeler Geologic Area, a spectacular, colorful rock formation set aside to perpetuate the beauty and uniqueness of this area. Access to the headwaters of West Bellows and Wheeler Geologic Area is from Wagon Wheel Gap on Hwy 149 on Forest Road 600. This 4WD road is sometimes closed in the spring when the road becomes boggy.

East Bellows Creek flows just east

of West Bellows. It is a swift, 5-foot-wide stream. It is a unique stream because it doesn't freeze over. It is fed by warm (50-degree) spring waters. Access to the upper reaches of East Bellows is by 4WD, north from Wagon Wheel Gap.

GOOSE CREEK

Goose Creek enters the Rio Grande from the south at Rio Grande Palisades near Wagon Wheel Gap on Hwy 149. A rough road follows the stream south to its headwaters and lakes in the Weminuche Wilderness. Goose Creek is about 12 miles long and about 6 feet wide, supporting cutthroat and brook to 12 inches. The water is open with a few beaver dams. Campsites are plentiful and scenic, but the lower stretches, from **Humphreys Lake** (private) at the wilderness boundary downstream, are private holdings and require permission to fish.

Fisher Creek is a main tributary of Goose Creek about 2 miles above Humphreys. It heads near South River Peak on the Continental Divide. Both **Lake Humphreys** and **Hay Press Lake** are closed, private lakes. A 9-mile trail from Lake Humphreys into the wilderness leads up Fisher Creek to **Goose Lake** (11,600 ft; 25 ac). The lake is a fluctuating reservoir with a maximum depth of 20 feet. It is usually kept full. The lake is rated good for cutthroat 16 to 18 inches. Campsites available. The easiest access to Goose Lake is from the Ivy Creek campground by Ivy Creek Trail (USFS 805).

SOUTH FORK

The **South Fork of the Rio Grande** enters the Rio Grande from the southwest at the town of South Fork and the junction of Hwy. 149 and U.S. Hwy 160, about 20 miles east of Creede. Twenty miles of fishing are available. The lower 10 miles parallel U.S. 160. The portion of the river upstream, but not adjacent to the highway is accessible by a trail from Big Meadows Campground on Big Meadows Reservoir. Averaging 15 feet wide, South Fork is easily fished, but rated only fair for 10-inch brown, rainbow and some brook in the higher reaches. Sections of South Fork require permission to fish. There are several campgrounds along the highway and stream, south from South Fork to Wolf Creek Pass on the Continental Divide.

Millions Reservoir (8,700 ft; 4 ac) is a small pond located less than a mile east of South Fork on the Beaver Creek Road—USFS 360. It is stocked with put-and-take rainbow.

A major tributary of South Fork is **Beaver Creek**, which is stocked with rainbows. It enters from the east, about 1-mile south of South Fork. Access is by taking Forest Road 360 a mile south of the town of South Fork. **Beaver Creek Reservoir** (8,763 ft; 110 ac) is about 2 miles from the confluence of Beaver Creek and adjacent to Cross Creek Campground. From the South Fork, go 1 mile on U.S. 160, then 5 miles on USFS road 360. It is a long, narrow reservoir with steep sides that is subject to considerable fluctuation. It is stocked with brook, rainbow, brown and some kokanee. A steep boat

Nice Rainbow

Photo Courtesy of the Morrison Angler

ramp is located at its southern end. Snagging for kokanee is permitted from October 1 through December 31. The road follows Beaver Creek southeast to its headwaters.

About 10 miles upstream at Beaver Creek headwaters is **Poage Lake** (11,100 ft; 12 ac). This natural lake produces huge cutthroat, though they are difficult to catch; most are between 9 and 12 inches. It's a short walk to gain access.

Race Creek is a tributary of Beaver Creek that enters Beaver from the east about 5 miles downstream from Poage Lake. It is rated fair to good for small brook and cutthroat. The upper reaches are accessible by a rough road from Poage Lake or by a 4WD road from Cross Creek near Beaver Creek Reservoir. At the headwaters of Race Creek are **Crystal Lakes** (11,300 ft; 10 ac). Upper Crystal has brook, although it sometimes winterkills, and Lower Crystal Lake is good fishing for brook to 12 inches.

Cross Creek is another tributary of Beaver Creek, which enters from the east about a mile upstream of Beaver

Creek Reservoir. Cross Creek is a narrow 3-foot-wide stream that is brushy and offers poor fishing.

PARK CREEK

Entering the South Fork from the southeast about 7 miles south of the town of South Fork at Park Creek Campground, **Park Creek** is paralleled by Forest Road 380 to its headwaters near Summit Pass. The creek averages 6 to 12 feet wide. The rough road parallels the stream to its headwaters, and then loops back to Del Norte, a beautiful all-day drive. Park Creek is stocked with catchable rainbow, and offers good fishing for browns, cutthroat and brook. It receives heavy fishing pressure.

Lake Fork enters the South Fork from the west, about 10 miles south of the town of South Fork, and is rated good for small brook. An excellent choice for beginning fly fishers. **Hunters Lake** (11,400 ft; 8 ac) sits 7 miles to the north of Big Meadows Reservoir. It is rated good for brook, but sometimes winterkills. Take the road north from Big Meadows to reach Hunters Lake.

A mile downstream from Big Meadows Reservoir, **Hope Creek** enters the South Fork from the west. A road (FR 430) going north from Big Meadows leads to Hope Creek; the headwaters are reached by horseback or on foot. Just north of Hope Creek, **Shaw Reservoir** (9,850 ft; 20 ac) can be reached by road. Shaw suffers from periodic winterkill, but it has ample feed and offers good fishing for cutthroat and rainbow.

About 8 miles north of Wolf Creek Pass to USFS road 410 near the Twin Bridges off U.S. 160 is **Big Meadows Reservoir** (9,200 ft; 114 ac), which has brook to 8 inches and rainbow to 12 inches.

Archuleta Creek flows into Big Meadows Reservoir from the southwest. The 4-foot stream has small cutthroat. The regulations for Archuleta Creek on the Coleman Ranch is fishing by artificial flies or artificial lures only and all fish caught must be returned to the water immediately. At its headwaters, requiring a 5-mile hike, **Archuleta Lake** (11,700 ft; 13 ac) in the Weminuche Wilderness Area is rated good for 10- to 16-inch cutthroat and brook.

About 12 miles south of the town of South Fork, the road leaves the South Fork and follows **Pass Creek**. Pass Creek enters the South Fork from the southeast. Forest Road 390 proceeds east and goes past Tucker Ponds Campground to the headwaters of Pass Creek. The partially brushy stream averages 6 to 8 feet wide. Fishing is fair for rainbow, brook and cutthroat. Fishing is by artificial flies and lures only, all cutthroat must be returned to the water immediately.

Several small lakes are along the stream, including **Pass Creek Lake** (9,500 ft; 1.5 ac), which lies on U.S. 160 about 4.5 miles north of Wolf Creek Pass. The lake sometimes winterkills, but is rated fair for 6- to 10-inch rainbow. The 2 **Tucker Ponds** (9,700 ft; 1.5 and 2.5 ac) lie off Forest Road 390. Access to the ponds and the Tucker Ponds Campground is by taking the access road about 4.5 miles north of Wolf Creek Pass. These ponds are stocked with rainbow and some brook.

Alberta Park Reservoir (10,200 ft; 30 ac) can be reached by turning off U.S. 160 onto FDR 391 about 1.5 miles north of Wolf Creek. This reservoir is near the headwaters of Pass Creek and is rated fair for 6- to 12-inch cutthroat, rainbow and brook. Artificial flies and lures only, catch and release on all cutthroat.

Willow Creek flows into the Rio Grande from the south about a mile east of the town of South Fork. Its upper reaches are accessible by a rough road south from Gerrard on U.S. 160. Willow is a brushy stream with little or no fishing.

North of the town of South Fork, **Alder Creek** enters the Rio Grande. Its lower 3 miles are on private land and posted. Forest Road 610 follows **West Alder Creek**, and then forks east to provide access to the upper reaches of all branches of Alder Creek. Alder and all its forks are rated fair for small rainbow, brook and brown.

DEL NORTE AREA

The **Rio Grande** flows southeast into the San Luis Valley as it leaves Del Norte. As water is drained for irrigation purposes, the river flow is greatly reduced. East of Monte Vista, **Sherman Lake** (7,627 ft; 67 ac) is located in the town of Homelake on Soldiers Home Road. It is stocked with pike, channel catfish and rainbow. The best fishing on Sherman Lake occurs in the spring when pike up to 4 pounds are caught.

Embargo Creek enters the Rio Grande from the north between the towns of Del Norte and South Fork. A rough road from U.S. 160 leads to the headwaters of this stream and Cathedral Campground. The lower portion of Embargo cuts through private land, and 5 miles of the headwater stream are open by trail only. From U.S. 160, turn north to cross the Granger Bridge on Road 18. Drive 10 miles to Cathedral Campground on Forest Road 650/640. Road continues about 1 mile to the Embargo Creek trailhead. Embargo Creek is rated fair for cutthroat in the higher reaches, and browns in the lower reaches.

Pinos Creek enters the Rio Grande from the south, 3 miles west of Del Norte. A paved road (14) southwest of Del Norte parallels the creek to its highest reaches. Pinos is rated fair for brook and brown to 10 inches. Approximately 10 miles upstream from the Pinos/Rio Grande confluence, **Burro Creek** enters Pinos from the east. It is rated fair for small brook. Also accessed by the road paralleling Pinos is **Fuchs Reservoir** (9,700 ft; 20 ac). Often drained to low levels creating fish loss, Fuchs may otherwise be good for rainbow.

At Del Norte, San Francisco Creek comes in from the south offering fair fishing for cutthroat. At the headwaters, the three **San Francisco Lakes** (11,900 to 11,980 ft; 4 to 6 ac each) are rated fair for cutthroat. The creek and the lakes are restricted to artificial flies and lures only, all fish must be returned to the water immediately. Lakes are reached by CR 13 to Middle Fork trailhead. South on trial by a 6 mile hike.

SAN LUIS VALLEY

In the San Luis Valley north of Hwy 160, many streams flow from the Sangre de Cristo Mountains that forms the valley's northeastern boundary. **Cottonwood Creek**, **Lower Cottonwood Lake** (11,800 ft; 2 ac), **Upper Cottonwood Lake** (12,310 ft; 2 ac), Deadman **Creek**, **Lower Deadman Lake** (11,680 ft; 6 ac), **Upper Deadman Lake** (11,780 ft; 14 ac), **Sand Creek**, **Lower Sand Creek Lake** (11,450 ft; 20 ac), **Upper Sand Creek Lake** (11,475 ft; 24 ac) and **Little Sand Creek Lake** (12,240 ft; 13 ac) are all located southeast of Crestone. This area is part of the Baca Grant, limited permission to enter this area can be gained at the administration office in Cottonwood. Cutthroat and brook are the most common.

Also south of Crestone is **South Crestone Creek**; it, too, flows through parcels of private land. The upper stretches contain brook trout and can be reached by trail about 1 mile southeast of town. Located at the headwaters of South Crestone is **South Crestone Lake** (11,800 ft; 10 ac) and **Willow Creek Lake** (11,550 ft; 8 ac), which can be reached only via steep, rugged 5 mile trails. Winterkill may affect South Crestone Lake, which is normally rated fair to good for 10- to 12-inch rainbow and cutthroat. Willow Creek is rated good for 12-inch cutthroat.

Twelve miles east of Moffat, **North and South Crestone Creeks** flow from the mountains. Fair to good fishing for cutthroat, rainbow and brook to 10 inches for 5 miles along North Crestone. Five miles from North Crestone Campground via a steep, marked trail is **North Crestone Lake** (11,800 ft; 15 ac). From the town of Crestone, a road leads about 2 miles northeast of North Crestone Creek Campground, and a trail leads from that point upstream to the **Lake Fork of Crestone Creek**. Another trail heads north to **San Isabel Lake** (11,650 ft; 5 ac) and **Rito Alto Lake** (11,300 ft; 7 ac). Rito Alto Lake and San Isabel Lake provide fair to good fishing for cutthroat.

Several other streams flow from the Sangre de Cristos south of Valley View Hot Springs, but again access is limited due to private land. Most of these streams have a lake at their headwaters. **Cotton**, **Wild Cherry** (locally referred to as **Short Creek**), **Rito Alto** and **San Isabel Creeks** are a few of the better-known streams. These brushy streams are rated fair to good for rainbow and cutthroat; a few have brook. **Cotton Lake** (11,500 ft; 11 ac) and **Cherry Lake** (11,800 ft; 8 ac) are at the headwaters via very steep trails. Lunker rainbows are possible from Cotton Lake. Inquire locally about access and fishing.

Near the town of Mineral Hot Springs, about 5 miles south of Villa Grove, **Garner**, **Major** and **Black Canyon Creeks** have fair fishing for small brook. They may be accessed by driving west from Mineral Hot Springs to Valley View Hot Springs.

SAN LUIS CREEK

From Poncha Pass at the north end of the valley, **San Luis Creek** roughly parallels U.S. 285 southward. The entire length of the stream is within private property, and permission is seldom granted for its marginal fishing.

Clover, **Alder** and **Spring Creeks** are small streams with beaver ponds on the west side of the valley south of Poncha Pass near the town of Alder. 4-wheel-drives are needed to reach streams with small brookies.

Entering San Luis Creek from the west about 10 miles south of Alder on U.S. 285 is **Kerber Creek**. The town of Bonanza, reached from a road running to the west from Villa Grove, has several tributaries entering Kerber, including **Upper Kerber**, **Brewery**, **Slaughterhouse** and **Elkhorn Gulch Creeks**. All are rated good for small brook. Numerous roads provide access, consult good topo map for access. Below the town of Bonanza, Kerber Creek passes through private land, but it is virtually fishless.

SAGUACHE CREEK

One of the longest and best fisheries in the valley is **Saguache Creek**, which provides 50 miles of stream between its headwaters in the Rio Grande National Forest to the town of Saguache in the northwestern part of the valley. (A regional museum, housed in a decommissioned county jail in Saguache, makes note of much of the history of this mining region. Alferd Packer, the Colorado cannibal, was imprisoned in this jail in 1874.)

Saguache Creek is reached by driving west from the town of Saguache on Hwy 114 to North Pass, then an additional 5 miles beyond the summit of North Pass, look for sign to Stone Cellar Campground, or by another route, from Gunnison 8 miles east on U.S. 50, then south on Hwy 114. About 5 miles before the pass summit, a sign along the highway indicates Forest Road 804 leading to Stone Cellar Campground and Saguache Park via Forest Road 787. From the sign, the campground is 15 miles, at the confluence of Middle and North forks of Saguache Creek. The water from this creek and tributaries drains into the San Luis Aquifer near the Great Sand Dunes. Regulations for Saguache Creek from the confluence of California Gulch upstream to the headwaters of the Middle and South Fork tributaries are fishing by artificial flies or artificial lures only. **East Pass Creek** parallels Hwy 114 from the top of North Pass. Catch and release on all cutthroat, artificial flies and lures only.

The headwaters of the **Middle Fork Saguache Creek** are in La Garita Wilderness. Stocked rainbows and populations of cutthroat and brook are found in the stream. From the campground upstream to the wilderness boundary, artificial flies and lures only. Middle Fork has numerous beaver ponds.

Machin Lake (12,300 ft; 10 ac), pronounced "machine", is located at the headwaters of Middle Fork, about 15 miles from the campground, the last 8 by trail. Although occasionally suffering from winterkill, the lake is stocked with cutthroat and produces 5- to 6-pounders.

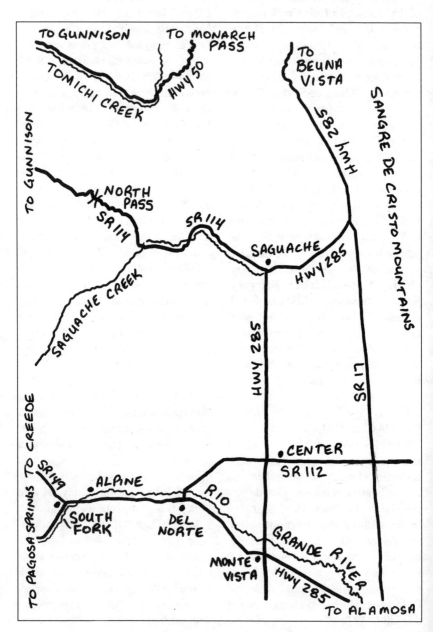

RIO GRANDE RIVER

Paralleling 8 miles of trail upstream from the campground is **North Fork Saguache Creek**, a 5-foot-wide stream with fair fishing for brook and cutthroat.

The **South Fork Saguache Creek** can also be reached from Stone Cellar Campground. A road more or less parallels the creek to the wilderness boundary, a distance of about 7 miles. Brook and cutthroat fishing is good. At the point where South Fork flows into the wilderness, **Wannamaker Creek** enters from the southeast. Both streams are small and brushy. Rated good for brook, Wannamaker also has a limited number of cutthroat.

Below the campground, a 4WD road parallels Saguache Creek until it flows through a deep, rugged canyon (sometimes called Box Canyon), accessible only by trail. A road leading southwest from Hwy 114 about 21 miles west of Saguache also provides access to the stream and canyon mouth. When the road forks 1.5 miles from the highway, take the right (west) fork to the creek. The road crosses the creek and continues for another mile, but leads away from the creek and canyon. Some of the tributaries from the southeast are **California Gulch**, **Johns** and **Bear** creeks, all with beaver ponds and good fishing for small brook.

Saguache Creek flows through private land for 21 miles as it turns east toward Saguache. If permission to fish is obtained, anglers will find some excellent fishing for brown.

Entering the Saguache from the north, 21 miles west of the town of Saguache, is **Sheep Creek**. A dirt road follows upstream about 2 miles until the road forks; the west fork leads another 6 miles to the upper portion of the stream, which has brook. **Spanish Creek**, a western tributary of Sheep, has no fish.

Trail 771 from the upper Saguache Forest Service Station in the Gunnison National Forest leads 12 miles up Sheep Creek and over the Continental Divide to **Baldy Lake** (11,250 ft; 5 ac), which periodically suffers from winterkill. It is stocked and rated good for 12 to 16-inch rainbow.

Ten miles east of Sheep Creek, **Middle Creek** enters the Saguache from the north. A maintained dirt road follows the creek 10 miles to the national forest, from where a trail leads another 5 miles to the headwaters. Portions of the creek accessible from the trail offer good fishing for cutthroat and brook. **East Middle Creek** and **Indian Creek**, two of the eastern tributaries of Middle Fork, provide similar fishing conditions. East Middle Creek from waterfall, about 2.5 miles upstream from the confluence with Middle Creek to headwaters is catch and release for all cutthroat, artificial flies and lures only.

Ford Creek, which enters the Saguache from the north 0.25 mile east of Middle Fork, flows through private land, but its upper tributary, **Turtle Creek** is on Forest Service land. Fishing is by artificial flies and lures only, all cutthroat must be returned to the water immediately.

Much of the water has been diverted by the time Saguache Creek enters the town of Saguache; and what's left quickly soaks into the valley floor.

LA GARITA CREEK

Flowing out of the La Garita Mountains, **La Garita Creek** is reached via U.S. 285 17 miles north of Monte Vista. Turn west at the sign to the town of La Garita. From La Garita, rough roads parallel the stream and its tributaries. This small, brushy creek has many ponds with fair fishing for cutthroat, brown and brook.

Middle, South, and North Carnero Creeks, are small meadow streams with beaver ponds. They are tributary streams of La Garita Creek flowing from the northwest. They are rated fair for cutthroat. Catch and release on all cutthroat, artificial flies and lures only. The lower 15 miles pass through private property. Tributaries of Carnero Creeks, including **South Fork**, **Cave Creek** and **Miners Creek**, are small, with beaver ponds that offer good fishing for brook.

A conglomerate of lakes known as **Russell Lakes** are northeast of La Garita and south of Saguache about 10 miles on U.S. 285. These are primarily waterfowl habitat without fish. East of Russell Lakes are the **Mishak Lakes**, which are often dry.

ALAMOSA RIVER

To reach the **Alamosa River** in the National Forest, take Hwy 15, 12 miles south of Monte Vista, then 8 miles west on USFS road 250. A 25- to 30-foot-wide river, it has rather poor fishing near its mouth. Pollution from mining has ruined this stretch. Above the lower 3 miles, the Alamosa River is rated

poor to fair for 8- to 10-inch rainbow and, in lesser numbers, cutthroat and brook. The **Alamosa Reservoir** (8,250 ft; 150 ac), also known as **Terrace Reservoir**, fluctuates considerably and is dry at times. The Alamosa River above the reservoir has no fish, killed by mining pollution from Summitville, but below it there are some cutthroat and rainbow. The lower reaches of the river pass through private land and are not stocked. The Alamosa River, Alamosa Campground and Alamosa Reservoir can be reached by turning west off U.S. 285 onto Hwy 15, about 12 miles south of Alamosa and then on USFS 250.

As the Rio Grande moves toward the New Mexico state line, **Culebra Creek** joins the river about 30 miles southeast of Alamosa, entering the Rio Grande from the east. It flows primarily through private land.

Regulations state that from Culebra Creek from the State Highway 159 bridge downstream approximately 3 miles to Jaquez Bridge fishing by artificial flies or artificial lures only. All trout caught shall be returned to the water immediately. Landowner permission on a Colorado Courtesy Card is required before access is permitted. As the landowners' agent, the San Luis Visitor Center is authorized to issue courtesy card permission.

Sanchez Reservoir (8,278 ft; 4200 ac) is on **Ventero Creek**, a tributary of Culebra. To reach Sanchez, go 20 miles south of Alamosa on U.S. 285, take Hwy 142 east about 30 miles to San Luis. The reservoir is about 5 miles south of town. Closed between Febru-

Photo Courtesy of Dana Agren

High in the San Juans

ary 15 to July 15 for waterfowl nesting. The fishing for yellow perch and northern pike is excellent at Sanchez, with the perch reaching 14 inches, and pike to 30 pounds. Walleye may also be caught.

TRINCHERA CREEK

Entering the San Luis Valley on U.S. 160 from the east, there are two reservoirs on **Trinchera Creek** about 30 miles east of Alamosa. **Smith Reservoir** (7,721 ft; 700 ac) is located 7 miles west of Mountain Home Reservoir and 3 miles south of the town of Blanca, also on U.S. 160. The fishing for rainbows at Smith remains very good with the trout averaging 2.5 pounds. Both Smith and Mountain Home reservoirs receive large annual stockings of 8-inch rainbows. Smith also produces catfish. Fishing prohibited November 1 through the last day of waterfowl season except within 200 yards of dam. Public prohibited February 15 to July 15 on north and east shores.

Nearby, **Mountain Home Reservoir** (8,145 ft; 639 ac) is located 3 miles south of Fort Garland off Hwy 159. Rainbow trout are the primary fish, with a few brook and cutthroat. **West Indian Creek** drains down from the national forest, at its headwaters is **Forbes Park Lake** (9,450 ft; 10ac). Access is 3 miles southwest of Russell on Hwy 160. All fish must be returned to the water immediately, artificial flies and lures only.

North of Hwy 160 and coursing through the eastern edge of the Great Sand Dunes National Monument is **Medano Creek**, approximately 20 miles east of Mosca, on Hwy 17. From the Pinyon Flats and Dunes campgrounds at the end of the road at the monument, Medano Creek is 12 miles of brushy stream to its headwaters. Small brown and cutthroat are found in the swift water. All cutthroat must be returned to the water immediately, artificial flies and lures only. 10 miles by a rugged 4WD road, beginning at the campground, is Medano Pass, where a 3-mile trail takes the angler to **Medano Lake** (11,500 ft; 4 ac), which has fair fishing for small brook.

Sego Springs is located 3 miles east of Manassa on Hwy 142, then 0.5 mile on the access road. Limited stream fishing on the Conejos.

LA JARA CREEK

La Jara Creek flows from the west and enters the Rio Grande east of the town of La Jara, 13 miles south of Alamosa on U.S. 285. Hwy 15 west from La Jara provides access to La Jara Creek and its headwaters. Stocked with brown trout.

At the headwaters of La Jara, **La Jara Reservoir** (9,700 ft; 800 ac) is a shallow, open, but weedy, lake with 10-inch brook and rainbow. Boats and motors are permitted, but no concession provides this service. Primitive campsites adjoin the reservoir, and a spring at the upper end of the reservoir provides drinkable water. From Monte Vista, take Hwy 15 twenty miles south and a rough access road 232 west 10 miles up Ra Jadero Canyon. Several small streams feed into La Jara Reservoir, including **Upper La Jara Creek**, which contains brook. **Jim** and **Torsido**

Creeks, into which Rio Grande cutthroat have been introduced, are rated fair. Regulations for Jim Creek and Torsido Creeks are fishing by artificial flies or artificial lures only. All cutthroat trout caught must be returned to the water immediately. A limit of brook trout may be taken.

About 2.5 miles downstream from the reservoir, **Jarosa Creek** feeds into La Jara Creek from the west. It is rated good for brown and brook. Below the reservoir, La Jara Creek is rated fair for brook.

CONEJOS RIVER

The **Conejos River** is the largest and may be the best of the Rio Grande tributaries, with headwaters near the town of Platoro, about 25 miles southwest of Del Norte. From Platoro, the Conejos flows south through the Rio Grande National Forest, adjacent to the South San Juan Wilderness, then cuts east along Hwy 17 near the town of Antonito, where it crosses U.S. 285. From there the river flows mostly north through private land to meet the Rio Grande River. In all, the Conejos River is more than 75 miles long. The best fishing is west of Antonito.

Most of the eastern portion of the Conejos flows through private land, but the section of the river west of Mogote, on Hwy 17 about 5 miles west of Antonito, to its headwaters provides about 60 miles of river that is open to the public. Over 20 miles of the river have undergone stream habitat improvements, which have greatly improved fishing conditions. This is a scenically beautiful area with exceptional fishing. The river through this stretch has numerous pools and riffles and average is 60 feet wide. The upper portion primarily offers brown trout, while the lower portion has good fishing for both brown and rainbow.

Except during high-water spring runoff, the Conejos is easily waded and fished. About 20 miles west of Antonito on Hwy 17 at Elk Creek Campground, Forest Road 250 swings north to the headwaters of the Conejos.

Regulations for the Conejos River state that on the Bear Creek subdivision, H.E.B.O. Corporation properties and the Douglas properties from Aspen Glade Campground upstream approximately 4 miles to Menkhaven, all public use is prohibited except for fly fishing. Fishing by artificial flies only. The bag, possession and size limit for trout is two fish, 16 inches in length or longer.

From the Saddle Creek bridge downstream to and including the Hamilton property at the confluence of the Conejos River and the South Fork of the Conejos River. All waters on the Hamilton property shall be restricted to fishing by artificial flies or artificial lures only. The bag, possession and size limit for trout is two fish, 16 inches in length or longer.

ELK CREEK

Elk Creek enters the main Conejos from the south at Elk Creek Campground off Hwy 17 where the Conejos turns from the north and heads east. Elk Creek is about 25 miles west of Antonito. Meandering through 3 meadows, Elk Creek averages 12 feet in

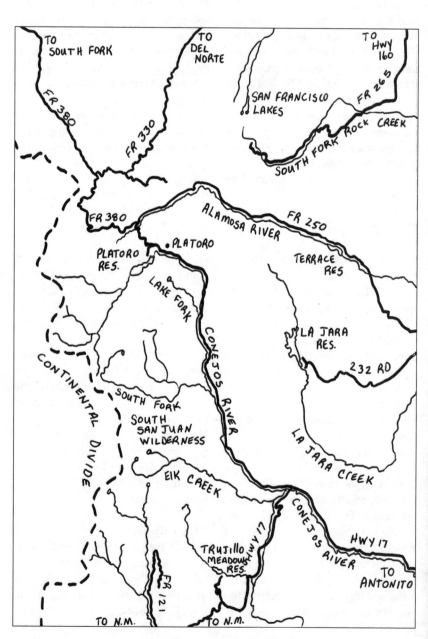

RIO GRANDE EAST

width. Small brook and brown provide the action on this excellent fly water, particularly above the second meadow, reached by trail from Elk Creek Campground. Several lakes feed the creek, including **Beaver Lake** (9,600 ft; 4 ac), which is rated fair for 10- to 12-inch cutthroat, and **Rock Lake** (9,900 ft; 10 ac), another moody lake, holding cutthroat up to 11 pounds. Both lakes are found just within the South San Juan Wilderness boundary and can be reached from Elk Creek Campground. It is about a 3-mile hike. Nearby, **Duck Lake** (10,000 ft; 15 ac) has good fishing for brook.

South Elk Creek enters the main creek at first meadow. It is a 3-foot-wide stream that offers fishing similar to Elk Creek. There is no trail up South Elk, but the trail leading to La Manga Creek's headwaters and Red Lake also provides access to the upper reaches of South Elk Creek.

BORDER STREAMS

Providing 6 miles of fishing for brook and a few small cutthroat, **La Manga Creek** is an 8-foot-wide, open stream that enters Elk Creek about 2 miles west of Elk Creek Campground. In the vicinity of its headwaters, **Red Lake** (11,550 ft; 15 ac) contains 12- to 16-inch cutthroat and rainbow and is rated good. Located in the wilderness area, it can be reached by a 7-mile trail from Hwy 17 about 5.5 miles west of Elk Creek Campground.

Situated in Colorado and New Mexico with the major portion in Colorado, the **Rio de Los Pinos** joins the Conejos northeast of Antonito. The stream averages about 10 to 15 feet wide. Regulations for that portion of the Rio de Los Pinos and the North Fork of the Rio de Los Pinos within the boundaries of the Cumbres subdivision are fishing by artificial flies only. All fish caught must be returned to the water immediately. A second area restricted to fishing by artificial flies and lures, catch and release is from the waterfall at the South San Jaun Wilderness boundary to the headwaters. Less than 15 miles of the stream's headwaters are in Colorado. **Trujillo Meadows Reservoir** (10,000 ft; 70 ac), with cutthroat, rainbow, and brown is near the river's headwaters and can be reached by a 4wd road going north past Neff Mountain near Cumbres Pass on Hwy 17. It is not as temperamental as the alpine lakes to the north.

Two waters of note are **Cascade Creek** and **Osier Creek**; both are designated as Wild Trout water. Both creeks are located east of Cumbre Pass, 6 and 7 miles respectively. Access is best gained from New Mexico then back to USFS 103 in Colorado. Catch and release on all cutthroat, artificial flies and lures only.

In this same area, the headwaters of the **Chama River** edge into Colorado from New Mexico. Forest Service Road 121 from Lobo Lodge, 5 miles northeast of Chama, New Mexico, leads into the forest where the stream is open to public fishing. The Chama, which has pools and riffles, is about 10-feet wide and fairly open as it flows through meadows. It is good for cutthroat and rainbow averaging 10 inches. The **Chama Lake** (11,700 ft;

18 ac) at the headwaters of the Chama River offers poor fishing. Periodically the lake goes dry due to drought.

SPECTACLE LAKE

Spectacle Lake (9,100 ft; 10 ac) is located near Spectacle Campground on the Conejos River Road (Forest Road 250). Catch and release only. A strictly a put-and-take lake. Stocked with 8- to 12-inch rainbow, Spectacle receives heavy fishing pressure.

No Name Lake (11,350 ft; 10 ac) lies south of the South Fork Conejos. Accessed by a 7-mile trail from near the Spectacle Lake Campground on the Conejos River Road. Winterkill can be a problem, but No Name can also be excellent for cutthroat.

The same trail that leads to No Name Lake also leads 5 miles to **Ruybalid Lake** (11,150 ft; 12 ac). Brook trout are stocked at this heavily fished lake. **Alver Jones Lake** (11,180 ft; 12ac) is by a 4-mile trail to west at mid point to No Name Lake. Fair fishing for cutthroat.

SOUTH FORK CONEJOS RIVER

Thirty-two miles west of Antonito and 6 miles downstream from Lake Fork Campground, the **South Fork of Conejos** enters the main river from the west. Averaging 12 feet in width, the South Fork flows for 14 miles through the scenic country of the South San Juan Wilderness. A trail from the Conejos River follows the stream to its headwaters and several of its headwater lakes. The South Fork is easily fished for rainbow, cutthroat and brook and some brown to 11 inches. It is rated very good.

A tributary of South Fork, **Hansen**

Creek feeds into the South Fork 3 miles above its mouth from the north. It provides 4 miles of fishing in a 6-foot-wide stream, brushy at its lower end and rated good for 10- to 12-inch cutthroat and brook. No trails lead into this drainage.

Canyon Verde, the next tributary up the South Fork, offers very good fishing for small rainbow and cutthroat. Follow TR 724 up the South Fork Conejos 5 miles, and then turn south 3 miles on TR 726 up Canyon Verde drainage to **Green Lake** (11,550 ft; 15 ac), at the head of Canyon Verde. Rated good for small cutthroat, rainbow and brook averaging 12 inches. **Trail Lake** (12,000 ft; 20 ac) is a long, narrow, temperamental lake at the top of the Continental Divide, 3 miles past Green Lake on same trail to TR 727. Rated fair for rainbow from 15 inches to 5 pounds.

Canyon Rincon is a tributary stream of the South Fork entering from the north. It is a small, fast stream that supports only a few small cutthroat.

Rated fair to good for 12-inch cutthroat and rainbow is **Timber Lake** (11,300 ft; 12 ac), up Canyon Rincon. It is located 2 miles south of Twin Lakes, 12 miles from the Conejos.

Twin Lakes (11,700; 2 ac each), at the headwaters of Canyon Rincon, are good for rainbow averaging 12 inches; the western lake is the best.

Glacier Lake (11,950 ft; 15 ac), at the head of the South Fork and less than a mile from Twin Lakes, is rated fair for rainbow from 12 to 15 inches.

Blue Lake (11,000 ft; 30 ac) is 5 miles up TR 718 flanking the South Fork. The best access is from Platoro Reservoir, following the Rito Azul drainage. Blue is rated good for brook and a few cutthroat.

Lake Ann (11,910 ft; 16 ac) lies 6 miles up TR712 at the headwaters of the Middle Fork. Fair for cutthroat

Saddle Creek enters the Conejos from the west upstream from the South Fork. Forming the northeast border of the South San Juan Wilderness, it is a very swift, brushy, difficult stream in which to fish, but rated good for cutthroat, rainbow and brook. Forest Road 105 follows the creek for about 6 miles. Sign reads Conejos Peak and Tobacco Lake.

Reached by TR 720 from FR 105, **Bear Lake** (11,500 ft; 25 ac) feeds Saddle Creek near the confluence with Conejos River. **Tobacco Lake** (12,250 ft; 20 ac) is at the headwaters of Saddle Creek, just inside the wilderness. TR 719 leads southwest of FR 105 to the lake. Both Bear and Tobacco are temperamental high mountain lakes. When the fishing is good, it is very good for rainbow and cutthroat.

Entering the Conejos from the west about 8 miles south of the town of Platoro is the **Lake Fork of Conejos**. Rio Grande cutthroat have been introduced into the stream, and is designated as Wild Trout Water. Any cutthroat caught from Rock Lake upstream to the headwaters must be immediately released. The stream also has brook, rainbow and brown to 12 inches.

From Lake Fork Campground, go south 1 mile to USFS road 105, west across Conejos River for .5 mile and north 1 mile through private property to the trailhead for Lake Fork. **Rock Lake** (9,600 ft; 4 ac) is .75 mile from the trailhead and 2.25 miles further is **Big Lake** (9,800 ft; 15 ac). Both lakes have been stocked with Rio Grande cutthroat,

designated wild trout waters and are restricted to artificial lures and flies. Regulations for the Conejos River Lake Fork state that from the headwaters including Big Lake, downstream to Rock Lake including Rock Lake and the outlet, fishing by artificial flies or artificial lures only. All cutthroat caught must be returned to the water immediately. The headwaters of Lake Fork can be reached by USFS 4WD road 100 that intersects road 105 about 5 miles west of the Conejos River.

Near the headwaters of the Conejos, **Platoro Reservoir** (9,970 ft; 416 ac) is located west of the village of Platoro. It fluctuates greatly, but still provides very good fishing for brown, kokanee, and rainbow.

North Fork, Middle Fork of Conejos and **El Rito Azul**, known locally as the **Three Forks**, are upstream from Platoro Reservoir. Forest Road 247 circles north of Platoro Reservoir and continues on to the Three Fork's trailhead, which enters the South San Juan Wilderness via trail 712. **Adams Fork**, which enters Platoro Reservoir from the west, also is accessible by trail 713 only. These streams average 6 to 18 feet in width and, combined, offer 25 miles of fishing. They contain cutthroat, brook and brown.

Mix Lake (9,970 ft; 25 ac) is located at the east end of Platoro Reservoir, with Mix Lake Campground on its north shore. Because it occasionally winterkills, it is a put-and-take rainbow lake. Northeast of Mix Lake is **Kerr Lake** (11,300 ft; 50 ac), which is rated excellent for cutthroat. It is restricted to artificial flies and lures; limit on trout is 2 fish. Access is from FR 250, the Mix Lake road to FR 257, a rough 4WD road.

UPPER COLORADO RIVER
BLUE RIVER

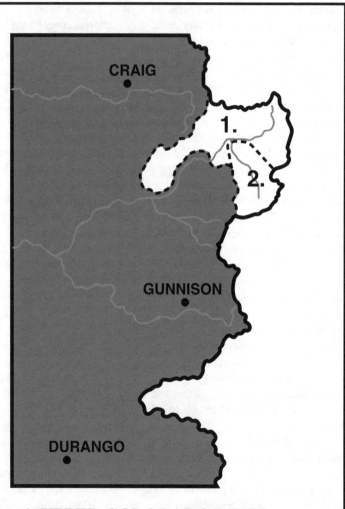

1. UPPER COLORADO RIVER
2. BLUE RIVER

UPPER COLORADO RIVER

High in the snowy mountains of northwest Rocky Mountain National Park from sparkling clear tributaries, the Colorado River, first south and then westerly, cuts its way across the Colorado Plateau en route to the Grand Canyon. Eventually it reaches the salty Sea of Cortez in Mexico. In its namesake state, the Colorado provides some of the best stream and reservoir fishing in the country.

The 60-mile-long upper Colorado River corridor provides numerous and varied recreational opportunities. Unlike the famous downstream sections of the Colorado River known for big waves and rocky canyon isolation, the upper Colorado is popular for its combination of easy access, unique scenery, whitewater, wildlife and fishing.

County roads and a railroad parallel this section of river. Most of the private land is in agricultural production and very few developments exist on public land. Thus, though evidence of man exists, the river corridor remains primarily natural.

Much of Colorado's Western Slope remained undeveloped and occupied by the Ute Indians until the late 1800s. Gold and silver discoveries and the westward extension of railroads attracted many fortune hunters to the area. The fertile land along the Colorado River, then called the Grand River, convinced many people to stay, home-

stead and graze livestock on the abundant rangelands.

In 1906, the famous "Moffat Road" railroad was surveyed through upper Gore Canyon. Surveyors used suspended bridges along the sheer walls to locate the roadbed. The railroad was blasted out from the canyon's granite walls. Huts at the pump-house end of the canyon that housed men who built the railroad are still visible. The historic log cabins seen along the Colorado River are reminders of where pioneers lived at the turn of the century.

Following heavy rains, the mineral composition of surrounding soils gives the river a variety of colors. Near Catamount Bridge, the high silica content turns the water milky white. Downstream the river becomes red from the maroon silt.

Game fish in the upper Colorado include rainbow, brown, cutthroat and brook trout and mountain whitefish. Carp and suckers also reside there.

U.S. 40 is the primary access route to this section of the Colorado River from Granby to Kremmling. Inside Rocky Mountain National Park, Colorado River headwaters offer little fishing as it heads down Kawaneechee Valley toward the town of Grand Lake.

Flowing into the Colorado River from the west out of the Never Summer Mountains, **Baker Creek** has poor brook trout fishing, with some cutthroat in the upper end. At the headwaters in Routt National Forest, **Parika Lake** (11,450 ft; 3 ac), in the Never Summer Wilderness, is fair for cutthroat. It's a 6.4-mile hike from Bowen/Baker Trailhead in Rocky Mountain National Park.

To the south, **Bowen Creek**, like Baker, is small and brushy and has some brook and maybe a brown in the lower end, cutthroat higher up. Upstream, **Bowen Lake** (11,000 ft; 10 ac) and to the northeast **Blue Lake** (10,650 ft; 5 ac) have some cutthroat. Access is via the Bowen/Baker Trailhead in Rocky Mountain National Park. It's a 12-mile trip to Bowen Lake; a northwesterly hike to Blue Lake is 7 miles by trail off the east side of Bowen Lake. Beautiful country.

Near Bowen, USFS road 120 crosses three branches of **Supply Creek**, which is fair to poor for brook and maybe a rainbow or two. Farther south, **Stillwater Creek** is fair for cutthroat higher up; brook on lower reaches. Like Supply Creek, it is small and brushy.

ARAPAHO NATIONAL RECREATION AREA

As the Colorado River exits Rocky Mountain National Park and flows south, it enters the Arapaho National Recreation Area.

Anglers can find most of what high-country lake fishing is all about in the "big lakes" of the 36,000-acre area. Among them, Shadow Mountain Lake and Lake Granby have mackinaw, brown, cutthroat, rainbow and brook trout, as well as some of the best ko-kanee salmon action anywhere. Willow Creek Reservoir is also part of the area.

SHADOW MOUNTAIN LAKE

Shadow Mountain Lake (8,367 ft; 1800 ac) is a reservoir with rainbow, brown, cutthroat, kokanee and some mackinaw, but not as many mackinaws as in Grand Lake, because Shadow Mountain is only about 30 feet deep. Large rainbows are fairly common. It is often choked with weeds in late summer, but the fish are there. Best for rainbow and brown through July, later in the year kokanee fishing is better. Two marinas with boat rentals. Popular for fishing is the submerged Colorado River channel and shoreline. Some boating areas are restricted. Ospreys can be seen on the summer but do not approach their nests. Ice fishing often is good, but only portable shelters are allowed. They must be removed at the end of each day. Many fee campsites are available.

Connected to Shadow Mountain by channel is **Grand Lake** (8,376 ft; 500 ac), a beautiful blue-water natural lake in an idyllic mountain setting. Just outside Rocky Mountain National Park and the Arapaho National Recreation Area, it has long been a tourist haven and summer-home center. Nearly 300 feet deep, it has rainbow and kokanee salmon and is one of the best mackinaw (lake trout) fisheries in the state. Fish up to 20 pounds or more caught nearly every year. Some enormous mackinaws are believed to be in the lake.

Fishing regulations for Grand Lake including inlet and outlet streams follow. The bag and possession limit for mackinaw is four fish, only one may be over 36". From October 1 to June 30, all lake trout between 26 inches and 36 inches in length must be returned to the water immediately. No gaffs or tail snares are permitted. Ice fishing shelters must be portable. Shoreline access is limited by private property, but there is a marina with boat rental. Rainbow fishing is best in spring. The channel usually is good fishing, but there are some suckers. Trolling and inlet fishing usually produce best.

In general, fishing is best early in the spring through June to mid-July. Wet flies and lures are good for brown and rainbow. Sucker meat tempts mackinaw. Ice fishing is popular. Access is from U.S. 40 from the south or west, and U.S. 34 from the north and east.

As part of the Colorado Big Thompson Water Diversion Project, the lakes in the recreation area are linked together by channels and pipelines. They divert water from the upper Colorado River Valley on the west side of the Continental Divide through the Adams Tunnel to the Big Thompson River on the eastern slope.

The Arapaho National Recreation area is adjacent to Rocky Mountain National Park and Indian Peaks Wilderness area. ANRA recreation facilities include four developed campgrounds with 340 overnight camping spaces, six public boat launching ramps (boating regulations are posted), eight picnic areas and 14 miles of hiking trails. Also open to the public are numerous marinas.

LAKE GRANBY

Lake Granby (8,280 ft; some 4000 ac), when full, has 41 miles of shoreline. Fishing is mostly for rainbow, kokanee and mackinaw, although there are some large brown trout. Mackinaw fishing has picked up with many fish exceeding 30 pounds. Trolling is the best method. The bag and possession limit for lake trout and splake is 4 fish, only one fish may be over 36". From October 1 to June 30 all mackinaw caught between 26 inches and 36 inches in length must be returned to the water immediately. No gaffs or tail snares are permitted. Five marinas with rentals. Fishing is similar to Shadow Mountain, although Lake Granby is generally deeper, and the lake level fluctuates due to water project withdrawals. Fishing is prohibited in Columbine Bay to the Twin Creek inlet from October 15 through December 31. Ice shelters must be portable.

At the southeast tip of Lake Granby, **Roaring Fork**, **Grouse** and **Irving Hale Creek** enter the reservoir. The lower reaches of each creek are too fast for fish, and fishing at the upper ends is limited mostly to cutthroat. To reach Roaring Fork Creek, Monarch Lake and the Buchanan Creek trailhead, turn east off Hwy 34 at the sign about 5 miles north of Granby, and follow the south shore road along Lake Granby to its end. Bring mosquito repellent. **Watanga Creek**, a tributary to Roaring Fork Creek, and **Watanga Lake** (10,800 ft; 3 ac) have cutthroat, but access is over a steep, very rough trail that follows Roaring Fork Creek to the Watanga Creek confluence.

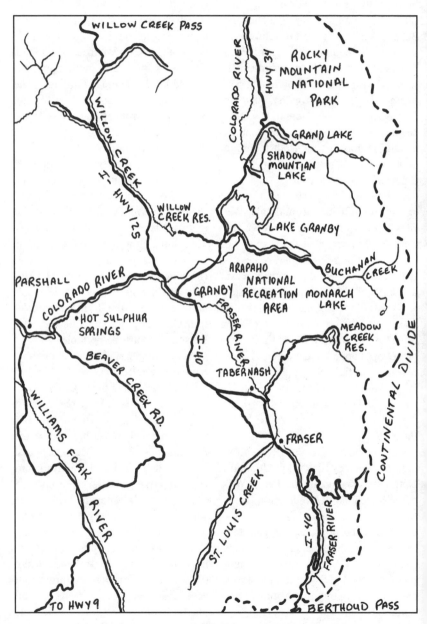

UPPER COLORADO RIVER (EAST)

MONARCH LAKE

A mile southeast of the southeast tip of Lake Granby is **Monarch Lake** (8,300 ft; 130 ac) and the west trailhead to the Indian Peaks Wilderness to the east and southeast. Monarch is a pretty, quiet water littered with downed timber on the south and west ends. It offers good fly-fishing for brook 6 to 15 inches. People fish from the dam with bait, but results often are poor. Flies are better.

A few hundred yards of stream between Monarch Lake Dam and Lake Granby are all that remain of the **South Fork of the Colorado River,** Lake Granby inundates the rest. From Monarch Lake downstream to the County Highway Bridge fishing is by artificial flies or artificial lures only. All trails from Monarch Lake lead into Indian Peaks Wilderness Area where a permit is required for camping.

A mile south of Lake Granby in Arapaho National Forest is **Strawberry Lake**. The lake is private, winterkills and probably has no fish.

BUCHANAN CREEK

Flowing into Monarch Lake are **Buchanan Creek** from the northeast and **Arapaho Creek** from the southeast. Buchanan has brook in its lower reaches, some rainbow and cutthroat at the higher elevations. It is heavily fished despite steep sections of trail leading to the Continental Divide and Indian Peaks Wilderness Area.

Two miles upstream from Monarch Lake, **Hell Canyon Creek** flows from the north into Buchanan. A very steep, rocky trail roughly parallels the creek 3 miles to **Long Lake** (9,920 ft; 6 ac), rated fair for rainbow and cutthroat, as is **Crawford Lake** (10,110 ft; 3 ac), another 0.5 mile upstream. About 2 miles farther upstream, and a little easier climb than the very arduous stretch to Long Lake, is **Stone Lake**. (10,683 ft; 7 ac) A few hundred yards farther is **Upper Lake** (10,730 ft; 8 ac). They have somewhat better cutthroat fishing than the two lower lakes. Very scenic country. The creek itself above Crawford Lake offers some fishing for cutthroat.

About a mile east of Hell Canyon Creek on Buchanan Creek, **Cascade Creek** gushes in from the southeast. Five miles up at its headwaters are **Mirror Lake** (10,350 ft; 1 ac) and **Crater Lake** (10,400 ft; 10 ac). Mirror has small brook; Crater has brook, rainbow and small mackinaw. Fishing pressure is periodically heavy from backpackers and a few horsemen. A mile below Mirror, a trail heads up a small tributary 1.5 miles to **Pawnee Lake** (11,000 ft; 12 ac), which is only fair fishing for brook. Streams in the area are not stocked.

Back at the Buchanan Creek-Cascade Creek confluence, Buchanan continues northeast toward the Continental Divide. About 2 miles upstream, a sign points to the Gourd Lake Trail, a very steep, rough hike 2 miles up to **Gourd Lake** (10,850 ft; 15 ac). A deep lake surrounded by timber and giant rocks, it has big cutthroat, if they can be tempted. Difficult to fish. Limited camping sites. A trail leads north to **Island Lake** (11,500 ft; 16 ac) for small

Colorado River Rainbow

cutthroat. Spectacular terrain.

At Monarch Lake, **Arapaho Creek** comes from the southeast through timber at Arapaho Pass. It is shallow and has poor fishing for brook. It and tributary streams are not stocked.

About 3.5 miles due south of Monarch Lake is **Meadow Creek Reservoir** (9,990 ft; 140 ac), a fair fishery for brook and rainbow to 12 inches, with best fishing in early summer. Reach by CR 83 north from junction with U.S. 40 about 1 mile east of Tabernash. Less than 0.25 mile from the highway turn left onto CR 84 and go about 8 miles to the reservoir. Inside the National Forest, the road is USFS 129. Below the dam, Meadow Creek is good for brook for about a mile. Farther down it is de-watered by irrigation diversions.

Upstream of the reservoir 3 miles at timberline is **Columbine Lake** (11,000 ft; 8 ac), which gets heavy fishing for 12-inch cutthroat. The stream also has cutthroat.

North of Granby, **Willow Creek Reservoir** (8,130 ft; 260 ac) is a private open-irrigation reservoir that fluctuates in summer. It has a zone around most of it that is open to the public so anglers can cast for rainbow and brook. Motor-powered boats are allowed at wakeless speed. Campground on lake shore. Turn off Willow Creek Road to the east about 5 miles north of U.S. 40 to reach the reservoir. Ice fishing shelters must be portable.

Willow Creek flows into the Colorado River from the northwest. It is stocked with rainbow and brook and has some brown trout on the lower reaches. It has several small, brushy tributaries. **Pass Creek** and **Cabin**

Creek are the best of these and are fair for small brook. Access is via Hwy 125 (Willow Creek Pass Road), which leaves U.S. 40 about 2 miles west of Granby and follows the stream most of the way to the top of Willow Creek Pass, about 20 miles. Cabin Creek Road goes off to the west about 9 miles north from U.S. 40. Pass Creek parallels the road for about 4 miles until its juncture with Willow Creek about 16 miles from U.S. 40.

FRASER RIVER

The **Fraser River** originates at the northwest side of Berthoud Pass and flows past Winter Park Ski Area to join the Colorado River just west of Granby. The upper reaches are stocked with catchable rainbow, and some brook at higher elevations. Brushy with willows and trees, the river offers delightful fishing, although it's close to U.S. 40 for about half of its 7 miles above Idlewild. Below, the river is mostly on private property.

Fishing in **Fraser Canyon** downstream from Tabernash is for rainbow and brown. Classified as Wild Trout water. The canyon receives heavy fishing pressure. Some private land is posted. Walking the Denver and Rio Grande Railroad grade is not permitted. Access to the lower end of the canyon is from CR 84 to Strawberry Access Road provides the best access. The river is often low after midsummer because of water diversions.

The first tributary upstream from the town of Granby is **Strawberry Creek**, which has small brook trout. Access is by CR 60, from the town of Granby

to Hankinson Reservoir, then south along a trail.

Several other small creeks enter the Fraser from the east, mostly via Ranch Creek. They include the **South, Middle** and **North forks of Ranch Creek**, **Little Cabin**, **Cabin**, **Hamilton**, **Hurd** and **Trail** creeks. They are small, brushy and with small, if any, trout. Tributary streams on upper reaches are too steep and swift for fish. The **North Fork of Ranch Creek** is catch and release for cutthroat.

East of Winter Park via the Rollins Pass road are **Deadman Lake** (11,300 ft; 7 ac), **Pumphouse Lake** (11,300 ft; 8 ac) and **Corona Lake** (11,200 ft; 9 ac). Deadman, closest to the road, has cutthroat, but tends to winterkill. Pumphouse has brook and cutthroat, and Corona has rainbow and cutthroat. The lakes are visible from the pass and are readily reached by hiking old roads or trails. Snow usually keeps the road closed until July. The road is blocked to vehicles on the east side, so access from South Boulder Creek on the east side of the Continental Divide is by foot.

On the west and south sides of the Fraser River there are numerous streams including **Elk**, **St. Louis** and **Crooked** and **Pole** creeks. All but St. Louis Creek have water diversion and and offer little fishing.

Vasquez Creek, from the Denver water Board diversion upstream to the headwaters is catch and release for cutthroat.

St. Louis Creek is a beautiful forest stream with brook, Colorado River cutthroat and rainbow. It is the only one

Williams Fork near Kremmling

stocked. It is reached by a good road from Fraser, CR 73, then USFS road 1602 that runs a dozen miles into the Fraser Experimental Forest, a research area for the U.S. Forest Service. There is eight miles of fishable creek inside the forest. There are two campgrounds. **St. Louis Lake** (11,400 ft; 4 ac) at the head of the creek is reached by a steep, 3-mile-long trail from the end of the road. Fair for cutthroat. Lower reaches of St. Louis Creek are on private land, brushy and hard to fish for brown and rainbow. Permission is needed.

West of Granby from Windy Gap to the confluence with Troublesome Creek, 3 miles east of Kremmling, the **Colorado River** is classified as a Gold Medal trout stream with large browns and some rainbow. The designation is possibly the result of modest fishing pressure, as most of the adjacent land is private and posted.

BYERS CANYON

West of Hot Sulphur Springs, the Colorado River provides fishing for rainbow and brown in cold, dreary **Byers Canyon** along the highway and railroad. Fishing there is popular. From the lower boundary of Byers Canyon approximately 3 miles west of Hot Sulphur Springs to Troublesome Creek, fishing by flies and lures only. All trout caught must be returned to the water immediately.

Below Byers canyon the best public access is at the Lone Buck State Wildlife Area 3.5 miles west of Hot Sulphur Springs. Public access extends downstream from the Beaver Creek Road bridge to Little Muddy Creek. Fishing

is rated good in this stretch for the large rainbow and brown in May and June but usually deteriorates to fair or poor by August when fish move into deep holes and are difficult to entice. Breeze State Wildlife Area just east of Parshall, and Kemp State Wildlife Area just to the west of Parshall offer access to the Colorado River. There is not an abundance of deep holes and fish are very wary. Low water levels in the fall make fishing difficult.

Several small streams enter the river above Hot Sulphur Springs, but do not offer much in the way of fishing.

Little Muddy Creek is small and brushy at lower levels, but in the forest beaver ponds and the stream have brook and rainbow. Access is by Williams Fork River Road and Keyser Creek Road to Church Park. Upriver a mile, **Beaver Creek** comes into the Colorado at the west end of Byers Canyon. USFS road 133 follows the creek upstream for 12 miles. Fishing is fair for brook.

WILLIAMS FORK RESERVOIR

Williams Fork Reservoir (7,800 ft; 690 ac when full) is a fluctuating reservoir of the Denver Water Department; nonetheless, it has rainbow and brown trout, northern pike and kokanee. Fishing is good and occasionally excellent for kokanee trolling during July and August, or, through winter ice. Northern pike up to 20 pounds have been caught. Regulations for Williams Fork Reservoir: Snagging of kokanee salmon is permitted from September 1 through December 31. All northern pike between 26 and 34 inches in length must be returned to the water immediately. Boat ramp, camping and state recreation areas are on the west side.

The Williams Fork River below the dam to the Colorado River provides good fishing on private land. Permission to fish is necessary. Public land is limited to State Wildlife Areas near the Colorado River. Regulations for Williams Fork from the dam downstream to the confluence of the Colorado River are fishing by artificial flies or artificial lures only. All trout caught must be returned to the water immediately.

The river, reservoir and creeks can be reached from the north on good roads that branch off U.S. 40 about 0.75 mile east of Parshall. Also, there is access by USFS road 132 east from Hwy 9 about 5 miles south of Green Mountain Reservoir (on the Blue River). The road crosses the Williams Fork Mountains at Ute Pass and intercepts the stream at mid-way near the Henderson mill.

Sometimes the headwaters can be reached from the east by 4WD over Jones Pass. Take the Henderson Mine road off Hwy 40 near Berthoud Falls on the east side of the Continental Divide. Local inquiry is advised, as the road can be impassable on the west side of the divide, even in midsummer, because of snowdrifts and flooding. Even 4-wheelers get stranded.

WILLIAMS FORK RIVER

The **Williams Fork River** flows north to enter the Colorado River near the village of Parshall, about 2.5 miles below Williams Fork Reservoir. The headwaters for this 25-mile-long stream are among the 12,000- and 13,000-foot peaks of the Williams Fork and Vasquez Mountains

The Williams Fork is a clear sparkling stream with good riffles and some holes. It remains one of the better insect-producing waters because of environmental safeguards that were put in place during the 1960s and 1970s when AMAX Henderson Mine facilities were constructed. The river downstream to the reservoir generally has good access, although there is some posted land.

The Denver Water Department has diverted the headwaters in several places. Above the diversions, fishing for cutthroat can be good in **McQueary**, **Bobtail** and **Steelman creeks** and in the **Middle** and **South forks** of the Williams Fork itself. The cutthroat in Bobtail and Steelman are the threatened Colorado River Cutthroat. Fishing is by artificial flies or artificial lures only. All cutthroat trout caught must be returned to the water immediately. **McQueary Lake** (10,960 ft; 3 ac) can be excellent for cutthroat to 14 inches. The trail to the lake is steep, and the ice leaves late.

The lower reaches of these creeks have some brook, rainbow and brown. Although the water department voluntarily maintains minimum stream flows, about 200 yards of **Bobtail Creek** are dry. Steelman has a reproducing brook population below the diversion.

The higher tributaries join the river near the Sugarloaf and South Fork campgrounds. Take USFS road 138.

Passenger car access continues up the South Fork for approximately 4 miles on USFS road 142.

The **Kinney Creek** drainage is heavily fished for brook, rainbow and some cutthroat. Fishing is by artificial flies and lures only. Cutthroat are catch and release only. Access by USFS road 141 off USFS road 138. **Horseshoe Lake** (11,250 ft; 5 ac) and **Evelyn Lake** (11,200 ft; 4 ac) are good for cutthroat to 14 inches. Evelyn is accessible from Keyser Creek Road (USFS 139) below the Kinney Creek drainage. **Keyser Creek** is fair for cutthroat and rainbow trout.

Amax Corp. sold some of its holdings on **Lost, Mule, Skylark, Battle, Bull Run and Copper creeks.** Public access is no longer permitted.

Troublesome Creek enters the Colorado from the north, between Parshall and Kremmling. It and a host of tributary streams are brushy and often difficult to fish, but they have lots of small brook. A road (CR 2) going north from U.S. 40 about 6 miles west of Parshall provides access. Most of the stream is on private property. The upper reaches of Troublesome Creek in the Arapaho National Forest flow through excellent elk and black-bear country.

GORE CANYON

West of Kremmling, the Colorado River enters **Gore Canyon** where it offers excellent fishing for good-size trout, mostly browns. Access is via trail up from Pumphouse Recreation Area on BLM land off Trough Road. From the upper end of Gore Canyon downstream to State Bridge is wild trout fishing, and it's often very good.

Gore Canyon also can be reached by driving south of Kremmling about a mile on Hwy 9 and turning west on Trough Road. At 8.5 miles, a sign identifies the Bureau of Land Management Pumphouse Recreation Area, where many floaters put into the river. The road goes to the river for fishing either upstream or downstream. Streamers, nightcrawlers and big flies are all worth a try.

Coming into the Colorado at Kremmling, opposite the Blue River confluence, is **Muddy Creek**. Its lower reaches are fair for rainbow and brown, but are mostly on private land. On the upper reaches, there are many small streams and ponds with brook, rainbow and cutthroat, but are often brushy and hard to fish for small trout. U.S. 40 roughly parallels the stream for nearly 30 miles through sagebrush and some timber to Muddy Pass. About 5 miles upstream from Kremmling, on US 40, is **Wolford Mountain Reservoir** (7,500 ft; 1,450 ac). Completed in 1995, the reservoir is owned by the Denver Water Board, and has done a great job cleaning up Muddy Creek. Wolford Reservoir is a structured lake made for easy fishing for large rainbow to 2 pounds, brown and an occasional brook. Best fishing in the early morning or in the evening as daytime temperature can become quite hot. North end of reservoir contains a wildlife area. This is a fee area. Camping, boat ramp and rental boats are available.

Six miles north of Kremmling on

U.S. 40, turn west on SR 134 to CR 19 which changes to USFS road 100 and then branches northwest onto USFS road 101 to **Red Dirt Reservoir** (8,400 ft; 182 ac) (also called **McMahon Reservoir**). Rated good for catchable rainbows and small brook.

Sheephorn Creek enters the Colorado less than a mile above Radium. A dirt road leads some 20 miles southeast up the creek to the edge of the Gore Eagles Nest Wilderness. Most of it is private land. **Gutzler Lakes** are not fishable. Upper reaches have numerous beaver ponds and small lakes such as **Walters Lake** (9,550 ft; 4 ac) and **Lone Lick Lakes** (9,770 ft; 4 ac) and some small streams. Fishing is mostly for small brook and some cutthroat.

Canyon Creek and **Blacktail Creek** enter the river from the northwest, but offer only fair fishing for brook trout. Blacktail is accessible from Gore Pass on Hwy 134 at the campground west of the summit about 0.75 mile. It is brushy, full of beaver ponds, and fishing is difficult.

Piney River flows from the southeast into the Colorado just above State Bridge. It drains Piney Lake, most easily reached from Vail. Piney is a decent stream with brown, rainbow, brook and, on the upper reaches, cutthroat. Three miles south of State Bridge on Hwy 131, a dirt road leads east; after about a mile it crosses the river. It's private land. To reach Piney's headwaters, some 15 miles distant take the Piney Lake-Meadow Creek Road (USFS 700) heading north from Vail.

Meadow Creek, **East Meadow Creek**, **North Fork Piney River**, **East Fork Piney River** and **Horseshoe Creek** all have trout, but fishing is fair and the most likely places are heavily fished by hikers, since the area, except for Piney Lake, is in the wilderness. Regulations for East Meadow Creek: fishing by artificial flies and artificial lures only; all cutthroat trout caught must be returned to the water immediately.

Piney Lake (9,295 ft; 35 ac) is about 15 miles north from Vail on USFS road 700 to USFS road 701, taking the right hand fork to the lake. The southwestern portion of the lake is private, but the rest is the National Forest, and fishing for brook is fair. Forest trails 1889 and 1885 lead from the north side of the lake to upper reaches of East Meadow Creek and Piney River, respectively. Both are heavily fished for cutthroat.

DERBY CREEKS

Between State Bridge and Burns, several small, muddy creeks enter the Colorado. They have small brook and some rainbow in brushy, hard-to-fish waters. Access is via private land. About 0.75 mile downstream from Burns, **Derby Creek** enters the Colorado after draining a southeast portion of the Flat Tops Wilderness. Derby Mesa Road out of Derby Junction at the mouth of the creek eventually leads 9 miles to Derby Guard Station and the creek. From here, the access to its upper reaches is by USFS road 613, a 4WD road, to the wilderness boundary and then by trail. This is very rugged country with some excellent fishing. It's also scenic.

South Fork Derby Creek is best reached from USFS road 613 (4 WD) west from the Derby Mesa Loop south of Derby Creek. USFS road 616 (4 WD) goes south intersecting USFS trail 1817. Two miles down the trail **Buck Lake** (9,900 ft; 11 ac) lies to the north. Two miles to the northwest of Buck is **Bull Lake** (9,900 ft; 4 ac) Both have Colorado River Cutthroat.

South Derby Creek heads at **Mackinaw Lake** (10,780 ft; 5 ac) and **Crescent Lake**, (10,750 ft; 14 ac) more than 10 miles by rough road into a wilderness "cul de sac." Both lakes have cutthroat and mackinaw, with mackinaws to 22 inches being taken from the namesake lake. Three miles down the creek; **Emerald Lake** (9,600 ft; 2 ac) has small brook. The creek itself has brook and cutthroat. This is bighorn sheep country, so a glimpse of Colorado's state animal is possible.

From the Derby Guard Station, a rough road (USFS 610) goes up **Middle Fork Derby Creek** five miles to the juncture with North Fork Derby Creek. USFS trail 1858 goes 5 miles up Middle Fork providing access to several lakes with no fish. Some of these, including **Muskrat Lake** (10,240 ft; 1 ac) and **Mud Lake** (10,320 ft; 1 ac), are stocked, but winterkill. These are accessible 0.75 mile off the main trail by USFS trail 1842. **McMillan Lake** (10,250 ft; 2 ac) stocked with cutthroat.

Deer Lake (11,150 ft; 4 ac) is a beautiful lake with good cutthroat. It is about 4 miles up from the Muskrat Lake turnoff. South of Deer Lake are **Upper Island Lake** (11,250 ft; 26 ac)

and **Lower Island Lake** (10,800 ft; 19 ac). Upper has cutthroat to 20 inches or so; the lower offers rainbow and cutthroat. Best fishing is late in the season. The Island Lakes are 3 miles from the Muskrat Lake cutoff over a good trail (USFS 1842). The final leg to Upper Island is steep, while USFS trail 1857 connects Island Lakes to Mackinaw Lake. Middle Fork itself offers good angling for cutthroat, especially in hard-to-reach sections of deep canyons.

North Fork Derby Creek flows through canyon for much of the 5 miles to **Hooper Lake** (11,100 ft; 18 ac), barren, and **Keener Lake** (10,740 ft; 30 ac), which has rainbow; some good ones to 5 pounds—if you can get them. About 1.5 miles east of these lakes is **Edge Lake** (10,960 ft; 7 ac), which also has cutthroat and large rainbow, and **Bailey Lakes** (10,760 ft; 1 to 4 ac), which have small brook. Access to North Fork Derby Creek is over a very rough 4WD road (USFS 610) from about 5 miles north of the Derby Guard Station to Stump Park and the wilderness boundary. From there it is a strenuous 6-mile hike to most of the lakes (USFS trail 1860). About 2 miles up from Stump Park and to the west is **Solitary Lake** (10,640 ft; 2 ac), which has brook and rainbow. USFS road 1842 is the best access. A trail (USFS 1846) off the road to the lake is easily located. The three **Sunnyside Lakes**, (10,300 ft; 2.5 to 7 ac) reached by USFS road 915 from the northeast and Routt County Road 3, have small brook trout.

For 7 miles downstream from Derby

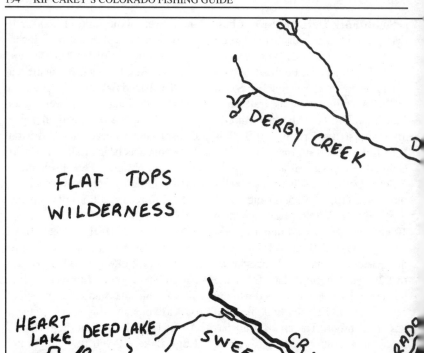

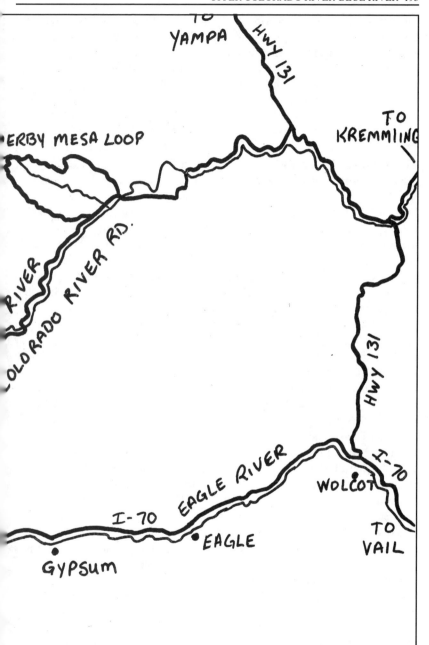

TO YAMPA

HWY 131

TO KREMMLING

ERBY MESA LOOP

RIVER

COLORADO RIVER RD.

HWY 131

I-70

EAGLE RIVER

WOLCOT

I-70

TO VAIL

GYPSUM

EAGLE

Junction, the Colorado River is in a narrow canyon. There is fishing for rainbow and brown from either side, but the stream is not wadable. East side access is at Burns and via the railroad grade. A good road follows the stream on the west.

SWEETWATER CREEK

Sweetwater Creek enters the Colorado from the west, 7 miles north of Dotsero. Sweetwater Road, RD 40, leads up 12 miles through private land to **Sweetwater Lake** (7,711 ft; 80 ac), and campground; a very pretty lake in an idyllic geological setting. The lake is deep and has fishing for brook, kokanee and rainbow, some sizable.

From Sweetwater, trails lead up the creek into the Flat Top Wilderness. About 8 miles up, on USFS trail 1854 to USFS trail 1856, is barren **Indian Lake** (10,560 ft; 7 ac); **Rim Lake** (10,824 ft; 14 ac), about 2.5 miles farther on USFS trail 1856, is deep and, although it was once stocked, it no longer is because it could not sustain fish. **Shepherd Lake** (10,750 ft; 20 ac) is a mile west of Rim Lake, west off USFS trail 1816, is good for cutthroat and mackinaw. Trails to lakes are rough and steep.

Turret Creek, a mile above Sweetwater Lake, is brushy with mostly small rainbow, brook and cutthroat. Best access from USFS trail 1832.

DEEP CREEK

Deep Creek flows into the Colorado River 1.75 miles above Dotsero and I-70. A good road, USFS road 600 also called Coffee Pot Springs Road, parallels it for about 1.5 miles before swinging around to the south and west and eventually reaches **Deep Lake** and **Heart Lake** on top of the Flat Tops after some 30 miles. Upper reaches of **Grizzly Creek** (also mentioned in Lower Colorado section) are also reached via several trails leading west off USFS road 600.

Deep Creek runs north of the road in a deep, wild canyon that has few visitors. It is tough fishing for small brook. West of the road is many small ponds and beaver ponds, which are barren.

White Owl Lake (10,650 ft; 12 ac) is fair for rainbow. It is stocked, but often winterkills. It is less than a mile off the Heart Lake-Deep Lake Road (USFS 600), about 3 miles south of Deep Lake. **Kline's Folly Lake** (10,650 ft; 4 ac) is alongside the road about 0.25 mile from Heart Lake. It has rainbow, often winterkills, but is stocked early in the season.

Supply Basin Lake (10,750 ft; 5 ac) is similar to Kline's Folly and is reached by an easy, 1-mile trail south from Heart Lake. **Bison Lake** (10,780 ft; 20 ac) is due west of Heart Lake and was fair for stocked rainbow, but stocking has ceased. **Heart Lake** (10,700 ft; 122 ac) is poor fishing for brook and is not regularly stocked.

Deep Lake (10,450 ft; 45 ac) has big mackinaw, and each spring ardent anglers wade through snowdrifts to get there soon after the ice out. That's when the fishing is best. Macs (lake trout) to 20 pounds and larger are there along with catchable-size rainbow and some brook.

By 4WD road (USFS 602) south from the Heart Lake Road at Heart Lake is **Grizzly Lake** (10,550 ft; 6 ac) and a mile farther, **Monument Lake** (10,746 ft; 13 ac). Grizzly Lake can also be reached by taking USFS road 632, a 4WD road, west from USFS road 600 north of Crane Park. Both lakes tend to winterkill, but there may be some brook trout.

To the southeast 3 miles by USFS trail 2025 is **Palmer Lake** (10,650 ft; 8 ac), which has some cutthroat, and good campsites. To the east, the **Grizzly Creek** and **South Grizzly Creek** area is accessible by USFS road 602 almost 2 miles north of Crane Park on USFS road 600, about 6 miles southeast of Heart Lake. Both streams have brook and rainbow but are hard to get to, even on foot, because of deep canyons.

BLUE RIVER

Summit County is best known for its mining history of the last century and its current status as a world-class ski destination. The resorts of Breckenridge, Arapaho Basin, Keystone and Copper Mountain are well known to skiers throughout the country. Not as familiar to many outside Colorado is the excellent fishing in the area.

The major tributary of the Colorado River from Summit County is the **Blue River** which flows north from Hoosier Pass into Dillon Reservoir, from the town of Silverthorne to Green Mountain Reservoir, and finally joins the Colorado River about 2 miles south of Kremmling. Its 60 miles of fishing are closely regulated to provide Gold Medal quality fishing. Because of its easy accessibility and quality fishing the DOW has put many regulations in place to preserve quality fishing. From three miles above Breckenridge downstream to the Colorado River, excluding Dillion and Green Mountain reser-

voirs, artificial flies and lures only. Read specific sections for other regulations. Highway 9 generally follows the stream except below Green Mountain Reservoir.

Only a 1.5-hour drive from Denver via I-70, the Blue River Valley, its tributary streams and adjacent lakes receive some of the heaviest fishing pressure in the state. Including the two reservoirs, the area offers rainbow, cutthroat, brown, brook, mackinaw and a hybrid brook-cutthroat trout and kokanee salmon. The best fishing seems to be from July until September, with a number of the largest browns being taken during their fall spawning run out of the reservoirs.

UPPER BLUE RIVER

The **Blue River** begins on the north side of Hoosier Pass (11,539 ft) with the merging of several small streams. The most important ones flow out of the Ten Mile Range on the west side of the valley. Dotted among the 13,000-

Blue River "Boz" 19" long, 17" tall, 7lbs.

Photo Courtesy of the Morrison Angler

and 14,000-foot peaks are several small, high lakes.

Above the picturesque mining-camping-turned-ski-town of Breckenridge, the river flows through timber and brush on private land; most property is posted. Fishing for brook, rainbow and brown in the town itself can yield pleasant surprises, especially in spring and fall. This portion of the Blue is a reminder of the mining past, with tailings ever present along the river.

From the inlet to Dillon Reservoir upstream to Breckenridge, the Blue River is channeled through old gold dredge tailings for much of its length and offers good potential for spring rainbow and fall brown and brook. From three miles above Breckenridge downstream to Dillion Reservoir the minimum size limit for trout is 16 inches. Fishing is prohibited October

1 to January 31.

South fromBreckenridge along Hwy 9, the Tenmile Range flanks the upper Blue River to the west. Steep country, all of the area lakes are high and subject to winterkill. They are heavily fished for stocked rainbow.

Directly below the town of Breckenridge on the east side of the valley is **French Gulch Creek**, fishing to the headwaters is regulated to artificial flies and lures only, all cutthroat must be returned to the water immediately.

Crystal Lakes (11,991 ft; 5 ac) is reached from the Mohawk Road (USFS 225) off Spruce Creek Road. **Upper Crystal** (12,856 ft; 3 ac) is 1 mile above lower lake by old wagon road. Once stocked with golden trout fingerlings, fishing has been poor, as fish often do not survive the severe winters at that altitude. Fair for cutthroat.

Over a ridge to the south are the **Mohawk Lakes** (11,700 ft; 10 to 12 ac). These deep lakes are reached by trail from the junction of Spruce Creek Road and the Blue River about five miles south of Breckenridge on Hwy 9. Only the three larger lakes have fish. Drive 3 rough miles and then walk 1 mile to first lake, 1 mile farther to second lake and 440 yards more to the third. The three lakes are fair for cutthroat to 13 inches, some are larger if you can tempt them.

Blue Lakes (11,500 ft; 50 ac, 6 ac) are located in the Monte Cristo Creek drainage. You can drive the 2 miles to the dam at the upper lake from a marked junction on Hwy 9 about 7 miles south of Breckenridge at the foot of the north side of Hoosier Pass. Both are rated fair for rainbow and cutthroat.

The **Swan River** flows into the Blue from the southeast about 2 miles upstream from the Blue River arm of Dillon Reservoir in a brushy, hard-to-get-to, hard-to-fish area just east of Hwy 9. The stream is lined with dredge tailings for most of its length. On the lower 3 miles, the Colorado Division of Wildlife has reconstructed the river to improve spawning habitat and reproduction potential for kokanee salmon, brown and rainbow on the gravelly bottom. **Swan River (North Fork)** - fishing by artificial flies and lures only. All cutthroat must be returned to the water immediately. **Swan River** - fishing by artificial flies and lures only; minimum size limit for trout is 16 inches or longer; fishing is prohibited from the confluence with the Blue River up-

stream 3 miles from October 1 through January 31.

Access is off Swan Mountain Road, which crosses the Blue just to the south, where the river enters the reservoir, or by turning east on a good dirt road from Hwy 9 about 2.3 miles south of Swan Mountain Road. The dirt road passes a subdivision before heading south up the west side of the creek. The North Fork of the Swan is on public land. It and some ponds are fair for small cutthroat. Middle Fork and mainstream are fair for brook and cutthroat. Fishing pressure tends to be heavy.

DILLON RESERVOIR

Dillon Reservoir (9,000 ft; 3200 ac when full) was built in the 1960s by the Denver Water Department. It is a fluctuating reservoir that changes from a beautiful, large mountain lake rimmed by snowy peaks, when it is full, to an ugly, mud-rimmed pond when volume is down because of drought or heavy drawdown.

It can, nonetheless, provide very good fishing from boat and shore. It is heavily fished and heavily stocked. No fishing is allowed from the dam. The 25.4 miles of shoreline have numerous access points for anglers; there are boat launching ramps at Frisco Bay, Blue River Inlet and Pine Cove Campground.

Fishing for rainbow is good from the shore during early summer months. Dillon has brown trout up to 20 pounds, but they are hard to catch. The reservoir has a few kokanee. Snagging for kokanee salmon is permitted from September 1 through January 31.

The Arapaho National Forest operates five campgrounds for group camping around the lake on the east, south and west sides - Heaton Bay, Peak One, Pine Cove, Prospector and Windy Point. They are all easily reached by either Hwy 9, US 6 or the Swan Mountain Road, which connects the other two highways on the south and east sides of the reservoir.

Dillon Reservoir can be reached from the east by exiting I-70 at the Silverthorne exit. From the west, the access is via either of the two Frisco exits off I-70. The Silverthorne-Dillon exit also connects with Hwy 9 to the north, which follows the Blue River downstream from the dam. The Frisco exits link up with Hwy 9 southbound to Breckenridge.

Several streams enter the reservoir, but only one, Tenmile Creek, offers very good fishing.

TENMILE CREEK

Tenmile Creek, tributary to the Blue, enters Dillon Reservoir from the southwest near the town of Frisco. Paralleled by I-70 in Tenmile Canyon west of Frisco, the lower portion has been successfully rehabilitated into a decent fishery for brown in the fall spawning season. Good also for rainbow and brook. Easy access is from the highway or bicycle path on east side from Frisco to Wheeler Junction (Copper Mountain Ski Area). This area receives heavy fishing pressure. Ponds at Wheeler Junction are stocked with rainbow. Fishing above Wheeler Junc-

Todd Andersen with client on the Blue River

tion south to Fremont Pass is poor.

Clinton Reservoir (10,900 ft; 13 ac) is alongside Hwy 91, a mile north of the summit of Fremont Pass and about 17 miles south of Wheeler Junction. It may have lunker cutthroat in addition to the 8- to 10-inch variety. It opened to public fishing in 1984. The bag and possession limit for trout is 2 fish. No boating allowed.

West Tenmile Creek flows down from the east side of Vail Pass to Wheeler Junction. Easy access, but fishing for small brook is fair at best.

Copper Mountain Village has implemented good stream improvements, but the creek remains private. They operate a kid's pond, open to the public, that's got some good trout in it.

North Tenmile Creek comes into the main creek from the west at Frisco. Fast and brushy with some ponds, it is fair to good for brook and rainbow to 8 inches. **Officer's Gulch Pond** (9,439 ft; 5 ac) is 4 miles west of Frisco on the north side of I-70. It is stocked with rainbow and brook, which tend to be small. Nearby **Uneva Lake** is private.

Lost and Wheeler lakes are in the Gore Eagles Nest Wilderness. **Lost Lake** (11,600 ft; 2 ac) at the head of Officer's Gulch Trail is 3 miles up the creek from Officer's Gulch Pond via a steep, rough trail. It has cutthroat to 12 inches and brook and rainbow.

The two **Wheeler Lakes** (11,000 ft; 7 ac) are up the Wheeler stock trail, about 4 miles from I-70 at Wheeler Junction. The lakes are 0.25 mile from the main trail by a marked side trail. They are about 0.25 mile apart by connecting trail. The first lake has plenty

of 15-inch cutthroat, but they are difficult to catch. Lost Lake is 1.5 miles farther along the main trail and is stocked with cutthroat. Parking is along I-70 and Hwy 91 junction at Copper Mountain ski area. The climb is steep and arduous from a marked trailhead.

Rainbow Lake (9,100 ft; 3 ac) lies south of the town of Frisco on **Miners Creek**. Signed road leaves Hwy 9 one mile south of Frisco; 1.5 miles to lake. Good for 8- to 12-inch stocked rainbow.

SNAKE RIVER

The **Snake River**, one of the prettier tributaries of the Blue, enters Dillon Reservoir on the east side. Because of development and pollution, fishing is poor. **Soda Creek** and **Reynolds Lake** are on private land. The creek flows into the Snake River arm of the reservoir. The higher reaches in Arapaho National Forest have rainbow, brook and some cutthroat. Fishing is only fair. Access is by a dirt road to the south about 300 yards east of the Swan Mountain Road turnoff from Hwy 6 at the east end of the reservoir.

Keystone Creek comes into the Snake River in the midst of a condominium development about a mile west of the ski area. It is brushy with some ponds, especially at high elevations. It is reached via an old road up Keystone Gulch. Fair for small brook.

US Hwy 6 generally follows the **North Fork** of the Snake River from the east arm of Dillon Reservoir past Keystone Ski Area to the foot of Loveland Pass. From 15 to 20 feet wide, it is in timber or brush. It runs fast and has some holes and beaver ponds. Stream and road part 6.5 miles east of Dillon. Good gravel road to the right goes 6 miles to Montezuma, generally following the main stream. The whole lower valley, about 4 miles, is developed by the ski area and associated building activity. The South Fork is not stocked because of mine pollution. Beaver ponds on upper reaches have small brook.

Among the upper tributaries to the Snake are **Deer Creek**, which comes in from the south about 2 miles above Montezuma townsite, and **Peru Creek**, which is about 5 miles from Hwy 6. Both are affected by mine drainage, and fishing for small brook is poor.

Chihuahua Creek flows into Peru Creek about 2 miles upstream from the turnoff. Just past the creek is a rough, steep 4WD trail 4 miles up to **Chihuahua Lake** (12,200 ft; 10 ac). Must walk the last 2 miles. Stream is steep and fast, and there is fair fishing for cutthroat. Lake is fair for 9- to 12-inch cutthroat.

Up a fairly good dirt road 6 miles along Peru Creek is **Gray's Lake** (12,500 ft; 1.5 ac). It snuggles right up against the Continental Divide at the base of 14,270-foot-high Grays Peak. Small and overfished, it has been stocked with brook and rainbow and some cutthroat.

LOWER BLUE RIVER AND WILDERNESS FISHING

From Dillion Reservoir to the Colorado River the Blue River is classified as Gold Medal. From Dillon Dam downstream to the northern city limits of Silverthorne all trout caught must be returned to the water immediately. From the north city limits of the town of Silverthorne downstream to the Colorado River, excluding Green Mountain Reservoir, the minimum size limit for trout is 16 inches. Snagging for kokanee salmon is permitted from Green Mountain Reservoir upstream to the first Hwy 9 bridge over the Blue River, September 1 through December 31.

Downstream from Dillon Dam, the Blue River meanders through developed property and ranchlands, and often is posted. Beginning at Dillon Dam and downstream through the city limits of Silverthorne, the angler who doesn't mind a crowd of fishermen and spectators can enjoy fishing for some large rainbows and browns—fish who have gorged on mysis shrimp from the outflow of Lake Dillon.

Below Silverthorne, the Division of Wildlife has leased 0.75 mile of river adjoining the national forest, which provides more than a mile of open fishing from Blue River Campground downstream. Rainbow, brook and some hybrid cutthroat are found.

Other public water in the area includes the Sutton Unit of the Blue River State Wildlife Area, about 7 miles north of Silverthorne, and the Eagles Nest Unit, about 9 miles north of Silverthorne. Another DOW lease opens almost 2 miles of the river's east bank between Brush Creek and Green Mountain Reservoir.

In the stretch between Dillon Dam and Green Mountain Reservoir 18 miles downstream, the Gore Mountain

Range and its Gore-Eagles Nest Wilderness Area dominate the landscape to the west. On the east are the Williams Fork Mountains. A mile or more of ranchland separates the river from the national forests and public access to several small streams and lakes. The creeks coming in from the west are better fishing; creeks from the east side are probably not worth fishing.

GORE RANGE

North of Dillon Reservoir and west of the Blue River, the Gore-Eagles Nest Wilderness is a very rough, harsh area. Access into the often-rocky barrens with few trees is across open terrain with some aspen and coniferous forest. Hiking in summer can be hot and tiring. The lower reaches of the creeks usually are brushy and difficult to fish. Water quality tends to be high, however. The higher elevations are austere.

Because it is so close to Denver, the area, especially the north end, is heavily used. Trails are good. There is much opportunity for cross-country hiking; use of topographic maps is recommended.

South, Middle and **North Willow Creeks,** the two **Willow lakes** (Lower 11,271 ft; 9 ac, Upper 11,283 ft; 7 ac) and **Salmon Lake** (11,200 ft; 11 ac) are good for 8-inch brook at the lower elevations, and, in the lakes, cutthroat to 10 to 12 inches. Access is via the Dillon-Wheeler and Gore Range trails that begin as dirt roads on the west side of Silverthorne. After 1.8 miles to the wilderness boundary, the trail crosses South Willow Creek, where the Dillon-Wheeler Trail goes upstream to the

west to Buffalo Pass. The Gore Range Trail continues northerly, crossing Middle and North Willow creeks. The trail leaves North Willow for about 2 miles and loops back south to Salmon Lake in a basin between two 13,000-foot peaks. It's about a 5-mile hike and a 2200-foot elevation rise.

Access to the Gore Range Trail also is possible a little north of the Silverthorne town limit just before Hwy 9 crosses Willow Creek. A dirt road heads west for less than a mile.

About 6 miles north of Silverthorne on Hwy 9, a dirt road across from the Blue River Campground traverses west for about 2.7 miles to the wilderness boundary. This provides access to **South** and **North Rock Creeks** and **Pebble Creek**, all of which have small ponds with brook and, usually, cutthroat in their upper reaches.

A couple of miles farther north on Hwy 9, a dirt road goes west, up **Boulder Creek**. A mile or so of private property is posted. It is about 2.3 miles to the wilderness boundary and about 2 more miles by trail to **Boulder Lake** (9,730 ft; 15 ac). The trail continues on a mile or so to a waterfall in the creek. Some small ponds in the higher reaches have cutthroat. Like other areas in the wilderness, this drainage is heavily fished for small brooks, cutthroats and hybrids.

Upstream from Green Mountain Reservoir, **Slate Creek** and the **Slate lakes** are reached by taking the Boulder Creek Road to the wilderness boundary and hiking north on the Gore Range Trail for about 3 miles to Slate Creek. A trail up the stream leads to the

Photo Courtesy of the Morrison Angler

Todd Andersen of the Morrison Angler with client on Blue River with I-70 in background

lakes at the foot of steep, rocky mountainsides. The trail to the upper lake is very steep and rough. **Slate Lake** (9,800 ft; 20 ac) has good-sized rainbow and brook, and a few mackinaw may lurk in the depths. **Upper Slate Lake** (11,000 ft; 15 ac) has brook and cutthroat, which also may be found in the creek above the lake.

Green Mountain Reservoir (7,950 ft) is a popular fishing spot. It is a fluctuating reservoir and varies from 2100 acres when full to 224 acres in drought years. It usually is full in summer and drawn down by varying degrees by autumn. It is a shadeless setting for the most part, being surrounded by sagebrush-covered, rolling terrain. Fishing for kokanee salmon is excellent, and in the fall spawning season, snagging is a major attraction. Kokanee here are among the largest in the state at about 2 pounds and up, and there are a lot of them. Snagging salmon is permitted only September 1 through December 31.

The reservoir, which may be fished by boat, has a few big browns, rainbow, a few mackinaws and a lot of suckers. Green Mountain is popular with ice anglers because it is so easy to reach. The reservoir is well stocked, and fishing at inlets or tributary streams is usually good, especially when the ice recedes in the spring. It is heavily fished. There is a campground, resort accommodations, boat ramps, boat rental and picnic ground. Below Green Mountain Dam, the Blue River is good for rainbow and brown. Some of the browns can be quite large. The first 2.5 miles below the dam is classified as wild trout waters. Releases of water from the reservoir make fishing unpredictable. Mostly private land below Green Mountain.

A paved road exits Hwy 9 about 13 miles north of Silverthorne to Green Mountain Reservoir. The road also provides access to Black, Cataract, Elliott and

Martin creeks. Campgrounds are Davis Springs, McDonald Flats, Elliot Creek, Willows, Cow Creek and Prairie Point.

GORE RANGE LAKES

West of Green Mountain Reservoir, **Black Lakes** (8,891 ft; 60 ac) are 4.5 miles up **Black Creek** by road. They are private and not open to the public. **Blue Lake** (8,743 ft; 20ac) is outside the wilderness and is stocked with brook, cutthroat and hybrids. A few brown trout may be present. Upstream into the wilderness are several tributary streams and ponds that reportedly have small cutthroat. **Cliff Lake** (10,740 ft; 3 ac) and its cutthroat are reached by a very strenuous cross-country trek from Dora Lake or north-westerly from a tributary of Black Creek.

Otter Creek is another fast tributary (with brook, cutthroat, hybrids and possible browns) that drains **Surprise Lake** (10,000 ft; 8 ac) and **Dora Lake** (12,225 ft; 12 ac). Both are most easily (and it isn't that easy) reached by Gore Range Trail going south from Cataract Creek Trail. Dora is good for cutthroat and brook to 15 inches. Surprise has some brook and cutthroat.

Cataract Creek is a good-sized, fast flowing stream that provides access to the very popular north end of the wilderness. A 1.8-mile road (USFS 1725) leads up from the reservoir road just north of the bridge over the creek to **Lower Cataract Lake** (8,630 ft; 60 ac). There is a 4-unit campground at the creek. The creek and lake have brook, brown, cutthroat and hybrid trout and, in the lower reaches of the stream, kokanee in the fall.

The lake is a main jumping-off place for hiking into the Eaglesmere lakes, Tipperary Lake, Upper Cataract Lake,

Mirror Lake and, just outside the wilderness, Mahan Lake—all in especially scenic, rugged terrain.

Upper Cataract Lake (10,700 ft; 40 ac) is a deep lake that can be very good for brook and good-sized cutthroat when the trout are striking. It and **Tipperary Lake** (9,750 ft; 10 ac), which also has some rainbow, are 4 and 2 miles, respectively, above Lower Cataract Lake by steep trail up the tributary to the main stem of the creek. Upper stretches of the creek are fair to good for small cutthroat. **Mirror Lake** (10,550 ft; 5 ac) is shallow but sometimes good for cutthroat.

The **Eaglesmere lakes** require a 4-mile hike with one good, steep section. **Upper Eaglesmere** (10,950 ft; 20 ac) and **Lower Eaglesmere** (10,250; 12 ac) are heavily fished for cutthroat, rainbow and brook.

Mahan Lake (11,028 ft; 5 ac), which can also be readily reached by the Spring Creek Road going west from the north end of Green Mountain Reservoir, is shallow, flat, weedy, and tends to winterkill. Possibly some brook there.

Flowing into the Blue above its confluence with the Colorado River, **Elliott, Martin, Deep, Spring** and **Spruce creeks** offer some brook, rainbow and hybrid cutthroat fishing. Much of the fishing is on private land and some of it is posted. Permission to fish is necessary, because public and private land boundaries are not always posted. The river is west of Highway 9.

Tough Road (CR 1), on the route to State Bridge, crosses the Blue River about a mile above the confluence with the Colorado River, but is completely on private property.

EAGLE RIVER
ROARING FORK RIVER

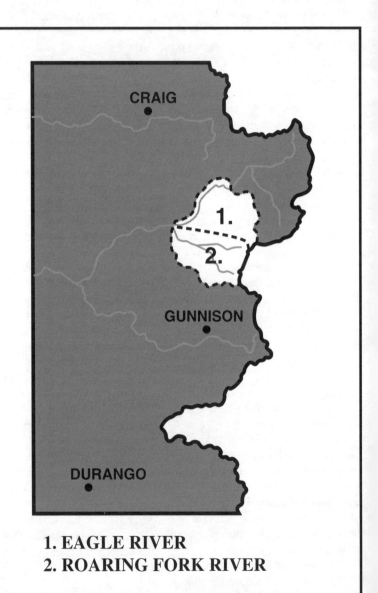

1. EAGLE RIVER
2. ROARING FORK RIVER

EAGLE RIVER

The **Eagle River** has long been one of the better trout streams in Colorado, despite the infusion of pollutants from mine tailings in its upper reaches, water diversions and real estate development. Somehow, the Eagle ignored these intrusions and remains a good stream for both rainbow and browns. Fishing on the Eagle is likely to get better as effluents from old mines have recently been brought under control.

The valley of the Eagle and its tributaries has been transformed over 30 years from a series of sleepy mountain ranching hamlets and pastoral bottom land into a world-class outdoor recreation destination. The towns of Vail, Avon and Edwards have replaced hay meadows. Condominiums crowd the edge of streams where only an occasional beaver previously resided. Construction of I-70 through the valley encroached on its streambed in many places, occupying a wide swath of valley land.

The quality of outdoor experience the Eagle-Vail area offers is a testimonial to the resilience of Mother Nature, especially when augmented by thoughtful planning. Elk still winter in the valley, though today their winter home is probably a championship golf course. Trout still lurk in the deep holes, many of which were created during habitat enhancement projects by man. Deer frequent the slopes skiers'

use in winter and even a bear is occasionally seen.

The Eagle River rises in heavy timber on the north side of Tennessee Pass, about 11 miles north of Leadville. Its two principal tributaries are the South Fork of the Eagle River and Homestake Creek. Gore Creek, the river's other principal headwater stream, originates on the northwest side of Vail Pass. Gore Creek merges with the Eagle just west of Vail near Minturn. Brush and Gypsum creeks are major tributaries in the lower stretches.

From the confluence of Gore Creek, downstream for 14 miles to Wolcott, the Eagle River is fair to good fishing for 10- to 14-inch rainbow and brown; many larger fish are taken. Some posted access, so ask permission to cross private land. Best access is to take US 6, which generally follows the river down the valley, instead of I-70. A mile of the river runs through state land just below the confluence of Gore Creek and the river. Slow down by the bridge for a sharp turn onto Hwy 24 and the service road by the river.

Fishing is good in the Eagle from Minturn down to Gypsum Creek. Good dry fly fishing for rainbow and browns up to 14 inches, with many larger. Heavy population of caddis flies. Below Gypsum Creek the river bottom gets silty, insect populations decline and so does the fishing. Below Eagle

Vail Area Waterfall

Photo Courtesy of Kevin Rummell

and past Gypsum to the Colorado, fishing can be good, but permission is required. From Gypsum to the Colorado River, 6 miles, the BLM owns the south bank and has a campground and 1 mile of public fishing on both sides of the river, a mile west of Gypsum. The stream contains rainbow, brown and suckers. Brushy; waders needed.

GYPSUM CREEK

Six miles up the Eagle from its confluence with the Colorado River, **Gypsum Creek** flows in from the south. The lower 6 miles are occasionally stocked with 10-inch rainbows. Rated poor. The next 3 miles have small brook. The **Gypsum Ponds State Wildlife Area** consists of three ponds totaling 10 acres. The ponds contain Snake River cutthroat and rainbow.

USFS road 425 (4WD), off USFS road 412 from Gypsum, takes you south to **Red Creek** and Red Table Mountain. About 7 miles up USFS road 425 is **Red Lake** (10,800 ft; 2 ac) which has brook, but often winterkills.

To the west, **Rim Lake** (10,700 ft; 8 ac), **Sugarloaf Lake** (10,710 ft; 7 ac), **Sourdough Lakes** (9,450 ft; 1 ac total), and **Shingle Lake** (10,500 ft; 4 ac) lie below the rim of Red Table Mountain and offer brook, cutthroat and rainbow. Access is from USFS road 514, which runs to the southwest of the lakes (4 WD), or from CR 412 to trail 1862. **Borah, Erikson, Cherry** and **Muckie's lakes,** are all barren.

USFS road 412 leads from the town of Gypsum 18 miles to **LEDE Reservoir** (9,500 ft; 28 ac). It is stocked with

rainbow. To the west, coming off Red Table Mountain, are many small irrigation and stock watering channels, which have no fish. The ponds at their heads are little more than watering holes. There are fish in two of the lakes, if you can find them in the timber. **Lost Lake** (10,900 ft; 5 ac) is stocked with brook. It is reached by hiking west from Lede Reservoir to **Ragged Lake** (9,661 ft; 6 ac) and then up the creek that flows into the southwest corner of Ragged Lake (not the creek coming in from the south) on trail 2224.

BRUSH CREEK

Brush Creek, which flows from the south into the Eagle River just west of Eagle, has brook, rainbow and, at lower levels, brown. The lower dozen miles where the stream flows through meadows that are brushy and are private property. Permission to fish is necessary. Access is via USFS road 400, which parallels the stream. The stream forks 2 miles into the forest, as does the road, where it becomes USFS road 415 along **East Brush Creek**, rated good for brook, some to 9 inches. Stream meanders through very brushy meadow with many small beaver ponds. **Hat Creek** splits off East Brush towards the south. A catch and release, flies and lures only stream managed for native Colorado River cutthroat restoration. USFS road 416 reaches the stream from USFS road 415.

East Brush Creek continues southeast another 12 miles past beautiful Yeoman Park and Fulford Cave campgrounds. Beaver ponds upstream and downstream from the bridge to the campground offer good fishing for brook, and some stocked rainbow.

At the headwaters of East Brush Creek is **Mystic Island Lake** (11,300 ft; 30 ac) and **Lake Charles** (11,000 ft; 16 ac), both in the Holy Cross Wilderness and accessible by USFS trail 1899 that runs to the southeast from Fulford Cave Campground. Both are fair to good for cutthroat and brook. The stream itself has brook and cutthroat. The area is heavily fished; many beaver ponds.

Three miles up East Brush Creek, **Nolan Creek** comes in from the east. It has about 3 miles of fishing in stream and ponds for brook and cutthroat. Fishing by artificial flies and lures only. Cutthroat are catch and release only. Nolan is paralleled by an old mining road, now USFS road 419, to Fulford. A 3-mile trail from Fulford to the southwest leads to **Nolan Lake** (10,800 ft; 7 ac) at the headwaters of the creek. It is deep and has good brook-trout fishing.

Nolan Creek also provides access to New York Lake to the east via old mining roads. The climb is over a 12,500-foot saddle, very tough climb. Fulford is outside the wilderness; Nolan Lake is just inside.

Triangle Creek is another East Brush tributary. A 4WD road about 1 mile north from Fulford leads to Triangle Park where Triangle Creek is extensively dammed by beaver. Rated fair for small brook.

West Brush Creek, up USFS road 400, is rated fair for brook and rainbow; it tends to be brushy—hence its name. Many beaver ponds. Four miles

up West Brush Creek is **Sylvan Lake** (8,510 ft; 42 ac) State Park. Lake is stocked with rainbow and brook. Sylvan Lake provides good ice fishing. Rainbows to 2 pounds are sometimes caught. Brook trout in the lake are prolific. Fishing is prohibited in the inlet and upstream 0.5 mile from September 1 through November 30.

USFS road 400 continues above the lake following the creek to Crooked Pass and the Fryingpan River Valley. The pass is dangerously slippery when it rains.

Antoine's Cabin Creek enters West Brush Creek just below Sylvan Lake. **Antoine's Cabin Lakes** have no fish.

The **Eagle River** from Wolcott to Eagle has good fishing for rainbow and brown to 14 inches; many larger. Rainbow fishing is best in fall and spring, but the river in this stretch becomes muddy from tributaries after rain. Some of the best water has been leased by the state. It begins a mile east of Eagle and extends 6.3 miles, as posted, on the north side of the river only. From the south bank, 2 to 3 miles are open. Signs indicate public waters. Inquire in Eagle. Other stretches are open by permission.

LAKE CREEK

Upstream from Wolcott **Lake Creek** flows into the Eagle from the south below Edwards. Two miles south from Edwards and US 6, it forks into **East Lake Creek** and **West Lake Creek.** Access is from CR 25 To USFS 423. Lake Creek has brown, rainbow and cutthroat.

USFS road 423 follows **West Lake Creek**. The road goes 6 miles up from the confluence with East Lake Creek, 4WD is recommended for entire distance. West Lake Creek is fair for brown at lower levels, cutthroat higher. At its headwaters is **New York Lake** (11,300 ft; 40 ac), good for cutthroat. To get there, go up West Lake Creek on the old road to Polar Star Mine. Just below the mine, the road forks. Take the east road up 1.5 miles to timberline, and continue east around a hill onto a saddle from which New York Lake can be seen below. Vertical differences of 700 feet to 800 feet makes it a rough hike down and back up again.

Middle Lake (11,200 ft; 18 ac) is between West and East Lake creeks and is best reached from the west by driving the road to its end, then taking USFS trail 2223 1.5-miles and than 2220 to lake. Fish the lake for cutthroat.

At upper elevations, the 5 **Gold Dust Lakes** (11,400 ft; 15 to 20 ac total) require a 2-mile climb to the west of small creek to a bench; follow stream south past the first two lakes to three larger ones that produce cutthroat to 15 inches. Don't count on a trail. To the north 0.5 mile is **Big Pine Lake** (11,280 ft; 5 ac), which is accessed via USFS trail 1880 to USFS trail 1896. Over a steep, high ridge is **Lake Thomas** (11,600 ft; 15 ac), which also has cutthroat and big rainbow. Very remote and rugged country.

Three good cutthroat lakes lie about 2 miles south of Gold Dust Lakes on the other side of an unnamed 12,730-foot mountain. **Big Spruce Lake** (12,000 ft; 15 ac), **Horseshoe Lake** (11,600 ft; 8 ac) and **Big Lake** (11,600 ft; 11 ac) are reached by hiking cross-country from Gold Dust Lakes or up the unnamed creek that drains them from East Lake Creek.

Moving upstream past Edwards, **Beaver Creek** enters the Eagle from the south of Avon. Development of a ski area and related projects has left its lower reaches off-limits to public fishing. Upper reaches have cutthroat and brook. **Beaver Lake** (9,750 ft; 5 ac), 0.5 mile inside the Holy Cross-Wilderness, has good brook and cutthroat fishing. An old road leads to the boundary, then it's an easy hike on USFS trail 2109. Upstream from Beaver Lake, where USFS trails 2109 and 2129 meet, are the **Turquoise Lakes** (11,000 ft; 6 ac each), with cutthroat. Higher lake is deeper, better fishing.

VAIL AREA

Gore Creek joins the Eagle River 2 miles downstream from Minturn. The Gore is an astonishing stream, because the town of Vail and construction associated with Vail ski area has surrounded much of it with development. Still, it has brown, rainbow, cutthroat and brook trout. On its lower reaches in the town of Vail, it has been designated a Gold Medal water for quality fishing. This portion is from Red Sandstone Creek downstream to its confluence with the Eagle River, a distance of 4 miles. Artificial flies and lures only, with the minimum size limit for trout 16 inches. Catch and release is encouraged. Portions of the stream are posted.

Gore Creek originates in the southern end of the Gore-Eagles Nest Wilderness north of I-70 in the vicinity of

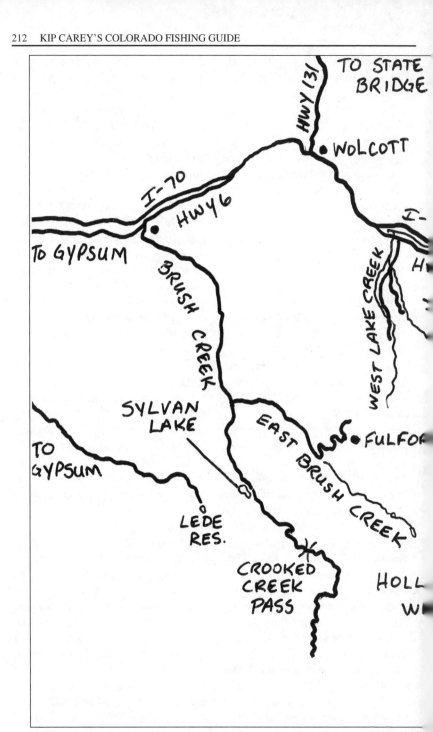

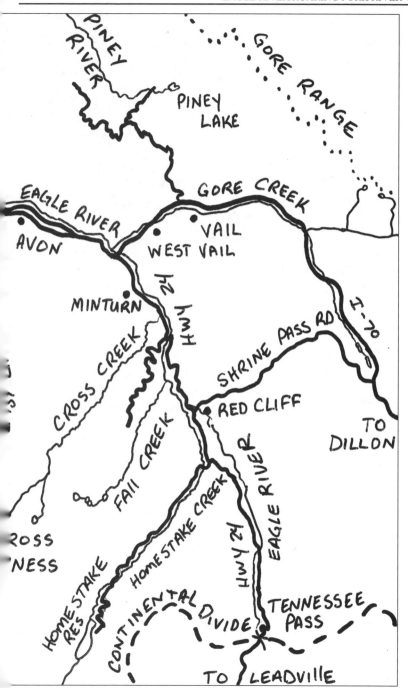

Jay at New York Lake

Photo Courtesy of Steve Carey

Red Buffalo Pass. North of the creek, **Gore Lake** (11,400 ft; 5 ac) and **Deluge Lake** (11,740ft; 5 ac) offer fair fishing for cutthroat. Both lakes can be reached from Gore Creek Campground via USFS 2015 and 2014. Other lakes in the area are barren. Five miles down through brush and timber, **Black Gore Creek** joins Gore Creek from the south after a 10-mile run from near the summit of Vail Pass. Near the summit, the two **Black Lakes** (Lower 10,394 ft; 11 ac, Upper 10,510 ft; 19 ac) can be seen at 10,400 feet elevation. They are heavily stocked with rainbow and heavily fished. They tend to be temperamental, but often provide good fishing. Easy access from I-70 via USFS road 228.

Downstream, **Bighorn** (USFS trail 2013), **Pitkin** (USFS trail 2012) and **Booth** (USFS trail 2011) creeks plunge down steep valleys to Gore Creek. They are too fast to fish at lower reaches, but in higher terrain have small cutthroat and some brook. Get off I-70 and use the north service road to find parking. **Pitkin Lake** (11,400 ft; 8 ac) is at timberline and requires a strenuous 6-mile hike. It and **Booth Lake** (11,500 ft; 5 ac) are both heavily fished for cutthroat. Booth Creek Trail provides access; roadside signs note creeks.

Lost Lake (10,300 ft; 18 ac) is a deep lake at the headwaters of **Red Sandstone Creek** that flows into Gore Creek west of Vail. It is a deep, beautiful lake reached by taking the Red Sandstone Creek Road (USFS road 700) 9 miles to the end of the road; then it's an easy 1 mile trail (1893) to the lake. Heavily fished.

Above the confluence of Gore Creek

and the Eagle and just north of Minturn, **Grouse Creek** joins the Eagle. USFS trail 2129 leads up **West Grouse Creek** 6 miles to **Olsen Lake** (11,200 ft; 10 ac), 0.25 mile off the trail in timber. Trail goes past Olsen to the two **Turquoise Lakes** (11,000 ft; 6 ac each), where it joins USFS trail 2109. These lakes are 4.5 miles from Olsen and have cutthroat. Higher lake is deeper, better fishing.

Grouse Lake (10,700 ft; 5 ac) is 5 miles up Grouse Creek by USFS trail 2127. This trail forks from USFS trail 2129 about a mile west from Hwy 24. Good fishing for small brook.

CROSS CREEK

Cross Creek is a productive rainbow, brown, brook and—at the upper levels—cutthroat fishery, it receives very high fishing pressure. At the north end of the Eagle River Canyon, where Hwy 24 crosses the river, a dirt road, USFS road 707 goes west to provide access to the Fall and Cross Creek drainages. Very rough road. The Eagle itself is in a deep narrow canyon with access only along the railroad track beside the river.

About 4 miles into the forest on USFS road 707 is Tigiwon Campground, a good place to leave the car, although the road goes on another 4 miles to Half Moon Trailhead and the Holy Cross Wilderness boundary. From Half Moon, trails go north, USFS 2009, to Cross Creek and the summit of Mount of the Holy Cross (14,005 ft), and south, USFS trail 2001, above Fall Creek to Lake Constantine. Another trail, USFS 2006, leaves USFS road 707 after a mile and also leads to Cross Creek. This entire area receives very heavy traffic and fishing pressure. Most lakes are stocked.

Cross Creek offers a variety of fishing: fast canyon water, open and brushy streams, beaver ponds and high mountain lakes. At the headwaters of East Cross Creek is **Lake Patricia** (12,500 ft; 10 ac); with cutthroat. It is about 5 miles from Half Moon Campground. Farther up is **Bowl of Tears,** a shallow pond without fish.

A steep, rugged trail goes 2 miles down the west side of East Cross Creek to the main stream trail. About 4 miles upstream, **West Cross Creek** enters the main stream above Reeds Meadows. Fishing by artificial flies and lures only. Cutthroat are strictly catch and release. It's strictly a no-trail situation upstream to four **West Cross Creek Lakes** (12,240 ft to 11,680 ft; averaging 12 ac). Best route is probably to continue up Cross Creek 5 miles to Blodgett Lake and then head north-northwest along the ridge to West Cross Creek. The four lakes then lie about 0.25 mile apart, all easy walking from Blodgett, for good cutthroat fishing.

Harvey Lake (11,000 ft; 20 ac) is about 3 miles upstream from West Cross Creek juncture. It is good for brook and cutthroat, including some big ones. Harvey is just off the mainstream 1.5 miles up a small creek and is accessed by USFS trail 2006, which parallels Cross Creek.

Another 2 miles upstream, beyond an old mill site, the creek forks. The left, or east fork leads 0.25 mile to **Treasure Vault Lake** (11,600 ft; 23 ac) and some good cutthroat. The right fork leads, a similar distance, to **Blodgett Lake** (11,650 ft; 25 ac) for similar angling.

These lakes are also accessible by a 4-mile hike on established trails from Holy Cross City via Fancy Pass or by a 6-mile hike from Missouri Lakes.

Lake Constantine (11,400 ft; 13 ac) is a 5-mile hike from Half Moon. It is fair for cutthroat, rainbow and brook. **Fall Creek,** downstream from the lake to the river, is in a deep canyon; though often brushy and very difficult to reach and fish, its beaver ponds are loaded with brook trout.

Above Constantine by steep streamside trail are the **Tuhare Lakes** (12,300 ft; 12 ac). The lower and, a short distance beyond, the upper (12,400 ft; 43 ac) are good for cutthroat, but are heavily fished by iron-legged, leatherlunged fishermen. It helps to have both hands free on the climb up from Constantine.

The **Seven Sisters Lakes** are accessible by taking USFS trail 2001 about 0.5 mile above Constantine. Tricky creek crossing.

GOLD PARK AND HOMESTAKE CREEK

Gold Park and Gold Park Campground is a major trailhead for hiking into the Holy Cross Wilderness and to scores of lakes to the west and north. On a summer weekend, 100 cars may be parked there, for the 122,600-acre wilderness is one of the most heavily used areas in Colorado. Fishing pressure is very heavy in summer and fall, largely because 19th century mining roads and trails provide ready, if strenuous, access to spectacular mountain country. Just below Redcliff, the clear waters of **Homestake Creek** enter the Eagle. Rated good for stocked rainbow.

USFS road 703 leads up Homestake Creek to Gold Park Campground and Homestake Reservoir from Hwy 24. About 4 miles up USFS road 703 from Blodgett Campground, USFS trail 2002 goes off to the north to the **Whitney Lakes** (10,600 ft; 5 to 15 ac), a steep 3-mile trail that climbs 1900 feet. The lower lake has brook, rainbow and cutthroat; the two upper two lakes, which require a tough hike without trails, have cutthroat and brook.

From Gold Park Campground, USFS road 704, a very rough road, goes 3.5 miles southwest up Missouri Creek to provide access to the Brady Lakes, Sopris Lake, Lake Esther, the four Missouri lakes, Fancy Lake and the two Mulhall lakes. Missouri Creek, Sopris Creek, Fancy Creek and French Creek contribute their waters to the Homestake Water Collection system. Most of their headwater lakes are fishable.

Other tributary streams to Homestake Creek tend to be too steep and fast for fish except at the higher elevations, where some small cutthroat and brook may be found in pools and ponds. The same conditions prevail on the east tributaries to the Eagle River between its east fork and Gore Creek at the junction of Hwy 24 and I-70.

French Creek dribbles (most of its water having been diverted) into Homestake at Gold Park after draining Cleveland Lake, Hunky Dory Lake and the Seven Sisters Lakes. An old road off USFS 759, both of which are 4WD, to Holy Cross City provides access to **Hunky Dory** (11,600 ft; 6 ac) and **Cleveland Lakes** (11,920 ft; 20 ac), which have brook and cutthroat. Cleveland, the better of the two, also has some rainbow. Both are on the edge of the wilderness. The road is easier to walk than drive, although a 4WD can make it from midsummer on.

Seven Sisters Lakes (11,840-12,700 ft; 6 to 12 ac) are on **French Creek** to the north of Hunky Dory. USFS trail 2001 leaves USFS road 759, which follows the creek leads to the Seven Sisters. Fishing at the three lowest lakes is for brook and some cutthroat. The fourth lake has brook and cutthroat; higher ones are barren. The lakes are heavily fished, because they are only a mile or so into the wilderness; all are above timberline. The trail continues over Fall Creek Pass to Fall Creek and Lake Constantine. About 4 miles south of Gold Park are the **Lost Lakes,** also known as the **Chain of Lakes** (10,500 ft; 4 to 15 ac). Best access is by a cross country hike from the water diversion pipes on the Isolation Lake Trail near Homestake Reservoir (4wd needed to reach trailhead). Lakes are very clear and the trout are wary, but there is good fishing for cutthroat and rainbow; uppermost lake is possibly the best of the four.

A quarter-mile below the Homestake Water System intake tunnel on Homestake Creek and above Gold Park a mile, **Fancy Creek** merges with Homestake. At its headwaters is **Fancy Lake** (11,500 ft; 4 ac). It can be reached

High mountain valley

Photo Courtesy of Dana Agren

by USFS trail 2006 up the creek or by an old road from Hunky Dory Lake and Holy Cross City to the north. Fancy Lake has brook. The **Mulhall Lakes** (11,920 ft; 2 and 4 ac) can be reached by going north on a trail 100 yards north of Fancy Lake to a stream, then upstream a total distance of about 0.75 mile. The Mulhalls have brook. They can be reached via Holy Cross City.

The **Missouri Lakes** (11,400 ft; 4 to 13 ac) are about 4 miles by USFS trail 2003 from the end of the road (USFS 704). The lowest lake is barren; the other three have brook and cutthroat.

Proceed up **Sopris Creek** from the end of the Missouri Creek Road (USFS 704) at the wilderness boundary. Follow the old road about a mile; then a faint trail accesses **Brady Lake** (10,890 ft; 8 ac). To the north 0.25 mile is **Sopris Lake** (10,890 ft; 5 ac), which is sometimes referred to as Brady Lake. Both have cutthroat. **Esther Lake** (11,280 ft; 4 ac) lies to the southwest a mile by a cross-country trek. Follow the stream up to the lake for good fishing for brook.

A trail parallels the **East Fork of Homestake Creek** for 5 miles. After about 3 miles, a trail breaks off to the east along a small stream. It's a mile along the east branch to **Isolation Lakes** (11,600 ft; 2 and 3 ac). Although above timberline, the lakes offer good cutthroat fishing. Two miles farther, at the headwaters of East Fork, is **Lonesome Lake** (11,520 ft; 10 ac), which also has cutthroat.

Homestake Reservoir (10,260 ft; 300 ac) lies in a 3-mile-long cul de sac in the Holy Cross Wilderness Area about 11 miles up USFS road 703 from Hwy 24. Last few miles to reservoir are rough and may require 4wd. The reservoir is rated fair for cutthroat and brook, and is lightly fished, with good reason. Fishing is difficult because of steep rock banks.

At the southwest corner of the reservoir, a small creek comes down from **Paradise Lakes** (11,200 ft; 2 to 20 ac). A very steep, 2-mile hike to these four above-timberline lakes can provide fair fishing for brook and cutthroat. There is heavy fishing pressure from hikers.

Three miles above Homestake Reservoir is **Upper Homestake Lake** (10,500 ft; 17 ac). Follow the creekside trail for good fishing for cutthroat averaging 15 inches in the upper reservoir. This is very rugged and scenic country.

UPPER EAGLE RIVER

Farther upstream on the Eagle, **Resolution Creek** enters the river at Camp Hale in Eagle Park. USFS road 702 follows the creek northeast. It has been stocked with fingerling Colorado River Cutthroat.

The **South Fork Eagle River** flows as a small forest creek 5 miles north from Tennessee Pass beside Hwy 24, often through heavy brush with beaver ponds. At Camp Hale, at the foot of the pass, East Fork Eagle River coming down from the Robinson tailings pond of AMAX Climax molybdenum mine joins it. For 3 miles it is channeled along the airstrip at Camp Hale, training center for the 10th Mountain Division in World War II. Fishing is for small browns and rainbow. The river is rated poor on the upper reaches, but fair near Camp Hale, because the river is stocked and the Forest Service has made stream improvements. There are two campgrounds: Camp Hale and East Fork. Stocked fishing ponds at Camp Hale are just off Hwy 24 and easy to fish for rainbow and brook.

ROARING FORK RIVER

A couple of the most recognizable names in trout fishing lore are found in the Aspen-Glenwood Springs area: the **Roaring Fork River** and **Fryingpan River**. They provide exceptional fishing for large brown and rainbow trout and have earned Gold Medal status as premium quality water.

This region is also well known to the rich and famous as the home of the Aspen-Snowmass ski resort area. This popular resort town is at the heart of many fine streams. Aspen is an idealistic setting for a resort town.

ROARING FORK RIVER

For more than half of its 59 miles from Glenwood Springs to its origins at Independence Pass near Hwy 82 on the Continental Divide, the **Roaring Fork River** defines what a premium freestone river is. Flowing through one of the most scenic valleys in Colorado, brown and rainbow trout to 20 inches are common in its riffles and pools, even though it is heavily fished. There is a substantial population of good-size mountain whitefish in the river, providing many a delicious meal of smoked fish.

From the confluence with the Colorado River at Glenwood Springs upstream 12 miles to the Crystal River confluence, the Roaring Fork is classified as Gold Medal water. The trout in this stretch are a mix of brown and rainbow, with fish averaging from 12 to 18 inches; larger fish are common. Whitefish average 2 to 3 pounds in this same water. **Carbondale State Wildlife Area** offers river access.

From the Colorado River to Upper Woody Creek bridge fishing is by artificial flies or lures only. The size limit for trout is 16 inches or longer. From the Upper Woody Creek bridge upstream to McFarlane Creek, fishing is with artificial flies only, and all fish caught must be returned to the water at

Photo Courtesy of the Morrison Angler

Todd Andersen of the Morrison Angler with large Fryingpan brown once.

County Road 109 at the confluence of the Crystal River and the Roaring Fork in Carbondale follows the river north on the west side of the Roaring Fork to Glenwood Springs. Hwy 82 runs along the east side of the river, but river access is by private road.

The Colorado Division of Wildlife has classified the 7-mile stretch between Aspen's Hallam Lake and the Upper Woody Creek Bridge as Wild Trout water and restricts anglers to artificial flies and lures only. All trout caught are to be returned to the river immediately.

Just above Aspen the river meanders through many beautiful meadows. There are a few ponds. There is also a mix of public and private land. Public fishing is allowed along much of the river on the north edge of town. Observe signs. Fishing for brown and rainbow in the town of Aspen itself can be good, depending on the volume of stream flow.

The river headwaters are on Independence Pass and the Roaring Fork roars and tumbles from there for 15 miles to Aspen. This upper stretch is rated fair to good for smaller brook and a few rainbows. Near Lincoln Creek junction, a few cutthroat might be found.

CRYSTAL RIVER

Upstream from Glenwood Springs, the first major drainage entering the Roaring Fork is the **Crystal River**. Flowing for more than 35 miles through some of the most scenic terrain in Colorado, it joins the Roaring Fork River from the south 2 miles below Carbondale.

The Crystal and its tributaries and lakes have rainbow, brook and cutthroat trout. Browns may be found close to the Roaring Fork. A swift stream, its valley is popular with tourists and anglers alike. It is heavily stocked, and trout over 13 inches are seldom caught except in the most out-of-the-way places.

Hwy 133 leaves Hwy 82 about 10 miles south of Glenwood Springs, 12 miles north of Basalt near Carbondale. It follows the river and is paved 20 miles to Bogan Flats at the foot of McClure Pass. A poorly paved road 314 continues 5 miles upriver to Marble and 5 more 4WD miles to Crystal. After that it is strictly 4WD up the river's south fork to Schofield Pass. Sections of the road above Marble are one-way traffic and dangerous for the inexperienced.

Downstream from the hatchery south of Carbondale, the Crystal River is on private property to its junction with the Roaring Fork. **Prince Creek** enters the Crystal just below the fish hatchery south of Carbondale. A road from Hwy 133 to the east parallels it through private land toward **Dinkle Lake** (8,580; 9 ac). Prince Creek has cutthroat in the upper reaches; brook in the lower. The three **Thomas Lakes** (10,200 ft; 13 ac each) at the headwaters of Prince Creek are good for cutthroat. Take 2.5-mile trail from Dinkle Lake (USFS trail 1957 to 1958). About a mile up, watch for the trail to Thomas Lakes at an angle to the west. It's a 1.5-mile walk to access trails between the lakes, which are a quarter mile apart.

The best fishing in the Crystal River drainage is probably in the **Thompson Creeks**, which flow into the river from the west 4.5 miles south of Carbondale. Angling is for rainbow and cutthroat in small streams, reached by taking CR 108 from Hwy 133 in Carbondale. After a couple of turns, the road veers west to Jerome Park and then south to Thompson Creek, a total distance of 12 miles. A good map is handy here. A dirt road (USFS 304) goes west up the creek into the forest and to **North Thompson Creek**. Off North Thompson Creek is **Yank Creek** with small brook trout.

Back at Jerome Park, going south about 1.5 miles south of the Cemetery Road to the west, a dirt road (USFS 305) goes off to the southeast. After 2 miles it comes to the creek and, after another mile, swings west toward **Middle Thompson Creek**. USFS trail 1950 parallels creek. Observe posted signs and gates. Good clear, swift water for mostly rainbow, but also cutthroat. **Lake Ridge Lakes**, up USFS road 305, have no fish.

Avalanche Creek flows into the Crystal north of Redstone from the east. Fishing in the creek and in **Avalanche Lake** (10,700 ft; 6 ac) at its headwaters is poor. USFS trail 1959 leads up the creek to lake. The lake usually winterkills.

Above Redstone, **Hawk, Big Kline** and **East Creeks** are too precipitous to fish. **Coal Creek** is sterile and a source of pollution to the river. Between Redstone and Marble there are beaver ponds and some posted stretches. The USFS and DOW have cooperated on stream improvements to improve fishing.

Below Marble, off Hwy 133, is **McKee Pond** (7,400 ft; 2 ac), a put-and-take rainbow fishing hole with rainbow and brook. Heavily fished; stocked by Colorado DOW

Along the USFS road 314 about 1.75 miles short of Marble, **Island Lake** (7,800 ft; 3 ac) is stocked and trout seem to respond best to bait.

Lily Lake, a mile below Marble Cemetery, off USFS road 314 is private and usually winterkills.

Beaver Lake (7,950 ft; 30 ac) is a state fishing area at Marble that is stocked with brook and rainbow. It is heavily fished. Boats are allowed, but no motors; also no camping.

Yule Creek is good fishing for cutthroat to 12 inches. It races into the Crystal River from the south at Marble. Walk 4 miles up an old road past the marble quarries and 4 miles more in rough terrain. Four miles past the quarries and off the trail to the northeast are the **Yule Lakes** (12,000 ft; 3 to 8 ac) with cutthroat. Fishing is poor, but there may be some fair sized trout. Take a dim trail up the second creek coming into Yule Creek above Thompson Flat. The northernmost lake has no fish.

In view, just off the road between Marble and Crystal, is **Lizard Lake** (10,000 ft; 3 ac). Usually, heavily fished and stocked with brook and rainbow.

At the ghost town of Crystal, the north and south forks of the main river merge. The **North Fork of the Crystal River** flows 7 miles from its origins to join the South Fork at Crystal.

The North Fork has many beaver ponds open, but difficult fishing in a canyon for cutthroat. It is heavily fished. A dangerous 4WD road above the river is often blocked by snow until midsummer.

Geneva Lake (10,950 ft; 33 ac) is reached by driving 2.5 miles up the North Fork from Crystal to Lead King Basin. Leave vehicle and hike north up a steep switchback trail to lake. A deep lake with shallow shoreline and brook trout to 12 inches.

From the inlet to Geneva Lake it is 2 miles upstream to **Little Gem** (or **Upper Geneva Lake**) (11,700 ft; 3 ac), with some cutthroat, but fishing usually is poor. Over a ridge 0.5-mile northwest of Geneva Lake is **Snowfield Lake** (11,600 ft; 1 ac), with brook. No trail.

A very dangerous road that often is snow-filled and impassable until late July parallels the South Fork of the Crystal River. Fishing in the fast water of Crystal Canyon is for brook and cutthroat.

Galena Lake (12,000 ft; 12 ac) is temperamental for cutthroat. Above timberline, it is reached by a trail going over a ridge to the northwest at Elko Park near the summit of Schofield Pass. It is about 2 miles. Be prepared for cold weather.

Back on Hwy 82, upstream from the Crystal River and Carbondale 2 miles west of Basalt, **Sopris Creek** joins the Roaring Fork. About 8 miles up **West Sopris Creek** is **Dinkle Lake** (8,400 ft; 6 ac), a pothole irrigation reservoir with rainbow and brown. Best fishing is early in the year. Creek is private below lake, but fair fishing above for cutthroat, brook and some rainbow.

Hardscrabble Lake (10,150 ft; 4 ac) with its poor fishing for cutthroat is a 0.75 mile walk from the wilderness boundary at Capitol Creek. Sign indicates trail. **Williams Lake** (10,800 ft; 7 ac) is a mile southwest of Hardscrabble by USFS trail 1960 from the inlet. It has brook and cutthroat.

Christine Lake (6,725 ft; 3 ac) is on the west edge of Basalt town limit just off Hwy 82 on the blacktop road to the east, west of gas station. Stocked with rainbow and brown. Moss can be bad at times.

FRYINGPAN RIVER

The **Fryingpan River** enters the Roaring Fork at Basalt. It is a designated Gold Medal trout stream from its confluence with the Roaring Fork upstream 14 miles to Ruedi Reservoir Dam. From the dam downstream to the river's confluence with the Roaring Fork, all trout, except brown trout, must be returned to the water immediately. The bag, possession and maximum size limit for brown trout is 14 inches in length. Fishing is restricted to flies and artificial lures only.

There are some brook and cutthroat in the waters below the dam that run to 18 inches, with only a few large sized rainbows remaining from the days when Mysis shrimp fed a hoard of football-shaped rainbows that frequently topped 15 pounds. As might be imagined, this section of the river continues to be heavily fished most of the year. Until restrictions on possession and catch-and-release fishing were imple-

Photo Courtesy of the Morrison Angler

Fishing near Basalt

mented, this stretch of the Fryingpan was in danger of being fished out except for put-and-take fishing.

The green drake fly hatch in late summer and early fall often results in spectacular angling for the accomplished fly fisher along much of the length of the Frying Pan.

Ruedi Reservoir (7,750 ft; 1000 ac when full), rated slow and poor fishing for rainbow and brown, it is now used more by pleasure boaters. Since it was filled in 1969 with water from one of the best trout fisheries in the world, it has largely been a disappointment to anglers but has produced some lake trout over 30 inches and browns to 18 inches. It also has rainbow and kokanee salmon. Fishing is from both shore and boats. The inlet area in the early spring may be the best.

Past private land 2 miles above Ruedi Reservoir, the Fryingpan flows some 17 miles through national forest from its origins along the Continental Divide in the Hunter-Fryingpan Wilderness. A good road (USFS 105) follows upstream nearly 12 miles to the wilderness boundary.

Upstream from the reservoir, the Fryingpan River fluctuates in volume because of water diversions through tunnels to Turquoise Lake on the east side of the Continental Divide. Minimum stream flows are maintained to the benefit of the fishery. The stocking of rainbow and cutthroat in the upper reaches has resumed below the diversions. Cutthroat, brook and rainbow are found in streams above the diversion of the river and its tributaries.

Two miles above Ruedi, **Lime Creek** enters the Fryingpan. Lime Creek rises 10 miles to the northeast in the Holy Cross Wilderness at **Strawberry Lakes** (11,200 ft; 4 ac total), where there are brook.

Just west, at the base of Avalanche Peak, is **Sherry Lake** (11,800 ft; 7 ac), with brook. Further downstream from Strawberry are **Fairview Lake** (10,640 ft; 10 ac), **Eagle Lake** (10,600 ft; 12 ac) and **Wood Lakes**. Woods Lake is private. The others, all in the wilderness, have brook and cutthroat. Below Woods Lake, off USFS road 507, Lime Creek runs through a deep canyon and is difficult to reach.

USFS road 400 from Thomasville off USFS road 105 at east end of Ruedi Reservoir provides access to Lime Creek. USFS road 506 also runs north from USFS road 105 east of Ruedi Reservoir and joins USFS road 507. USFS trail 1915 begins at USFS road 507 and provides access to Eagle Lake. From the town of Eagle, USFS road 400 over Crooked Creek Pass follows Lime Creek past Crooked Creek Reservoir to the Flying Pan. It is perilously slippery when wet.

Above Ruedi and the village of Thomasville, both the main road and the Fryingpan River fork. Brushy **Last Chance Creek** joins the North Fork Fryingpan River just above the fork. It has brook. Eight miles upstream via

USFS trail 1917 is **Lake Josephine** (11,420 ft; 2 ac) with brook. To the northwest 2 miles, **Tellerium Lake** is barren.

The **North Fork Fryingpan River** flows 10 miles from the **Savage Lakes** (11,300 ft; 15 and 25 ac). The lakes have brook trout. The North Fork drainage is accessed by USFS road 501 from USFS road 105.

Diemer Lake (9,900 ft; 12 ac) is a weedy pond a mile by trail above Elk Wallow Campground. It is stocked with brook and rainbow. **Sellar Lake** (10,170 ft; 7 ac) is shallow and rated fair for stocked rainbow. It is a mile southwest of Diemer Lake, via USFS road 502.

Joining the North Fork a mile above the Elk Wallow Campground, **Cunningham Creek** flows in from the southeast. It has fair fishing for brook. Regulations for Cunningham Creek in Pitkin County are fishing by artificial flies and lures only and all cutthroat must be returned to the water immediately. Much of its water is diverted to the Eastern Slope.

Farther up USFS road 501 **Mormon Creek** drains **Mormon Lake** (11,400 ft; 14 ac) another 4 miles upstream to the southeast. It has brook, but is rough hiking through brush. Savage, Carter and Mormon lakes are all just inside the wilderness.

From Norrie Colony on USFS road 105, USFS road 504 winds southeast to Chapman Gulch and **Chapman Lake** (9,200 ft; 15 ac) (which should not be confused with Chapman Dam and Campground 2 miles away on the main river). The lake is fair to good for

Big ol' 9 lb. brown from the Fryingpan

Photo Courtesy of the Morrison Angler

brook and cutthroat. A clear trail to it is evident 2 miles up from the fork in the road. Good road continues on for 2 more miles, then a trail (USFS 1920) to upper reaches of Chapman Gulch. All of it offers good fishing.

At the fork in USFS road 504, the west fork goes 2.75 miles up **Chapman Creek**, a fast stream with some cutthroat. In the wilderness 2 miles southwest of the end of the road, where there are water diversion structures, is **Sawyer Lake** (11,050 ft; 12 ac), with cutthroat. It is a rough hike up Sawyer Creek from this point. An easier trail goes southwest 7 miles from Chapman Campground on the Frying Pan, through the timber and across Twin Meadows to Sawyer. **Chapman Dam** (8,536 ft; 10ac) and Campground has a 15-acre pond, which is good for rainbow and brook. Stocked and heavily fished.

The **South Fork of the Fryingpan River** rises 12 miles southeast of the Hunter-Fryingpan Wilderness 12 miles southeast of the village site of Nast. Much of the river is good fly-fishing with riffles, pools, rapids and quiet stretches with rainbow and cutthroat. The river canyon is steep, deep and rough going in many sections. Access is by USFS road 504 south from Norrie.

USFS road 105 follows the main river southeast above Chapman Campground. The road generally stays high on the canyon rim. **Ivanhoe Creek** flows into the river from the east. USFS road 105 generally follows the creek 5 miles to its headwaters at **Ivanhoe Lake**, (10,900 ft; 30 ac) on the way to Hagerman Pass. The lake has rainbow

and receives moderate fishing pressure. It lies along the old Colorado Midland Railroad grade. History buffs may be advised that the locomotive that went off the track and down into Hell Gate Canyon (3 miles downstream) has been salvaged despite legends to the contrary. The creek is rated fair fishing for rainbow and brook.

Lyle Creek flows into Ivanhoe Creek 2 miles below the lake. Up Lyle Creek 1.5 miles in the Holy Cross Wilderness is **Lyle Lake** (11,600 ft; 10 ac). It and the stream are rated fair for brook. The lake also has mackinaw.

Tributary streams from the south, **Marten Creek** and **Granite Creek,** and the two **Granite Lakes** (11,700 ft; 3 and 5 ac) have small brook in the 6-inch range. Access is by wilderness trail off USFS road 505 south of USFS road 105.

The **Fryingpan Lakes** (11,000 ft, 2 ac total) are about 5 miles up pack trail USFS 1921 from the Boustead Tunnel West Portal and the end of the road. They are teeming with small brook and an occasional cutthroat. Regulations for Fryingpan Lakes 2 and 3 are fishing by artificial flies and lures only and all cutthroat trout must be returned to the water immediately. Colorado River Cutthroat Recovery Water.

MAROON BELLS/SNOWMASS WILDERNESS AREA

Continuing Upstream from Basalt on Hwy 82, the **Snowmass Creek** drainage enters the Roaring Fork from the south. It has many beaver ponds, though brushy. Rainbow fishing rated good, brook trout excellent. Snowmass

Maroon Bells

Photo Courtesy of Dana Agren

Creek Road (CR 11) parallels the creek for a distance to trailheads that access **East and West Snowmass Creeks**, both rated poor fishing. **Snowmass Lake**, (10,980 ft; 84 ac) at the headwaters of the main stem of the creek, is rated good. Deep and in a glaciated pocket of the mountains, the lake has rainbow to 20 inches and larger and some smaller cutthroat. The lake is 7 miles into the wilderness from the end of the road. Turn south from the Snowmass store on Hwy 82 where the creek enters the river. USFS trail 1975 runs from end of road to Snowmass Lake. There is no longer a campground at this location.

The first creek inside the wilderness, **West Snowmass Creek** drains **Moon Lake** (11,720 ft; 9 ac), which has cutthroat. Ignore streamside trail and go on up the main Snowmass Creek Trail (USFS 1975) to the second creek, **Copper Creek,** and follow the trail up it to timberline, about 3 miles. Take the draw to the right. At the end of a break in the top of the ridge to the northwest, Moon Lake is visible to the north, 0.5 mile away across rockslide.

Directly west of Moon Lake over a steep ridge is **Capitol Lake** (11,600 ft; 21 ac), a deep lake with good-sized cutthroat. Access is up Capitol Creek Road (CR 9), which follows **Capitol Creek** from its juncture with Snowmass Creek about 2 miles south of Hwy 82. Four miles up, at the monastery, take the northwest fork in the road 3 more miles to Cow Camp. Then hike into the wilderness up Capitol Creek, 5 miles to lake. Capitol Creek has small brook and is brushy at lower elevations.

Nickelson Creek, off Capitol Creek, is catch and release fishing only with artificial flies and lures; Colorado River Cutthroat Recovery Water.

Up Snowmass Creek above the confluence with West Snowmass Creek, **Bear Creek** drains the **Pierre Lakes** (12,300 ft; 18, 27 and 15 ac) from the west, southwest. The lakes have cutthroat. Access is steep and rugged. It entails walking an old, closed-off road 1.5 miles up Snowmass Creek from the wilderness boundary to Bear Creek, the third stream coming in from the west. Leave the main trail to Snowmass Lake and go up the north side of the creek about 4.5 miles to the lakes. The largest and highest lake tends to have the best fishing, though all three are good.

Woody Creek flows into the Roaring Fork from the east and **Brush Creek** from the west, downstream from Aspen. Both are poor fishing for small trout closer to Aspen. Maroon Creek Road (USFS 125) leads from town and parallels **Maroon Creek**. It's the principal access to the Maroon Bells-Snowmass Wilderness and receives heavy backpacker, but not necessarily angler, traffic. Unless you're camping at Maroon Lake, Silver Bar, Silver Bell or Silver Queen campgrounds, access is by shuttle bus during the summer months.

Maroon Creek, East Maroon Creek and **Maroon Lake** (9850 ft; 15 ac) have mostly rainbow and a few brook. The famous Maroon Bells, the mountains surrounding Maroon Lake, are a photographer's dream. Fishing is often good on both the lake and stream for stocked, catchable-sized rainbows in summer. Not as heavily fished as in the past. From June to September the access road (Maroon Creek Road) is closed from

8:30 am to 5 pm. Shuttle transportation is provided from Ruby Park in Aspen.

West Maroon Creek and **Crater Lake** have few, if any fish. USFS trail 1975 leads from Maroon Lake to Crater Lake.

Willow Creek joins Maroon Creek a mile up the road from Aspen Highlands parking lot. Good horse trail follows it for 9 miles to **Willow Lake** (11,705 ft; 18 ac) and good fishing for brook and cutthroat; some large ones are in this alpine lake. Willow Lake is reached by USFS trails 1975 to 1978 from Crater Lake.

ASPEN AREA

Castle Creek enters the Roaring Fork from the south on Aspen's southwest side after a 15-mile dash out of the 12,000 and 13,000-foot peaks of the Elk Mountains above Ashcroft. A winding, paved road (USFS 102) from Hwy 82 follows the creek a dozen miles. The stream is fair to good for cutthroat, rainbow and small brook; it's brushy in places, with some beaver ponds and private lands.

Conundrum Creek is a substantial stream, less de-watered by irrigation than Castle Creek, but offers only fair to poor fishing for most of its 10 miles. USFS road 128 leads up Conundrum Creek from USFS road 102, then USFS trail 1981 parallels creek.

Above Ashcroft just over a mile, **Pine Creek** flows in from the west and **Cathedral Lake** (11,855 ft; 17 ac). A steep 1-mile road leads to the lake, where fishing for rainbow, brook and cutthroat has been increasing in recent years. Camping is no longer permitted here. **American Lake** (11,365 ft; 8 ac) is due west of Ashcroft, but is most readily reached by a 3-mile trail from Elk Mountain Lodge downstream from Ashcroft about a mile. American has rainbow and surprisingly little fishing pressure.

Northeast of Aspen, **Hunter Creek** enters the Roaring Fork on Aspen's north edge. It offers fair fishing for cutthroat and brown on lower reaches and for cutthroat higher in the Hunter-Fryingpan Wilderness Area. A fair road leads from Aspen, but quickly becomes 4WD and vehicle access is open only during big game hunting season. This leads to several trails that service Hunter Creek, including USFS trail 2194.

UPPER ROARING FORK RIVER

At the headwaters of the Roaring Fork and 1.5 miles below Independence Pass on Hwy 82, there is parking space on a curve and a trailhead to **Linkins Lake** (12,008 ft; 11 ac), 0.75 mile by steep trail. Follow a sign up to the left. Fishing for brook and stocked rainbow is best on the deeper side. From the same trailhead, 2 miles up the river, **Independence Lake** (12,490 ft; 9 ac) has brook trout to 16 inches if not winterkilled. A half-mile north by easy trail, **Lost Man Lake** (12,450 ft; 10 ac) also has rainbow. **Lost Man Creek** has small rainbow, brook and cutthroat downstream to **Lost Man Reservoir** (10,590 ft: 6 ac), which is heavily fished for rainbow and brook. North of the reservoir, **Scott Lake** (12,020 ft; 5 ac) is above the creek on a bench to the west about midway between Lost Man Lake and reservoir; a steep climb for good, small brook fishing.

Heading back toward Aspen off Hwy 82 to the south, 10 miles below Independence Pass, USFS road 106, a 4WD dirt road requiring high clearance, crosses the

river and follows **Lincoln Creek.** It's stocked with 10-inch rainbows. Take USFS road 106 six miles to **Grizzly Reservoir** (10,560 ft; 28 ac). Best fishing is early summer for rainbow.

South above the reservoir a mile by road, **Truro Creek** joins Lincoln out of **Truro Lake** (12,300 ft; 7 ac). The lake is good for cutthroat, as is **Jack Lake** (12,150 ft; 3 ac). Both lakes are to the west and up a steep slope. Directly across the valley to the east is **Grizzly Lake** (12,560 ft; 8 ac) producing rainbow. Access to Grizzly Lake is via a circuitous trail (USFS 1990) up Grizzly Creek from the east side of Grizzly Reservoir.

A mile farther up Lincoln Creek, a trail follows a creek coming in from the west to two lakes. At the fork in the creek, about a mile up, the south fork goes to **Anderson Lake** (11,814 ft; 9 ac), which is fair for small rainbow. The North Fork leads a mile to **Petroleum Lake** (12,300 ft; 12 ac) and good rainbow fishing. The area is rarely open until mid-July, when the ice goes out and snowdrifts melt. **Ruby Lakes** at the top of the drainage are barren.

Two miles downstream from Grizzly Reservoir, **Tabor Creek** flows into Lincoln Creek from the south. Three miles by trail up the creek; a smaller creek comes in from the west out of **Tabor Lake** (12,320 ft; 6 ac), which has cutthroat.

Down the Roaring Fork 1.75 miles from Lincoln Gulch is Weller Campground and a trail leading south 0.5 mile to **Weller Lake** (9,520 ft; 5 ac), which is fair for rainbow. The river is in a deep canyon and hard to fish for its small cutthroat and rainbow.

YAMPA RIVER
WHITE RIVER

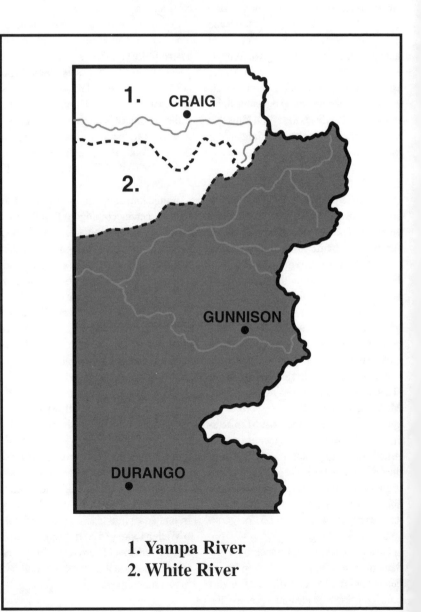

1. Yampa River
2. White River

YAMPA RIVER

The **Yampa River** (referred to locally as Bear River) originates in the Flat Tops Wilderness, tumbling out of its eastern boundary and rushing toward Steamboat Springs through one of the more scenic valleys in Colorado. The waters of the Elk River drain the west side of the Mount Zirkel Wilderness area and enter the Yampa west of Steamboat Springs. Other tributaries drain the Elkhead Mountains and join the Yampa just east of the city of Craig. From Craig, the river rolls and winds through dry, brushy hills into Dinosaur National Monument on the Colorado-Utah state line. There the clearer flow of the Green River absorbs the Yampa's murky waters.

All told, the Yampa has over 100 miles of fishing, and includes trout in the mountains, big pike in the slow meanders west of Steamboat and catfish in the slow, silty western section. The river also offers native whitefish. Often overlooked, they run to 2 pounds in many of the river's stretches. They go for small flies and are fun to catch. Smoked, they are delicious.

The Yampa headwaters in the Routt National Forest vary between 20 and 50 feet wide and tease anglers with challenging fly-fishing from midsummer on. Rainbow, brook and brown to 10 inches are there for the taking. In many cases, lakes and some reservoirs offer larger trout than the river itself.

When the Yampa swings west of Steamboat Springs, it averages 100 feet wide with deep holes. Spinning is grand; worms, grasshoppers, fly larvae and minnows are favorite trout cuisine. In the stretch of the river between Craig and Hayden, northern pike are big and numerous. They are found in the backwater sloughs, especially during spring's high water.

Including a large portion of national forest, thousands of square miles of BLM lands and a number of state wildlife areas, the Yampa River drainage provides a substantial area of public land. The Yampa River lies below 9,426-foot Rabbit Ears Pass to the east, 9,527-foot Gore Pass to the southeast, and Ripple Creek and Nine Mile passes along its southern edge. It is a complete mix, ranging from pine-covered mountains to sagebrush flats.

U.S. 40 is the major east-west artery, passing through Steamboat Springs, Hayden, Craig, then forking at Maybell. From the southeast, Hwy 131 enters the region from the south of Toponas and continues north of the Yampa River. Access from the north is from Hwy 13 south of Baggs, Wyo., to Craig, and then continues down to Meeker. A tremendous number of mule deer also use this highway, so caution should be observed from dusk to dawn.

Fishing regulations for the Yampa River from the Elk River to Catamount

Photo Courtesy of Kevin Rummell

Mountain Lake in upper Colorado River Drainage

Dam is a 2-trout limit. From Catamount Lake to Stagecoach Dam fishing is by artificial flies and lures only with a two-trout limit.

UPPER YAMPA RIVER

The upper Yampa is accessed from the town of Yampa on Hwy 131. From this point the river is called the Bear River, a name old-timers still call the entire river. County Road 7 parallels the stream all the way to Stillwater Reservoir.

Stillwater Reservoir (9,700 ft; 165 ac when full) is almost surrounded by the Flat Tops Wilderness. It is 18 miles southwest of Yampa, and is rated good for brook and cutthroat from 10 to 12 inches. It is heavily fished. There is a USFS campground and boat ramp at the reservoir; only electric motors al-

lowed on boats. The area is a jumping-off point for trips into the wilderness.

A 1.5-mile trail north from Stillwater Reservoir leads to **Little Causeway Lake** (10,750 ft; 5 ac), which is rated fair for brook and cutthroat averaging 10 inches. It sometimes winterkills. USFS trail 1119 continues beyond the lake over the Devils Causeway ridge to the headwater lakes of the Williams Fork River drainage.

Just below Stillwater Reservoir and Little Causeway Lake, **Smith Creek** feeds into the Bear River from the north. At Smith Creek headwaters, **Smith Lake** (10,355 ft; 11 ac) is rated very good fly-fishing for small cutthroat and brook to 16 inches.

Down the Bear River from Stillwater Reservoir about 2.5 miles is **Upper Stillwater Reservoir** (9,700 ft; 47 ac), which sometimes is referred to as the **Yampa Reservoir**. It is called the "upper" even though it is the lower of the two reservoirs. It is rated fair fishing for rainbow averaging 9 inches, a few brook and cutthroat and a large population of whitefish to 14 inches. Bear Lake campground is located there.

At the Yampa headwaters are more reservoirs and several lakes. Two marked trails, 1122 and 1120, leave from the dike at Stillwater Reservoir. These trails lead to numerous lakes, as well as, to lakes at the headwaters of the North Fork of Derby Creek on the Colorado River. Other Yampa headwaters' lakes include **Mosquito Lake** (10,600 ft; 13 ac), which is fair for brook to 13 inches. **Skillet Lake** (10,700 ft; 7 ac) lies to the north of Mosquito about 0.5-mile, and is rated fair for brook from 10 to 12 inches. **Little Skillet Lake** (10,800 ft; 2 ac) lies 0.5 mile west of Skillet. No trail; rough terrain. Little Skillet is deep and rated good for brook to 12 inches. **Rainbow Lake** (10,800 ft; 2 ac) is a small pond nestled against a ridge. Good for rainbow to 14 inches.

Mandall Creek feeds into the Yampa Reservoir from the north. At its headwaters are seven **Mandall Lakes,** not all lakes have fish. Trail 1121 leads 3 to 4 miles to the lakes. At the highest reaches, **Black Mandall Lake** (10,830 ft; 6 ac) is good for rainbow to 16 inches and some mackinaw. Southwest of Black, **Slide Mandall** (10,659 ft; 9 ac) has cutthroat to 12 inches. Below Slide, **Upper** and **Lower Twin Mandall Lakes** (Upper 10,553 ft; 5 ac, Lower 10,550 ft; 7 ac) have brook, and fishing is rated fair. **Beaver** (10,540 ft; 4 ac) and **Mud Mandall** (10,555 ft; 8 ac) lakes are rated fair for brook.

Yamcolo Reservoir (9,593 ft; 155 ac), just downstream from Upper Stillwater Reservoir was completed in the fall of 1980. It offers fishing for whitefish, rainbow and a few brook and brown. The Yampa below the Yamcolo is about 15 to 20 feet wide. The Yampa Valley Flyfishers Club and the Forest Service have completed stream improvement work in this section. Good fishing for trout averaging 9 inches with some larger browns.

Just below the Yamcolo, **Rams Horn Lake** (9,700 ft; 4 ac) can be reached over a rough road of less than a mile from the Bear River Road. Rainbow fishing can be good. Ice fishing is good for brook trout.

Below Rams Horn, **Gardner Park Reservoir** (9,630 ft; 65 ac) is also accessible by a good road, USFS 910. It winterkills, but plenty of feed promotes fast fish growth for fish stocked each summer.

Several county roads, USFS roads and a major highway provide good access to the river and many of its tributaries. At the town of Yampa, **Phillips Creek** joins the river. It is a small stream flowing mostly through private property; permission required to fish. Fair for 10- to 11-inch rainbow and brown with some large brown taken.

North of the town of Yampa, **Watson Creek** enters the Yampa River from the southwest. It is 10 to 20 feet wide, but irrigation draws leave it muddy and dry; consequently, there's not much fishing. But at the Watson Creek headwaters, **Heart Lake** (9,900 ft; 24 ac) offers challenging fishing for trophy size rainbow. On its northeast shore is Heart Lake Campground. This 18-foot-deep lake has plenty of food, so trout thrive. There are some big fish here. The trick is to get them. Take USFS trail 1110 from the end of CR 11 past McChivis Reservoir. **McChivis, Bull Park**, and **Burnt Mesa Reservoir** do not offer any fishing opportunities.

A southern tributary of Watson is **Moody Creek**, and at its headwaters is **Blue Lake**. Neither Moody nor Blue has fish.

HUNT CREEK

Downstream of the Watson confluence and north of the town of Yampa about 5 miles, **Hunt Creek** enters the Yampa River from the southwest. Hunt has three forks that are all rated good, but they are tightly posted. The road from Phippsburg on Hwy 131 reaches the forks, and secondary roads to the west follow **North** and **Middle Hunt Creek Forks**. At the headwaters of North Hunt Creek, **Crosho Lake** (8,900 ft; 50 ac) offers good ice fishing; campsites below the lake. Grayling are restricted to 2 fish 16 inches or longer. Fishing is mostly for cutthroat, however. The land behind the locked gate and over the cattle guard is private posted land.

About 200 yards west of the gate, a trail leads 0.75 mile to **Allen Basin Reservoir** (8,700 ft; 87 ac), which lies on the Middle Hunt Creek. It is a fluctuating irrigation reservoir, rated very good for cutthroat, brook and rainbow averaging 13 inches; good fly water.

This doesn't look like much of a fishery, but it could be the best accessible fishing in the drainage. The walk up is easy.

Near the headwaters of South Hunt Creek via FR 940 (4wd), **Chatfield Reservoir** (10,500 ft; 12 ac) pools below a towering cliff. It occasionally winterkills, but has a few cutthroat to 14 inches. It is three miles south of Chapman Reservoir.

CHAPMAN RESERVOIR

Oak Creek enters the Yampa from the southwest 19 miles north of the town of Oak Creek. This small stream, 10 to 15 feet wide, has a plethora of ponds. It is rated fair for small cutthroat, rainbow and brook. About 14 miles southwest of the mining town of Oak Creek, at the headwaters of Trout Creek are **Sheriff Reservoir** (9,700 ft; 25 ac), which is rated fair to good for brown trout to 10 inches; **Oak Lake** (10,100 ft; 3 ac), which is also good for rainbow and cutthroat to 14 inches; and **Chapman Reservoir** (9,100 ft; 25 ac), which can be reached by rough road, FH 16 off of Hwy 131. Chapman is heavily fished, but rated good for rainbow to 12 inches; best for larger fish in the early spring and especially late fall. Boats are allowed on Chapman, but not available for rent; only electric motors are allowed. All of these headwater lakes are located in the Routt National Forest just outside the Flat Tops Wilderness Area.

North of Phippsburg, the Yampa River angles northeasterly. Yellow Jacket Pass Road (CR 14) from the east intersects Hwy 131 about 2 miles north

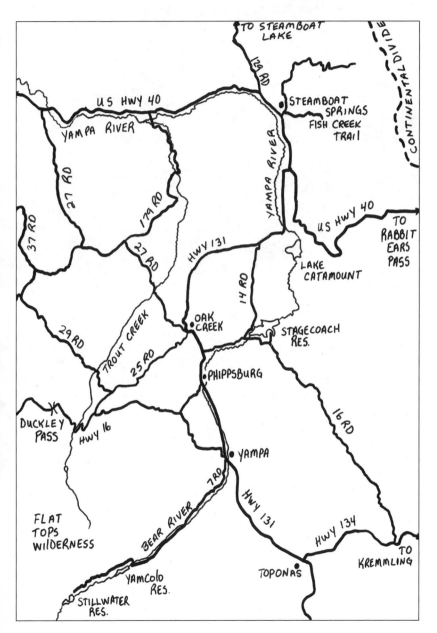

YAMPA RIVER SOUTH

Rainy day fishing near Yampa

of Phippsburg and runs alongside the river, eventually rejoining Hwy 131 south of Steamboat Springs. About 5.5 miles east on Yellow Jacket Pass Road, **Little Morrison Creek** enters the Yampa from the south. Small and brushy, it is rated good for brook to 10 inches in the early spring and poor to fair for the rest of the year. Access is on a good road, USFS road 270, to the southeast up the creek for 18 miles or so to Lynx Pass and Lynx Pass Campground.

About a mile east of Yellow Jacket Pass Road, a rough road turns north off the Lynx Pass Road to provide access to Service Creek. **Lynx Pass Lake** (8,940 ft; 2 ac) is stocked with 10-inch rainbow trout.

Seven miles east of Oak Creek is the 1989-completed **Stagecoach Reser-**

voir (7,200 ft; 775 ac) and **Stagecoach State Recreation Area**. It has 100 campsites, a concrete boat ramp and a small marina. Stagecoach Reservoir offers very accessible inlets and coves for the bank fisherman or float tuber. Rainbows and Snake River cutthroats, average 12 to 14 inches with many in the 16- to 20-inch class. From Stagecoach dam downstream .6 miles fishing is catch and release. Evening midge hatches in summer make for good fly-fishing. Northern Pike have also reached large sizes. Good fishing for brook, kokanee, and white fish. Trolling also produces good results.

The Yampa River from Stagecoach Dam to Catamount Lake inlet is restricted to artificial flies and lures only. From Walton Creek downstream 4.8 miles to the James Brown bridge in

Steamboat Springs is restricted to artificial flies and lures only, catch and release.

Service Creek flows into the Yampa about three miles downstream from Little Morrison Creek near Blacktail Mountain. Service is rated excellent for small brook in the upper stretches in Routt National Forest. It is about 15 feet wide and has some beaver ponds. The lower portion is heavily fished. USFS Trail 1105 follows the creek for 15 miles. Upper part is easily fished; lower part features good, fast water.

Green Creek enters the Yampa River south of US 40 and north of Service Creek. Its lower portions are too fast for fish, though a few ponds harbor trout. The upper stretches are excellent for small brook. Green Creek is about 15 feet wide.

Harrison Creek enters the Yampa about 2 miles downstream of Green Creek. Its lower parts are swift, too fast to fish. The creek is rated fair to good for small brook with some cutthroat in the upper stretches. Best fishing is late season. Access to Harrison and Green creeks is easiest from the big bend of US 40, six miles west of the summit of Rabbit Ears Pass at the Harrison Creek Campground.

Lake Catamount is a private reservoir at the foot of Rabbit Ears Pass, which offers fishing for large stocked rainbows.

Walton Creek enters the Yampa River from the east two miles south of Steamboat Springs. Its upper tributary is **Fishhook Creek.** The upper reaches, northwest of the Rabbit Ears Pass summit, are accessible by a rough 4WD road, USFS 313. Drive north to Dumont Lakes; follow the road north from there. The last mile or two must be hiked. Walton Creek averages 15 feet to 30 feet wide, meandering through many meadows. Its midsection cuts through a rough canyon. Walton has many small forks, and its tributaries are all rated good for small brook in the upper parts and rainbow and brook in the lower reaches. The lower reaches are on private land; request permission to fish.

At the headwaters of Fishhook Creek is **Lake Elmo** (10,000 ft; 14 ac). It is good for 8- to 12-inch brook, with some weighing 2 pounds. Other headwater lakes include **Fishhook Lake** (9,900 ft; 16 ac) and **Lost Lake** (9,900 ft; 20 ac). Both are good for brook to 11 inches. Fishhook is shallow (5 feet deep), and may experience winterkill.

Fish Creek feeds into the Yampa from the south, just downstream of Walton Creek and a mile south of Steamboat Springs. A road east at the eastern edge of Steamboat Springs, USFS 320, is marked "Fish Creek Falls." Fish Creek is easily fished, good for small brook above falls, but is usually poor in the lower stretches due to low water. The creek forks just above Fish Creek Falls Picnic Ground. Trail 1102 follows the south fork, the main creek, for 7 miles to **Long Lake** (9,900 ft; 40 ac), which can be good to excellent for small brook. Long Lake is restricted to hand-propelled and electric motor-powered boats.

Fish Creek Reservoir (9,900 ft; 40 ac), on the **Middle Fork of Fish Creek**, is a fluctuating body of water owned by the city of Steamboat Springs. Drive north from Steamboat to the reservoir by the Buffalo Pass Road (USFS 60). Drive past Dry Lake Campground, about 7 miles, to Buffalo Pass. From the pass, take USFS road 310 past the Dinosaur Lake trailhead, about 6 miles south, to Granite Campground, located on the east side of the reservoir. Fish Creek Reservoir is stocked with brook trout. **Lake Dinosaur** (10,150 ft; 20 ac) is at the headwaters of the **North Fork of Fish Creek**, and is rated fair for 9-inch brook trout. The North Fork enters Fish Creek near Fish Creek Falls Campground. It is fast and rough to fish, but excellent for small brook. The same roads taken to Fish Creek Reservoir reach the North Fork's upper reaches and Dinosaur Lake. A map is recommended for even short cross-country hikes in this area.

Spring Creek and **Butcherknife Creek** enter the Yampa River at the town of Steamboat Springs. They are both very small, deep streams producing small rainbow and brook.

Soda Creek enters the Yampa at the north edge of Steamboat Springs. Its headwaters are north of Buffalo Pass on the Park Range about 2.5 miles. Access to the headwaters is by taking the USFS trail 1101 north from Buffalo Pass. The North Fork has small cutthroat, the South Fork has small brook. Both are rated good. The main creek averages 20 feet wide and has several ponds.

ELK RIVER

Almost 6 miles downstream from Steamboat Springs the Yampa's largest tributary enters the main stream. The Elk River drains the northwest side of the Mount Zirkel Wilderness Area, and tends to offer the best fishing after August. The river varies from 50 feet to 100 feet wide. It has unusually slippery footing, and sports a great range of water from fast and turbulent to deep and quiet. The upper Elk offers about 12 miles of public access in its headwaters in the national forest, and is rated good for 10-inch rainbow, a few brook and cutthroat. The lower river is also good for whitefish averaging 11 inches. Some large brown and rainbow are taken early in the season. The best fishing on the Elk probably is in the vicinity of Hinman Campground, 5 miles east of Glen Eden, and upstream for 4.5 miles to Seedhouse Campground along USFS road 400. The river is mossy in the late season. From the forest boundary to its confluence with the Yampa, the Elk flows mostly through private land. A Division of Wildlife lease, the Christina State Wildlife Area, provides almost 2 miles of access to the lower Elk. County Road 129 parallels the Elk River to Glen Eden about 18 miles north of Steamboat. Take USFS road 400 east for access to the Elk's headwaters.

The **North Fork of the Elk River** enters the Elk at Seedhouse Campground. About 30 feet wide, it is a partially brushy stream that flows through mountain parks and small canyons. The lower part is rated fair to good, and the upper is excellent for 8-inch brook and rainbow. Late season fishing is best. Access is by turning north at Seedhouse

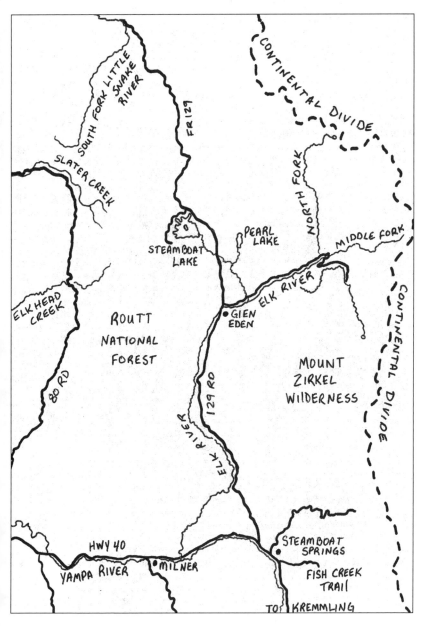

YAMPA RIVER NORTH

Campground on USFS 431 that parallels the stream to the Mount Zirkel Wilderness boundary. Tributaries of the North Fork include **English, Lost Dog** and **Trail creeks**. All are small with some beaver ponds. They can also be accessed by USFS road 433 just to the northeast of Seedhouse Campground. Trail Creek is rated best.

At the headwaters of Trail Creek, **Sanchez Creek** flows west from **Sanchez Lakes** (10,500 ft; 4 ac total) in the Mount Zirkel Wilderness. The two Sanchez lakes are about 0.25 mile apart, and are reached by driving north along the North Fork to Diamond Park at the wilderness boundary. From there, hike north on a trail about 3.5 miles along the Continental Divide. The lakes lie just under the west side of the Continental Divide. The upper lake is good for 12-inch cutthroat, while the lower lake has cutthroat and rainbow averaging 9 inches.

The **South Fork of Elk River** enters the Elk about 0.25-mile southeast of Hinman Campground. Several tributaries feed the South Fork. At its headwaters, to the southeast, there are several small lakes in the wilderness area about 5 miles southeast of Box Canyon Campground. Take USFS trail 1169. **Ptarmigan Lake** (10,700 ft; 5 ac) is rated fair for small cutthroat. In the same locale, **Dome Lake** (10,080 ft; 17 ac) is 12 feet deep and rated fair for cutthroat to 11 inches. Due to good growing conditions, it has some large fish; occasionally 5- to 10-pound fish are taken. **Wolverine Creek** flows into the South Fork from **Wolverine Basin** and **Wolverine Lake** (10,240 ft; 7.3 ac). This 25-foot-deep lake is rated good for 12-inch Colorado River cutthroat.

Southeast of Wolverine, **Pristine Lake** (11,040 ft; 9.7 ac) is rated good for small brook. This is a self-sustaining lake and is not stocked. Northernmost of this group of lakes is **North Lake** (10,300 ft; 6 ac), rated excellent for small brook. Access to these headwater lakes is by driving east from Box Canyon Campground about 3 miles to trailhead; signs specify main trails.

Three Island Creek feeds from the east into the South Fork near Box Canyon Campground. At its headwaters three miles upstream, **Three Island Lake** (10,000 ft; 35 ac) is rated excellent for 9-inch brook. Fish the east side of the lake, where it is wadable. The creek below the lake is good for small brook. Follow trail USFS 1163, southeast for two miles from Three Island Lake to reach **Beaver Lake** (10,400 ft; 6 ac). It is good for 12-inch brook.

Burn Creek enters the South Fork from the southeast about 2 miles from the South Fork's confluence with Elk River. Burn is a small, brushy stream rated good for small cutthroat and brook.

Hinman Creek enters the Elk River from the north about 2 miles downstream from the South Fork at Hinman Campground. It has several tributaries, including **Scott Run**. Hinman and its tributaries are small and brushy; rated good for small cutthroat and brook. **Himan Lake** is barren.

The largest tributary of the Elk River, **Willow Creek**, is also the best fishing tributary. Draining Steamboat Lake, it is 25 feet to 30 feet wide with many ponds. Willow is a good early season and summer stream. It is rated good for 9-inch rainbow, brook and cutthroat. Access is via CR 129 north out of Glen Eden.

Several streams flow into Steamboat Lake, including **Floyd, Mill, Dutch** and **Larson creeks**. These streams are rated poor and offer no fishing, except for Mill, which is rated good for rainbow to 8 inches.

Pearl Lake (8,000 ft; 190 ac) is 3 miles east of Steamboat Lake. The access road is well marked to this state park. The 80-foot-deep reservoir has plenty of feed, and has a good population of fat cutthroat. Sometimes it is difficult to entice the fish because the food supply is so ample in the reservoir. Cutthroat from Pearl weigh from 1.5 pounds to 6 pounds, with a few large rainbow and 13-inch brook taken. Fishing by artificial lures or flies only, with the bag limit of two fish 18 inches or longer.

Farther south below Glen Eden, **Big Creek** enters the Elk River from the north and east, about 9 miles north of Steamboat Springs along CR 129. The lower end of Big Creek is mostly posted, but the upper 6 miles are on public land with the exception of a 1-mile stretch. Big Creek is rated good for small brook with a few cutthroat in the upper reaches.

STEAMBOAT LAKE STATE PARK

Steamboat Lake (8,000 ft; 1053 ac) is about 3 miles west of Pearl Lake. It is fed by several small streams that offer little fishing. Steamboat Lake is stocked with several strains of rainbow trout as well as Snake River cutthroat, and offers good sport the entire summer for 8- to 17-inch rainbow and 11- to 17-inch cutthroat. Both boat and shore angling have resulted in good fishing. Supplies and a 220-site campground are found at the northeast end of the lake at the village of Hahns Peak. Because it is a state park, a parks pass or daily fee, (also valid for Pearl Lake) is required. It is a popular boating and water skiing area. There is a marina.

Above Steamboat Lake is **Hahns Peak Lake** (8,200 ft; 38 ac), which was built by the Colorado Division of Wildlife. The lake has a brushy bottom and offers easy bank fishing; rated fair with flies. Hahns Peak is reached by USFS road 486, which leads to Hahns Peak Lake Campground, off of CR 129. Hahns Peak Lake is stocked with creel-size rainbow and small Snake River cutthroat. Fish show little growth. Motor-propelled boats and rafts are prohibited.

About 6 miles northwest of Steamboat Springs, **Mad Creek** enters the Elk River. It flows from the east out of the Mount Zirkel Wilderness Area. The lower 3 miles of the Mad are tightly posted. A road follows the Mad for about 2 miles, and from there USFS trail 1100 follows the stream along its North Fork into the wilderness area. Fishing is excellent for brook on both the **North Fork** and **South Fork of Mad Creek**. No trail along the South Fork. At the headwaters of both forks lie several lakes requiring 13 to 16 mile hikes. These lakes including **Big Creek**

Kevin near Steamboat

lakes (10,600 ft; 8 ac), **Lake of the Crags** (10,900 ft; 6 ac), **Luna Lake** (10,500 ft; 38 ac), **Lake Elbert** (10,800 ft; 19 ac), **Rosa Lake** (10,000 ft; 5 ac), **Mirror Lake** (10,000 ft; 12 ac), (10,000 ft; 10 ac), **Lake Margaret** (10,000 ft; 10 ac), **Snowstorm Lake** (10,000 ft; 10 ac) and **Fish Hawk Lake** (10,000 ft; 9 ac). Fishing regulations for Big Creek Lake (lower); limit for lake trout 1 fish, all lake trout between 22 and 34 inches in length must be returned to the water immediately.

These lakes are interconnected by trails, with the primary access by USFS trail 1168. Margaret and Edward lakes are good for small cutthroat. Luna Lake is good for small cutthroat also, and is perhaps the most scenic in the area. Big Lake is excellent for small cutthroat to 12 inches. Lake of the Crags often winterkills, Elbert Lake is good for small cutthroat. Fish Hawk Lake and Snowstorm Lake are good for small brook. And Rosa Lake is good for 12-inch brook and cutthroat.

West of Steamboat Springs about 10 miles along US 40, **Trout Creek** enters the Yampa from southwest of Milner. Its upper reaches stretch to Oak Creek and can be reached by a good-weather only road. All 18 miles of Trout Creek are fishable; the upper parts are best. Good fly water in the national forest area. The lower stretches have smaller volume and murky water with brushy banks. Trout Creek is rated fair for 8- to 12-inch rainbow, brook and a few brown. From the west, **Fish Creek** is the largest tributary of Trout Creek and is rated fair for small rainbow and cutthroat. Its headwaters can

be reached from Milner or Hayden by driving south on county roads. Good fishing north of the Yampa River ends about here.

Haley Reservoir (8,800 ft; 13 ac), at the headwaters of Trout Creek, is also accessible from the East Fork of the Williams River via 1109 and a 3-mile hike. It is stocked with small brook trout.

Elkhead Creek enters the Yampa a few miles east of the town of Craig and, along with the rest of the north-draining streams to the west, is silt-laden and spasmodic in flow. Elkhead Creek is a small 12-foot-wide stream that can be fished easily. A few rainbow and cutthroat inhabit its upper reaches; lower reaches are rated poor for cutthroat and brook. Elkhead enters the Yampa about 35 miles west of Steamboat Springs and 10 miles west of Hayden. Tributaries include **First, Armstrong, Knowles, Jokodowski, Stuckey, Circle, Torso** and **Hole-in-the-Wall creeks**. The tributaries are near the headwaters. Road access to the lower reaches is by turning northeast off US 40 about 9 miles west of Hayden, or 6 miles east of Craig.

Elkhead Reservoir (6,300 ft; 440 ac) is about 3.5 miles up Elkhead Reservoir Road. It is a turbid, non-fluctuating lake offering some fishing for fall-planted rainbows, a few catfish and a few northern pike. Some decent largemouth bass and smallmouth bass have been tempting anglers, some of whom have done well. Bass must be 15 inches in length or longer. Parks pass required.

The **North Fork of Elkhead Creek** is rated fair for cutthroat. Access to the headwaters in the Elkhead Mountains is by driving north out of Hayden. Road forks after 0.75 mile. Follow the right fork, CR 80, and continue 17 miles. This road continues for access to **Slate Creek** and other tributaries of the Little Snake River.

Fortification Creek is a small brushy stream that flows through Craig and into the Yampa from the north. It is rated fair to poor for small cutthroat. Hwy 13 and 789 follow the creek north from Craig. **Cottonwood Creek** and **Little Cottonwood Creek** enter Fortification about 15 miles north of Craig. Little Cottonwood has a few cutthroat. At the headwaters of Little Cottonwood, **Freeman Reservoir** (8,750 ft; 14 ac) is stocked with cutthroat and rainbows and sometimes offers good fishing for 10- to 12-inch fish. Fishing is prohibited within 50 yards of the inlet and upstream 0.25-mile from January 1 through July 31.

Little Bear Creek flows out of the Elkhead Mountains north of Craig and into **Ralph White Lake** (6,300 ft; 90 ac). Ralph White Lake is rated fair to good for rainbow to 12 inches. Stream has very little fishing.

South of Craig, **Axial Basin Reservoir** (6,250 ft; 24 ac) is stocked with 10-inch rainbow trout. In Craig, **Craig City Ponds** (6,200 ft; 5 ac) are also stocked with 10-inch rainbow trout.

WILLIAMS FORK RIVER

South of the Yampa, the west-flowing **Williams Fork River** originates from tributaries flowing northward out of the high country just north of the Flat Tops Wilderness. The best fishing is in the upper reaches of the East Fork of the Williams Fork, the South Fork of the Williams Fork and some of the smaller associated streams and lakes.

The river flows westward through Hamilton and then north to merge with the Yampa River about 10 miles southwest of Craig. The Williams Fork upstream from Hamilton is 20 feet to 30 feet wide and is good fishing for rainbow and cutthroat. Almost all but the uppermost reaches are on private or leased land.

The river is reached by driving north on the Poose Creek-Vaughn Lake Road from the White River, or south on Hwy 13 and 789 between Meeker and Craig. At Hamilton turn east for ready access to the river and its major tributaries. From Oak Creek, it is reached by going west over Dunckley Pass.

A mile south of Pagoda, the **East Fork** and the **South Fork** converge to form the Williams Fork River. Good roads go up each fork. The south road (CR 67) follows the South Fork of the Williams Fork about 10 miles through private land to where a lower quality road goes off to the southeast following the mainstream. After a mile, the road forks again. Take the west fork, still following the stream, about 2 miles into the national forest. Trails then provide access to small streams with cutthroat, brook and rainbow. Fishing is usually good.

South Fork tributaries include **Beaver**, **Indian Run** and **Pine creeks**. The tributaries and South Fork are brushy, small, often with fast water, and with some ponds. Fish mostly are small, but some make it to 10 inches. Best fishing is early spring; poor thereafter.

The **East Fork of the Williams Fork** is over a steep wall northwest of Stillwater Reservoir, and flows northwesterly out of the Flat Tops Wilderness. There are several deep lakes that offer good fishing for brook, rainbow and cutthroat.

The East Fork is about 24 miles east up the Williams Fork from Hamilton. It is 13 more miles on a good road to Pyramid Ranger Station and public fishing in Routt National Forest. The lakes are another 7 miles to 10 miles by trail to the south and are, perhaps, more readily reached from the White River access near Trappers Lake. From Pyramid Ranger Station, hike up the stream for fair fishing for 9- to 12-inch brook, cutthroat and rainbow. Marked trail leads to the headwater lakes. Lakes include **West Lost Lakes** (8,500 ft; 17 and 20 ac), the five **East Lost Lakes** (8,700 ft; 7 ac), **Round Lake** (8,100 ft; 7 ac) and **Causeway Lake** (9,000 ft; 20 ac). West Lost Lake is the closest and best fishing. A good but steep trail leads to the lakes; it forks just before West and East lakes. East Fork trail leads 3 miles to Round Lake. Causeway Lake is one mile farther. The trails, numbers 1116 and 1119, make a loop to hit all lakes. West Lake has brook and cutthroat, East Lake has rainbow, and all are stocked with cutthroat.

Dunckley-Dubeau Reservoir (8,950 ft; 3 ac), **Shaffer Reservoir** (8,830 ft; 5 ac), and **Sellers-Cromwell Reservoir** (9,025ft; 6 ac) south of the town of Dunckley, are accessed from CR 29 by USFS trail 1111. The reservoirs are stocked with small brook trout. **Gill Reservoir** (9,035 ft; 8 ac) may be accessed by continuing south

Lake at first morning light

Photo Courtesy of Kevin Rummell

on USFS trail 1111 from Dunckley Reservoir. It may also be reached by taking USFS trail 1111 north from CR 19, which parallels the East Fork of Williams. Gill Reservoir is 8 acres and is stocked with brook trout.

Poose Creek enters the East Fork of Williams downstream about 6 miles from Pyramid Ranger Station on the Vaughn Lake Road. Poose is a small, brushy and fast stream, and is rated good for small cutthroat and rainbow. Restricted to artificial flies and lures only, all cutthroat must be returned to the water immediately. A road to its headwaters and to **Vaughn Lake** (9,500 ft; 36 ac) parallels Poose creek. Vaughn Lake is stocked with creel-size rainbow and cutthroat. The limit on cutthroat is 2 fish.

LITTLE SNAKE RIVER

About 23 miles east of Maybell, US 40 crosses the Yampa as the stream and highway wind through high, arid land. About 15 miles west, the **Little Snake River** joins the Yampa from the north in very eroded, desolate country favored by antelope and sage grouse.

This long river reaches into Wyoming, and its tributaries spread back into Colorado in the Routt National Forest. Its upper reaches in Colorado are accessible by Hwy 13 north from Craig, or a secondary road (CR 129) northeast of Steamboat Springs. The Little Snake varies from 50 feet to 100 feet wide with many types of water. It offers marginal fishing due to tremendous fluctuations from irrigation draws. As the water returns from irrigation use, it is warm and murky,

hardly a suitable home for trout. There are several tributaries of the Little Snake, including **Slater, Willow, and Fourmile creeks** and the **South** and **Middle Forks**. Slater is stocked with creel-size rainbow, but offers only poor to fair fishing. The lucky angler might find a brook in the Middle or South Forks. Little fishing is to be found in Fourmile Creek. Tributaries of the Middle Fork are **King Solomon, Box, Summit, Smith, Independence, Little Red Park, Silver City** and **Whiskey** creeks. All of these tributaries are rated good for 7- to 9-inch brook and cutthroat, especially in the upper reaches. County Road 129 north from Steamboat Springs crosses several of these creeks.

LOWER YAMPA RIVER

East of Craig the **Yampa River** runs wide with deep holes, some fast water does exist. The river through this stretch is home to large northern pike, which were accidentally released into the river several years ago. The pike have made themselves quite at home here, feeding on the populations of smaller fish in the river. Whitefish through this section are large and well fed, some over two pounds. Public access is available at Double Bridges (one of eight State Park accesses on the river) 2 miles west of Hayden. Parks pass required.

West from Craig, the lower **Yampa River** is heavy, wide and somewhat turbulent, taking on the appearance of coffee with cream. Fishing is spotty, but there are plenty of whitefish and catfish. An occasional squawfish, a pro-

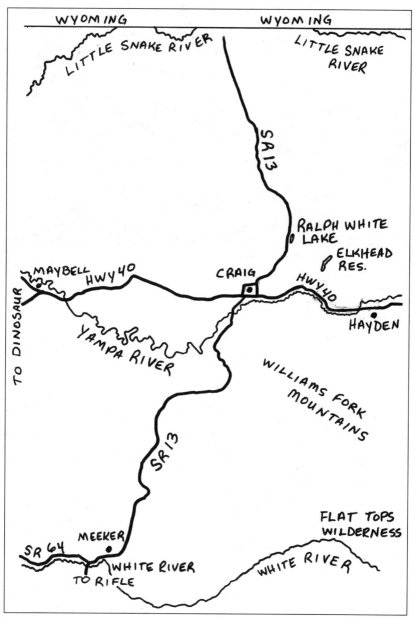

CRAIG

Photo Courtesy of Kevin Rummell

A beautiful valley near Steamboat

tected species, may be landed. Some scrappy 15-pound northern pike have been caught in the backwaters and ox-bows of the Yampa both east and west of Craig. Late evening fishing is best.

The remaining 7 State Park accesses are located west of Craig. The Yampa is popular floaters' stream, especially west of Craig. The Cross Mountain stretch northwest of Maybell and US 40 is perilous, and access is limited. Local inquiry is recommended. South Beach, Duffy Mountain, Juniper Canyon, and Maybell Bridge are all located west of Craig. Limited foot access at Juniper Canyon and Maybell Bridge. West of Maybell is Sunbeam and East Cross Mountain accesses. Park Pass is required at all locations.

West of the Little Snake River confluence, the Yampa River flows into **Dinosaur National Monument**,

which is named for remarkable deposits of fossil bones. The petrified remains of crocodiles, turtles and 14 species of dinosaurs have been excavated from the 140-million-year-old Morrison Formation.

Access to the Yampa as it enters the monument is by driving northwest 11 miles from US 40 about 15 miles west of Maybell. From the point that the Yampa enters the Monument, it wanders about 40 miles west before meeting the Green River. This stretch of the Yampa is home to channel catfish and northern pike as well as a few Colorado protected species. Fishing is marginal until reaching the confluence of the Green and Yampa, where the fishing is good for catfish. The Yampa is dotted with campgrounds on its banks as it winds through the rough and dry canyon. It is a floater's favorite.

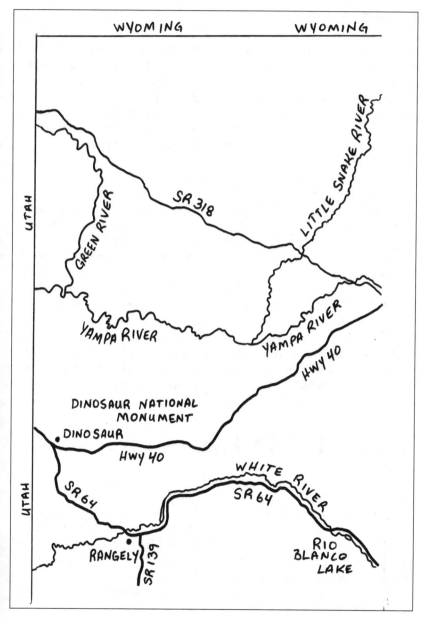

DINOSAUR

GREEN RIVER

The favored fishing in this area is in **Jones Hole Creek** just over the Colorado-Utah state line and requires a Utah fishing license. It can be worth the price. It enters the Green below the Yampa-Green confluence in Utah from the east. Its headwaters run along the state line. This stream is a favorite of anglers who lay claim to catching 15-inch brown and rainbow on a regular basis. Access is limited to hiking. Inquire at Jensen, Utah, on US 40.

The **Green River** is much clearer, cooler and faster than the Yampa. The Flaming Gorge Reservoir Dam in Wyoming and the northeast corner of Utah determine its flow. The river has healthy populations of 13- to 17-inch rainbow and 20-inch cutthroat. The Browns Park National Wildlife Refuge is very good in the early season. Campsites are available at Swinging Bridge and Crook campgrounds. Browns Park is accessible via Hwy 318, which forks from US 40 at Maybell.

From Hwy 318, via USFS road 10N, you can access **Talamantes Creek**. Stocked with brook trout.

After passing through the refuge, the Green enters the Dinosaur National Monument. It immediately cuts through the famous Gates of Lodore, where the river canyon walls become nearly vertical, and there is no landing. A permit is required to float the canyon. Inside the Monument, the Green can be reached only by boat. This stretch of the river has trout, but it is mainly used by whitewater boaters.

Midway through the monument, the muddy Yampa joins with the clearer Green River. The Green River enters Colorado from the extreme northwest corner of the state and flows south to meet the Yampa at Echo Park. Reach Echo Park by turning north at the Dinosaur National Monument Headquarters on US 40 about 5 miles east of the Utah state line. Where the Yampa meets the Green at Echo Park, the two rivers merge and become the Green River as it flows back into Utah.

WHITE RIVER

The **White River** has its origin in one of the best trout fisheries in Colorado—Trappers Lake on the edge of the Flat Tops Wilderness. The Flat Tops Wilderness is a 196,000-acre "high island" between Steamboat Springs and Glenwood Springs, which produces some of the best fishing in Colorado. Because it is classified as a wilderness area, the Flat Tops are only accessible by horseback or foot. Many of its most productive waters, therefore, are difficult to reach. There are numerous lakes, beaver ponds and streams in the wilderness. Many waters offer superb fishing for cutthroat, rainbow and brook trout, particularly in late summer and early fall. A maze of pathways, soggy bogs, timbered ridges, hidden ponds and brushy marshes indicates that

"Flat" is a bit of a misnomer. During normal years the Flat Tops receives huge amounts of snow and early-season visitors will find snow banks surrounding most lakes. Melting snow creates a tremendous amount of standing water, which accounts for the huge number of mosquitoes and other insects. The rainbow, cutthroat, brook and mackinaw trout in these streams and lakes, despite a rather short growing season, make the most of a rich diet of insects growing very large and healthy.

From the high country of the Flat Tops, the White River flows west toward Meeker, passing through valley pastureland. Whitefish are the predominant fish from Meeker downstream; rainbow and cutthroat are stocked near Meeker. The rivers overall fishing quality declines rapidly west of the junction of Hwy 13 and 64 south of Meeker. As it passes Rangely and enters Utah, the river becomes silt-laden and slow moving.

The **Piceance Creek** Basin, a major tributary to the White River, lies west of Rio Blanco. Paralleled by Hwy 13 for most of its length, the creek and Piceance State Wildlife area offers little fishing opportunities in this low, dry country.

RIO BLANCO LAKE

Downstream from Meeker in the White River, fishing is generally poor. About 20 miles west of town, and above the junction with Piceance Creek and Hwy 64, is **Rio Blanco Lake** (120 ac) and State Wildlife Area. It has rainbow stocked in the spring, and large

and smallmouth bass, crappie, perch, northern pike, channel catfish and bullheads. Fishing is generally slow, but some good bass to 4 pounds are reported along the dike. All largemouth and smallmouth bass under 15 inches must be immediately returned to the water.

Located in the Douglas Creek valley south of Rangely, **Canon Pintado** (painted canyon) is listed on the National Register of Historic Places. It is an outstanding example of rock art created by the Fremont people between 600 and 1300 AD. Reached by Hwy 139.

Meeker Pasture State Wildlife Area, a small easement 3 miles east of Meeker, provides fishing on the White River for rainbow, brown, brook, cutthroat, and white fish.

Upstream from Meeker to Buford, most of the **White River** is on private land - often pasture with cattle. A scenic area, permission to fish is required. The river is clear and is rated good for rainbow, brook, some cutthroat and whitefish. Whitefish run to 18 inches through this stretch, especially in deep holes and riffles.

Miller Creek is reached from CR 57 which turns into USFS road 215, 11 miles southeast of Meeker on road to the south off highway. Posted water from turnoff to forest boundary. Road forks after 4 miles. Right fork continues 2 miles, the one to the left for 1 mile. Both the **East Fork** and **Middle Fork** are fair for small rainbow, brook and cutthroat. The creeks are about 6 feet wide, fast and a little brushy. There are a few ponds about halfway up.

Good in early season using both bait and flies. Very clear water after July 1. Access to the upper reaches of East, Middle and West forks is possible in dry weather with 4WD.

North Elk Creek, about 10 feet wide, offers about 8 miles of fair to good fishing for 8- to 12-inch cutthroat and brook; a few larger cutthroat are possible. Access is via CR 59 out Of Buford with the best fishing 5 miles up from the White River. Creek has some ponds. Lower end private and posted. **Giley Lake** (8,305 ft; 8 ac) at the headwaters of North Elk creek, is also easiest reached from Buford on CR 59. Short half-mile hike for good brookie fishing on USFS 1833. **Shadow, Beaver, and Seventh** lakes are private.

Sleepy Cat Ponds State Wildlife Area (3 ac), is 1 mile downstream of Elk Creek Ranch between Meeker and Buford, stocked with brown, brook, and white fish. This area is closed from December 1 to July 15.

Lake Avery (6,985 ft; 264 ac), in the Oak Ridge State Wildlife Area, is also known as **Big Beaver Reservoir**. Rated good for 10- to 15-inch rainbow with some taken to 5 pounds. Some bank fishing, but trolling from boat gives best results. Boat ramp, campground, tables and dumping station are available, but no drinking water. Excellent fishing from the time the ice goes out until mid-June. Summer weed growth hampers bank fishing. Lake Avery is just north of the confluence of the North Fork of the White River and the South Fork, a mile below Buford. Good road (CR 82) to the north leads to lake, which is hidden from the highway by hills.

Above Buford, **Ute Creek** flows out of the wilderness meeting the North Fork of the White River about a mile west of Marvine Creek. A trail (USFS 1824) from the North Fork road (CR 8) leads up the stream to its headwaters. Ute is a small, brushy stream with a few small headwater ponds and is fair fishing for brook and cutthroat.

Fawn Creek, which enters the White River from the north, is artificial flies and lures only, all fish must be returned to the water immediately. Access is via FR 236.

MARVINE CREEKS

Marvine Creek enters the North Fork of the White River from the southeast at Sizemore Resort, 8 miles above the town of Buford. Marked road follows creek for 5 miles to USFS campground. Fishing is open to the public for 0.25 mile after crossing the first bridge; then it is private land to campground where stream forks. Stocked with rainbow to 8 inches. **West Fork of Marvine Creek** is 5 to 6 feet wide, brushy and meandering. This water and setting is as beautiful as an angler could ask for. Fair for brook and cutthroat. One of the best and easiest trails in the region follows the **Middle Fork of Marvine Creek**, which is about 10 feet wide and rated fair to good for 10-inch brook and cutthroat.

Near its headwaters are the Marvine Lakes. **Upper Marvine Lake** (9,325 ft; 65 ac) to the east is good for brook and rainbow averaging 14 inches. **Lower Marvine Lake** (9,325 ft; 88 ac), 6 miles from the Marvine Campground on the wilderness boundary and less than a 0.25 mile from Upper Marvine, is rated excellent for brook and cutthroat averaging 10 to 14 inches, though many larger ones are taken. Three miles above the lakes is **Slide Lake** (8,640 ft; 5 ac), and 4 miles is **Pine Isle Lake** (9,230 ft; 7 ac). Both lakes offer fair fishing for rainbow and brook.

Northeast of Marvine is **East Marvine Creek**, stretching about 8 miles from the Marvine Campground. It is a very fast and brushy stream generally rated poor, though it can be good in early season. To get there, follow Marvine Creek Road (CR 12). East Marvine and Marvine campgrounds are at the end.

At East Marvine's headwaters are several lakes. **Mary Loch Lake** (9,800 ft; 3 ac) is surrounded by heavy timber with a steep ridge wrapping around it high above. It is a good fly-fishing lake for rainbow averaging 10 inches and cutthroat to 14 inches. Downstream about a mile, **Shallow Lake** (9,950 ft; 1 ac), which lies east of the stream, is rated fair for cutthroat and rainbow to 11 inches. Just northwest of Shallow is **Rainbow Lake** (9,950 ft; 10 ac), rated excellent for 10- to 12-inch rainbow and cutthroat. Also a few brook. **Guthrie Lake** (9,270 ft; 13 ac) is shallow and is rated good for 10-inch brook. About a mile northwest of Guthrie, **Johnson Lake** (9,000 ft; 9 ac) is a murky lake with difficult fishing for small rainbow. Occasionally larger fish are caught.

Lost Creek flows into the North Fork from the north a little more than 1 mile above Marvine Creek. **Hahn Creek** is located 2.5 miles up Lost Creek. Fishing by artificial flies and lures only. All cutthroat trout must be returned to the water immediately. Colorado River Cutthroat Recovery water.

Snell Creek enters the White River from the north, 5 miles above North Fork Campground. A steep trail leads up this small, fast creek. The first 1.5 miles are very brushy. Fishing is poor in lower part; rated fair in upper for small brook and cutthroat. Fishing by artificial flies and lures only. Cutthroat are catch and release only. **Pagoda Lake** (10,000 ft; 55 ac) is a shallow lake at the bottom of a pine-timbered mountain park. USFS trail 1810 leaves road just above Snell Creek; look for sign: "6 miles to lake". Lies about 0.75-mile southeast of the junction of Snell and Ripple Creek trails. An easier trail (USFS 1804) takes off from the summit of Ripple Creek Pass 4 miles above Ripple Creek Lodge. Trail is marked. It leaves west of the road opposite the sheep corrals. It's about 4 miles to lake. Pagoda is good for 10- to 14-inch brook and some cutthroat.

Ripple Creek, where CR 8 forks, 11 miles above Sizemore Resort, is small, fast and brushy. Poor for small rainbow and cutthroat, though over a mile of water is stocked periodically. A few hundred yards south of where the road forks, a trail (USFS 1821) heads west then swings south to **Mirror Creek**. At the headwaters of the 3-mile long stream is **Mirror Lake** (10,000 ft; 12 ac), a deep, beautiful crater lake rated excellent for small brook. Downstream

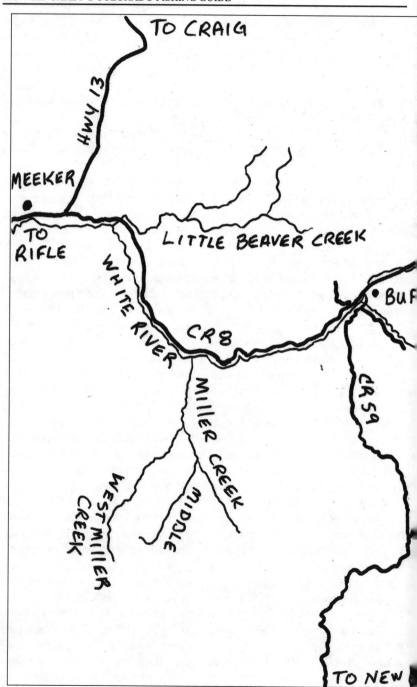

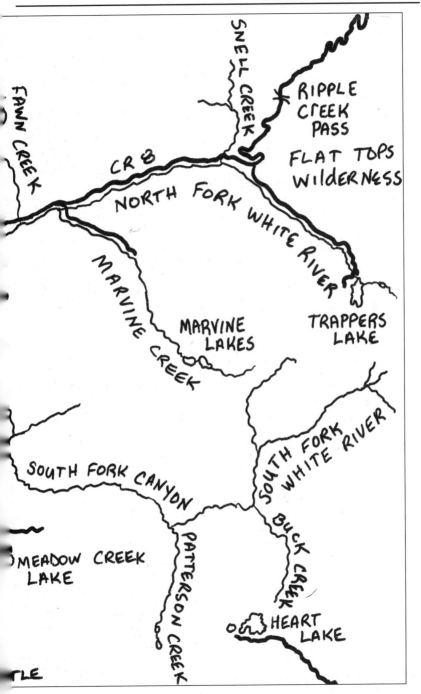

from Mirror Lake less than 0.5 mile, **Shamrock Lake** (9,900 ft; 2 ac) is a good fly fishing lake for fat brookies averaging 10 inches.

Sable Lake (9,882 ft; 7 ac), located south of the North Fork between Marvine Creek and Snell Creek, is stocked with small Colorado River Cutthroat. Reached by USFS trail 1820.

Big Fish Creek flows into the North Fork White River from the south at Himes Peak Campground. The creek is good fishing for 10- to 12-inch rainbow. **Boulder Creek**, a small tributary of Big Fish Creek, enters from the north. Some small cutthroat. At its headwaters is **Boulder Lake** (9,750 ft; 2 ac), that is rated good for 10- to 12-inch rainbow. From Himes Peak Campground take USFS trail 2262 from USFS trail 1819. **Doris Lake** (10,010 ft; 5 ac) is .5-miles south of Boulder Lake. Fair for small rainbow.

About 3 miles upstream from the Big Fish-North Fork confluence off USFS trail 1819, Big Fish Creek flows through **Big Fish Lake** (9,400 ft; 20 ac), rated fair for rainbow that average 10 inches, though lunkers to 8 pounds are occasionally taken. At the headwaters of Big Fish lies **Gwendolyn Lake** (9,750 ft; 2 ac), a deep lake with shallow areas. It is rated poor for 10- to 16-inch cutthroat. There is no trail, and the lake is difficult to find.

Above Big Fish Creek farther up USFS road 205, about 1 mile from Himes Peak Campground, is **Lake of the Woods** (9,000 ft; 10 ac), a small, shallow lake rated good for brook and cutthroat though heavily fished. There

is some rainbow, with reports of larger fish caught. Access is from the county road a mile upstream from Himes Peak Campground, where a sign indicates that it's a 0.25-mile hike to the lake.

Lynx Creek and **Skinny Fish Creek** enter the White River from the northeast, 0.5-mile and 2 miles, respectively, above Himes Peak Campground. They are fair for small cutthroat and rainbow. Skinny has small brook.

About 3 miles from the road, and just before crossing the last stream below Skinny Fish Lake, turn left and go up the hill. Follow along the creek for 0.75 mile to **Elk Lake** (10,125 ft; 4 ac). It is rated fair for 12-inch cutthroat. **McGinnis Lake** (9,500 ft; 10 ac), about 0.75 mile southeast of Skinny Fish Lake on the same trail (USFS 1813), is good for cutthroat and rainbow from 10 inches to 14 inches. The lakes are stocked with rainbow. **Skinny Fish Lakes** (lower 10,245 ft; 20 ac, upper 10,270 ft; 4 ac) are rated good for 12-inch rainbow, 13-inch cutthroat and a few small brook. Larger fish taken in lower lake.

TRAPPERS LAKE

Trappers Lake (9,627 ft; 200 ac) is one of Colorado's most picturesque lakes with actually good fishing. It is readily accessible by CR 132 east from Meeker 50 miles (through Buford) until the road dead-ends at the Trappers Lake, Shepherds Rim, Bucks and Trapline campgrounds.

Due to considerable fishing pressure, Trappers Lake has some restrictive regulations, including the use of artificial flies and lures only. Limit of 8 cut-

Nice fat Rainbow

throat, all fish longer than 10 inches must be returned to the water immediately. Fishing is prohibited in all inlets and upstream for 0.5 mile and within 100 feet of inlet and outlet streams and in the outlet and downstream to the first falls. There is no bag limit on brook trout.

Trappers is classified as Wild Trout water that produces cutthroat to 14 inches. There is a launching area for carry-in boats a short walk from the parking area. Rental boats are also available, but motors are not allowed.

East of Trappers Lake about a mile up a trail, **Little Trappers Lake** (9,941 ft; 30 ac) can be reached by an easy 1.5-mile trail. Follow **Little Trappers Creek**, which is moderately fast and brushy. Best fishing is in the upper part just below Little Trappers Lake. The shallow lake and stream are rated fair for 10- to 12-inch cutthroat and rainbow, with a few larger ones taken.

Fraser Creek, flanked by USFS trail 1816, is a tributary just south of Trapper's Lake. Fair for small cutthroat.

En route to Little Trappers Lake, **Coffin Lake** (9,700 ft; 10 ac) is on the north side of the stream about 0.5 mile east of Trappers Lake. Coffin Lake is full of natural feed and has cutthroat to 5 pounds. The average is about 16 inches.

Surprise Lake (11,200 ft; 9 ac) is about 2 miles southeast of Little Trappers Lake. Take trail southwesterly to top of the rim where the trail turns south. The lake lies in timber just below the rim. It is rated good for rainbow to 12 inches.

Due west of Trappers Lake is **Anderson Lake** (9,400 ft; 4 ac), which is rated poor for brook and occasional rainbow. It's a mile hike on a well-defined trail from Trapline Campground.

South of Trappers Lake, about 2

Nice Catch.

miles up the North Fork, is **Wall Lake** (10,980 ft; 12 ac), a very deep lake that is rated good for 14- to 16-inch cutthroat; many weighing up to 3 pounds are taken. A steep 5-mile trail from Trapline Campground accesses Wall Lake.

SOUTH FORK WHITE RIVER

The **South Fork of White River** is followed by a marked CR 10 that leaves the New Castle-Buford Road 1-mile southwest of Buford. The road follows the stream much of the way for 9 miles to South Fork Campground, a handicapped accessible USFS campground just before the wilderness area. There are 16 miles of good trail to the headwaters. The river is 20 feet to 30 feet wide, fast, and with many deep pools. Much of the stream flows through wide, deep canyons and is brushy much of the way to headwaters from the campground. Good to excellent for brook, cutthroat and rainbow to 14 inches and whitefish to 11 inches. The Colorado DOW stocks the Colorado River cutthroat. The upper end is very good for 1-pound cutthroat and rainbow. The South Fork Canyon also is accessible by trail from Deep Lake and Trappers Lake.

Moving up canyon, **Bailey Lake** (8,800 ft; 15 ac) is reached via USFS trail 1825 south from an old Buford schoolhouse that is now a community center. It is a steep 4 miles to lake, 0.5 mile more to **Swede Lake** (8,850 ft; 4 ac). Both are good for brook and rainbow to 12 inches. Connecting trail USFS 1826 leads to **Peltier Lake** (9,000 ft; 13 ac) about 8 miles up South Fork Road (CR 10). Good trail, but very steep. Lake is shallow with open shoreline. Rated good for brook, 10 inches to 12 inches, and best early and late season.

Entering the South Fork from the north, **Lost Solar Creek** is only 5 miles east of South Fork Campground. A trail follows Solar Creek to its headwaters. The creek has very few fish.

Patterson Creek enters the South Fork from the south about 8 miles east of the South Fork Campground. At its headwaters are the **Elk Lakes** (10,400 ft; about 5 ac each). Only one has fish, rated fair for 10- to 12-inch rainbow. Downstream, **Jet Lake** (10,450 ft; 7 ac) lies to the west of the creek. It is rated fair for 12-inch rainbow and brook. Reached from USFS 601 (4wd) or from Heart Lake by way of 640.

North of Jet and west of Patterson Creek are **Shadow Lake** (10,450 ft; 14 ac), which is deep and lightly fished, rated poor for small rainbow; **Blair Lake** (10,640 ft; 28 ac), fair for 12-inch rainbow, brook and cutthroat, and **Crater Lake** (11,146 ft; 30 ac), rated fair for brook with some mackinaw taken to 15 pounds. These lakes rest on the southwest boundary of the Flat Top Wilderness and can also be approached by a 4WD road from Buford via USFS road 244 and USFS road 601. The last mile or two must be hiked on USFS trail 2098, because it becomes wilderness.

LOWER COLORADO RIVER
GUNNISON RIVER

CRAIG

1.

GUNNISON

2.

DURANGO

1. LOWER COLORADO RIVER
2. GUNNISON RIVER

LOWER COLORADO RIVER

The lower Colorado River accumulates water from a wide variety of streams and high country lakes. Characteristics of its tributaries and the topography of their origins varies considerably, offering equally ample fishing opportunities. Fishing can range from idyllic alpine lakes to swift, deep runs holding brutish size trout on the mainstream of the Colorado River.

Interstate-70 provides primary access from Glenwood Springs downstream to the Colorado-Utah state line. At 5,756 feet Glenwood Springs is surrounded by some rather tall country. To the north the spectacular Flat Tops rise above 10,000 feet. Up the Roaring Fork River valley to the south, Mount Sopris rises to 12,953 feet. Glenwood Springs is well known for its hot springs. Ute Indian Chief Colorow was a frequent visitor to the hot sulphur-laden springs located along the north edge of town. The outside swimming pool and bathhouse were built in 1891 and still today remain a tourist attraction.

West of Glenwood Springs, the Colorado River flows past rouge-red cliffs on the south side of the river that give way to dry, irrigated pasture west of New Castle. On the north bank, fruit orchards characterize small acreages. Fishing in the river is surprisingly good; anglers should use the old road and US 6 on the south side to access the stream. The river has attractive, long riffles, some boulders and deep pools. Bait fishing or fishing with bait and lures, as well as with spoons and spinners, can pull in some good size brown, rainbow, round-tail chub, carp and mountain whitefish. The river is too deep to wade, but there are sandbars and shale-rock stretches that provide some variation to straight bank fishing.

Between New Castle and the town of Silt, the river stays relatively clear. Fishing for large trout can be fairly good in this stretch. Fishing is generally poor nearer to Silt except in some isolated stretches. Tributary streams are fair fishing at best, except several miles upstream toward the headwaters. Land ownership is a mixture of private and BLM, so it would be prudent to confirm ownership before walking onto questionable land.

As it enters the Grand Valley east of Grand Junction, the **Colorado River** is tapped severely for irrigation water. Fishing below Roller Dam at Palisade begins to improve in the 2 miles above the confluence with the Gunnison River; fishing is excellent for catfish averaging 1 to 2 pounds, with some as large as 6 pounds. There are also some rainbow, brown, carp, the threatened and endangered razorback sucker and the protected Colorado River squawfish. West to the Colorado-Utah state line there is more than 30 miles of river with fishing for the same species.

Corn Lake, (4,720 ft; 10 ac) part of Corn Lake State Wildlife Area, is reached by going south off exit 37 on I-70 and the town of Clifton to 141. Continue south watching for signs after crossing the river. Stocked with rainbow trout.

West of Grand Junction, Highline State Recreation Area offers fishing in **Highline** (4,700 ft; 174 ac) and **Mack Mesa Lake** (4,730 ft; 20 ac) for rainbow, bass, crappie, and catfish. All largemouth bass must be 15 inches or longer in both areas. There is a boat ramp, 25-site campground and plenty of welcome shade. This is a fee area. This true oasis is reached by taking Hwy 139 north from Loma for 6 miles.

PLATEAU CREEK

Plateau Creek is a major tributary feeding the Colorado from the south. It flows from the east and stretches 25 miles along the valley north of the Grand Mesa. Plateau Creek is 20 to 25 feet wide and is paralleled by the Plateau Valley Road (Hwy 330) for most of its distance. Plateau offers fair fishing for rainbow and brown trout 10 inches to 12 inches at a few public access sites below Vega Reservoir. Two miles west of Molina on 330 is Jerry Creek State Wildlife Area and **Jerry Creek Reservoir** (5,410 ft; 28 ac). The reservoir is 1.5-miles from marked parking lot. Fishing is for bass and bluegill. Artificial flies and lures only, all fish must be returned to the water immediately.

Silver Spruce Trail and High Trail provide access to the upper reaches of

the stream as it plunges off Grand Mesa. Fishing there is fair for small brook and a few rainbow. The road east from Collbran follows **Buzzard Creek**, which has small brook trout. Another road north and then northeast from Collbran leads for 6 miles to **Hawxhurst Creek**, which has small cutthroat.

Driving north out of Collbran on CR 58.60 to the end gets you to USFS trail 523. Hiking north to the junction with USFS trail 527 and heading northwest takes you to the five **Battlement Reservoirs** (9,840 ft; 1 to 14 ac). Ranging in size from 1 to 14 acres, they have been stocked with fingerling Colorado River Cutthroat, a threatened native species. The reservoirs can also be reached from the north by way of CR 338 and USFS road 847 from the town of Parachute.

In the town of Parachute, **Parachute Pond** (3 ac) offers fishing for stocked 10-inch rainbow.

A paved road (330 E) leaves the north end of Collbran and heads east up a hill. After 7 miles, the road forks; the right fork, (CR 64.60) leads to **Vega Reservoir** (8,100 ft; 900 ac), which is rated good for rainbow and Snake River cutthroat averaging 12 to 16 inches, with some to 3 pounds. Trolling and shore fishing both give good results. It is heavily fished and a popular family outing site.

GRAND MESA AREA

Grand Mesa is one of the largest and most scenic flat-top mountains in the West. Rising 5,000 feet above the Gunnison and Colorado rivers, its

34,200 acres encompass over 200 lakes and streams sprinkled throughout alpine meadows and pine forests. The fishing for rainbow, brook, brown and splake can be outstanding.

Portions of "The Mesa" near the roads are almost park-like with paths, horse trails, picnic areas, campgrounds, resorts and summer homes. As one gets into the denser forests of Engelmann and blue spruce, alpine and Douglas fir, aspen and ponderosa pine, amid bogs and brush and rocky ridges, the terrain becomes more primitive. Elk, deer, bear, more than 200 species of birds and many smaller creatures may be the angler's companions. But there is no companion as affectionate and prolific as the mosquito. Come well prepared.

Ancient volcanic action formed many of the Grand Mesa's features, and the big-game animals have adapted to them. Along the lower west end of the Mesa, the semi-desert conditions have attracted a small herd of antelope, primarily between Grand Junction and Delta. The west end of Battlement Mesa has a small herd of bighorn sheep. Large numbers of deer and elk frequent the Mesa, of course, but it also holds dense populations of bear and mountain lion.

The Colorado Division of Wildlife actively stocks the numerous waters of Grand Mesa, primarily with rainbow trout, but brook and cutthroat are also plentiful in selected streams and lakes. Beaver ponds often hold surprisingly large cutthroat and brook.

Grand Mesa has no shortage of campgrounds. There are campgrounds near Island and Alexander lakes,

Bonham and Big Creek reservoir and the Mesa lakes. All are first-come, first-served.

The 2-mile-high oasis rising from the surrounding Colorado Plateau desert attracts thousands of visitors. In a normal winter, the mesa is literally buried in snow—5 feet to 10 feet or more.

In spring, the melting snow becomes the lifeblood of abundant apple, pear, cherry, peach and apricot orchards, vineyards and produce fields near Cedaredge, Delta, Palisade, Grand Junction and other communities at the foot of the mesa. Many lakes, consequently, actually are reservoirs that collect, store and release water through the growing season. Late summer anglers should inquire locally about water levels in lakes and reservoirs they plan to fish.

Grand Mesa is easily reached from the north by turning east off I-70 about 20 miles east of Grand Junction (or about 26 miles west of DeBeque) in DeBeque Canyon. From the south, turn east from US 50 at Delta onto Hwy 92. After 4 miles, turn north at the intersection of Hwy 65.

Most lakes on Grand Mesa are clustered and have similar fishing conditions. A detailed topo map of the area is most helpful. Most of the waters are accessible from Hwy 65, which cuts 25 miles across Grand Mesa, north and south. This description begins at the northwestern edge of the plateau and follows Hwy 65 to the village of Grand Mesa.

Mesa Creek, which flows through Sunset Lake, offers some beaver-pond fishing below the lakes. It flows north to enter Plateau Creek. Mesa Creek is brushy and difficult to fish. It is rated fair for 8- to 10-inch brook.

MESA LAKES AREA

At the top of a hill on the north side of the plateau, **Mesa Lakes,** at the headwaters of Mesa Creek, lie along Hwy 65 about 12 miles south of the town of Mesa. The Mesa Lakes are at an elevation of about 9,900 feet and are on both sides of the highway. The lakes, in light timber, are only a short distance apart.

Mesa Lake (9,870 ft; 37 ac), the largest, and **Beaver Lake** (9,824 ft; 7 ac), near the village of Skyway, receive the greatest fishing pressure, yet still offer the promise of large fish. South of Mesa Lake, **South Mesa Lake** (10,000 ft; 11 ac) and **Lost Lake** (10,036 ft; 6 ac) are stocked with catchable rainbow and fingerling brook. Both of these lakes are natural lakes accessible by marked trails from Glacier Springs Picnic Grounds on Mesa Lake. It's a mile to South Mesa Lake and another 0.5 mile to Lost Lake. **Sunset Lake** (9,784 ft; 12 ac) has stocked rainbows. **Glacier Springs Pond** (9,870 ft; 2 ac), **Jumbo Lake** (9,777 ft; 3 ac) and **Water Dog Lake** (9,934 ft; 23 ac) are also grouped near Skyway. All are stocked with catchable rainbows and browns. Glacier Springs Pond contains cutthroat. Jumbo and Beaver maintain constant water levels; Sunset, Mesa and Water Dog fluctuate with irrigation demands. With the exception of Lost Lake, boats are available on all lakes. Fishing pressure in this area is very heavy.

On Hwy 65 south about 2 miles east from Mesa Lakes, a sign marks the Griffith Lakes to the north. The Griffith Lakes are at about 10,000 feet elevation. A 0.25-mile trail leads to **Griffith Lake** (10,052 ft; 62 ac), the closest lake. **Middle Griffith Lake** (10,036 ft; 36 ac), the only other fishery of the group is located about 100 yards below the dam of Griffith. Both lakes are rated fair, especially in the early season for 9- to 13-inch rainbow and some brook trout, but they are best known for the big browns taken on large wet flies at night. They are reached by trail from Water Dog Reservoir. Fishing by artificial flies and lures only. The limit for trout is 2 fish, 16 inches or longer. **West Griffith Lake** and **Monroe and Barnes Reservoirs** usually are drained each year.

Northeast of **Griffith Lakes** about a mile, the **Bull Creek Reservoirs** can be reached by trail leaving from the big bend in Hwy 65 about 2 miles east of Mesa Lakes. There are 12 reservoirs in this group, but only five have fish. **Bull Creek Reservoir No. 1** (10,134 ft; 15 ac) has rainbow to 2 pounds; **No. 2** (10,134 ft; 10 ac) is stocked with rainbow; and **No. 3**, which is drained each year, has no fish. Nos. 1 and 2 and their connecting channels are restricted to artificial flies and lures only, and have a bag and possession limit of 2 trout, 16 inches or longer. **Bull Creek Reservoirs Nos. 4** (9,850 ft; 31 ac) and **5** (9,652 ft; 18 ac) and **Bull Basin Reservoir** (10,015 ft; 10 ac) are east of Bull Creek Reservoirs. Nos. 1 and 2 and are rated poor for rainbow due to low wa-

1. Mesa Lakes
2. Griffith Lake
3. Middle Griffith Lake
4. West Griffith Lake
5. Waterdog Lake
6. Monroe & Barnes Reservoir
7. Bull Creek Reservoir #1
8. Bull Creek Reservoir #2
9. Bull Creek Reservoir #3
10. Bull Creek Reservoir #4
11. Bull Creek Reservoir #5
12. Bull Creek
13. Island Lake
14. Little Gem Reservoir
15. Rim Rock Lake

16. Granby Reservoir #1
17. Granby Reservoir #2
18. Granby Reservoir #5
19. Granby Reservoir #7
20. Granby Reservoir #12
21. Big Battlement Reservoir
22. Little Battlement
23. Carp Lake
24. Ward Creek Reservoir
25. Deep Slough
26. Ward Lake
27. Ward Creek
28. Alexander Lake
29. Hotel Twin Lake
30. Upper Hotel Lake

31. Forest Lake
32. Butts Lake
33. Town Grand Mesa
34. Baron Lake
35. Reed Reservoir
36. Kiser Slough Reservoir
37. Eggleston Lake
38. Upper Eggleston
39. Neversweat Reservoir
40. Big Meadow Reservoir
41. Kitson Reservoir
42. Cottonwood Reservoir #5
43. Cottonwood Reservoir #4
44. Cottonwood Reservoir #1
45. Cottonwood Reservoir #2

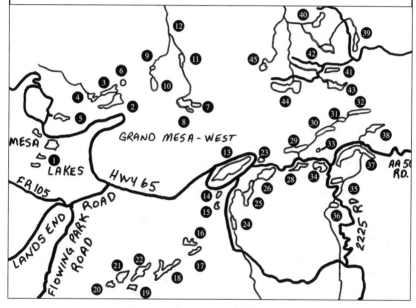

Grand Mesa West

ters.

About 2.25 miles south of the Bull Creek reservoir trailhead on Hwy 65, Lands End Road comes from the west to junction with Hwy 65. Turn west on this road for access to some of the western plateau lakes. Most of the lakes run dry at times, but **Carson Lake** (9,892

ft; 37 ac), in a steep-sided bowl at the headwaters of the westerly flowing Kannah Creek, has been a good producer of brook to 12 inches. No boats allowed. **Kannah Creek** flows about 9 miles west off the mesa and eventually empties into the Gunnison River. It has a series of beaver ponds below the Carson dam and is rated good for naturally produced cutthroat. Turn south off the Lands End Road onto the Carson Road to reach the lake.

Back on Hwy 65 traveling east from the Lands End Road, the highway skirts the largest lake on the Mesa. **Island Lake** (10,250 ft; 199 ac) is a good trolling and fly lake for 10-inch rainbow (though sometimes they are taken up to 18 inches) and brook. A few large splake are taken. A large sucker population is also present. Rental boats are available. Electric motor, sail or hand-powered boats are permitted. No outboards. Island Lake has two fully accessible fishing piers. It is also accessible by the trail from Little Bear Campground.

Little Gem Reservoir (10,000 ft; 13 ac) lies southwest of Island Lake less than 0.25 mile and is accessible by the road that encircles Island Lake. It is rated poor for 9- to 11-inch rainbow, brook, and splake. **Rimrock Lake** (10,100 ft; 12 ac), southwest of Little Gem, can often go dry. Fair for stocked rainbow.

Beyond Rim Rock Lake about 2 miles southwest on forest road #116 from Island Lake, the **Granby Reservoirs** at 10,000 feet are spread through a wide valley. Previously 12 reservoirs, the count now stands at 9. Reservoirs 4, 5, 10, and 11 are now combined to form **Granby Reservoir No. 5** (10,023 ft; 46 ac). Reservoir #5 is rated good for big brown and rainbow from 8 inches to 20 inches. **Nos. 6 and 7** (10,023 ft; 14 ac), which are combined, are rated poor for small rainbow, though there are large ones reported.

No. 9 is not stocked. **No. 12** (9,995 ft; 44 ac) is rated good for rainbow from 12 inches to 3 pounds. **Nos. 1, 2, 3, 8 and 12** (10,000 ft; 8 to 23 ac) are stocked with rainbow. Fishing after dark with big flies has resulted in catches of 2 pounders. No boats are available.

At the west end of the Granby reservoirs, the four **Battlement Lakes** are at about 10,000 feet elevation. Only **Big Battlement Lake** (10,082 ft; 37 ac) and **Little Battlement** (10,068 ft; 14 ac) have fish. Signs on the dams distinguish the lakes. Both of these lakes are rated fair for brook and rainbow.

Down USFS trail 115 going southwest from the Battlement Lakes, the trail splits. Take USFS trail 725 west to **Morris Reservoir**, (9,200 ft; 4 ac) on the upper reaches of **Oak Creek.** Morris has been stocked with rainbows. Further up Oak Creek is **Pitcairn Reservoir** (9,040 ft; 11 ac) which is stocked with brook.

At the northern end of Island Lake, Hwy 65 turns south and parallels the eastern shore for a short distance. After about 0.25 mile, it is intersected by a good paved road to the east (USFS 121) which leads to the village of Grand Mesa and the eastern end of the mesa itself.

Carp Lake (10,250 ft; 10 ac) lies northeast of Hwy 65 at the road junction to Grand Mesa village. It is rated fair for 10-inch rainbow; best results are with bait. No motor-propelled boats or rafts are permitted. South of Carp Lake about 2 miles, east of Hwy 65, **Ward Creek Reservoir** (9,774 ft; 26

ac) is rated fair for cutthroat and rainbow averaging 10 inches. **Ward Creek** has been stocked with cutthroat.

Southeast of Carp Lake about 0.25 mile is **Ward Lake** (10,300 ft; 55 ac). Ward is rated good for 8- to 16-inch rainbow and small brook. A rough USFS road leads around the west side to the south about 0.25 mile to **Deep Slough Reservoir** (10,000 ft; 27 ac). Fishing is rated good for rainbow to 14 inches.

Next to Ward Lake to the east is **Alexander Lake** (10,300 ft; 35 ac), which is rated fair for 12-inch rainbow. North of Alexander and north of the road is **Hotel Twin Lake** (10,350 ft; 25 ac). The name Twin Lake derives from the fact that at low water this lake becomes two. It is heavily fished and rated fair for stocked rainbow and brook to 14 inches. A trail from the parking lot at the east end of Twin Lake leads 0.25-mile northeast to **Upper Hotel Lake** (10,300 ft; 25 ac). It is rated fair for brook to 10 inches. No boats are available on this lake. A 1.5-mile trail northeast from Forest Lake leads to **Butts Lake** (10,500 ft; 18 ac), one of the prettiest lakes on Grand Mesa. It offers lots of sport for 10- to 12-inch cutthroat. No motor-propelled boats or rafts are permitted.

West of the village of Grand Mesa on the south side of the highway is **Baron Lake** (10,200 ft; 30 ac), rated good for rainbow and brook from 10 to 12 inches.

At Baron Lake, a road goes south to Hwy 65 and off the mesa. A northeast road leads to more lakes and eventually to the town of Collbran in the valley north of the Grand Mesa.

On the road south from Grand Mesa village to Cedaredge and Delta, the first lake encountered is **Reed Reservoir** (10,000 ft; 15 ac). Reed is rated good for 8- to 10-inch rainbow; however, it often is dry by late summer.

Kiser Creek drains Reed and other lakes near the village of Grand Mesa. **Kiser Slough Reservoir** (10,000 ft; 18 ac) is about 0.5 mile south of Reed. It is fair fishing for rainbow to 15 inches and stocked 10-inch rainbows. Boats are allowed on this lake, but it, too, is often drained by irrigation draws.

Across the road to the east from Baron Lake and the village of Grand Mesa is **Eggleston Lake** (10,200 ft; 130 ac), an elongated lake stretching along the south side of Collbran Road. Eggleston is rated good for rainbow from 10 inches to 12 inches, but some to 3 pounds. Boats are available, and campsites are nearby. On the north side of the road, a trail leads about 0.25 mile from Crag Crest Campground to **Upper Eggleston Lake** (10,400 ft; 25 ac), which is good fishing for cutthroat and brook to 16 inches and 12- to 13-inch rainbow. No boats are available.

A half-mile east of Eggleston at the head of Youngs Creek on the south side of the road are the three **Youngs Creek Reservoirs** (10,300 ft; 17 to 33 ac). They can be good for rainbow and cutthroat. Fishing is by artificial flies and lures only, all cutthroat must be returned to the water immediately. Best fishing is before July 4. The creek has been planted with small cutthroats. A 4wd on the east side of #3 leads a short way to **Pedro Reservoir** (10,380 ft; 12) which is stocked with brook. Pedro is subject to severe drawdown during the summer.

PARK RESERVOIR

As the Collbran road (USFS 121) continues east and begins to cut north, it passes **Park Reservoir** (9,950 ft; 80 ac). The reservoir is 0.5 mile from the road to the southeast, but can be seen from the road. It is good fishing for rainbow averaging 12 inches, brook, and cutthroat. To the northwest of the road in the same area is **Military Park Reservoir** (10,100 ft; 31 ac), which is fair for rainbow and cutthroat. It is subject to draw down during the summer. About 0.5-mile east, **Vela Reservoir** (10,150 ft; 25 ac) lies just south of Park Reservoir Campground. It is a put-and-take lake, rated good for 8- to 11-inch rainbow.

Near Trickle Park Reservoir Campground, a good dead-end road (USFS 126) travels east to the Twin Lakes and Weir and Johnson Reservoir. **Twin Lakes** (10,400 ft; 18 and 21 ac) are good fishing for small rainbow. They lie on the north side of the road, about 2 miles east of Trickle Creek Campground. Beyond the Twin Lakes, **Weir and Johnson Reservoir** (10,250 ft; 60 ac) is rated good for small brook and catchable size stocked rainbow.

South of Twin Lakes and Weir and Johnson Reservoir, and accessible only by foot from these lakes or from Trickle Park Reservoir, is **Bonita Reservoir** (10,000 ft; 64 ac), which has fair fishing for cutthroat to 15 inches; motor-propelled boats and rafts not permit-

ted. Southeast of Bonita 0.25 mile is **Cedar Mesa Reservoir** (9,950 ft; 35 ac), offering the same type of fishing. 1.5 miles farther east is **Trio Reservoir** (10,200 ft; 17 ac), with cutthroat fishing. Farther to the northeast about a mile over a hill, **Cole Reservoir No. 1** (10,400 ft; 25 ac) is rated good for cutthroat and rainbow averaging 10 to 12 inches.

About 0.75 mile northeast off Weir and Johnson Reservoir, accessible by trail, is **Leon Lake** (10,500 ft; 85 ac), a long and narrow lake that is one of the most consistent trout producers on the mesa. The upper end, where Leon Creek enters, usually offers the best fishing. Trolling usually is successful. No boats are available. It receives heavy fishing pressure, yet remains rated good for brook to 14 inches. At the headwaters of **East Leon Creek** is **Hunter Reservoir** (10,360 ft; 17 ac). Fishing is fair for cutthroat to 12 inches. Located on 4wd trail 4E up from Vega or a tough cross country hike from Leon Lake. Beautiful country.

Two small lakes about a mile west of Leon, **Finney Cuts Lakes** (10,500 ft; 3 and 6 ac), are rated fair for 10- to 12-inch cutthroat. To the northeast of Leon Lake about a mile is **Colby Horse Park Reservoir** (10,150 ft; 42 ac), which is accessible by the same trail from Weir and Johnson Reservoir. Colby is fair fishing for cutthroat averaging 10 inches. Boats are not allowed. Both Leon and Colby Horse Park Reservoir can be reached by a rough 4WD road south of Park Reservoir about 4 miles or from Vega Reservoir north of the Grand Mesa.

1. Youngs Creek Reservoir #1
2. Youngs Creek Reservoir #2
3. Youngs Creek Reservoir #3
4. Pedro Reservoir
5. Park Reservoir
6. Military Park Reservoir
7. Vela Reservoir
8. Twin Lakes
9. Weir & Johnson Reservoir

10. Bonita Lake
11. Cedar Mesa Reservoir
12. Trio Reservoir
13. Cole Reservoir
14. Leon Lake
15. Hunter Reservoir
16. Finney Cuts Lakes
17. Colby Horse Parks Reservoir
18. Monument Creek Reservoir

19. Kenny Creek Reservoir
20. Youngs Lake
21. Big Creek Reservoir
22. Silver Lake
23. 40 Acre Lake
24. Bonham Reservoir
25. Atkinson Reservoir

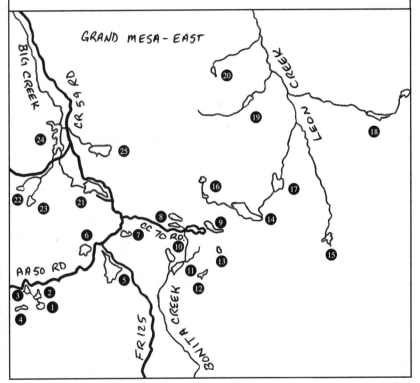

Grand Mesa East

Northeast of Colby Horse Reservoir about 3 miles is the **Monument Creek Reservoir** (10,200 ft 35 ac), and north about 2 to 4 miles are **Kenney Creek Reservoir** (9,900 ft; 18 ac) and **Youngs Lake** (10,200 ft; 8 ac). A network of 4WD roads connects these lakes and reservoirs. They are rated fair for rainbow, brook and cutthroat. The access to these lakes is by the 4WD road (USFS 260) east of the Collbran Road, about a mile north of Bonham Reservoir. This road swings to the east along Kelly Reservoir and on to Leon Creek.

Monument Reservoirs are accessible by trail from Leon Creek.

North of Trickle Park Reservoir Campground on the Collbran Road (USFS 121), **Big Creek Reservoir No. 1** (10,100 ft; 50 ac) is on the west shoulder of the road. It is rated fair in the summer for 10-inch rainbow and good in the fall.

North of Big Creek Reservoir about 1.5 miles, **Bonham Reservoir** (9,850 ft; 64 ac) is rated fair for 10- to 14-inch cutthroat and rainbow, with best fishing results in early season. A good road follows around the reservoir's south end about 5 miles to Cottonwood Lakes, which are east of the Griffith, Bull and Mesa lakes discussed earlier.

COTTONWOOD LAKES

Atkinson Reservoir (9,920 ft; 71 ac) is reached from USFS road 121 by trail to the east just short of the turnoff to Bonham Reservoir. Atkinson is fair for small rainbow, brook, and cutthroat. **Silver Lake** (10,150 ft; 11 ac), east of the Cottonwood group, is good fishing for 12-inch cutthroat. Fishing by artificial flies and lures only. Limit is 2 fish 16 inches or longer. This lake can be reached from the Bonham Reservoir by trail or by taking USFS road 257 from the Bonham Lake Campground and picking up a trail from the road. **Forty Acre Lake**, (9,840 ft; 11 ac) southeast of Silver Lake, can be reached by the same trail. Brook trout fishing, large ones, if you can tempt them.

Neversweat Reservoir (10,050 ft; 17 ac), to the northwest of Silver Lake on USFS road 258 about a mile, is fair fishing for stocked 10-inch rainbow

and holdover rainbows averaging 14 inches. Brook present as well. Northwest of Neversweat, **Big Meadow Reservoir**, (9,860 ft; 13 ac) at the end of USFS road 258, empties into Cottonwood Creek. Big Meadow has been stocked with fingerling brook trout. Nearby is **Kitson Reservoir** (10,050 ft; 28 ac), rated fair for brook and rainbow averaging 10 inches. Grayling are also present, limit is 2 fish 16 inches or longer. Just north of Kitson, **Cottonwood No. 5** (10,000 ft; 20 ac), offers slow fishing for 16- to 19-inch brook and cutthroat; **Cottonwood No. 4** (10,240 ft; 28 ac), is rated fair for 12-inch rainbow and brook, and reportedly is best in late season with flies; **Cottonwood Lake No. 1** (10,150 ft; 85 ac) is rated excellent for rainbow, cutthroat, brook, and splake averaging 12 inches; **Cottonwood Lake No. 2** (10,050 ft; 18 ac) has no fish.

All of these lakes and reservoirs are at the headwaters of Cottonwood Creek, which flows north into Plateau Valley. Cottonwood Creek has some beaver ponds below the reservoirs. Lower reaches of the stream are private.

COLORADO RIVER

Beginning east of Glenwood Springs and downstream from the confluence of the Eagle and Colorado rivers at Dotsero, access to the Colorado is across private land for 2 miles to Glenwood Canyon. There, behind Shoshone Dam, the river becomes broad and quiet. Fishing is from the roadside for rainbow, brown and suckers. Fishing, generally, is fair through

Photo Courtesy of the Morrison Angler

David Shiloh with 10 lbs rainbow

most of the canyon. Some whitefish start to show up about 3 miles below the dam at Grizzly Creek.

In the canyon, the river is heavy and unwadable but with plenty of rainbow and brown trout (including big ones) and lots of suckers. Bait, spinners, caddis fly dries and deeply drifted nymphs are effective, but fishing can be tedious.

Between Glenwood Springs and Dotsero, **Grizzly Creek** joins the Colorado River from the north within Glenwood Canyon. It has small brook and rainbow trout. A good trail follows the length of the stream up a steep canyon.

From Glenwood Springs going north, jeep road USFS 602 goes up to **Deer Lake** (9,760 ft; 5 ac) stocked with Colorado River cutthroat and **Yellow Lake** (10,400 ft; 8 ac) stocked with brook trout. At Glenwood Springs, the Roaring Fork River, a Gold Medal trout stream, enters the Colorado. **Mitcell Creek** on the western end of Glenwood

Springs is artificial flies and lures only, catch and release above the Glenwood Springs fish hatchery.

CANYON CREEK

About 9 miles west of Glenwood Springs on I-70, **Canyon Creek** enters the Colorado River from the north. Canyon Creek is a small, brushy creek rated fair for small brook and cutthroat. About 4 miles north of the highway, Canyon Creek forks in several directions, with its tributaries spreading near the boundary of the Flat Tops Wilderness. Reach the headwaters and the wilderness boundary by taking a dirt road north from the town of New Castle at Interchange 109 and I-70.

East Canyon Creek is an 8-mile-long tributary feeding into Canyon Creek from the northeast. It offers the same type of fishing as the main stream. At its headwaters is **Blue Lake** (10,406 ft; 9 ac), which is rated good for brook to 15 inches. Access is by hiking 5 miles from the road that follows the main stream along USFS trail 1844 or by taking USFS 602 (4WD) to 637 from Glenwood Springs.

To the northwest, **Adams Lake** (10,804 ft; 40 ac) feeds the west fork of Canyon Creek. The lake is rated fair for 12-inch brook, cutthroat and rainbow, with some lunkers taken occasionally. Access is by 6 miles on USFS road 640 (4WD) from sign at Heart Lake, near the headwaters of Deep Creek. Heart Lake is accessed via the Deep Creek Road (USFS 600) 2 miles north of Dotsero, east of Glenwood Springs, and contains a few brook trout. (See Upper Colorado chapter for details.)

Possum Creek, another tributary of Canyon Creek, lies farther east than East Canyon Creek. Possum offers fair angling for small brook and some cutthroat. It flows through some posted private land.

ELK CREEK

At New Castle, about 13 miles east of Rifle and 13 miles west of Glenwood Springs, **Elk Creek** enters the Colorado from the northwest. From New Castle, turn north on Buford Road (CR 245) to a right turn, where **Main Elk Creek** comes in from the north. Here, CR 243 goes northwest another 2.5 miles to the national forest boundary. From there, USFS road 603 winds another 5 miles into the national forest, then turns north for 15 miles before becoming 4WD. Access to Main Elk Creek is cross country 3 miles northwest for good fishing for small rainbow.

The Buford Road from New Castle forks 2.5 miles west of Main Elk Creek. The West Fork leads 4 miles to Harvey Gap Reservoir and on to Rifle Creek. The North Fork winds 22 miles before intersecting with a road from the east at Hiner Spring. **Cliff Lakes** and **Meadow Creek Lake** are 2.5 and 5 miles, respectively, to the east. Many roads wind through this area, but the primary access is on USFS road 244, with roads 601 and 823 leading to the lakes. A good map is required.

Cliff Lakes (9,650 ft; 6 ac) are shallow. Easily fished for 11-inch rainbow and brook. Fishing pressure is heavy. **Meadow Creek Lake** (9,550 ft; 55 ac) is rated good for rainbow and brook to 16 inches. There is a campground. Downstream from the reservoir, **Meadow Creek** offers fair fishing for 3 miles for small brook, rainbow and a few cutthroats. Access is from Buford on 244 to 601, 4wd to lake.

Harvey Gap Reservoir (6,402 ft; 380 ac) (also called Grass Valley Reservoir), is a good fishery in western Colorado. It has rainbow and brown trout, large and smallmouth bass, channel catfish, crappie and green sunfish. There are browns to 8 pounds and probably larger. Excellent bass fishing; all bass under 15 inches must be returned to the water. Boats are limited to 20 hp motors. The reservoir can be reached from the Buford-New Castle Road (CR 245) or by good road north from US 6 about 2 miles west of Silt (4 miles east of Rifle). The reservoir is 7 miles north.

RIFLE CREEK

Rifle Creek enters the Colorado River from the north at the town of Rifle. Hwy 25 goes about 17 miles to Rifle Gap Reservoir and State Recreation Area. It is a fee area. At the reservoir, the road forks, with the west road leading north to Hwy 13 to Meeker. North and east, State Road 325 follows East Rifle Creek past Rifle Falls.

Rifle Gap Reservoir (5,960 ft; 600 ac) is a clear-water reservoir favored by scuba divers, where underwater spearfishing is allowed year-round. The reservoir is framed in sandstone and shale cliffs. In the north shore area are several campsites as well as a boat ramp and public swimming. Auger-bearing anglers flock to Rifle Gap Reservoir for ice fishing. Fishing in the reservoir is for brown and rainbow, walleye and bass. All largemouth and smallmouth bass between 12 inches and 15 inches must be returned to the water immediately.

Below the reservoir, **Rifle Creek** flows through private land. Above the reservoir there are about 2 miles of public access to fishing along **Middle** and **West Rifle creeks.** Fishing pressure is heavy. **East Rifle Creek** enters the reservoir from the northeast through 5 miles of private land above the reservoir to Rifle Falls State Recreation Area and Fish Hatchery. Public fishing in the recreation area is for rainbow and cutthroat. The falls spill in three segments and cloak mysterious caves and rock formations. There are campgrounds in the park and two more within 4 miles north of the park. The road continues north to intersect at Triangle Park with Buford-New Castle road. Meadow Creek Lake is 12 miles northeast off a road that junctions to the east at Hiner Springs. Fishing pressure is heavy.

PARACHUTE CREEK

Parachute Creek joins the Colorado at the town of Parachute. It comes from a deep canyon to the northwest. A good road provides access to fishing from private land on the lower seven to eight miles. Permission is needed to fish for rainbow and brook.

From Parachute, the Colorado River moves south, swinging past the Roan Cliffs and the town of DeBeque.

ROAN CREEK

Roan Creek enters the Colorado from the northwest at DeBeque. Take a secondary road north from DeBeque. Keep left at the second fork. This road parallels the stream for about 15 miles. Roan offers poor fishing.

West of DeBeque the **Colorado River** enters DeBeque Canyon and some attractive water with mostly rough fish. Fishing pressure is very light. Just below the confluence with Plateau Creek is Island Acres Recreation Area between I-70 and the river. A pond is stocked with rainbow.

GUNNISON RIVER

The headwaters of the Gunnison River flow from the western flank of the Sawatch Range on the Continental Divide, from the southern slopes of the Elk Mountains and from the northern San Juan Mountains. This vast area of rugged peaks, high buttes and spectacular canyons has a well-known reputation among weathermen as being one of the coldest areas in the nation. It is also the home of huge herds of hardy deer and elk.

The Gunnison National Forest comprises the largest part of U.S. Forest Service lands within the Gunnison basin: A portion of the Uncompahgre National Forest, the Big Blue and La Garita Wilderness areas to the south and the West Elk, Maroon Bells-Snowmass and Collegiate Peaks wilderness areas to the north are also part of the area.

Access into the Gunnison area is primarily via US 50, although the basin may be reached from the south by Hwy 114 over North Pass above Saguache or north from Creede through Lake City on Hwy 149. The city of Gunnison is the center for information and supplies.

From Grand Junction to Austin, the Gunnison River is muddy and often shallow with mostly rough fish. Loads of heavy natural sediment, irrigation return flows and the arid terrain take their toll on the fishing.

Kannah Creek flows into the Gunnison about 10 miles above Grand Junction. Kannah Creek headwaters begin on the Grand Mesa. Near the Gunnison River the creek is on private property, access in the national forest in by way of GS.00 Rd off of Land Ends Road. Continue on Lands End Road up on the Grand Mesa to reach the creeks headwaters. The creek and its many tributaries offer fishing for small rainbow and brook.

In the same area, off of Lands End Road, about six miles from Hwy 50 is **Purdy Mesa Reservoir** (formerly **Hallenbeck Reservoir)** (5,650 ft; 52 ac) and **Juniata Reservoir** (5,750 ft; 87 ac). Both reservoirs are large offering fishing for bass, crappie, and bluegill. Both are restricted to artificial flies and lures, all bass must be 15 inches or longer.   Owned by the city of Grand Junction

UNCOMPAHGRE RIVER

The **Uncompahgre River** joins the Gunnison at Delta after a long, winding trip from the mountains near Ouray, some 60 miles to the south. It runs from the San Juan Mountains and is heavily contaminated from mine tailings above Ouray. It provides poor fishing for rainbow and brown between Ouray and Montrose, and public access is difficult because much of the valley is privately owned. Two areas are open to fishing: Riverbottom Park and Billy Creek State Wilderness Area near Colona.

From Ridgway Dam downstream to the USGS Gauge Station, fishing is prohibited, except as posted. From the USGS Gauge Station below Ridgway Dam downstream to the confluence with Cow Creek, fishing is catch and release with artificial flies and lures only. From CR 23 bridge downstream to Ridgway Reservoir, snagging of kokanee salmon is permitted from September 1 through December 31.

Confluence Lake, (5,100 ft; 70 ac) in Delta, was rebuilt from lagoons at the confluence of Uncompahgre and Gunnison Rivers. Stocked with rainbow. Easy drive to the lake. Bank fishing for kids is good.

Todd Andersen of the Morrison Angler with mysis shrimp fed Rainbow

Photo Courtesy of the Morrison Angler

Sweitzer Lake (5,100 ft; 127 ac), in the Sweitzer Lake State Recreation Area, is no longer a viable fishing area because of high levels of selenium which contaminated the fish. Warning signs against eating its fish have been posted. The Department of Wildlife does not stock any fish because of possible health hazards.

Chipeta Lake, (5,900 ft; 8.5 ac) recently renovated, is approximately 2 miles south of the city of Montrose. Stocked with rainbow, largemouth bass and sunfish. Has some catfish. Easy drive to lake. A designated state wildlife area with excellent access for children and handicapped anglers.

Upstream from Delta and Ridgway, the river is essentially part of the valley's irrigation system. **Fairview Reservoir** (6,270 ft; 20 ac) is just off US 50 about 5 miles east of Montrose. It is closed to fishing because it is a water supply lake and is not stocked.

Coming into the Uncompahgre from the southeast, 8 miles north of Ridgway, is **Cow Creek**. It rises 18 miles to the southeast, its upper 10 miles in national forest and open to public fishing for small rainbow and cutthroat. Several roads west from Hwy 550 lead to the creek at its intersection with the Owl Creek Pass Road (USFS 858). Upper reaches are reached through 4 miles of private land by 4WD road; then trail. Many small streams and beaver ponds in this area have small cutthroat offering good dry-fly fishing. Inquire in Ridgway about permission to cross private land.

Ridgway Reservoir (6,870 ft; 1000 ac) and Ridgway State Park on the

Uncompahgre River is 22 miles south of Montrose via Hwy 550. Facilities include a campground with 200 spaces, some with full hookups, a dump station, drinking water and a boat ramp. Excellent campgrounds and day facilities. The reservoir has rainbow trout, kokanee salmon and some browns. May fish from bank or boat. Snagging of kokanee salmon is permitted from September 1 through December 31.

The mile of Uncompahgre River between the dam and confluence of Cow Creek is catch-and-release water restricted to flies and lures. Fair fishing for rainbow to 14 inches and a few brown.

Dallas Creek joins the Uncompahgre from the southwest, about 3 miles upstream from Ridgway. Its upper portions and tributaries are reached by driving west from Ridgway on Hwy 62 for 5 miles and then south 2 miles to where the road forks. Take the west fork of the road (USFS 851) 7 more miles to the Uncompahgre Wilderness boundary.

The **East Fork of Dallas Creek** has fair fishing for cutthroat and rainbow inside the wilderness. At its headwaters farther south are the three **Blue Lakes** (11,000 to 12,000 ft; 3 to 5 ac), with fair fishing for cutthroat. Reached by East Dallas Road (USFS 851) and USFS trail 201 into the Mt. Sneffels Wilderness. **West Fork of Dallas Creek** has similar fishing via West Dallas Road (USFS 850), a private road that turns off Hwy 62 about 6 miles west of Ridgway, becomes a rough road for about 8 miles, then a trail.

Farther south, **Canyon Creek** flows

Fall in Colorado

into the river in Ouray and offers rainbow and brook trout fishing. Take the Camp Bird Mine Road (USFS 853) southwest from town. Most streams in the immediate Ouray area are too steep and fast for fish or too heavily polluted from past mining activity.

NORTH FORK GUNNISON RIVER

The **North Fork** and its tributaries drain a vast area to the east and north. It and many of its tributaries are tapped for irrigation water, and, because the terrain is readily eroded, the streams often are muddy. The headwaters of the North Fork comprise East and West Muddy creeks and Anthracite Creek, which merge just below Paonia Reservoir.

On the west side of the town of Hotchkiss, **Leroux Creek** enters the North Fork from the north. It stretches 22 miles to the south end of Grand Mesa. The creek is good for small rainbow at the lower end and cutthroat at the upper. At its headwaters are several reservoirs that are rated poor with the exception of **Goodenough Reservoir** (10,400 ft; 51 ac), which is accessible by road. It is rated fair to good for 10- to 12-inch cutthroat and rainbow. Some large browns are taken. Less than a few hundred yards west, **Dogfish Reservoir** (10,400 ft; 25 ac), about the same size as Goodenough, is rated fair for the same type of fishing.

West of Hotchkiss, the North Fork flows through mostly private land, and permission to fish is a good idea. Some good rainbow and brown are in the stream.

About two miles west of Somerset, **Hubbard Creek** enters the North Fork from the north. A rough road leading to the east end of Grand Mesa follows the creek for several miles. Hubbard is fair for brook trout on its upper reaches. The road, like others in the area, is slippery and treacherous during and immediately following a rain.

At the headwaters of Hubbard Creek is **Overland Reservoir** (10,800 ft; 170 ac), which is good for 10-inch cutthroat. Two miles southwest by trail from Overland is **Crater Lake** (10,000 ft; 6 ac). It is rated poor because few fish survive winterkills, but those that do may be 18 to 20 inches. Nearby streams are rated good to excellent fishing for brook, cutthroat and rainbow to 12 inches.

Muddy Creek rises 18 miles north of the reservoir in a host of small streams with brook and cutthroat. **Clear Fork Creek**, **Jones Creek**, **East Fork Muddy Creek** and **West Muddy Creek** join East Muddy Creek from the west and north. **Lee Creek** follows Hwy 133 down from McClure Pass, and **Spring** and **Dugout Creeks** flow in from the east. These streams have small brook, sometimes rainbow and cutthroat. There are many beaver ponds and, usually, open meadow as well as brushy segments.

Anthracite Creek joins the North Fork from the east. Its headwaters are in several tributaries high in rugged mountains. The creek is fair for rainbow, brook and some brown to 12 inches. The upper reaches primarily contain cutthroat and brook, and there are plenty of beaver ponds.

Tributaries include **North Anthracite Creek**, **East Anthracite Creek**, **Ruby Anthracite Creek** and **Middle Anthracite Creek**. Ruby is stocked with small cutthroats. Access is by the Kebler Pass Road between Crested Butte and the North Fork, where it comes in at Paonia Reservoir. The road is often closed by snow until late June. Foot trails lead up most creeks from Erickson Springs Campground, which is 5 miles by road east of the reservoir.

Dollar Lake (10,500 ft; 2 ac) is poor fishing for stocked brook. It sometimes winterkills. Northwest from Dollar, **Lost Lake** (9,870 ft; 8 ac) is 1 mile from the Lost Lake Campground on Lost Lake Slough. Lost Lake is good for 8- to 10-inch brook. **Lost Lake Slough** (9,625 ft; 53 ac) is a fluctuating reservoir. It has fair to good fishing for stocked rainbow and natural brook to 10 inches. Best results are early in the season. A campground is located on its north shore and is accessible by a rough road 2.5 miles from the Anthracite Creek Road and then 8 miles southeast of Erickson Springs.

Coal Creek enters the North Fork Gunnison River from the south just below Paonia Reservoir. It is rated fair to good for rainbow and brook to 12 inches. A dirt road follows the stream to its headwaters. Flowing into Coal Creek from the east, **Cliff Creek** provides small stream fishing for cutthroat, rainbow and brook to 10 inches. At its headwaters, **Sheep Lake** (10,505 ft; 10 ac) is just inside the West Elk Wilderness. It is reached by 8 miles of trail from the end of the road, near Coal Creek. It offers fair fishing for rainbow and cutthroat to 16 inches. It is a good fly fishing lake. **Little Gunnison**, **Cascade**, **Robinson** and **Willow Creeks** also feed into Coal Creek and offer similar fishing.

Paonia Reservoir (6,450 ft; 300 ac when full) is a poor place to fish. It is not stocked very often and is usually too muddy for trout. Rated fair for pike, which fair better in the muddy water.

SMITH FORK

Smith Fork Creek enters the Gunnison from the east about 11 miles downstream from the Black Canyon monument boundary. It drains the west side of the West Elk Mountains and isn't much of a fishing stream, although there are some rainbow and brook. The upper reaches and Smith Fork Campground are on a good road 7 miles east of Crawford. From Crawford west, access is on private, posted land where permission to fish is unlikely.

Little Coal Creek, which feeds the Smith Fork just inside the national forest 6 miles east of Crawford, is good fly-fishing, but tends to get fished heavily for brook and rainbow. **Crawford Reservoir** (6,550 ft; 340 ac when full) is a mile south of Crawford along Hwy 92. Good fishing for rainbow 8 to 12 inches, a few browns, some good catfish from 20 to 24 inches long and some 12 and 15 pounders caught nearly every year. Largemouth bass fishing fair in the spring. Excellent ice fishing for yellow perch in December and January. Other warm water fish are taken on bait. The lake is a state park with camping, trailer facilities and boat ramps; some ice fishing. A fee area. All small and largemouth bass

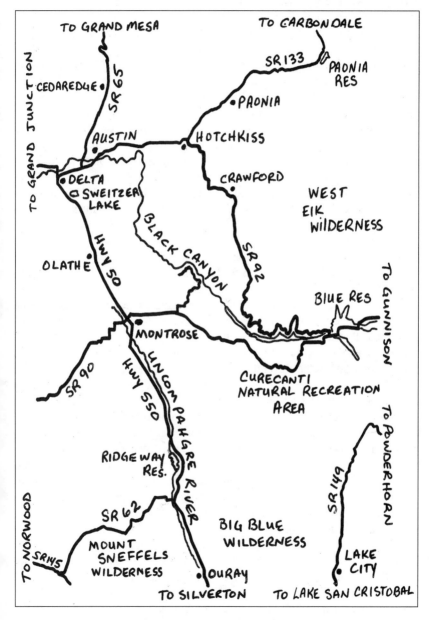

BLACK CANYON

must be 15 inches or longer. There is no daily limit on yellow perch. **Doug Creek** above reservoir, via road B80, is restricted to artificial flies and lures only, all cutthroat must be returned to the water immediately.

Gould Reservoir, just south of Crawford Reservoir, is private, often dry late in the year, and is not stocked. It may have some rainbow and perch. Permission to fish is needed.

Four miles downstream from Smith Fork Creek, the Gunnison leaves its canyon and is joined from the east by North Fork of the Gunnison. The 4 miles between Smith Fork and North Fork are heavily fished, being accessible by boat coming upstream from the North Fork confluence, and by trail and rough roads over BLM land from the town of Austin off Hwy 92.

Below the Black Canyon of the Gunnison is the Gunnison Gorge, an area specially managed by the BLM. Access can be either from Montrose, Olathe, or from Delta. Several good trails lead into the gorge, with the most popular being Bobcat, Duncan, Ute and Chukar from the Olathe and Montrose side. All lead into the gorge and are very steep - Ute Trail is the least steep. Good fishing continues all the way to the town of Austin. Fishing is rated good to excellent for rainbows to 20 inches and browns to about 15 inches. Rainbows are found in the riffles and runs rather than in deep pools and are best caught with big dead-drifted stonefly nymphs. The browns in the river are found in eddies and pools and take an occasional dry fly. Mepps and other spinners work well. No camp-

fires, a few good campsites. Practice minimum impact camping. Fishing is poor below Austin.

BLACK CANYON OF THE GUNNISON

Of all the wonderful Gold Medal quality water on the Gunnison, the Black Canyon stretch is the most famous for its fishing and the difficulty in getting to it. Crystal Reservoir marks the beginning of the **Black Canyon of the Gunnison**. For 53 miles, the canyon rim rises 1730 feet to 2700 feet above the river. For half of this distance, the river is gold medal trout fishing water from the eastern boundary of the Black Canyon of the Gunnison National Monument downstream 26 miles to the confluence of the river with the North Fork of the Gunnison. Special regulations exist for the gold medal portion of the river, which restrict fishing to the use of artificial lures or flies only. All fish between 12 and 16 inches must be released. You may keep 4 brown trout, 12 inches in length or smaller, or 3 trout less than 12 inches and 1 trout 16 inches or longer. All rainbow must be returned to the water immediately. Watch for bald eagles, bighorn sheep and mule deer in the canyon. Access is limited to spring, summer and fall only when the roads are dry.

The river through the Black Canyon of the Gunnison National Monument is difficult to get into, and fishing is quite limited. Limited accesses from both sides of the canyon via North or South Rim Roads require serious hikes down in and back out again.

Photo Courtesy of the Morrison Angler

San Isabel National Forest

Angling these waters must be a well-planned endeavor warranting investigation beyond the parameters of this fishing guide. An experienced guide service is recommended, fishing for large rainbow and brown can be outstanding, however.

Immediately above the canyon is **Crystal Reservoir** (6,759 ft; 165 ac), which was completed in the late 1970's as part of the Curecanti project. Its function is to stabilize the flows in the Black Canyon of the Gunnison River. Access to Crystal Reservoir is mostly limited to the short trail below Morrow Point Dam. To get there, travel to Cimarron on US 50, where the well-marked road leads to the dam. An interesting sidelight here is the old Denver and Rio Grande train, which has been preserved and stands on tracks at the dam. The train once ran through this spectacular gorge. Good kokanee run into Cimarron River from Crystal Reservoir in late October. Open to snag-

ging September 1 to December 31.

Crystal Reservoir requires some tricky work to get down to the river, but the climb down is less than that to Morrow Point. The water coming in from Morrow Point is swift, but soon the reservoir slows the flow and the trip is well worth it. The fishing is rated as good to excellent, with kokanee salmon and rainbow making up most of the catch. Trolling produces the best fishing, with shoreline fishing virtually impossible. The flow out of Morrow Point can be strong, and a good strong outboard, at least 10 hp, is often required to get back upstream.

Morrow Point Dam arcs across the Gunnison River 12 miles below Blue Mesa Dam and backs the river up about 11 miles to create **Morrow Point Reservoir** (7,200 ft; 820 ac). Built as part of the Uncompahgre Valley Water Users Association's Curecanti project, Morrow Point is about 400 feet deep in parts and is 12 miles long in a spectacular canyon. The fishing is equally spectacular and rated good to excellent. Kokanee salmon comprise a good percentage of the catch, most in the 2-pound class, with some larger. Snagging of kokanee salmon is permitted September 1 through December 31. The lake also has rainbow and some huge browns.

For the most part, access is limited to the Pine Creek Trail, off US 50 west of Blue Mesa Reservoir. A good road leads down to the trailhead and parking lot. The trail is actually a set of well-built stairs down to the river. However, access is very tough for boatmen, with only hand-carried craft possible. Boats should have a strong outboard to get back up against the strong current to the Pine Creek Trail. Fishing from a boat is the only way to go, and trolling spoons deep has produced good fish, such as some 20-pound browns. Fishing in the tailwater below Blue Mesa Reservoir in the spring has produced some nice fish for shore anglers.

CIMARRON RIVER

West of Big Blue Creek is the Cimarron River drainage. The **Cimarron River** flows into the Gunnison just below Morrow Point Dam and the power plant. Four miles east of the Cimarron Store on US 50, a good road goes south up the river almost 20 miles, providing access to **Little Cimarron River** and **Fall Creek**, which offer brook and cutthroat fishing. The middle, east and west forks are stocked with 10-inch rainbows. Snagging of kokanee salmon on the Cimarron River is permitted November 1 through January 31.

About 2.5 miles south from US 50, a road goes off to the southwest 18 miles to Silver Jack Reservoir and the Big Cimarron and Beaver Lake campgrounds.

Silver Jack Reservoir (8,800 ft; 250 ac) is at the juncture of the **West**, **Middle** and **East Forks of the Cimarron River**. Silver Jack Reservoir is reached by a long dirt road from near the town of Cimarron. The lake is located 18 miles from US 50 in a beautiful valley on the edge of the Big Blue Wilderness. It is a large irrigation reservoir, which is often nothing but muddy flats in the fall. For this reason, fishing is rated poor to fair, with best fishing coming in the early spring for stocked rainbow. The scenic Owl Creek Pass Road from near Ridgway and US 550 may also reach this lake. No boats are allowed on Silver Jack.

Beaver Lake (8,750 ft; 5 ac) is 3 miles down stream from Silver Jack Reservoir. It is fair fishing for stocked rainbow. No boats allowed; there is a campground.

To the west of the river, less than 2 miles, in the same area as Beaver Lake, are **Hampton Lake** (9,650 ft; 10 ac), which is good for brook to 12 inches, and **Fish Creek Reservoirs No. 1 and No. 2** (9,350 ft; 15 and 25 ac). The two reservoirs are less than 0.25 mile apart and are good fishing for 10- to 12-inch rainbow in early summer. The reservoirs are reached by 4WD road (USFS 862) heading west below Big Cimarron Campground.

Three miles of the Cimarron River are open to public fishing above its confluence with the Gunnison River. Water is clearest in late summer and fall, and fly-fishing is good. At Cimarron, a paved road winds down the canyon to the Gunnison and provides access to Crystal Reservoir.

Streams entering Morrow Point Reservoir include Curecanti and Blue creeks. **Curecanti Creek** flows in from the north and is accessible by walking or 4WD (USFS road 720) from Hwy 92 about 10 miles west of Blue Mesa Dam. The highway goes up Soap and Black mesas, and access to the reservoir from the extremely steep north side requires a treacherous, arduous effort down and up again. Although from a road map it looks short, it is not worth the effort. Where the highway heads north up Curecanti, 4 miles west of Blue Mesa Dam, the reservoir is 500 feet below. Curecanti offers fair fishing in the stream and its many beaver ponds for brook trout to 11 inches and stocked rainbows. It extends several miles to the north.

Blue Creek enters the Morrow Point Reservoir from the south across from the Curecanti Creek inlet. About 9 miles east of Blue Mesa Dam on US 50, a Forest Service road goes off to the south for some 30 miles providing access to rainbow, brook and cutthroat fishing in **Big Blue Creek**, **Soldier Creek** and many beaver ponds in Uncompahgre National Forest. At the confluence of Big Blue and Soldier creeks is the Big Blue Campground. This is high country, about 9800 feet elevation, where meadow fishing is rated fair. A trail goes up Big Blue Creek a dozen miles to its headwaters

at the foot of 14,300-foot Uncompahgre Peak.

BLUE MESA RESERVOIR

With 73 miles of shoreline, **Blue Mesa Reservoir** (7,519 ft; 9000 ac when full) is Colorado's largest body of water, however, in recent years, the lake has not filled. Blue Mesa is located about 15 miles west of Gunnison along US 50 and is part of the Curecanti National Recreation Area. The reservoir is 23 miles long and receives tremendous fishing pressure for brown, rainbow, mackinaw and kokanee salmon. More than 30 streams flow into it, providing food and spawning habitat. State and federal hatcheries annually stock hundreds of thousands of trout and kokanee fry. Many campsites in the area, with camping in the town of Gunnison, also. Several Marinas and boat ramps are available.

Fishing at Blue Mesa can run hot and cold. For good fishing, concentrate on fall of the year after the water cools, or spring and early summer. Forget about late summer, when the fishing is poor at best. Trolling for kokanee and rainbow is good in mid-summer. Spring fishing is excellent for trophy mackinaw and brown. Most of the rainbow in the lake averages 15 inches. Good kokanee salmon fishing early in the day with lead-core trolling line. Bank fishing is best in April and May, poor in summer, with best fishing at Soap Creek arm, the upper bridge and the Lake Fork bridge, several miles down the lake on US 50.

US 50 follows the reservoir for its length and gives easy access to the res-

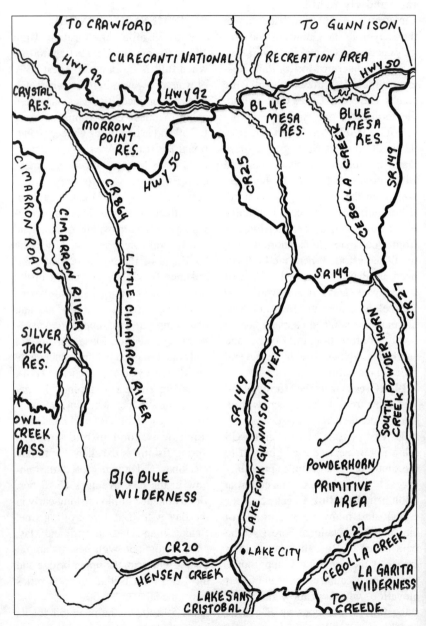

BLUE MESA

ervoir on the north side. However, most of the south side of this massive reservoir is tough to reach without a boat. Camping is allowed only on certain designated sites. The reservoir is divided into three large basins, **Iola**, **Cebolla** and **Sapinero basins**. Best bets for spring and fall fishing include trolling along the mouths of several inlet creeks, as well as trolling in the Sapinero and Iola basins. An occasional large mackinaw is taken, especially during the early spring.

Good facilities, plenty of parking and camping, are found on the western end of the lake. At the western end of the reservoir, a road leads across the dam toward Hotchkiss. A mile from the dam, a washboard dirt road (USFS 721) leads up the **Soap Creek Arm** of the reservoir, affording access to about 3 miles of shoreline before dipping away from the reservoir. This road (USFS 721) eventually leads into the south side of the West Elk Wilderness. Bank fishing in April and early May in Soap Creek arm is reportedly very good.

Boat access into the coves of **Soap Creek** and **West Elk Creek** can result in fast action on a fly rod during the evening hours at the inlets. No camping allowed, except in designated sites.

Ice fishing on Blue Mesa can be excellent for rainbow trout. Best areas for rainbow include **Dry Gulch**, **East Elk**, the **Bay of Chickens**, the **Gunnison River inlet area** and **Elk Creek**. Ice anglers should be very cautious on the ice, which is usually good from about mid-December until about mid-March. For trophy mackinaw, concentrate around the Lake Fork Bridge and around the Middle Bridge (Dillon Pinnacles).

Boaters should be aware that strong winds rake the reservoir into white caps early in the afternoon on most midsummer days, but abate by late afternoon, allowing evening fishing. The water level can fluctuate as much as 100 feet over a season, and can seriously affect kokanee fishing.

The setting for Blue Mesa Reservoir is one of western beauty with cliffs, stone outcroppings and escarpments crowning the northern shore. The south shore is austere, featuring rolling hills of sagebrush and scrub oak. Ice fishing shelters must be portable. The bag and possession limit for lake trout (mackinaw) is 8 fish. In Blue Mesa and its inlets at the reservoir high water mark upstream to the bridge at the junction of US 50 and Hwy 149, snagging for kokanee salmon is permitted from September 1 through January 31. The snagging bag and possession limit for kokanee is 10 fish. From the Coal Creek inlet at Blue Mesa Reservoir, fishing is prohibited from the high water line at the reservoir upstream 1 mile from January 1 through June 30.

NORTH OF BLUE MESA

Beaver, **Steuben**, **Willow**, **East Elk**, **Red**, **West Elk**, **Coal** and **Soap creeks** enter Blue Mesa Reservoir from the north and from what is some of the best big-game hunting country in the state. These streams tend to be small and brushy, with willow growth and only fair fishing for brook and some small rainbow and, occasionally, beaver-pond fishing for brook. Access is generally steep and rough by 4WD road or trail, except for Soap Creek where access is good via USFS road 721.

Dead-end roads up Red and East Elk creeks are not maintained and are considered better for hiking. The Dry Creek Road is a good 13 miles to **Rainbow Lake** (10,847 ft; 10 ac when full). Creek often dry; lake rated fair for brook when there's sufficient water. Nice campground.

There is a put-in campground on West Elk Arm that's reachable only by boat. There is private property upstream, and permission to cross it should be sought.

Soap Creek (Sapinero Creek on old maps) has a good gravel road north along its west side to Soap Creek and Commissary Gulch campgrounds. Turn off US 50, cross Blue Mesa Dam on Hwy 92 and go up a canyon a few hundred yards to sign. Turn back east; a road follows the reservoir about 7 miles before a turnoff that descends to the reservoir at Soap Creek inlet. Main road continues north, following the creek for 8 more miles to Big Soap Park. Trail continues 2 miles to West Elk Wilderness Area boundary.

Soap Creek is about 10 feet wide and is fair to good for brook and rainbow, especially early in the season. Generally, ample campsites are available in addition to campgrounds.

Upstream from Blue Mesa and west of the city of Gunnison about 6 miles along US 50 is **Beaver Creek**, which flows into the Gunnison River at the Beaver Creek Picnic area. Beaver Creek offers 8 miles of good fishing for brook in the national forest. Lower

section is posted. **South Beaver Creek** enters the Gunnison from the south and is on private property. **West Beaver Creek** has fair fishing for cutthroat, but the entire length is tough to fish and not well-accessed. Fishing by artificial flies and lures only, all cutthroat must be returned to the water immediately in all forks of Beaver Creek.

SOUTH OF BLUE MESA

Above the Lake Fork Arm of Blue Mesa, the **Lake Fork of the Gunnison** is in a deep canyon. The stream here is possibly the best stretch of the entire river, with some large brown and rainbow taken all summer long. It is tough to fish and requires a stealthy approach. A good road (Rd 3009) continues northwest from Gateview to join US 50 just west of the Blue Mesa Dam. Above the town of Gateview the Lake Fork is a substantial stream for more

8 lb Snake River Cutthroat from the Taylor River

than 25 miles to Lake San Cristobal. The river meanders through meadows and brushy sections, and much of it is posted as private property. The river is paralleled by Hwy 149 for many miles and is easily fished. Well-marked public and private sections.

Crystal Lake (11,700 ft; 18 ac) is located on a 4-mile trail (USFS 235) outside Lake City, which begins at the Riverside Estate Subdivision. The trail begins at the old cemetery and climbs for the duration of the hike. The trail can get confusing, so a good map is recommended. Fair to good fishing for rainbow and brook. Occasionally winterkills. Near the 3-mile mark, the trail passes tiny **Hay Lake** (10,100 ft; 1 ac), which contains small brook trout.

Larson Lakes (11,000 ft; 3 ac and 1 ac) are reached by a 4-mile hike on USFS 236, off the same trailhead, but are found north of Crystal Lake in another drainage. The lakes, one of which is tiny, offer fair fishing for rainbow and brook.

Thompson Lake (9,920 ft; 6 ac) is located on USFS 235 one mile from the cemetery on a good trail. This shallow lake can winterkill and is fair fishing for brook and rainbow.

At Lake City, **Henson Creek** races into the Lake Fork from the west. A well-marked road (Rd 3300) leads 16 miles up the historic mining valley past many abandoned mines and town sites. The lower reaches of the creek are in the canyon and difficult to reach below Treasure Falls. Above, it contains rainbow, brook and some browns to 13 inches. Best fishing during high clear flows in early summer. Narrow valley;

camping limited. **North Henson Creek** joins the stream at Capitol City townsite. Fair fishing for small brook and cutthroat. The entire area is a 4WD mecca and is heavily traveled, because the Henson Creek Road goes over Engineer Pass (about 13,000 feet) to Ouray. Most tributary streams are small, swift and too vertical to offer much fishing.

Just above Cooke Falls, a bridge spans the Lake Fork and connects with Park Creek Road to provide access to **Waterdog Lake** (11,100 ft; 11 ac). The 5-mile road begins at T Mountain Resort and heads northeast. The trail near the sewer plant in Lake City is an alternate route. (Inquire locally for directions.) The climb will take several hours and does pass through private property. Please stay on trail and respect the property of others. The lake has good fishing for brook and stocked rainbows.

Special regulations apply to the Lake Fork below Lake San Cristobal and Lake City. Approximately 12 miles below the lake, from High Bridge Gulch downstream to the BLM boundary below Gate campground and from Cherry Creek to upper Red Bridge campground boundary: the Lake Fork is restricted to fishing by artificial flies and lures only. Limit for brown trout is two fish, 16 inches or longer. All rainbow must be returned to water immediately.

LAKE SAN CRISTOBAL

Lake San Cristobal (8,995 ft; 350 ac) is a popular lake, formed naturally by the famous Slumgullion Slide,

Photo Courtesy of Kevin Rummell

Mountains in the fall near Paonia

which dammed up the Lake Fork. This lake is heavily fished and condos line the eastern shoreline. Most of the fishing is for stocked rainbow and brook. A public launch ramp is located on the west side of the lake. Heavy pressure can make this lake poor in the summer, but winter ice anglers are few and far between, and fishing can be good. Few large mackinaw. Boats are available. Just below the outlet is Argenta Falls. From Argenta Falls downstream to Blue Mesa Reservation, snagging for kokanee salmon is permitted from September 1 through January 31. Good road circles the lake. The Lake Fork from the inlet of Lake San Cristobal upstream to the first bridge crossing is restricted to fishing by artificial flies and lures only.

From Sherman to Mill Creek Camp-ground and the Castle Lakes and Williams Creek Campground, the Lake Fork is heavily fished and stocked with rainbow. There are also brook and brown. Brushy stretches alternate with some ponds and pools. Spectacular country. The Lake Fork from the waterfall at Sherman to the headwaters is restricted to artificial flies and lures only, all cutthroat must be returned to the water immediately.

The Lake Fork from American Basin to the beginning of the Cinnamon Pass Road is tough to fish, especially in the lower section where it goes through a spectacularly steep canyon with a trail. The brushy upper portion has fair fishing for cutthroat, with openings in the brush periodically. In the canyon, most of the fishing is tough, but good for brook. Below the canyon,

Cottonwood Creek enters the Lake Fork. Cottonwood Creek is reached from the ghost town site of Sherman by auto for about 3 miles. It provides about 6 miles of good fishing above the confluence with Lake Fork. The lower section is timbered, but the upper section has some beaver ponds and is easier to fish. It is a fast moving stream with good fishing for brook to 8 inches, a few larger. A 4WD road follows the stream for a couple of miles, where it becomes a footpath.

Cataract Creek flows into Cottonwood Creek near its confluence with the Lake Fork, also at Sherman. About 2 miles upstream are beaver ponds, usually good for small brook and some cutthroat. **Cataract Lake** (12,100 ft; 15 ac) is 5 miles upstream by trail. The first mile is steep, and then it's relatively easy walking. The lake is usually covered with ice until July. Rated fair for cutthroat. Several small ponds to the west may be worth checking out.

Sloan Lake (12,920 ft; 7 ac) in the American Basin 20 miles southwest of Lake City is the origin of the Lake Fork. Sloan Lake is reached by traveling out of Lake City on Hinsdale CR 30 for 12 miles to CR 4 Road, which is commonly called the Cinnamon Pass Road. This lake is reached by about 2 miles of trail and contains Colorado River cutthroat, a rare species of trout. Restricted to artificial flies and lures only, all cutthroat must be returned to the water immediately. Occasionally winterkills. Lovely area with views of several 14,000-foot peaks, including 14,048-foot Handies Peak to the north.

Cooper Lake (12,750 ft; 10 ac) is located north of the Cinnamon Pass road, and is found by parking just after crossing **Cooper Creek** near the old ghost town of Whitecross. The lake is reached by a steep 4-mile trail. The creek has some fishing for small brook. Cooper Lake is good fishing for Colorado River cutthroat and small brook. Fishing by artificial flies and lures only, all cutthroat must be returned to the water immediately. This is a tough lake to fish, with only a few areas affording easy fishing as most of the shoreline is up against steep cliffs.

Snare Lakes (12,400 ft; 3 ac each) are located on the headwaters of Snare Creek and are seldom fished. They are reached by following the creek for about 7 miles from the end of the 4WD road up through a large meadow. The largest lake is the only one worth fishing and has some good brookies.

CEBOLLA CREEK

Cebolla Creek rises east of Lake City and is reached via Hwy 149 over Slumgullion Pass. Or from Creede, go north on Hwy 149 over Spring Creek Pass to the headwaters. The creek here is very small, but it grows in size as it picks up a few tributaries, including the West Fork of Cebolla Creek and Mill Creek.

Cebolla Creek, from its headwaters downstream to Powderhorn, runs through private and public land. The upper stretches are approximately 9 miles in length on public land. Upper reaches are accessible off the Mill Creek Road (USFS 788) from Hwy 149 between Lake City and Creede.

Heavily fished for rainbow, brown

Photo Courtesy of the Morrison Angler

Todd Anderson of the Morrison Angler with a 30" Taylor River Rainbow

and brook in the public section along the road, but offers good fishing for 12-inch brown and 9-inch brook above the Mill Creek Confluence. You can wade Mill Creek, then hike up an obscure trail along Cebolla. There are numerous beaver ponds that are easy to fish. This portion runs through the La Garita Wilderness Area.

The **West Fork of Cebolla Creek** is small, with 4 miles of fair fishing for small brook. From Lake City, the creek is 15 miles along Hwy 149 where the highway crosses the creek. Most of the creek has no trail and is not fished much after the first mile.

Mill Creek is also small and has about 6 miles of fishable water. It is reached by taking Hwy 149 out of Lake City for 9 miles to the Mill Creek Road, a good gravel road leading to Cathedral. Forest Service improvement on

this road has made it passable for larger RVs, but caution is advised on tight corners. The creek has brown, rainbow and brook, and receives moderate pressure.

Calf Creek joins Cebolla Creek about 9 miles down the Mill Creek Road from Hwy 149. The creek is small, but has good fishing for small brook in some beaver ponds. This creek drains a large area known as the Powderhorn Primitive Area.

The Forest Service has five campgrounds in the upper reaches of Cebolla Creek between Slumgullion Pass and Cathedral townsite. The terrain ranges from rolling timber to steep rock cliffs and outcrops. There are numerous small creeks, such as **Brush Creek**. Some have small brook.

Deer Creek Lakes (10,500 ft; 6 lakes of 3 to 4 ac each) are stocked and easily fished for rainbow and cutthroat. **Mill Creek Ponds**, as well as Deer Creek Lakes, are reached from the Mill Creek Road. Stocked with catchable rainbows.

Spring Creek merges with Cebolla at Cathedral. Up to the falls on **Cascade Creek** about 6 miles, stream and beaver pond fishing can be good for cutthroat and brook. Some posted sections. Again, beautiful country. Ask permission to cross private land.

There is roadside fishing along the creek in the **Cebolla Creek State Wildlife Area** just north of Cathedral for brook and rainbow. From the Forest Service boundary downstream to Powderhorn, there are only 3 miles of public stream in the Cebolla State Wildlife Area. Reasonably open fishing for fly fishers.

POWDERHORN AREA

From Hwy 149, 2 miles northwest of Powderhorn, a dirt road heads south to **Powderhorn Creek** drainage. The road becomes a trail before entering the Powderhorn Primitive Area. The **East, Middle** and **West Forks of Powderhorn Creek** are good for small brook, and the upper portions contain cutthroat. Many beaver ponds.

Upper Powderhorn Lake (11,800 ft; 27 ac) is a beautiful lake, which contains cutthroat and brook averaging 12 inches, but some larger. Difficult lake to fish. The lake is reached off Hwy 149, 25 miles north of Lake City at mile marker 97. A sign here indicates Indian Creek Road, CR 58, and goes south 9 miles. It is good for most autos. The well-marked trail goes 5 miles to the lakes. **Lower Powderhorn Lake** (11,650; 9 ac) has good brook and some cutthroat fishing, and also is very beautiful. It's a scenic area where there is a good opportunity to see wildlife, including deer, elk and ptarmigan.

Devils Lake (11,900 ft; 43 ac) is reached by taking the Mill Creek Road to Deer Creek Lakes. Head north to where Brush Creek flows under the road. The trail (TR461) is seven miles long and good for horses. The lake lies below Calf Creek Plateau and often winterkills. Fair fishing for brook and cutthroat.

Powderhorn Creek meets the Cebolla at Hwy 149 north of the town of Powderhorn. A good road follows the creek for a short distance (less than a mile) to the junction of East and West Powderhorn Creeks. Another road, one that gets progressively worse and eventually turns into a 4WD road, follows the East Fork. Tough road when wet.

Ohio Creek flows into the Gunnison River north of the city of Gunnison. It is reached by taking the Ohio Creek Road off Hwy 135 about 3 miles north of Gunnison. The road leads northwest for 10 miles to the Mill Creek Road, where it becomes dirt and parallels Ohio Creek for another 12 miles. The creek flows through private ranch land for its duration and is poor fishing for rainbow due to the large amount of irrigation diverted from it during summer. Extreme upper reaches are in national forest and are accessible via the Ohio Pass Road to the summit of Kebler Pass. There is some cutthroat in the upper area.

The Ohio Creek Road (USFS 730)

continues over Ohio Pass to intersect with the Kebler Pass Road. It is an interesting trip, especially beautiful in the fall when the aspen leaves change color (mid-September). Before the valley narrows, the road passes the historic town of Baldwin, located on posted, private property. This coal-mining town is possibly the best-preserved ghost town in Colorado.

Mill Creek flows into the Ohio from the west at the Mill Creek Road. A road (USFS 727) follows Mill Creek to the West Elk Wilderness for about 5 miles. The fishing in the creek is poor and is posted at the lower end. Some brook higher. Great view of "The Castles", rising high on a ridge to the north.

Carbon Creek enters Ohio Creek 3 miles above the Mill Creek Road. The road follows the creek for 6 miles and crosses mostly private land with limited public access. Permission to fish is rarely given. In the upper stretch there is some good fishing on public land for brook and small cutthroats in beaver ponds, however, it is very narrow and brushy.

Castle Creek flows into the Ohio from the west about a mile above Baldwin. It is on private land. A locked gate has shut off all access from this point. To reach Castle Creek, one can travel another 3 miles north to the Beaver Ponds trailhead and follow a trail (USFS 439 to USFS trail 438) along the Anthracite Range for about 4 miles west and then south to Castle Creek. Good fishing for small brook and small rainbow.

Costo Lake (10,100 ft; 15 ac) is inside the West Elk Wilderness and was a good fishery; however, extreme pressure has depleted this lake which once was filled with large brook; now only has small brook. The lake is reached by the same trail (USFS 439) that leads to Castle Creek. A few good campsites on the lake, but they are heavily used.

Pass and **Little Pass** creeks are also accessed from the trailhead (USFS 439) and are good fishing for small brook. Wild trout in these streams require a very stealthy approach. Many campsites in the area. Numerous bears are in the area; store food overnight by hanging it from a tree.

Located about 3 miles from the Cow Camp on Castle Creek are two hidden lakes along Storm Ridge, deep in the West Elks. No developed trail. The lakes, known as **Long Lake** (11,040 ft; 8 ac) and the **Golden Lake** (11,080 ft; 3 ac), are located below Storm Ridge. The lakes are best reached hiking in from the north rather than walking through heavy timber. Use a topo map. This is one of the few places in the state that contains golden trout. Excellent camping in the area and along Castle Creek. Be certain to practice low-impact camping in this heavily used area.

Another method for reaching the Castle Creek drainage is via the Swampy Pass trail in the West Elks from the Horse Ranch Park on the west side of Kebler Pass. This is a very long route, but a scenic one that travels over Anthracite Ridge.

UPPER GUNNISON BASIN

The Upper Gunnison Basin north and east of the town of Gunnison, in-

Photo Courtesy of Kevin Rummell

Waterfall near Ouray

cluding, Cochetopa Creek, Tomichi Creek, East River and the Taylor River offers outstanding fishing and gorgeous scenery. The mountain town of Crested Butte offers its own unique blend of beautiful country, great restaurants, mountain hiking and other outdoor pursuits. The entire area is easily accessible from US Hwy 50 west of Monarch Pass.

Cochetopa Creek rises along the Continental Divide about 30 miles south of Tomichi Creek and flows north. Hwy 114 from US 50 parallels Cochetopa for about 18 miles before turning east. Entering Tomichi Creek at the intersection of US 50 and Hwy 114, the lower section runs through a beautiful, steep, wooded canyon. The stream is surrounded by private land in the lower reaches; and permission to fish must be obtained. Fishing is good for rainbow and brown but gets heavy fishing pressure.

The canyon gives way to a beautiful mountain park. In the park, the Coleman Ranch Lease is Wild Trout water, catch and release with artificial flies and lures only. This section is good for large rainbow and brown. Taking USFS road 3083 off Hwy 114 accesses this stretch. It is a good, gravel road and is passable for larger RVs.

The **Lower** and **Upper Dome Reservoirs** (9,000 ft; 16 and 22 ac) State Recreation Areas are just above the catch-and-release section of Cochetopa Creek. The reservoirs have large sucker populations, and offer fair fishing for rainbow and brown.

Los Pinos Creek, which enters the Cochetopa about 20 miles upstream from Cochetopa's confluence with Tomichi Creek, is fair for brook and, at higher elevations, some cutthroat. A good road (KK - 14) follows Los Pinos. Wild trout water and fishing is strictly catch-and-release with artificial lures or flies.

Pauline Creek and the upper sections of Cochetopa Creek are reached by taking USFS road 3086 southwest from the reservoirs. The road offers excellent access to both creeks, and travels through scenic parks with excellent campsites that provide views of the La Garita Wilderness. Both creeks are good for brook and a few cutthroat.

Tomichi Creek rises high in the mountains near the Continental Divide at the western foot of Monarch Pass above the summer resort of White Pine, about 11 miles north of US 50. The road going north out of White Pine is a rugged dirt road, which quickly deteriorates into a 4WD road, which parallels the creek through its length, affording easy access. This 5-foot-wide upper section can be good for 6-inch brook but fishing is difficult in the swift water and profusion of willows. Catchable size rainbows are stocked. This is basically the only portion of the creek open for public fishing. Below White Pine, permission is necessary from landowners. It enters the Gunnison 1-mile southwest of the town of Gunnison.

From its headwaters, Tomichi Creek drops quickly into cattle country and meanders through private land for about 35 miles to its junction with the Gunnison River west of Gunnison. The upper stretch is a beautiful stream, with high, shaded banks affording good fishing for brown averaging 12.

Though it is an extremely fertile river, it can have high water temperatures in late summer, resulting in a large number of suckers in the creek. Concentrate on fishing it in fall, when ranchers stop irrigating, water temperatures drop and stream flows stabilize. Overall, rated good.

Needle Creek enters Tomichi Creek from the south 4-miles above Doyleville, but nearly all the water is diverted into irrigation ditches during the summer through this section and there is no fishing. To reach the upper stretches, take the good dirt road leading south from Doyleville, known as the Doyleville Cut-Off Road. The route is marked for much of the way, consult a good map for complete directions. The creek offers fair fishing for brook. **Needle Creek Reservoir** (8,800 ft, 6 ac) is primarily used for irrigation and fluctuates greatly. The reservoir has fair fishing for rainbow and brook in a very scenic setting.

A rough 4WD road leading directly over to the Razor Creek Park for about 3-miles reaches **Razor Creek** from Needle Creek Reservoir. The creek winds through the park to its headwaters on the Continental Divide, and offers open fishing for brook. It's a good place to watch for elk. Early summer is the best angling time as low water in the late summer and fall makes fishing difficult. The creek also may be reached by following the Doyleville Cut-Off for about 6miles to the creek. Permission is required to fish this private stretch. Beautiful country with interesting dome-shaped mountains, including Razor Creek Dome and

Cochetopa Dome. Tomichi Dome is visible to the south.

Marshall Creek enters Tomichi from the southeast about 1 mile west of Sargents along US 50. Follow the road that turns south at Sargents and goes over Marshall Pass for 40 miles to Poncha Pass and Salida. It parallels the creek for about 10 miles. The lower stretches of Marshall provide good fishing for 12-inch brown, but 7 miles of it is on private land and permission is required. Upper reaches are good for brown, rainbow and brook to 10 inches. Good campsites.

Canyon and **Porphyry creeks** feed into the upper Tomichi south of White Pine. Both are small, brushy streams with limited fishing for brook to 10 inches. Both can provide good fall fishing, especially in the beaver ponds in the upper stretches. Porphyry Creek is tough to reach, however, and requires permission to cross private land. Canyon, with 5-miles of stream, is accessed by a good trail about 0.5-mile south of the Snowblind Campground near White Pine. Rated good.

Agate Creek is reached by a good trail off US 50 near Monarch Pass. The creek can be excellent fishing for brook, with a few rainbow in sections. The trail parallels the creek for about 8-miles after dropping sharply from the Monarch Pass road.

QUARTZ CREEK

Quartz Creek enters the Tomichi about 13 miles east of Gunnison on US 50 at the town of Parlin. A good highway, 162, parallels the length of Quartz and goes over the Cumberland Pass into Taylor Park and to Taylor Reservoir. The lower sections of Quartz Creek are on private ranch land. Permission to fish is required.

It's very brushy from Ohio City to Roosevelt Mine, 4.5 miles upstream. The creek averages 10 feet wide as it flows through one of the most picturesque valleys in the region. It has deep pools and undercut banks in some spots containing primarily rainbow and brook, with a few brown to 12 inches, particularly in the upper end.

Gold Creek enters Quartz from the north at Ohio City. It is paralleled by a good dirt road (USFS 771) for most of the way and has two Forest Service campgrounds on its banks. Fishing is fair for small brook. Several high mountain lakes are accessed from this drainage.

A trail leads 3 miles from the Gold Creek Campground to the **Lamphier Lakes**. **Upper Lamphier Lake** (11,700 ft; 4 ac) is a beautiful lake about 0.25 mile above **Lower Lamphier Lake** (11,250; 3 ac). Both have fair to good fishing for Snake River cutthroat to 12 inches, some larger. This rugged area is known as Fossil Ridge and is a good area in which to keep an eye out for mountain goat and elk. From Upper Lamphier, the visible notch that is seen in the ridge to the north is Gunsight Pass.

Hike 3 miles through the pass over a rough, steep trail to **Henry Lake** (11,700 ft; 13 ac), a deep, clear lake with Snake River cutthroat, some to 18 inches, but most smaller. Very temperamental fishing. Henry Lake is also reached from the Lottis Creek Campground in Taylor Canyon, 7 miles by good horse trail.

Boulder Lake (11,100 ft; 20 ac) is reached by 2.5 miles of well-marked trail from Gold Creek Campground. The lake is overstocked with naturally produced small brook. **Mill Lake** (11,600 ft; 7 ac) is reached from Boulder Lake Trail just before crossing Fossil Ridge, (north about 1 mile along Lamphier Creek drainage). Stocked with Snake River cutthroat.

Crystal Lake (11,250 ft; 3 ac) is reached from Willow Creek, which enters Quartz from the northwest about 0.5-mile below Ohio City. Use 4WD to go 5-miles up-creek to old Carbonate King Mine, and then hike 5 more miles by marked trail over and down Fossil Ridge. South of the trail, Boulder Lake can be seen. Crystal Lake is opposite Boulder Lake on the north side of the ridge. Crystal is rated good for Snake River cutthroat, but they can be tough to catch.

Near the town of Pitkin, portions of the creek are open to the public and rated good, especially in the fall and early spring. Excellent camping is available above Pitkin (16 miles north of Parlin) and at Quartz Creek (7 miles north of Ohio City), both on Hwy 162. This area was once the site of heavy mining activity and consequent logging, but few traces of the past are found today. The hills, which were deforested, have regrown with mature lodgepole pine. The hatchery near Pitkin is the oldest in the state.

Two miles above Pitkin, the road forks. The east fork (USFS 767) leads 2-miles to a campground at **Middle**

Quartz Creek. The creek is good for small rainbow and brook. To get to **South Quartz Creek**, which is good for small brook, drive another 0.5-mile. Both streams are 3 to 4 feet wide, with beaver ponds.

Quartz Creek above Pitkin is known as **North Quartz Creek**. It is paralleled by the Cumberland Pass Road (USFS 765) and can be good for small brook, rainbow and brown. It has many ponds, as does **Middle**, and **South Quartz** creeks.

TAYLOR RIVER

Taylor Canyon, formed by the Taylor River, is one of the most spectacular in the area, and an excellent viewing area for bighorn sheep, particularly in the fall and winter. From Taylor Dam downstream for 325 yards, fishing is prohibited as posted. From a point 325 yards below Taylor Dam downstream to the upper boundary of Sam's private property (approximately 0.4-mile), fishing is catch and release with artificial flies and lures only. It holds trophy fish; 2-4 pounds are average, some in the 10- pound range.

The **Taylor River** starts near the Continental Divide along Taylor Pass and runs about 35 miles before joining the East River at Almont to form the Gunnison River. The best route to the Taylor River is to travel north out of Gunnison on Hwy 135 to the Taylor Canyon Road at Almont. Good pay campsites abound along the river. The Taylor is a rarity in the area, as most of its waters are open to the public, with the remainder heavily posted by private resorts and where permission to fish is rarely granted. The lower river through the canyon offers fair fishing for 12-inch stocked rainbow, small browns and an occasional brook or cutthroat. The river receives heavy pressure.

Spring Creek enters the Taylor from the north at Harmel Resort, about 8 miles from Almont on Hwy 306. The lower end is privately owned, but the upper end has several miles of public access, next to a dirt road (USFS 744), which can become quite corrugated, and is not recommended for larger RVs. The creek offers fair fishing for rainbow to 12 inches and smaller brook. The creek receives heavy pressure, especially during the summer. Cabins are available at the lower end of Spring Creek, and there are ample campsites upstream.

Spring Creek Reservoir (9,900 ft; 82 ac) is reached by following the Spring Creek Road for about 12 miles. The reservoir, built by the Colorado DOW, fluctuates occasionally, but offers fair fishing for catchable rainbow and a few brown. It also receives heavy pressure.

Just to the south of the reservoir, the road forks and parallels **Rocky Brook Creek** for a distance. This swift stream has fair fishing for small brook. Approximately 7-miles from the fork is Star Trail, leading into the backcountry behind Forest Hill.

Rocky Brook and **Bear Creek** in Deadman's Gulch are tributaries of Spring Creek, entering it about 7-miles above its mouth. It is another small stream with beaver ponds and offers fair fishing for small cutthroat and brook.

Horsethief Lake (10,000 ft; 2 ac) is a small, hidden lake located just off the trail about a mile from the trailhead. However, it is very easy to walk right by it without ever seeing it. The lake offers good fishing for brook to about 8 inches. Excellent campsites in the thickly timbered shoreline.

Five miles up Star Trail is **Mysterious Lake** (10,800ft; 5 ac), which is situated in a meadow to the left of the trail. Mysterious Lake has a large population of small brook and provides excellent fly-fishing.

East Beaver Creek enters Taylor River from the south, opposite Spring Creek. It is 10 miles long, 3 feet wide. Lower reaches are brushy; beaver dams upstream offer fishing for small brook and brown. Can be very good fishing. Accessible from One Mile Campground off of Taylor Road. A 4WD road crosses the creek to continue south for four to five miles. Rated fair.

Lottis Creek joins the Taylor River at the Lottis Creek Campground, about 4 miles below Taylor Park Dam. The creek is fishable up through Lottis Canyon and into Union Park on **North Lottis Creek**. Contains brook. Rated fair. **South Lottis Creek**, on Gunsight Pass Trail, has cutthroat from three miles above campground to Henry Lake.

Several smaller streams, including **Cameron** and **Cross Mountain**, offer some fishing, but most are difficult to fish due to dense vegetation. These are also reached by a rough 4WD road from Taylor Park at the trading post, locally known as Cranorville.

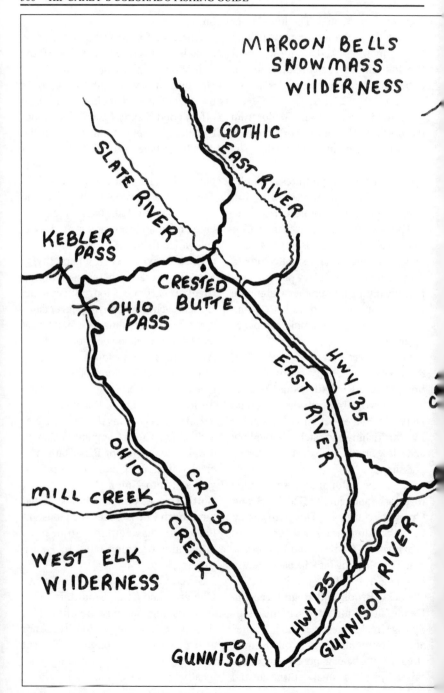

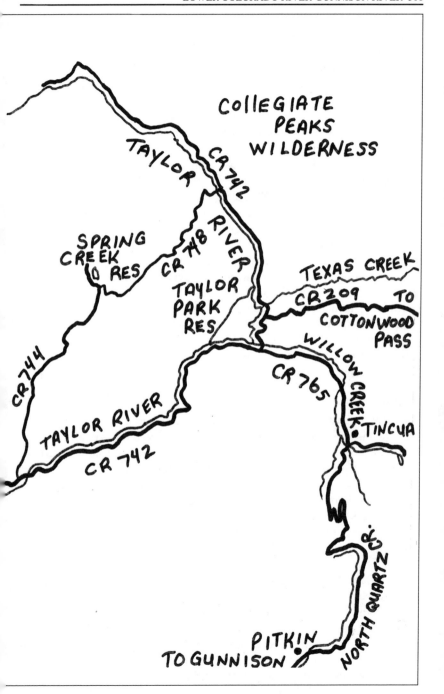

TAYLOR RESERVOIR

Taylor Reservoir (9,330 ft; 2000 ac), built in 1930, produces some nice fish. Part of this is due to the introduction of mysis shrimp several years ago. Better water management has improved the rainbow and kokanee fishing in the lake, which is now rated as good to excellent. Lake trout fishing is excellent. Mackinaw in the lake are in good shape and are caught just after ice-out (mid-May) or by ice fishing with sucker meat about 60 feet deep near the dam. The lake also contains a trophy-class northern pike fishery, which is very underutilized. Excellent in June in the shallow areas of the lake. Brown trout fishing is poor to fair with some occasional lunkers. The bag and possession limit for mackinaw is 3 fish, only one can be longer than 26". Snagging of kokanee salmon is permitted September 1 through January 31.

Willow Creek enters Taylor Reservoir from the east. It has 3.5 miles of water that is very good for brook and brown to 12 inches. Good for spawning browns in the fall when they swim up from the reservoir. A good gravel road (USFS 756) that follows West Willow Creek to Cumberland Pass parallels the creek. Stream forks at the town of Tincup. At the church in Tincup, a good gravel road (USFS 267) follows **East Willow Creek** for 3.5 miles to **Mirror Lake** (11,000 ft; 27 ac) and Mirror Lake Campground. The lake offers fair fishing for 10-inch brook and brown, with the occasional lunker. Beautiful area with excellent facilities; no motor boats. A pickup road (USFS 7562A) south from Tincup follows **Middle Willow Creek**.

All of the Willow creeks are small streams up to 10 feet wide, with much willow meadow and pond fishing for good brook populations. They contain small cutthroat in upper ends, with rainbow and brown in lower stretches. These are all good streams from midsummer on.

Pass Creek and **Cow Creek** enter Willow Creek from the north about 3 miles above Taylor Reservoir. Creeks are reached by short rough road from Hwy 162. They are small streams with beaver dams offering small brook and small cutthroat. Rated fair. Cottonwood Pass Road crosses Pass Creek 3 miles above Taylor Park Trading Post. **Cow Lake** (11,400 ft; 6 ac) is at the head of Cow Creek. Take Timberline Trail from the top of Cottonwood Pass south for 3 miles; look for sign. Good for 10-inch cutthroat and a few small brook.

TEXAS CREEK

Texas Creek flows into Taylor Reservoir from the east. Can drive 12 miles upstream (USFS road 755) with jeep or pickup, 6 miles by car. There are 16 miles of fishing in a stream about 10 feet wide. Good for rainbow, brook and cutthroat to 10 inches. Very good for brown in the fall.

Texas Creek Lakes (10,500 ft; 2 to 3 ac) lie hidden in timber 8 miles upcreek on the south side, across the stream from the road. There are three small lakes. Numbers 2 and 3 stocked with rainbows; Texas Lake north stocked with cutthroat. No boats or rafts allowed. Rated fair for brook to

10 inches with some bigger trout possible, especially in the center lake. They are shallow; good fly lakes, though temperamental.

Illinois Creek enters Taylor River from the east, 2 miles above the upper end of the reservoir. The creek offers 6 miles of fishing for small brook and brown in 4-foot-wide stream. Rated fair. Campsites. **Illinois Lake** (10,720 ft; 2 ac) is 1.5 miles by trail from the end of the road. Not shown on most maps. Good for cutthroat to 12 inches. Lake has heavy fishing pressure.

Red Mountain Creek enters Taylor River from the northeast about 3 miles above Pie Plant Cow Camp. Drive 1.5 miles up marked dirt road (USFS 742 8H). This 3-foot-wide stream is fishable for another 3 miles by trail. Beaver ponds. Fair for small brook.

Pot Hole Lakes (9,724 ft; 3 and 5 ac) are located 5 miles above Taylor Reservoir off the road to Dorchester. Heavily stocked, they are rated good for rainbow to 12 inches.

Italian Creek junctions from the west with Taylor about 2 miles below the Dorchester Ranger Station. Five miles of good fishing in a 4-foot-wide stream for brown and brook to 12 inches, some cutthroat and stocked rainbow.

Tellerium Creek joins the Taylor River less than a mile below the ranger station. About 6 feet wide with ponds. Eight miles of fishing can be reached by 4WD trail (USFS 584). The creek is fair to good for cutthroat in the upper stretches and small brown in lower. **Tellerium Lake** (12,300 ft; 6 ac), sometimes called **Ptarmigan Lake**, is a deep lake above timberline on the west fork of the creek. A rough road and a steep hike reach it, but it's beautiful. Good (but temperamental) for medium-sized cutthroat. Campsites below lake.

Pine Creek enters Taylor from the north, 0.5 mile below the ranger station at Dorchester. It is a 4- to 6-foot-wide stream with beaver ponds, and offers 4 miles of fair fishing for small cutthroat and brook. Trail is only fair.

Bowman Creek, entering Taylor at Bowman, is small and swift. It is rated fair for small brown, rainbow and cutthroat. A trail follows the creek.

Taylor Lake (12,400 ft; 30 ac) is 4 miles from Bowman by 4WD road. No buildings are left at this old ghost town site, just good campsites. Bowman is located at the confluence of Bowman Creek and Taylor. Taylor is rated good for rainbow and brook to 13 inches. Campsites are located below and around the lake. No boats or rafts allowed. Heavily fished.

EAST RIVER

The **East River** flows south from Crested Butte and joins the Taylor at the village of Almont, 10 miles northeast of Gunnison. The lower section is primarily private, with a stretch of quality water near the Roaring Judy Fish Hatchery a couple of miles above Almont. Permission is sometimes granted on the other portions but probably not likely. Fair to good fishing for brown to 18 inches. The river has a temperature problem in late summer. From the upstream property boundary at the Roaring Judy Hatchery downstream to its confluence with the Taylor River, fishing is with artificial flies only and the bag and possession limit is 2 trout of 12 inches in length or less. Early summer and late fall is the best times to fish the river. The taking of kokanee salmon is prohibited.

Cement Creek enters East River from the east at Crested Butte South, a collection of homes and condos on a plateau above the East River. The creek is followed by a good dirt road (USFS 740) for 9 miles, and by jeep road for another 9. The lower creek is brushy with fair fishing in the lower brushy end for cutthroat and rainbow. Higher up it flows through an open meadow and is good fishing for small brook. Numerous campsites including Cement Creek Campground, which is about a dozen sites and drinking water. Be especially careful to keep an extra clean campsite, however, as there are many bears in the area.

The Brush Creek road (USFS 738) reaches the upper East River, at Skyland Resort. Here, in the East River Valley, the fishing is good to excellent for brown and rainbow as the river meanders through hay meadows lined with willows. A bouncy 4WD road through private property that is usually accessible parallels this portion of river. Another way to reach this portion of the river is take USFS road 317 north out of Crested Butte over to Mt. Crested Butte and on toward Gothic. The upper river above Gothic has some brook and is rated only fair.

Gothic is an interesting place; it is a ghost town turned outdoor laboratory. Gothic is the headquarters of the Rocky Mountain Biological Laboratory, where scientists converge annually to study various effects of high altitude.

The Gothic Road eventually leads over Schofield Pass to Marble, a nasty jeep road (one of the toughest in the state), but in one of the most scenic areas. The road traverses a historic route that was once the connection between the marble quarries and Gothic as well as the supply town of Crested Butte. This road also gives access to the Maroon Bells-Snowmass Wilderness in the heart of the Elk Mountains.

Copper Creek enters East River at Gothic from the east. It is small and swift and offers poor to fair fishing for small cutthroat and rainbow. **Copper Lake** (11,450 ft; 10 ac) is up Copper Creek, 6 miles from Gothic by 4WD on 739. It contains cutthroat to 12 inches, rated fair. Forest Service campground at lake. **East Maroon Lake** (12,500 ft; 5 ac) is located 2 miles north of Copper Lake on good, marked trail; has cutthroat averaging 12 inches. Rated good. No campsites of any value. Often iced over into midsummer.

Brush Creek is reached by the Skyland Resort road, which is a good road (USFS 738) to the junction with the creek, but quickly turns into a rough jeep road. The creek is fast, with some good pools. Previously the creek was good for rainbow to 12 inches, but heavy pressure has demoted the fishery to only fair. Road from mouth of creek goes for 3 miles up **West Brush Creek**. Can 4wd within 3 miles of Twin Lakes at the head of **Middle Brush Creek** at the base of Teocalli Mountain (13,208 ft). Four-wheel-drive roads go up both Middle and **East Brush Creeks**. West Brush averages 6 feet wide. Good results are reported as far up as the falls for small rainbow, brook and cutthroat. Middle Brush is rated fair to good for small brook, cutthroat and rainbow. **Twin Lakes** (11,800 ft; lower 3 ac, upper 7 ac) are reached by 3 miles of trail (USFS 402) from Middle Brush Creek Road at the foot of Pearl Pass Road to Aspen, and are located 3 miles inside the Maroon Bells-Snowmass Wilderness Area. These beautiful lakes lie in a high alpine valley and can be tough to fish. Stocked with rainbow, some cutthroat, they offer fair fishing. Typical of high mountain lakes, the Twin Lakes can be very temperamental. Some large fish in the upper lake. Campsite below lakes.

Spencer Lake (10,000 ft; 3 ac) is located in timber. It is situated up Middle Brush Creek and is difficult to find. Not shown on forest map. Faint trail leaves Middle Brush Road 0.5 mile west of where Twin Lakes Trail leaves the road. Rated fair to good for small brook.

East Brush Creek enters Middle Brush 5 miles from the mouth of Brush Creek. It has 6 miles of fishing in a 4-foot stream with a few beaver ponds and much brush. East Brush is hard to fish, but is rated good for cutthroat to 11 inches.

The road along Middle Brush Creek eventually goes to Aspen via Pearl Pass (which isn't much of a pass at all and is usually not passable even for jeeps).

Farris Creek enters the East River on private land about 2 miles south of Brush Creek. Rough 4WD road from Brush Creek accesses the creek. The

Marilee with beautiful Taylor River Rainbow

Photo Courtesy of the Morrison Angler

road is about 4 miles up the Brush Creek Road from the intersection of Hwy 135. Turn right 0.75 mile above Veltrie Ranch; then it is 3 miles to the creek at the Forest Service boundary. There is private posted land downstream, where permission to fish is generally not granted. The creek averages 5 feet wide and is good for small brook, ponded in the upper end. The road quickly turns into a trail, which follows the creek for 3 miles of fishable water.

CRESTED BUTTE AREA

Slate River enters East River 6 miles below Crested Butte and is accessible by good dirt road (USFS 734) north from town. Road crosses the creek just east of town and then parallels Slate River northwest for 9 miles to Pittsburg and 2 miles beyond. Eight feet wide,

the stream is open above, brushy near mouth. Contains brook, brown and rainbow to 10 inches. Some Snake River cutthroat and small brook in upper reaches. Rated fair to good. **Nicholson Lake** (8,900 ft; 13 ac), a small lake, is located about 3 miles north of Crested Butte on the Slate River Road to Pittsburg, which goes right around it. Has brook to 10 inches. Rated fair, many rough fish.

Coal Creek, which parallels Road 12 for several miles, has some good brown trout and possibly a few hold-over stocked rainbows. It appears to be recovering from acid mine drainage pollution. It is often overlooked as a fishery, even in the town of Crested Butte, where it flows into Slate River.

Oh Be Joyful Creek enters Slate River about 6 miles northeast of

Crested Butte; accessible by dirt road (USFS 754) north of town. By 4WD it's 7 miles upstream. Beautiful small stream, 6 to 8 feet wide, offers small cutthroat and brook. Rated fair.

Blue Lake (11,100 ft; 5 ac) is reached by a good 2-mile trail from the end of the road up the Oh Be Joyful Creek. Stocked with small rainbow and cutthroat. Rated fair. No campsites at lake. Ice is late to leave—usually July.

Peeler Creek joins Oh Be Joyful Creek from the west, 2 miles above the mouth. Small and seldom fished. **Peeler Lake** (10,800 ft; 5 ac) is located up Peeler Creek by a good steep trail 4 miles from the end of the road. Lake is off main trail to the left or south 0.5-mile in timber, very difficult to find. Contains brook from 8 inches to 10 inches, with some fish to 16 inches. Rated good, but very temperamental.

Washington Gulch Creek enters Slate River east of Crested Butte; accessible from marked dirt road (USFS 811 off Gothic Road) 2 miles north of town. Offers 2 miles of fishing in a stream 4 feet wide, brushy at mouth and open upstream. Fair for small brook.

Meridan Lake (9,700 ft; 40 ac) is reached by traveling a dirt road up Washington Gulch north of Crested Butte. The road forks 2 miles from town; take the left fork 2 more miles to where a trail can be seen across the creek. It leads 0.25 mile to the lake. Steep hike. Fishing for rainbow from 10 to 12 inches.

Emerald Lake (10,500 ft; 12 ac) is on Schofield Pass, about 4.5 miles above Gothic in Gothic Natural Area, along a rough road that is often snow-bound. Rated fair for catchable rainbow and cutthroat, with a few large ones. Ponds in the area are research sites and closed to fishing. Campsites.

Lake Irwin (10,350 ft; 51 ac), sometimes called Lake Brennand, is west of the town of Crested Butte at the site of the historic town of Irwin, one of the largest silver-mining towns of the 1800's. President U.S. Grant visited Irwin during its heyday. Now all that is left are summer homes. The lake is reached by a good road (USFS 826) that forks off the Kebler Pass Road, then travels a mile to the Forest Service campground at the lake. Passable for RVs, this lake is a recommended stop for its scenery. Fishing can be excellent early in the year after ice out (mid-May) for rainbow and Yellowstone cutthroat to 12 inches. Excellent action from the banks in the early season, as well as from a canoe at one of the two inlets. Boats without motors permitted.

The Kebler Pass Road continues up and over the top, passing the Irwin cemetery. A field of glacier lilies can cover the ground immediately after the snow melts. The road travels over Kebler Pass through one of the largest continuous aspen stands in the state. Beautiful area with numerous campsites.

Green Lake (10,560 ft; 5 ac) at the headwaters of **Wildcat Creek** is good for small cutthroat. It is reached by trail from Kebler Pass Road about 3 miles west of Crested Butte. Most of Wildcat Creek is on private land. It provides fair fishing for small brook and cutthroat in the national forest area.

SOUTHWESTERN COLORADO

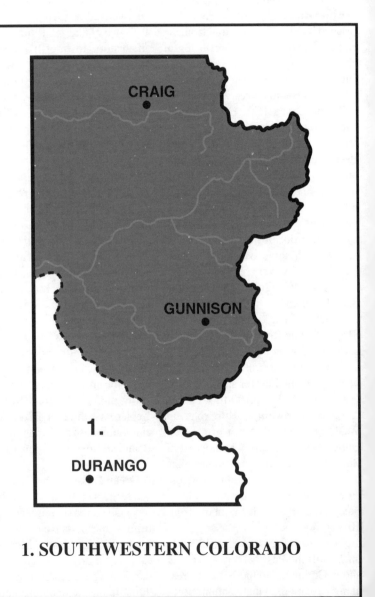

CRAIG

GUNNISON

1.

DURANGO

1. SOUTHWESTERN COLORADO

SOUTHWEST RIVERS

Southwestern Colorado offers some of the best, most under utilized fishing in the state. Ten large streams flow southward from the high, rough country of the Continental Divide. These streams, moving from east to west, are the Navajo, Rio Blanco, San Juan, Piedra, Los Pinos, Vallecito Creek, Florida, Animas, La Plata, Mancos and Delores rivers. They flow out of the pine and aspen of the San Juan National Forest into the vast, semi-arid pinon-juniper country, and, as they do, the fishing goes from delightful to scant. All these streams, except for Vallecito Creek and the Dolores, pass through the Southern Ute or Ute Mountain Indian Reservations.

The Southern Ute Tribe has developed an extensive tourist program, stocks some of the better angling waters and manages campgrounds and other facilities. Fishing on reservation waters requires a permit.

Three major bodies of water provide fishing and other recreation in this area between Pagosa Springs, Durango and Mancos: Navajo Reservoir on the Colorado-New Mexico state line, and Vallecito and Lemon reservoirs northeast of Durango. Echo Canyon and Pastorius reservoirs and Capote Lake also offer convenient angling and other water recreation.

Logging and Forest Service roads web the area, but in the Weminuche Wilderness Area, north of US 160, access is by foot or hoof only. The Weminuche Wilderness Area, the largest in Colorado, is in the San Juan and Rio Grande national forests along the Continental Divide.

The San Juan National Forest teems with wildlife. One of the largest elk herds in the state is found here, as well as mule deer, black bear, bighorn sheep and mountain lion. Small mammals, such as porcupine and beaver, are also found in large numbers. In the early fall, waterfowl frequent lower elevation waters.

The San Juan Mountains, one of the richest mining areas in Colorado, have produced $750 million worth of base and precious metals over the last 120 years. The mining operations mainly have produced gold and silver, with lesser amounts of copper, lead and zinc. Another mineral, pyrite or "fools gold," has oxidized and stained the mountain slopes with brilliant hues of red, orange and yellow. Mining operations have left many ghost towns in the region.

Four-wheel-drive enthusiasts will enjoy the several hundred miles of rough roads in the San Juans. The "Loop Road," which is the primary artery connecting Ouray, Lake City and Silverton via Engineer and Cinnamon passes, is the most popular route for motorists. Many rugged roads that spur off the Loop Road are challenging, leading into many isolated areas with obscure but productive creek or high lakes fishing.

SAN JUAN RIVER

The **San Juan River** has widely dispersed tributaries as it drains a vast area of the eastern San Juans. The East and West forks join at Saddle Back Ranch, 13 miles north of Pagosa Springs. The river then flows southward and, at the New Mexico State line, enters Navajo Reservoir in Colorado near Arboles. Not very swift, rather shallow and rocky bottomed, it is easily worked and usually wadable except in early season. The San Juan offers 40 miles of fishing for rainbow, brown, a few brook and cutthroat averaging 10 inches; some larger have been taken below Pagosa Springs. US 160 parallels the river for 9 miles from Pagosa Springs toward Wolf Creek Pass. About 20 percent of the river above Pagosa to the Forest Service boundary is tightly posted. The rest may be open by permission only.

Northeast of Pagosa Springs, the **East Fork of San Juan** is about 10 miles long and unwadable until mid-July. It muddies rapidly after rainfall. This fly-fishing stream contains rainbow, cutthroat and brook to 13 inches, and an occasional brown. Turn east off US 160 about 11 miles northeast of Pagosa Springs to East Fork Campground.

Crater Lake (11,000 ft; 22 ac), at the head of East Fork, is stocked and rated good for cutthroat to 12 inches. Access is by 4-mile hike from Elwood Pass. **Quartz Creek** enters the East Fork of San Juan about 8 miles upstream from East Fork Campground. It is a 5-mile creek paralleled by a good trail. Quartz Creek is a heavy, canyon stream offering cutthroat to 10 inches on flies. Rated good.

Quartz Lake (11,500 ft; 3 ac) is reached by a good but steep trail 5 miles from the junction of Quartz Creek and East Fork. It is a timberline lake with cutthroat to 13 inches. Rated fair to good. Best access is by trail at the end of Mill Creek Road. This gravel road junctions with US 84 about 0.25 mile south of US 160 at Pagosa Springs. Road runs 12 miles, then it's a 4.5-mile hike on trail to lake; first 2 miles are steep. **Sand Creek** enters the East Fork from the south 3 miles upstream from East Fork Campground. A small mountain stream 3 to 5 feet wide, it offers 6 miles of trail fishing for small cutthroat. Rated fair.

The **West Fork of the San Juan** joins the East Fork at the Saddle Back Ranch on US 160, 11 miles north of Pagosa Springs. It has 12 miles of good fishing through canyon country with fine pools and sharp drops. Accessible by rugged trail. Wadable only during low water. Good for rainbow and cutthroat averaging 10 inches, slightly larger through the canyon. It's reached by turning west off US 160, 6 miles south of Wolf Creek Pass summit, at West Fork Campground. Rough road continues beyond campground about 1 mile to Borns Lake. The lower 4 miles of the West Fork, from its junction with the East Fork to the campground, is tightly posted private land.

Beaver Creek enters the West Fork

from the east, 4 miles above the end of the road at Borns Lake. It offers 6 miles of trail fishing in very rough country with numerous waterfalls. Stream is 4 to 6 feet wide and rated good for cutthroat to 10 inches. **Cimarron Creek** enters the West Fork from the west 5 miles above the end of road at Borns Lake. This 3-foot-wide stream offers good fishing on flies for small cutthroat. **Borns Lake** (8,371 ft; 10 ac) is poor fishing because of winterkill. There is a parking lot here to allow access by foot to the upper reaches of the West Fork. Below Borns Lake at the West Fork Campground are the small **Hatcher Lakes** (8,050 ft; 3 ac). These lakes have been stocked with rainbow, but fishing is for brook.

Turkey Creek enters the San Juan River about 2 miles downstream from the East and West Fork branches, about 8 miles north of Pagosa Springs on US 160. The highway crosses a bridge marked Turkey Creek. The creek contains small brook and rainbow, and some brown and cutthroat. This 12-foot stream flows through a mountain canyon and offers good fly-fishing. Good trail follows the creek upstream beginning at a sign 0.25-mile north of Turkey Creek bridge. Trail continues northwest 16 miles to Turkey Creek Lake. 4WD can travel first few miles.

Turkey Creek Lake (11,135 ft; 23 ac), a crater lake at timberline, produces fine catches of small brook trout and a few mackinaw. Campsites are nearby. Lake seems to be overpopulated and could use more fishing pressure. Best access is from Fourmile Lakes.

Fourmile Creek enters the San Juan about 4 miles north of Pagosa Springs off Hwy 160. Access to creek by rugged road (Snowball Road) at north end of Pagosa Springs. No public access in lower reaches of creek. At the Fourmile Creek headwaters, **Lower Fourmile Lake** (11,400 ft; 12 ac) is fair for cutthroat, and **Upper Fourmile Lake** (11,700 ft; 12 ac) is good for cutthroat up to 14 inches; fish are difficult to catch. Both lakes are stocked and are reached by a paved road (Fourmile Road) leaving north edge of Pagosa Springs through beautiful country. Creek has numerous waterfalls.

Five miles by trail from end of Snowball Road to headwaters, **Snowball Creek** enters Fourmile Creek from the north about 5 miles above the San Juan River.

On the west side of US 84 moving south of Pagosa Springs about 3 miles is **Echo Canyon Reservoir** (7,200 ft; 118 ac). It offers excellent early spring fishing for cutthroat to 14 inches. It is becoming a warm water fishery with bass, perch, crappie and carp competing with trout. Two-pound bass are frequently taken. Catfish run up to 18 pounds. Stocked with rainbows. Boats allowed. All largemouth and smallmouth bass caught between 12 and 15 inches in length must be returned to the water immediately. There is no daily bag and possession limit for yellow perch.

South of Pagosa Springs (1.5 miles) **Mill Creek** flows into the San Juan River. Access is by dirt road from Pagosa Springs rodeo grounds. Marginal fishing.

White water stream

NAVAJO RIVER

The San Juan River's far eastern fork is the **Navajo River**. There are several small streams feeding the Navajo that offer good fishing. Some of the higher streams are seldom fished. Much of the river, which flows on private lands, is stocked in exchange for public access. Check before casting. From the headwaters downstream to Bridal Veil Falls, fishing is by artificial flies and lures only. All cutthroat must be returned to the water immediately.

The western forks of the Navajo River offer marginal fishing. Where the Navajo River meets the San Juan River on the Southern Ute Indian Reservation, provides good catfishing. The Navajo River intersects US 84 about 3 miles northwest of Chromo.

RIO BLANCO

The **Rio Blanco** has terrible fishing because the San Juan-Navajo diversion tunnel takes most of the water. Higher elevations have beaver dams. The Rio Blanco meets the San Juan River at the northeast corner of the Southern Ute Indian Reservation. The **Rito Blanco**, a tributary of the Rio Blanco, can be reached by taking US 84 at Pagosa Springs and turning east at the rodeo grounds; follow Mill Creek road about 5 miles. Turn south on USFS road about 5 miles to upper part of Rito Blanco where the stream is 5 to 6 feet wide. Poor fishing for small cutthroat in lower part due to irrigation diversions, but fair in upper reaches. Lower section of the Rito Blanco is tightly posted.

Fish Creek enters the Rio Blanco near the end of Blanco Basin Road. Blanco Basin Road can be reached by turning northeast off US 84 at Rito Blanco Creek on USFS road 657. Fish Creek has two main forks. The main stream is very small but fishable for 6 miles by trail for small cutthroat and brook. Rated fair. The **North Fork of Fish Creek** is paralleled by Fish Lake Pack Trail about 7 miles. At its headwaters is **Fish Lake** (11,800 ft; 9 ac), rated good for cutthroat to 18 inches. Campsites below lake.

White Creek enters the Rio Blanco at the Hamlin Ranch, via the Blanco Basin Road. White Creek offers 2 miles of small-stream and beaver pond fishing for small cutthroat and brook. **Opal Lake**, (9,250 ft; 1 ac), at the headwaters of White Creek, is reached by 2 miles of unmarked trail. Rated good for brook and rainbow to 11 inches. The **Big Branch** of the Rio Blanco is fed by **Buckles Reservoir** (9,350 ft; 10 ac) and **Harris Reservoir** (9,450 ft; 37 ac). They are reached by USFS road 663 that joins US 84 about 22 miles south of Pagosa Springs; marked with sign. Short hikes to reservoirs. Buckles is fair to good for rainbow and cutthroat; a few brook to 20 inches. Although Harris fluctuates greatly, it has been a good producer of cutthroat, rainbow and brook to 13 inches, some larger. Harris often is choked with weeds by August. Fair campsites.

Navajo Reservoir (6,085 ft; 3000 ac) on the Colorado side of the Colorado-New Mexico State line is a fluctuating water body formed behind Navajo Dam. The reservoir is fed by the Piedra, Los Pinos and San Juan rivers.

A Ute Indian fishing permit is required.

The New Mexico side of the 35-mile-long reservoir has some 12,600 surface acres. A New Mexico fishing license is required of anglers in that part of the reservoir.

The reservoir has large- and small-mouth bass, rainbow and brown trout, bluegill, northern pike, kokanee, channel catfish, and crappie. Boat registration and inspection stickers from either state are valid on the reservoir. The boat ramp at Arboles is huge, and there is a visitor center and camping with showers and flush toilets, as well as RV dump facilities.

May and June is a good time for crappie near Arboles Marina. The Piedra and San Juan arms of the reservoir offer large catfish. The small, brushy coves on the north side of the reservoir offer good bass and northern pike fishing. Spring and fall on the Piedra arm are good for trout.

Located on pinon-juniper land, the reservoir fluctuates considerably. The area is very hot and dry in the summer. Service facilities are available at Arboles, just west of the reservoir.

Accessibility is from Pagosa Springs by a 40-mile gravel road west and north of the San Juan River. From Chimney Rock, access is 7 miles east on US 160 and then south on Hwy 151. From Durango, take Hwy 172 southeast via Ignacio about 35 miles.

PIEDRA RIVER

About 15 miles west of the San Juan River, the **Piedra River** is a 40-mile stretch that has trout fishing its entire length. The headwater tributaries are in the Weminuche Wilderness, and the lower river is on reservation lands. US 160 crosses the Piedra River 22 miles west of Pagosa Springs just past Chimney Rock. The section of the Piedra River below US 160 is noted for large browns taken on bait and lures. Rainbows to 10 inches also are caught using bait and flies. The river averages 30 feet wide, is rather slow moving and has alternating pools and rocky riffles; good stonefly hatch in spring. A gravel road follows the east side of the river north for 12 miles to First Fork of the Piedra River and Piedra Hunter Campground. A good time to fish the tributaries is immediately after summer showers. A 20-mile section of the river from Piedra River bridge on Forest Service road 631 (Piedra Road) downstream to the lower boundary of Tres Piedra Ranch (1.5 miles above US 160) fishing is by artificial flies and lures only.

The lower country streams and creeks feeding the Piedra River, including **Stollsteimer**, **Martinez Heflin, Same Reservoir**, and **Sullenburger Reservoir** are not worth fishing as all of the streams flow through private land and are not stocked. Martinez may offer some potential for cutthroat.

The **Middle Fork of Piedra River** can be reached from the Piedra Road (631), which goes north from US 84 about one mile west of Pagosa Springs. Road follows stream for about 6 miles. No trail to upper 6 miles of stream; very rough country.

The headwaters of the **East Fork of the Piedra River** are near the northeast boundary of the Weminuche Wil-

Photo Courtesy of Kevin Rummell

Wemanuche Wilderness

derness Area. The East Fork is 9 feet wide and about 10 miles long. The upper reaches are accessible by trail that follows the Continental Divide from the Middle Fork. Wadable and rated excellent with flies for cutthroat to 10 inches. Catch and release on all cutthroat, artificial flies and lures only. There are several backcountry tributaries, including **Deadman**, **Pagosa** and **Plumtaw Creeks** that offer good fishing for cutthroat and brook.

Williams Creek enters the Piedra River about 1 mile down river from the juncture of Middle and East forks. It's a 16-mile, 10-foot-wide stream rated fair to good for rainbow and cutthroat to 10 inches and is also stocked with brook. Fishing is excellent below Williams Creek Reservoir during rainbow spawning period in May. Road follows stream to Cimarrona Campground. Three other campgrounds are along stream. **Williams Fork Lake** (11,500 ft; 3 ac) at timberline is 7 miles north from the end of the road at Cimarrona Campground. Good trail parallels Williams Creek to lake. This lake is not stocked, but has a very good, self-sustaining cutthroat population. **Indian Creek** joins Williams Creek about 4 miles above the end of the road. Good for small cutthroat at lower end. **Williams Creek Reservoir** (8,242 ft; 343 ac) is rated excellent for 9- to 14-inch rainbow and brook. Cutthroat and kokanee are also available. Boats and motors allowed.

Weminuche Creek forks north from the Piedra River about 2 miles downstream of Williams Creek Fork. Access is by following USFS road 631 to Williams Creek Reservoir and cutting west before reaching reservoir. Upper part is stocked with cutthroat and rainbow. Lower part, in Weminuche Valley, is on private lands.

LOS PINOS RIVER

Midway between the Piedra River and Durango, the **Los Pinos River** intersects US 160 at Bayfield. The 25 miles of public fishing water above Vallecito Reservoir to the north in the Weminuche Wilderness average 20 feet in width with pools, riffles and rapids. Rated good for brown, rainbow and cutthroat to 14 inches. Los Pinos River from its headwaters to the Weminuche Wilderness boundary is fishing by artificial flies and lures only.

Near the northern boundary of the Weminuche Wilderness, **Snowslide**, **Rincon La Vaca**, **North Fork**, **Rincon La Osa**, **Canon Paso** and **Sierra Vandera** are small tributaries at the headwaters of Los Pinos. These streams are rated fair for small cutthroat. They are located in the Weminuche Wilderness Area and are accessible by long trail from the Pine River Campground northeast of Vallecito Reservoir. Three small lakes requiring 12 to 15 mile hikes are the headwaters for these creeks, including **Granite Lake** (10,400 ft; 35 ac), **Elk Lake** (11,550 ft; 6 ac) and **Divide Lake** (10,000 ft; 3 ac), are stocked by air and rated fair to good for cutthroat and rainbow. All three lakes are in exceptionally beautiful settings.

Flint Creek enters Los Pinos about 12 miles north from the end of the road at Pine River Campground. This typical, fine mountain stream, 6 to 8 feet wide with deep pools and fast riffles, offers good cutthroat fishing. It is fed by **Big Flint Lake** (11,650 ft; 38 ac), which is reached by a steep 8-mile trail up Flint Creek. Excellent for 10- to 14-inch cutthroat. Not open before middle of June. **Little Flint Lake** (11,870 ft; 10 ac) is across the canyon from Big Flint Lake. Trail connects. Fair for 10- to 12-inch cutthroat. Camping is best below lake along trail; however, there are ample campsites on lake.

Lake Creek enters Los Pinos from the north about 6 miles above the end of the road at Pine River Campground. It is a 5-mile stream with many large pools. Good for small cutthroat and rainbow. **Moon Lake** (11,700 ft; 12 ac) and **Half Moon Lake** (12,200 ft; 2 ac), are at the headwaters of Lake Creek. They have small rainbow, cutthroat and stunted brook. Three miles downstream two premier Wild Trout water exists, **Big Emerald Lake** (10,033 ft; 280 ac) has a good reproducing cutthroat-rainbow hybrid population. Big Emerald Lake is 242 feet deep, the second deepest natural lake in the state. **Little Emerald Lake** (10,000 ft; 15 ac) is south of Big Emerald Lake only a few hundred yards. **Dollar Lake** (11,550 ft; 10 ac) drains into Big Emerald Lake from the west. Dollar has been stocked with the Emerald Lake strain of hybrid cutthroat-rainbow. All three lakes offer good fishing, but are restricted to artificial flies or lures only, and the limit is two fish 14 inches or less in length. Fishing is prohibited in the Lake Creek inlet for 0.5 mile above Big Emerald Lake from January 1 through July 15.

Below Vallecito Reservoir to Bayfield, the Los Pinos meanders through private lands. This 12-mile stretch holds rainbow to 16 inches and some big brown. Wadable except in spring. It averages about 30 feet wide with fine riffles and pools. Public access is very limited.

From Bayfield south, the river enters the Southern Ute Indian Reservation. It is heavily stocked by the federal government, and fishing requires a Ute Indian tribe permit. County Road 511 south of Bayfield to Ignacio roughly parallels the river. Because of ideal fish habitat—suitable spawning sites and plenty of food—fish populations are virtually self-sustaining.

VALLECITO RESERVOIR

Vallecito Reservoir (7,500 ft; 2700 ac) is about 19 miles north of Bayfield. The reservoir can be reached by turning north off US 160 in Bayfield onto County Road 501; stay on the county road until reaching the reservoir. The reservoir is fished principally by trolling, but fishing from rocky points on shore is excellent at times. Rainbow are stocked. Pike were stocked in the early 1960s and are now self-sustaining. Browns are not numerous, but can be quite large. Boats and motors are available. Cabins, resort and five forest service campgrounds on east side. Spring and fall are the best seasons in this popular area.

VALLECITO CREEK

Vallecito Creek enters Los Pinos at Vallecito Reservoir and stretches north to the Divide offering 22 miles of fish-

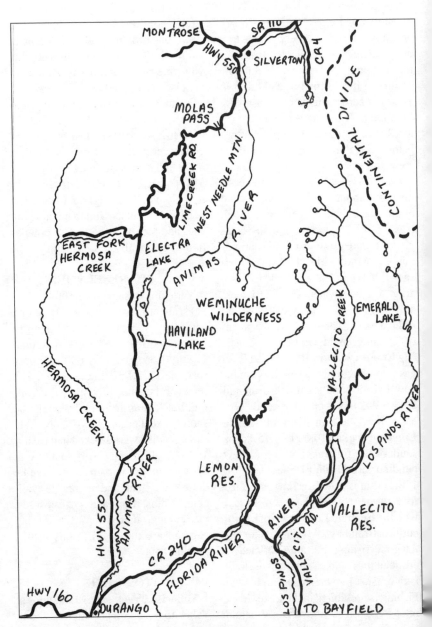

ANIMAS

ing, 19 miles of trail. From the reservoir to Vallecito Campground is private property. Vallecito is fast, heavily fished, wadable in shallows and averages about 15 feet wide with plenty of pools and riffles. It contains rainbow, brook and cutthroat to 10 inches and is rated a good fly stream. From the inlet of Vallecito Reservoir upstream the taking of kokanee salmon (including snagging) is prohibited except from November 15 through December 31. From the Weminuche Wilderness boundary to the headwaters fishing is by artificial flies and lures only.

Irving, **Johnson**, **Sunlight**, **Leviathan**, **Rock** and **Storm King creeks** are the principal fishing tributaries. Each offers about 4 miles of small-stream fishing and some beaver ponds. Fine fly-fishing for small cutthroat and few rainbow. There are a number of good lakes in the upper reaches of these creeks, requiring very hard 17 to 25 mile hikes. Many are accessible by horse from the Vallecito Campground at the north end of Vallecito Reservoir. Most of the alpine lakes are stocked with cutthroat by air. They include **Storm King Lake** (12,300 ft; 13 ac), **Silex Lake** (12,400 ft; 4 ac), **Mystery Lake** (12,600 ft; 5 ac), **South Leviathan Lake** (12,100 ft; 8 ac), **North Leviathan** (12,400 ft; 6 ac), **Sunlight Lakes** (11,650 ft; 18 ac combined), **Vallecito Lake** (12,010 ft 14 ac), **Trinity Lake** (12,250 ft; 16 ac), **Annie Lake** (12,200 ft; 12 ac), **Betty Lake** (12,167 ft; 7 ac), **Rock Lake** (11,834 ft; 30 ac), **Hazel Lake** (12,450 ft; 10 ac), **Columbine Lake** (12,400 ft; 4 ac) and **Irving Lake** (11,650 ft; 7 ac), and

are nestled in the rugged Needle Mountains. Trails connecting lakes are steep. On the east side of Vallecito Creek, **Hidden Lake** (12,000 ft; 15 ac) and **Lost Lake** (11,800 ft; 10 ac) are rated good for cutthroat and rainbow. These lakes are two of the most popular fishing holes in the Needle Mountains.

FLORIDA RIVER

The **Florida River** originates more than 20 miles north of Durango and enters the Animas below Durango from the northeast. It is a typical mountain stream about 10 feet wide. Logging roads along the ridges on both sides of the Florida River offer access. At its headwaters, **City Reservoir** (10,960 ft; 100 ac) is rated excellent for small brook and a few cutthroat. Access is from Lemon Reservoir on trail 534. Other lakes in the area, **Castilleja Lake**, **Stump Lakes** and **Lost Lake**, do not offer good fishing due to winterkill.

Lemon Reservoir (8,150 ft; 400 ac when full) has good rainbow and kokanee to 15 inches. The reservoir can be reached by following a good paved road, CR 240 (also called Florida Road), northeast out of Durango, that junctions with CR 243, which leads to the reservoir. Three campgrounds, Transfer Park, Florida and Miller, are located near or on the reservoir. Florida River below the reservoir flows through private land. Above Lemon, **Virginia Gulch Creek**, is a recovery area for greenback cutthroat. Catch and release, artificial flies and lures only.

Wilderness waterfall

Photo Courtesy of Kevin Rummell

ANIMAS RIVER

To the west of Los Pinos River and flowing through Durango, the **Animas River** has about 75 miles of fishable water. Heading near Silverton, the river is east of Hwy 550 and flows south through Durango, leaving Colorado below Bondad. Up to 100 feet wide in places, it can be waded at some riffles when the water is low. The river is stocked downstream from Elk Creek drainage, south of Silverton about 4 miles. Near Silverton the river runs deep into the West Needle Mountains and then joins with US 550 again below Bakers Bridge.

The Silverton Narrow Gauge Railroad parallels the Animas river through the Needle Mountains. This 100-year-old route provides anglers novel access to some of the Animas river drainages in the Needle Mountains. From June through August, the train runs four times a day. Reservations should be made 4 weeks to 6 weeks or more in advance.

This stretch of the Animas, winding through scenic canyons, contains rainbow and cutthroat 8 to 14 inches and some brown; it is rated good. Water is fast with pools and riffles abundant. From Trimble Springs, on US 550, south 9 miles to Durango, the Animas is slow, meandering and deep with rainbow averaging 10 inches. Mosquitoes are thick from late spring until September. Below Durango the river is less polluted than it was a few years ago. Excellent brown fishing from Durango to the Southern Ute Indian Reservation border.

Fishing Regulations for Animas River south of Durango from its confluence with Lightner Creek to Purple Cliffs are fishing by artificial flies and lures only and the minimum size limit for trout is 16 inches in length, or longer. This section of the river is registered as Gold Medal.

NORTH OF SILVERTON

At the Animas headwaters, north of Silverton, there are several small lakes, including **Denver Lake** (12,000 ft; 0.2 ac), but because of heavily mineralized water, fish populations do not do well; consequently, this area is not stocked.

Cunningham Creek enters the Animas from the southeast at Howardsville, about 7 miles northeast of Silverton. It is reached by Hwy 110, then a dirt road southeast along the creek for 3 miles. Cunningham is a 5-mile creek averaging 6 feet wide. Fair for small rainbow. At the end of the road, a steep marked trail leads south 3 miles to **Highland Mary Lakes** (12,000 ft; 47 and 11 ac). These lakes are rated excellent for brook, cutthroat and rainbow from 10 to 16 inches. Exposed campsites. One mile farther south of the Highland Mary Lakes over a grassy ridge are the **Verde Lakes** (12,000 ft; 15 and 13 ac). There is no defined trail connecting the lakes. Excellent for small brook and a few 8- to 10-inch cutthroat and rainbow. **Lost Lake** and **Silver Lake** are barren.

SOUTH OF SILVERTON

Mineral Creek enters the Animas from the west just below Silverton. Accessible by US 550. Highway follows creek north to Red Mountain Pass.

Above Timbline Lake near Animas River

Columbine Lake (12,700 ft; 22 ac) lies at the head of **Mill Creek**, a fork of Mineral Creek, southwest of Chattanooga. Five mile steep hike to lake. The lake is near the Divide. Good for brook and small cutthroat. Southwest of Columbine is **Crystal Lake** (12,064 ft; 4 ac), near Ophir Pass. It is accessible by a dirt road from US 550 at **Middle Fork**. The **South Fork of Mineral Creek** is rated good for brook and rainbows. A good road west off US 550 follows the South Fork to South Mineral Campground. From there a good trail continues up South Fork Mineral Creek to **Ice Lake** (12,300 ft; 15 ac), **Little Ice Lake** (11,400 ft; 2 ac), **Island Lake** (12,400 ft; 5 ac) and **Fuller Lake** (12,600 ft; 12.5 ac). North of the South Mineral Campground, a 4WD road leads to **Clear Lake** (12,000 ft; 30 ac), which has been stocked with

brook and rainbow. All of these lakes are good for cutthroats and brook trout and require a steep 3 mile hike.

Elk Creek enters the Animas from the east about 7 miles south of Silverton. It can be reached by narrow-gauge railroad or by a USFS trail from Molas Lake on Molas Pass, located on US 550 about 3 miles south of Silverton. The hike is about 4 miles south to the mouth of the creek. The creek varies from 8 to 10 feet wide and is easily fished. The lower part is good for cutthroat, brook and rainbow to 10 inches; upper reaches are too mineralized. At the headwaters of Elk creek are the two **Eldorado Lakes** (12,500 ft; 14 and 2 ac) by a 10 mile hike from the top of Molas Pass on the Colorado Trail. Both lakes are fair for small rainbow.

Molas Lake (10,600 ft; 20 ac), **Little Molas Lake** (10,900 ft; 7 ac) and **Andrews Lake** (10,800 ft; 10 ac) lie on Molas Pass 3 miles south of Silverton. All three are easily reached from US 550. They are good and heavily fished for rainbow and brook. **Tenmile Creek** enters the Animas from the east about 3 miles downstream of Elk Creek. It is about 4 miles long and averages 4 feet wide. Lower end is fast water and is rated fair: upper stretches meander, with some beaver ponds, rated excellent for rainbow from 6 to 10 inches. At its headwaters is cobalt-blue **Balsam Lake** (11,435 ft; 100 ac), which has no fish due to the high mineral content of the water. Good camping.

Noname Creek flows into the Animas about 2 miles south of Tenmile

Creek, about 13 miles north of Tacoma. The creek runs 6 miles, and is similar to Tenmile Creek. Brook, rainbow and rainbow/cutthroat hybrids. To the south of Noname Creek, **Ruby Lake** (10,850 ft; 8 ac) is at the headwaters of **Ruby Creek**, and can be reached from Noname Creek. Some small rainbow and rainbow cutthroat hybrids are available at the lower end. The lake is good for 1- to 2-pound rainbow. Access is by railroad from Durango.

Needle Creek enters the Animas River from the east just south of Needleton and 15 miles upstream from Rockwood. Access by railroad; leave train at Needleton. Creek rated fair for rainbow and cutthroat to 10 inches; about 10 feet wide and wadable except in the spring. **Webb Lake** (10,960 ft; 10 ac), **Jewell Lake** (12,000 ft; 10 ac), **Pearl Lake** (11,575 ft; 14 ac) and **Little Emerald Lake** (11,270 ft; 14 ac) are accessible by following a good trail up the north side of Needle Creek. About 2 miles up the creek, ford the stream at the old water wheel. Take steep Lime Mesa Trail along tributary. About an hour's hike from the ford. Lakes are rated good for rainbow to 13 inches and stocked with cutthroats. Camping is best at Webb Lake.

Three miles above Electra Lake, **Cascade Creek** forks north from the Animas. US 550 crosses this tributary. Take USFS road 785 north to Cascade Summer Group Home, a couple of miles north of Purgatory Ski Area. Access road off US 550 follows the creek for about 2 miles; from there take 4WD road. Creek is about 5 miles long, averaging 6 feet wide. Fair for small cut-throat, rainbow and brook. Artificial flies and lures, catch and release on cutthroat. **Lime Creek** enters Cascade Creek below Purgatory Campground at Purgatory Ski Area. Creek is about 5 feet wide and more than 12 miles long. Accessible from Lime Creek Road off US 550. Numerous pools in rugged canyon. Some beaver ponds. Rated fair for small rainbow and some brook. **Potato Lake** (9,800 ft; 9 ac) lies above Lime Creek Road along with the four **Twilight Peaks Lakes** (11,500 to 12,000 ft; 4 ac each). Lakes are rated fair for rainbow and brook to 15 inches, but some involve difficult climbs up **Twilight Creek**.

Farther south, **Canyon Creek** flows into the Animas from the east just below Tacoma Power Plant on the Animas. To access the upper creek, turn east off US 550 at Trimble Springs, cross the Animas and drive north on Missionary Ridge Road about 4 miles. Stream, marked by sign, is narrow, 3 feet wide, but good for small brook. Above the road, **Henderson Lake** (10,000 ft; 5 ac), is good in early spring for fat 10- to 12-inch rainbow and brook. Poor to fair in late season; suffers some winterkill.

Beautiful **Electra Lake** parallels US 550, but along with **Columbine Lake** and **Ignacio Lake** is private.

South of Electra, **Haviland Lake** (8,150 ft; 20 ac) is owned and developed by the Colorado DOW. It is 1 mile east of US 550 and 21 miles north of Durango, marked by a sign. The lake is rated good for rainbow to 12 inches. Motors are not allowed, and rental boats are not available. Campground is located on the southeast shore. Haviland is located on **Elbert Creek**. Elbert is a small, brushy and ponded creek good for brook and brown to 11 inches. It joins with the Animas about 6 miles below Canyon Creek.

Hermosa Creek enters the Animas from the northwest at Hermosa on US 550, about 10 miles north of Durango. The stream originates more than 20 miles north. Upper reaches are accessed by turning west at Purgatory Ski Resort on USFS road 578. Follow road about 5 miles to Sig Creek Campground. You can fish headwaters from here, which rate fair for small cutthroat. Road follows the **East Fork of Hermosa Creek**. The creek, including **Pasture Creek**, from its headwaters downstream to its confluence with Sig Creek is fishing by artificial flies and lures only and all cutthroat must be returned to the water immediately. Lower part of Hermosa Creek can be reached from US 550 at Hermosa. Eleven miles north of Durango, follow USFS road 576 about 4 miles to where fishing is fair for small rainbow. Trail follows upstream about 15 miles to Sig Creek Campground. Creek runs through a deep canyon up to where the South Fork joins it. Hermosa Creek varies from 4 to 12 feet wide. **Dutch Creek** and **Deer Creek**, about 5 miles from the Hermosa-Animas fork, enters Hermosa Creek from the north. They are small tributary streams, which are fair for cutthroat and a few rainbow. Both streams are artificial flies and lures only, all cutthroat must be returned to the water immediately. **Big Bend Creek** entering from the west

offers similar fishing with the same restrictions.

Junction Creek enters the Animas at the northwest edge of Durango. A good road (25th Street) opposite the fairgrounds proceeds west 4 miles to Junction Creek Campground and Recreation Area. From Junction Creek Campground, the road does not follow the stream but runs northeast of the creek about 8 miles to the headwaters at Neglected Mine. There is no trail along the stream. It's rocky and clear, rated fair for small cutthroat and rainbow.

South of Durango, **Pastorius Reservoir** (6,850 ft; 53 ac) is on reservation land but a tribal permit is not necessary. Turn south off US 160 at Loma Linda. Proceed south about 2.5 miles; Pastorius is to the west about 1 mile. First stocked in 1966, Pastorius has nice northern pike, some bluegill, yellow perch, bass and rainbow. Limited number of channel catfish. All smallmouth and largemouth bass possessed must be 15 inches or larger.

LA PLATA/MANCOS RIVERS

West of the Animas River, the La Plata and Mancos rivers offer marginal fishing. The **La Plata** intersects US 160 about 12 miles west of Durango at Hesperus. Graded dirt road goes north at Hesperus along La Plata's west bank for about 8 miles. Kroeger Campground is about 6 miles up. From Hesperus it is about 12 miles to La Plata's headwaters. Water is posted from Hesperus 3 miles north to Mayday mine and is rated poor. From Mayday north, river offers fair fishing for

Photo Courtesy of Kevin Rummell

Beautiful waterfall in Wemanuche Wilderness

small rainbow and a few brook.

The **Mancos River** forks just above the old sawmill in the town of Mancos at the intersection of US 160 and Hwy 184. Two forks, the west and middle, afford fair fishing. The **West Mancos River**, the longest fork, accessible by about 40 miles of logging roads, is fair in the upper reaches for rainbow, cutthroat and brook. The **Middle Mancos River** in Echo Basin has many small ponded tributaries that offer fair fishing for small rainbow and cutthroat. Gravel roads parallel lower 15 miles.

Several reservoirs dot the Mancos River drainage. **Jackson Gulch Reservoir** (7,825 ft; 217 ac) and State Wildlife Area is a popular spot. At one point it was drained to clear out the pike population and then stocked with rainbow and catfish. Catches of 2- to 3-pound rainbow are reported. **Joe Moore Reservoir** (7,680 ft; 35 ac), north of Hwy 184, is good for rainbow, brown, white amur and bass. Other reservoirs include **Summit Reservoir** (7,388 ft; 350 ac), which has northern pike, walleye, catfish, bass and rainbows and **Puett Reservoir** (7,261 ft; 150 ac) which is heavy stocked with pike, walleye, and rainbow. New Mexico anglers heavily fish these reservoirs during long holiday weekends. Weekday fishing offers quiet, serene settings. Local anglers have taken an interest in bass. At Summit all smallmouth and largemouth bass must be 15 inches in length or longer.

West of Pagosa Springs, **Capote Lake** is private.

South of US 160, the La Plata and Mancos flow through private and tribal lands and are not worth the trouble.

SOUTHERN UTE INDIAN RESERVATION

The Piedra, Los Pinos and Animas rivers flow through the Southern Ute Indian Reservation. These waters can be fished, but, in addition to a Colorado fishing license, a tribal permit is required. Some streams and reservoirs have specific regulations, and anglers should contact the Wildlife Conservation Office, Southern Ute Tribal Affairs Building (on Hwy 172, downtown Ignacio), P.O. Box 737, Ignacio, CO 81137; (970) 563-0130 or 563-0131 for information.

Fishing on reservation lands without a state license is punishable by state law. Persons fishing on the reservation without a tribal permit are subject to federal court fines.

DOLORES RIVER

The **Dolores River** begins at Lizard Head Pass (10,000 ft) beside Hwy 145 at the Dolores-San Miguel county line. It gathers waters from the south sides of Wilson Mountain, Dolores Peaks and Sheep Mountain, and from the west side of Hermosa Peak, then flows southwest in two forks, which join below the village of Stoner. The Dolores then flows southwest through the town of Dolores, turns northwest to join the Colorado River in Utah. Confined to Dolores and Montezuma counties, the main Dolores, its West Fork, McPhee Reservoir and Ground Hog Reservoir are the main fishing waters of the drainage.

Dolores River offers 35 miles of fish-

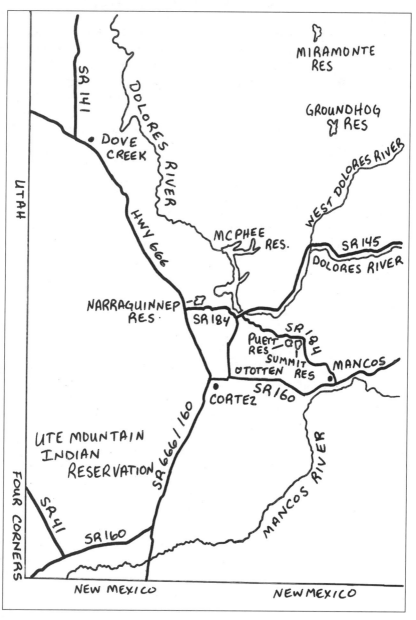

MACPHEE

ing in Montezuma County. It has been rated fair in spring for rainbow and brown to 1.5 pounds, though occasionally fish up to five pounds are taken. USFS road 504 follows the west side of the river downstream from Dolores. It averages 40 feet wide and is wadable except in the spring. It has brown and rainbow from 6 to 14 inches. Much land is posted, but permission is sometimes granted upon request. From its confluence with the West Fork Dolores River downstream to McPhee Reservoir, snagging for kokanee salmon is permitted from September 1 through December 31. From Mcphee Reservoir downstream to Bradford bridge is fishing by artificial flies and lures only, all trout must be returned to the water immediately.

Hwy 145 from Dolores to Lizard Head Pass (54 miles) parallels the main Dolores. There are Forest Service camping facilities at Forks Campground and at Priest Gulch Campground (22 miles north of Dolores). Cayton Campground is at Barlow Creek near Lizard Head Pass.

The upper Dolores has rainbow and cutthroat to 12 inches. Several small streams enter the river from the east above the old mining town of Rico.

Barlow and **McJunkin Creeks** from the south and **Lizard Head, Snow Spur, Slate, Coke Oven** and **Coal Creeks** from the north are small creeks with cutthroat and brook. Barlow Creek is rated good, the others fair. Some sections of the river are polluted below the town of Rico.

Scotch Creek enters the Dolores from the east three miles below Rico.

It offers four miles of fishing in a 3-foot-wide stream for small brook and cutthroat. Rated fair.

Ryman Creek enters the Dolores from the southeast. It offers four miles of small-stream fishing for cutthroat and brook up to seven inches. Rated fair. **Roaring Fork Creek** joins the river above the Priest Gulch Campground. USFS road 435 makes 10 miles of stream accessible. Fair for 7- to 12-inch cutthroat and brook.

Priest Gulch Creek enters the Dolores 10 miles above Stoner from the north at Priest Gulch Campground. It has five miles of trail fishing for small cutthroat and brook trout. Rated fair.

Entering the Dolores from the east eight miles above Stoner, **Bear Creek** has 25 miles of small stream fishing for small rainbow, cutthroat and brook. Restricted to artificial flies and lures, all cutthroat must be returned to the water immediately. Rated fair. Nearby **Rio Lado Creek** has the same restrictions.

Taylor Creek enters the Dolores River from the north four miles above Stoner. Can drive six miles upstream. A small stream with small cutthroat, brook and stocked rainbows. Rated fair. **Little Taylor Creek** is fishing by artificial flies and lures only, all cutthroat must be returned to the water immediately.

Stoner Creek enters Dolores from the north near Stoner Guard Station, 17 miles north of Dolores on Hwy 145. Ten miles of fair fishing in a stream up to six feet wide for small cutthroat. Trail is blocked by private land.

About 1.5 miles below Stoner, the West Fork of the Dolores joins the main stream.

WEST FORK

The **West Fork of the Dolores** is accessible from Hwy 145, 13 miles northeast of Dolores. Turn off on marked Dunton Road, which parallels West Fork for 28 miles. Fishing in the stream, which averages 15-feet wide, for small rainbow, cutthroat and brown, with a larger fish on occasion, is rated good. There are about eight miles of posted water. **Cold, Kilpacker** and **Meadow Creeks** enter West Fork above Dunton, 35 miles upstream from turnoff at Hwy 145. Eleven miles of trail fishing for cutthroat and rainbow to 10 inches. Rated fair.

Navajo Lake (11,150 ft; 10 ac) is at the foot of 14,159-foot El Diente Peak. In a spectacular setting, it is reached by a steep 5-mile trail beginning at Burro Bridge USFS Campground 2.5 miles northeast of Dunton. Usually ice-covered until July 1. Stocked with brook. Restricted to artificial flies and lures. Fishing below the lake is poor. **Ground Hog, Little Fish** and **Willow Creeks** enter West Fork about 12 miles up Dunton Road from the turnoff at Hwy 145. About 30 miles of trail fishing in streams three to four feet wide with beaver dams. Rated fair.

Fish Creek, which has some 14 miles of water, can be reached by a road that turns off at the mouth of Ground Hog Creek to go up Fish Creek for 4.5 miles, ending at the campground. The upper end is reached by a USFS road that turns west at Dunton to cross the upper creek. A pretty mountain stream about 15 feet wide with many beaver ponds, it is good for rainbow and cutthroat to 12 inches.

Downstream from McPhee Dam to Bradford Bridge, an 11-mile stretch, the Dolores River is easy to read. In the past, it has been one of the state's best late-season streams for browns and rainbows, although recent low summer flow regimens have been a worrisome concern as the river can warm to critical temperatures without sufficient water. Fishing is with artificial flies or lures only and all fish must be returned to the water immediately.

SAN MIGUEL RIVER

The **San Miguel River** rises in several high basins beneath 12,000- and 13,000-foot peaks above the town of Telluride in some of the most scenic country in Colorado. The mountains are steep, the valleys narrow and winding.

The area is heavily mineralized, as is evident from present and past mining operations and their workings, tailings ponds and aerial tramway lines. There are ghost towns in picturesque settings.

At higher elevations, sedimentary rock formations contribute considerable sediment to the streams, especially after heavy summer rains and during spring snowmelt. The San Miguel and the **South Fork** of the San Miguel, which originates just below the town of Ophir, can be clear, beautiful streams one day, torrents on another.

These natural conditions don't offer the prime trout fishing such beautiful

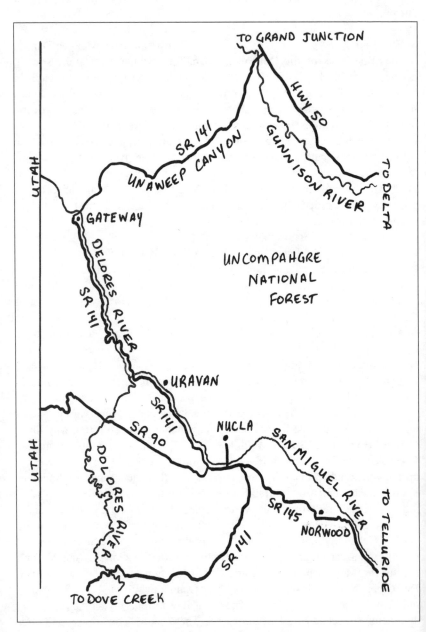

UNCOMPAHGRE

Nice catch and release Rainbow

Photo Courtesy of the Morrison Angler

terrain would seem to have. The river is heavily stocked with catchable size rainbow up to 12 inches.

LAKE FORK

The **Lake Fork of the San Miguel** parallels Hwy 145 as it rises in the vicinity of Lizard Head Pass. It is small and brushy with small brook and rainbow. **Trout Lake** (9,750 ft; 200 ac) is beside the highway and offers 8- to 12-inch rainbows, some brook and an occasional cutthroat. This is a pretty site. Boats and camping are available, and fishing can be good. **Lake Hope** (11,900 ft; 35 ac), at the headwaters of Lake Fork is reached by a 3-mile hike on trail 410. Fishing is fair for cutthroat.

The **Howard Fork** of the river comes down through Ophir to merge with **East Fork** and form the South Fork. Fishing is poor. Above Ophir at timberline are the **Alta Lakes** (11,250 ft; 11-15 ac). These are shallow lakes with rainbow. They are reached from 632 near Aims. A 6-mile-long road off Hwy 145 near Telluride also goes to Alta Lakes; it is usually open early in July.

TRIBUTARIES

Numerous creeks feed, from steep slopes, into the San Miguel. Many of them, such as **Bilk Creek** (which enters the river just below the confluence of the South Fork), **Deep Creek**, **Bear**

Creek and Fall Creek are 4-6 feet wide, fast, brushy and contain small brook and cutthroat. Dirt roads 638 and 639 from Hwy 145 provide access to Deep Creek in good weather. Deep Creek is restricted to artificial flies and lures only, all cutthroat must be returned to the water immediately. The Fall Creek Road provides about 12 miles of access into rugged terrain beneath Mt. Wilson (14,017 ft).

Woods Lake (9,400 ft; 30 ac), containing rainbow, brook and occasional cutthroat and brown, is a stocked lake of the Colorado Department of Natural Resources. It is reached by a 9-mile-long dirt road that leaves Hwy 145 about three miles above Placerville. Camping is available off state property below the lake. Fishing is good in late summer; artificial flies and lures only.

About seven miles below Telluride at Placerville, Leopard Creek enters the San Miguel. Although readily accessible by Hwy 62, which parallels it, Leopard Creek offers only fair to poor fishing. Some portions of the river are privately stocked, and summer-fall fishing is good where stream improvements have been made.

Saltada and Beaver Creeks enter the San Miguel five and two miles, respectively, above Norwood. These are small, brushy streams with small fish.

Gurley Reservoir (8,264 ft; 400 ac when full) has stocked rainbow and brook, and northern pike and bass. It is a fluctuating irrigation reservoir, where boats are allowed and fishing can be good. The reservoir is reached by driving south on the Norwood-Dolores Road, which goes south from Hwy 145

about 0.5 mile east of Norwood. There is camping.

MIRAMONTE

Miramonte Reservoir (7,755 ft; 420 ac) is a state recreation area and probably offers the best fishing in the San Miguel area. It has good size rainbow, although most are in the 10- to 14-inch range. There is a good boat ramp. It is 18 miles south of Norwood via the Norwood-Dolores Road. Camping is allowed. This is a fee area.

The San Miguel River below Norwood offers generally poor fishing, although some channel catfish are taken. Mineralization and siltation drastically diminish the stream well before its juncture with the Dolores River below the uranium-mining town of Uravan.

GROUND HOG RESERVOIR

Ground Hog Reservoir (8,700 ft; 670 ac), west of Dunton, has very good fishing for rainbow, cutthroat, brown and brook. Fishing pressure has been modest. Camping and boat ramps are available.

Below the confluence of the West Fork and the Dolores, the Dolores River flows through private land, where permission to fish is necessary. Lost Canyon Creek flows into the Dolores just south of the town of Dolores. This often brushy, 4- to 5-foot-wide creek is fair for cutthroat. It is mostly on private land and fishing is diminished by irrigation fluctuations. Upper reaches in national forest are fair for small trout.

Eight miles west of Dolores,

Narraguinnep Reservoir (7,050 ft; 386 ac) is an irrigation reservoir reached by Hwy 147. It offers rainbow, perch, crappie, northern pike, bluegill, channel catfish and some walleye. There is no camping.

Disappointment Creek, which joins the river in the high country northeast of the river below Dolores, offers poor fishing. To the Utah state line, the winding river is scenic but silt-laden, often slow-moving and with banks, cliff clefts and canyon rims crawling with rattlesnakes in spring, summer and fall.

South of the town of Dolores on Hwy 145 is the city of Cortez in the heart of the Montezuma Valley. **Totten** (250 ac)**, Summit** (402 ac) and **Puett** (162 ac) reservoirs east of the community are fair fisheries. Totten has good size panfish, some northern pike, walleye, channel catfish, largemouth bass, and white amur. Summit has walleye, perch, crappie, bass, channel catfish, northern pike and bluegill. Puett has some walleye, bass and catfish. Boating is allowed. All small and largemouth bass must be 15 inches or longer.

Denny Lake (6,085 ft; 11 ac) in the city of Cortez has bass, crappie, catfish, bluegill and some rainbow. It is heavily stocked; trout and other species are good in the spring. Non-powered boats are permitted.

MCPHEE RESERVOIR

McPhee Reservoir (6,800 ft; 4470 ac) was opened to public fishing in 1986, and has remained the region's best water. The reservoir holds Lake McConaughy rainbow trout, small and largemouth bass, crappie, bluegill, channel catfish, a cutthroat-rainbow hybrid and a growing population of kokanee salmon. Rainbow average 12 inches, but many have already topped the 4-pound mark. The Sage Hen Flats area may be the best for bass. All bass less than 15 inches in length must be immediately returned to the water. Snagging for kokanee salmon permitted from September 1 through January 31. There is no daily bag and possession limit on yellow perch. The McPhee Recreation Area has a 6-lane boat ramp, 114-car parking lot and 80 camping units in four camping areas. Another center, at House Creek, offers a 4-lane boat ramp, 75-car parking lot and two campsites with 56 units.

Index

A

Abyss Lake 97
Adams Fork 179
Adams Lake 274
Adobe Creek Reservoir 142
Agate Creek 297
Alamosa Reservoir 172
Alamosa River 172
Alan Lake 124
Albert Lake 40
Alberta Park Reservoir 167
Alder Lake 39
Alder Creek 167, 169
Alexander Lake 269
Allen Basin Reservoir 236
Alpine Lake 129
Alta Lakes 331

Alvarado Creek 134
Alver Jones Lake 178
American Crystal Sugar
    Pond 142
American Lake 230
Anderson Lake 231, 259
Andrews Lake 322
Anges Lakes 34
Anglemeyer Lake 128
Animas River 22, 321
Ann Lake 124
Annie Lake 319
Antero Reservoir 86
Anthracite Creek 279
    East Fork 280
    Middle Fork 280
    North Fork 280

Anticline Lake 140
Antoine's Cabin Creek 210
Antoine's Cabin Lakes 210
Apache Creek 146
Apishapa River 138
Aqua Fria Lake 41
Arapaho Creek 39, 110,
        185, 186
Arapaho Lakes 111
Archuleta Creek 166
Archuleta Lake 166
Arkansas River 119, 124,
        125, 129, 135, 139
    East Fork 119
    South Fork 130
Armstrong Creek 245
Arrowhead Lake 68
Arvada Reservoir 104
Atkinson Reservoir 272
Aurora Reservoir 103
Avalanche Creek 221
Avalanche Lake 221
Axial Basin Reservoir 246

B

Badger Creek 135
Bailey Lake 261
Bailey Lakes 193
Baker Creek 181
Baldwin Creek 129
Baldwin Lake 129
Baldy Lake 171
Balman Reservoir 132
Balsam Lake 322
Banana Lake 113
Banjo Lake 133
Banner Lakes 77
Babour Ponds 105
Bard Creek 108

Barker Reservoir 112
Barlow Creek 328
Barnes Meadow Reservoir 64
Baron Lake 269
Barr Lake 105
Battle Creek 191
Battlement Lakes 268
Battlement Reservoirs 264
Bear Creek 37, 95, 109,
        155, 171, 230, 299,
        328, 331
Bear Creek Reservoir 102
Bear Lake 66, 122, 128,
        148, 179
Bear Lakes 37
Bear Track Lakes 110
Beaver Creek 39, 41, 43, 62,
        85, 101, 135, 136,
        164, 189, 211, 246,
        254, 287, 288, 310,
        332
    South Fork 288
Beaver Creek East 51
Beaver Creek Reservoir 164
Beaver Lake 177, 211, 221,
        242, 266, 284
Beaver Mandall Lake 41
Beaver Reservoir 116
Bellaire Lake 60
Bellows Creek 163
Ben Tyler Gulch Creek 97
Bench Lake 45, 66, 72
Bennett Creek 157
Betty Lake 113
Big Battlement Lake 268
Big Beaver Reservoir 254
Big Bend Creek 324
Big Blue Creek 285
Big Branch 313
Big Creek 42, 243

Big Creek Lakes 42, 243
Big Creek Reservoir No. 1 272
Big Dutch Creek 71
Big Emerald Lake 317
Big Fish Creek 258
Big Fish Lake 258
Big Flint Lake 317
Big Kline Creek 221
Big Lake 179, 211
Big Meadow Reservoir 272
Big Meadows Reservoir 166
Big Pine Lake 211
Big Rainbow Lake 48
Big Spring Creek 157
Big Spruce Lake 211
Big Thompson Ponds 75
Big Thompson River 68, 117
        North Fork 117
Big Union Creek 123
Bighorn Creek 214
Bighorn Lake 37
Bilk Creek 331
Bill Moore Lake 108
Billings Lake 130
Bird Farm Ponds 142
Bison Lake 196
Black Canyon Creek 168
Black Canyon of the
        Gunnison 282
Black Creek 205
Black Gore Creek 214
Black Hollow Creek 62
Black Hollow Reservoir 75
Black Lake 67, 70
Black Lakes 205, 214
Black Mandall Lake 235
Blacktail Creek 192
Blair Lake 261
Blodgett Lake 216
Blue Creek 285

Blue Lake 37, 45, 116, 123,
        142, 148, 178, 182,
        205, 236, 273, 307
Blue Lakes 137, 199, 278
Blue Mesa Reservoir 285
Blue River 22, 24, 197
Bluebird Lake 67
Bob Lake 113
Bobtail Creek 190
Boedecker Reservoir 74
Bonham Reservoir 272
Bonita Reservoir 270
Bonny Reservoir 78
Booth Lake 214
Borns Lake 311
Boss Lake Reservoir 130
Boswell Creek 51
Boulder Creek 114, 203,
        258
        Middle Fork 112
        North Fork 114
        South Fork 110
Boulder Lake 203, 258, 298
Boulder Reservoir 105
Bowen Creek 182
Bowen Lake 182
Bowl of Tears Lake 215
Bowman Creek 303
Box Creek 248
Box Lake 67
Boyd Lake 74
Boyd Rose Pond 146
Brady Lake 217
Brainard Lake 115
Brewery Creek 169
Brook Creek 68
Brown Lakes 160
Brownlee State Wildlife
        Area 34, 37
Browns Creek 129

Browns Lake 62
Bruno Gulch 97
Brush Creek 133, 209, 230,
  292, 304
  East Fork 305
  Middle Fork 304
  West Fork 210, 304
Brush Creek Lake 132
Brush Hollow Reservoir 138
Buchanan Creek 185
Buck Creek 157
Buck Lake 193
Buckeye Lake 120
Buckhorn Creek 61
Buckles Reservoir 313
Buckskin Creek 83
Buffalo Creek 38, 96
Bull Basin Reservoir 266
Bull Creek Reservoirs 266
Bull Lake 193
Bull Park Reservoir 236
Bull Run Creek 191
Bundy Lake 39
Burchfield Lake 146
Burn Creek 242
Burning Bear Creek 97
Burns Reservoir 40
Burnt Mesa Reservoir 236
Burro Creek 167
Butcherknife Creek 240
Button Rock Reservoir 116
Butts Lake 269
Buzzard Creek, 264
Byers Canyon 189
Byron Lake 108

C

Cabin Creek 187
  Roaring Fork 68

Cache Creek 123
Cache la Poudre River 24, 53,
  56, 62, 71
  North Fork 56
  South Fork 60
Calf Creek 292
California Gulch 171
Camp Lakes 48
Canadian River 33
Canon Paso Creek 316
Canon Pintado 253
Canyon Creek 192, 273, 278,
  297, 323
Canyon Rincon Creek 178
Canyon Verde Creek 178
Capitol Creek 229
Capitol Lake 229
Capote Lake 326
Carbon Creek 294
Carbondale State Wildlife
  Area 219
Carey Lake 45
Caribou Creek 114
Carnero Creek 172
Carp Lake 268
Carson Lake 267
Carter Lake Reservoir 74
Cascade Creek 24, 64, 71,
  146, 177, 185, 280,
  293, 323
Castilleja Lake 319
Castle Creek 230, 294
Castle Rock Lake 157
Cataract Creek 205, 291
Cataract Lake 291
Cataract Lakes 205
Cathedral Lake 230
Causeway Lake 247
Cave Creek 172
Ceanothuse Lake 42

Cebolla Creek 291, 292
Cebolla Creek State Wildlife
      Area 293
Cedar Mesa Reservoir 270
Cement Creek 304
Chain of Lakes 217
Chalk Creek 128, 129
Chalk Lake 128
Chama Lake 177
Chama River 177
Chambers Lake 44
Chapin Creek 71
Chapman Creek 228
Chapman Dam 228
Chapman Lake 226
Chapman Reservoir 236
Chase Gulch Reservoir 107
Chasm Lake 67
Chatfield Reservoir 101, 236
Chedsey Creek 40
Cheesman Canyon 92
Cheesman Dam 92
Cheesman Reservoir 91
Cherry Creek Reservoir 102
Cherry Lake 168
Chicago Creek 107
Chicago Lakes 107
Chief Creek 79
Chihuahua Creek 202
Chihuahua Lake 202
Chinns Lake 108
Chipeta Lake 277
Chiquita Lake 70
Christine Lake 224
Cimarron Creek 311
Cimarron River 284
City Reservoir 319
Clay Creek 145
Clayton Lake 111
Clear Creek 33, 35, 33, 48,

      106, 108, 124, 157
   North Fork 106
   South Fork 109
Clear Creek Reservoir 124
Clear Fork Creek 279
Clear Lake 33, 322
Clear Lake Reservoir 109
Cleveland Lake 217
Cliff Creek 280
Cliff Lake 39, 205
Cliff Lakes 274
Clingingsmith Ponds 141
Clinton Reservoir 201
Cloyses Lake 124
Coal Creek 221, 280, 287,
      306, 328
Cochetopa Creek 24, 295
Coffin Lake 259
Colby Horse Park Reservoir 270
Cole Reservoir No. 1 270
Coloney Lakes 135
Colorado Creek 40
Colorado River 22, 24, 189,
      263, 275
   North Fork 71
   South Fork 185
Columbine Lake 186, 319,
      322, 323
Comanche Lake 62, 134
Comanche Ponds 146
Comanche Reservoir 62
Como Creek 114
Cone Lake 108
Conejos River 24, 175, 178,
      179
   South Fork 178
Coney Creek 116
Coney Lakes 116
Confluence Lake 277
Continental Reservoir 157

Conundrum Creek 230
Cony Creek 67
Cony Lake 67
Cooney Lake 85
Cooper Creek 291
Cooper Lake 291
Copper Creek 229, 304
Copper Lake 304
Corn Lake 264
Cornelius Creek 57
Corona Lake 187
Corral Creek 63
Costo Lake 294
Cotton Creek 168
Cotton Lake 168
Cottonwood Creek 126, 134,
      135, 168, 246, 291
      Middle Fork 126
      North Fork 128
Cottonwood Lake 126
Cottonwood Lake No. 1 272
Cottonwood Lake No. 2 272
Cottonwood Lake No. 4 272
Cottonwood Lake No. 5 272
Cottonwood Lakes 168
Cow Creek 277, 302
Cow Lake 302
Craig City Ponds 246
Craig Creek 96
Crater Lake 185, 230, 261,
      279, 310
Crater Lakes 111
Crawford Lake 185
Crawford Reservoir 280
Creedmore Lakes 56
Crescent Lake 193
Crestone Creek 168
Crestone Lake 168
Croke Reservoir
      (Carlson Reservoir) 104

Crooked Creek 156, 187
Crosby Creek 40
Crosho Lake 236
Cross Creek 165, 215
      West Fork 215
Crystal Creek Reservoir 137
Crystal Lake 70, 123, 124,
      289, 298, 322
Crystal Lakes 165, 198
Crystal Reservoir 283
Crystal River 220, 221
Cucharas Creek 148
Cucharas Reservoir 148
Cucharas River 148
Culebra Creek 172
Cunningham Creek 226, 321
Curecanti Creek 285

D

Dallas Creek 278
Davis Creek 43
Deadman Creek 49, 157, 316
Deadman Lake 168, 187
Deckers Lake 120
Deep Creek 39, 163, 196,
      205, 331
Deep Lake 39, 196
Deep Slough Reservoir 269
Deer Creek 96, 202, 324
Deer Creek Lakes 292
Deer Lake 193, 273
Del Norte State Wildlife
      Area 153
Delaney Buttes Lakes 37
Deluge Lake 214
Denny Creek 126
Denny Lake 333
Denver Lake 321
Derby Creek 192, 195

North Fork 193
Devils Lake 293
Devil's Thumb Lake 114
DeWeese Reservoir 133
Diamond J State Wildlife
    Area 34
Diamond Lake 112, 120
Diemer Lake 226
Dillon Reservoir 199
Dinkle Lake 220, 224
Disappointment Creek 333
Disappointment Lake 39
Divide Lake 316
Dixon Reservoir 55
Dogfish Reservoir 279
Dollar Lake 280, 317
Dolores River 326, 329
    West Fork 329
Dome Lake 242
Dome Reservoirs 295
Donut Lake 68
Dora Lake 205
Doris Lake 258
Dorothy Lee Pond 107
Doug Creek 282
Douglas Reservoir 75
Dowdy Lake 57
Dream Lake 68
Dry Creek 134
Dry Lakes 134
Duck Lake 97, 177
Dunckley-Dubeau
    Reservoir 247
Dutch Creek 243, 324
Dye Reservoir 142

E

Eagle Lake 67, 226
Eagle River 207, 210

South Fork 218
Eaglesmere Lakes 205
East Beaver Creek 299
East Brush Creek 305
East Canyon Creek 273
East Delaney Butte Lake 38
East Fork Dallas Creek 278
East Fork Muddy Creek 279
East Fork Piney River 192
East Fork Williams Fork 247
East Inlet Creek 72
East Leon Creek 270
East Lost Lakes 247
East Maroon Creek 230
East Maroon Lake 304
East Marvine Creek 255
East Meadow Creek 192
East Middle Creek 171
East Pass Creek 169
East Rifle Creek 275
East River 24, 303
East Willow Creek 302
Eaton Reservoir 57
Echo Canyon Reservoir 311
Echo Lake 107
Edge Lake 193
Eggleston Lakes 269
El Rito Azul Creek 179
Elbert Creek 324
Eldorado Lakes 322
Electra Lake 323
Elevenmile Reservoir 88
Elk Creek 96, 175, 177,
    187, 274, 287, 322
Elk Lake 258, 316
Elk Lakes 261
Elk River 240, 248
    North Fork 240
    South Fork 242
Elkhead Creek 245

Elkhead Reservoir 245
Elkhorn Creek 60
Elkhorn Gulch Creek 169
Elliott Creek 205
Embargo Creek 167
Emerald Lake 24, 68, 123,
        193, 307
Emmaline Lake 62
Empire Reservoir 77
Encampment River 43
English Creek 242
Envy Lake 116
Equalizer Reservoir 74
Erikson Lake 209
Esther Lake 218
Ethel Lake 108
Eureka Lake 134
Evelyn Lake 191
Evergreen Lake 110

F

Fairview Lake 226
Fairview Reservoir 277
Fall Creek 44, 45, 62,
        216, 284, 332
Fall River 70, 107
Fall River Reservoir 108
Fancy Creek 217
Fancy Lake 217
Farmer's Union Reservoir 153
Farris Creek 305
Fawn Creek 254
Fay Lakes 70
Fern Creek 68, 160
Fern Lake 68
Fifth Lake 72
Finger Lake 39
Finney Cuts Lakes 270
Fish Creek 51, 239, 245,
        313, 329
Fish Creek Reservoir 239
Fish Creek Reservoirs 284
Fish Hawk Lake 245
Fish Lake 313
Fisher Creek 164
Fishhook Creek 239
Fishhook Lake 239
Flagler Reservoir 79
Flat Lake 39
Flint Creek 316
Florida River 319
Fooses Creek 130
Forbes Park Lake 174
Ford Creek 171
Forest Lakes 110
Fortification Creek 246
Forty Acre Lake 272
Fountain Creek 135
Fountain Lakes 140
Fourmile Creek 86, 114,
        126, 135, 248 311
Fourmile Lakes 311
Fourth Lake 72
Frank Easement Ponds
    North and South 75
Fraser Canyon 187
Fraser Creek 259
Fraser River 24, 187
Freeman Reservoir 246
French Creek 216, 217
French Gulch Creek 198
Frozen Lake 97
Fryingpan Lakes 228
Fryingpan River 22, 219,
        224, 226, 228
    North Fork 226
    South Fork 228
Fuchs Reservoir 167
Fuller Lake 322

G

Galena Lake 122, 224
Gardner Park Reservoir 235
Garner Creek 168
Gem Lake 43
Geneva Creek 97
Geneva Lake 224
George Creek 57
Georgetown Lake 109
Ghost Lake 161
Gibraltar Lake 116
Gibson Creek 134
Gibson Lake 101
Giley Lake 254
Gill Reservoir 247
Glacier Creek 68
Glacier Gorge 67
Glacier Lake 114, 178
Glacier Springs Pond 266
Glenmere Lake 75
Gold Creek 297
Gold Dust Lakes 211
Golden Gate Canyon State Park
        (Ralston Creek) 106
Golden Lake 294
Goodenough Reservoir 279
Goodwin Creek 134
Goodwin Lake 134
Goose Creek 37, 91, 164
Goose Lake 115, 164
Gore Canyon 191
Gore Creek 22, 211
Gore Lake 214
Gould Reservoir 282
Gourd Lake 185
Grace Creek 51
Granby Reservoirs 268
Grand Lake 182
Granite Creek 228

Granite Lake 316
Granite Lakes 228
Grape Creek 134
Grass Lake 130
Grassy Run Creek 38
Gray Creek 131
Gray's Lake 202
Green (Georgetown)
        Reservoir 109
Green Creek 130, 239
Green Lake 178, 307
Green Lakes 115
Green Mountain Falls 136
Green Mountain Reservoir 204
Green River 252
Griffith Lake 266
Griffith Lakes 266
Grizzly Creek 38, 39, 129,
        197, 273
Grizzly Lake 129, 197, 231
Grizzly Reservoir 231
Gross Reservoir 111
Ground Hog Reservoir 332
Grouse Creek 215
Grouse Lake 215
Gunnison River 22, 24, 287
        Lake Fork 288
        North Fork 279
        Smith Fork Creek 280
Gurley Reservoir 332
Guthrie Lake 255
Gutzler Lakes 192
Gwendolyn Lake 258
Gypsum Creek 209
Gypsum Ponds State
        Wildlife Area 209

H

Hagerman Lake 122

Hague Creek 64, 71
Hahn Creek 255
Hahns Peak Lake 243
Hale Ponds 79
Haley Reservoir 245
Halfmoon Creek 123
Halfmoon Lake 317
Hallenbeck Reservoir 276
Halligan Reservoir 56
Hampton Lake 284
Hancock Lakes 129
Handcart Gulch Creek 101
Hang Lake 45
Hankins Gulch Creek 91
Hansen Creek 178
Hardscrabble Creek 137
Hardscrabble Lake 224
Harris Reservoir 313
Harrison Creek 239
Harrison Flats Lake 124
Hartenstein Lake 126
Harvey Gap Reservoir 274
Harvey Lake 215
Hassell Lake 109
Hasty Lake 144
Hat Creek 209
Hatcher Lakes 311
Haviland Lake 323
Hawxhurst Creek 264
Hay Lake 289
Hay Press Lake 164
Hazel Lake 319

Heart Lake 111, 157, 196,
        236
Hell Canyon Creek 185
Henderson Lake 323
Hennequin Creek 134
Henry Lake 297
Henry Reservoir 141

Henson Creek 289
Herman Lake 109
Hermit Lake 134, 160
Hermosa Creek 324
Hiawatha Lake 60
Hidden Lake 319
Hidden Lakes 40
Hidden Valley Creek 67
Highland Mary Lakes 321
Himan Lake 242
Hinman Creek 242
Hog Park Creek 43
Hohnholz Lakes 50
Hohnholz State Wildlife
        Area 50
Holbrook Reservoir 141
Hole-in-the-Wall creeks 245
Home Lake 120
Homestake Creek 216, 218
Homestake Lake 218
Homestake Reservoir 218
Hooper Lake 193
Hope Creek 166
Horn Creek 134
Horn Fork Creek 128
Horse Creek 92
Horse Creek Reservoir 142
Horse Paster Ponds 75
Horseshoe Creek 114, 192
Horseshoe Lake 74, 134,
        191, 211
Horseshoe Reservoir 148
Horsethief Lake 299
Horsetooth Reservoir 55
Hotel Twin Lake 269
Hourglass Reservoir 62
House Creek 156
Hubbard Creek 279
Huerfano River 138, 146
Humphreys Lake 164

Hunkydory Lake 130, 217
Hunt Creek 236
Hunt Lake 130
Hunter Creek 231
Hunter Reservoir 270
Hunters Creek 66, 67
Hunters Lake 166
Hutcheson Lakes 67

I

Ice Lake 108, 322
Iceberg Lake 49
Iceberg Lakes 111
Idaho Springs Reservoir 107
Ignacio Lake 323
Illinois Creek 303
Illinois Lake 303
Illinois River 35
Independence Lake 231
Indian Creek 171, 316
Indian Lake 196
Indian Run 246
Irvine State Wildlife Area 41
Irving Creek 35, 319
Irving Hale Creek 183
Irving Lake 319
Island Lake 45, 115, 120, 130, 185, 221, 268, 322
Island Lakes 193
Isolation Lakes 218
Italian Creek 303
Ivanhoe Creek 228
Ivanhoe Lake 228
Ivy Creek 161

J

Jack Creek 35

Jack Lake 231
Jackson Creek 94
Jackson Gulch Reservoir 326
Jackson Reservoir 77
James Creek 115
James Peak Lake 111
Jarosa Creek 175
Jasper Creek 113
Jasper (Reservoir) Lake 114
Jefferson Creek 82
Jefferson Lake 81
Jenny Creek 110
Jenny Lake 110
Jerry Creek Reservoir 264
Jet Lake 261
Jewel Lake 70
Jewell Lake 323
Jim Creek 174
Joe Moore Reservoir 326
Joe Wright Creek 44, 63
Joe Wright Reservoir 63
John Martin Reservoir 144
Johns Creek 171
Johnson Creek 51, 319
Johnson Lake 255
Jonah Lake 40
Jones Creek 279
Jones Hole Creek 252
Julian Lake 71
Jumbo Lake 266
Jumbo Reservoir Annex 78
Junction Creek 324
Juniata Reservoir 276

K

Kannah Creek 267, 276
Karval Reservoir 141
Kathleen Lake 39
Keener Lake 193
Kelly Creek 33

Kelly Lake 33
Kenney Creek Reservoir 271
Kenosha Creek 101
Kerber Creek 169
Kerr Lake 179
Ketner Lake 104
Keyser Creek 191
Keystone Creek 201
Kidney Lake 39
King Lake 113
Kinney Creek 191
Kinney Lake 140
Kirby Gulch Creek 97
Kirkpatrick Pond 144
Kiser Creek 269
Kiser Slough Reservoir 269
Kite Lake 83
Kitson Reservoir 272
Kline's Folly Lake 196
Kroenke Creek 128
Kroenke Lake 128

L

La Garde Creek 50
La Garita Creek 172
La Jara Creek 174
La Jara Reservoir 174
La Manga Creek 177
La Plata River 324
Lake Adams 72
Lake Albion 115
Lake Ann 179
Lake Arbor 104
Lake Avery 254
Lake Caroline 107
Lake Catamount 239
Lake Charles 210
Lake Constantine 216
Lake Creek 123, 210, 317

Lake Daigre 148
Lake Dinosaur 240
Lake Dorothey 149
Lake Dorothy 113
Lake Eileen 43
Lake Elbert 245
Lake Elmo 239
Lake Emma 83
Lake Erie 60
Lake Estes 117
Lake Fork Creek 120, 123, 124
Lake Fork Conejos 24
Lake Fork Gunnison 288
Lake George 88
Lake Granby 183
Lake Haiyaha 68
Lake Hope 331
Lake Humphreys 164
Lake Husted 70
Lake Irwin 307
Lake Isabel 138
Lake Isabelle 115
Lake John 37
Lake John State Wildlife Area 37
Lake Josephine 226
Lake Katherine 37
Lake Loveland 74
Lake Margaret 245
Lake Nanita 66, 71
Lake Nokomis 60
Lake Nokoni 71
Lake of Glass 68
Lake of the Clouds 71
Lake of the Crags 245
Lake of the Woods 258
Lake Patricia 215
Lake Quivira 107
Lake Ramona 60

Lake Ridge Lakes 221
Lake San Cristobal 289
Lake Solitude 70
Lake Thomas 211
Lake Verna 72
Lake Wahatoya 148
Lakes of the Clouds 133
Lamphier Lakes 297
Laramie Lake 45
Laramie River 25, 44, 50
Larson Creeks 243
Larson Lakes 289
Last Chance Creek 226
Lathrop State Park 148
Lawn Lake 70
LEDE Reservoir 209
Lee Creek 279
Left Hand Creek 115
Left Hand Park Reservoir 115
Lemon Reservoir 319
Leon Lake 270
Leopard Creek 332
Leroux Creek 279
Letitia Lake 60
Leviathan Lakes 319
Lilly Lakes 146
Lily Lake 34, 221
Lime Creek 161, 226, 323
Lincoln Creek 231
Lincoln Lake 110
Line Creek 43
Linkins Lake 231
Little Battlement Res. 268
Little Bear Creek 246
Little Beaver Creek 60
Little Cabin Creek 187
Little Causeway Lake 234
Little Cimarron River 284
Little Cochetopa Creek 131
Little Cottonwood Creek 246

Little Crystal Lake 70
Little Echo Lake 111
Little Emerald Lake 317, 323
Little Fish Creek 329
Little Flint Lake 317
Little Gem Lake 224
Little Gem Reservoir 268
Little Grizzly Creek 39
Little Ice Lake 322
Little Molas Lake 322
Little Morrison Creek 238
Little Muddy Creek 189
Little Pass Creek 294
Little Rainbow Lake 47
Little Rock Lake 68
Little Ruby Lake 160
Little Sand Creek Lake 168
Little Skillet Lake 235
Little Snake River 248
Little Squaw Creek 156
Little St. Charles Creek 138
Little Taylor Creek 328
Little Trappers Creek 259
Little Trappers Lake 259
Lizard Head Creek 328
Lizard Lake 221
Loch Lomond Lake 107
Lon Hagler Reservoir 74
Lone Lick Lakes 192
Lone Pine Creek 37, 60
Lone Pine Lake 72
Lonesome Lake 218
Long Draw Creek 63
Long Draw Reservoir 63
Long Hollow Gulch 92
Long Lake 39, 115, 185,
     239, 294
Loomis Lake 68
Los Pinos Creek 25, 295
Los Pinos River 316

Lost Canyon Creek 332
Lost Creek 110, 255
Lost Dog 242
Lost Lake 40, 45, 70, 113,
        146, 201, 209, 214,
        239, 266, 280, 319,
        321
Lost Lake Slough 280
Lost Lakes 160, 217
Lost Man Creek 231
Lost Man Lake 231
Lost Man Reservoir 231
Lost Solar Creek 261
Lost Trail Creek 155
Lottis Creek 299
Love Lake 161
Loveland Pass Lake 109
Lower Big Creek Lake 42
Lower Cabin Creek
        Reservoir 109
Lower Camp Lake 48
Lower Cataract Lake 205
Lower Chicago Lake 107
Lower Coney Lake 116
Lower Cottonwood Lake 168
Lower Eaglesmere 205
Lower Fourmile Lake 311
Lower Island Lake 193
Lower Lake Agnes 34
Lower Lamphier Lake 297
Lower Marvine Lake 254
Lower Michigan Lake 82
Lower Mitchell Lake 116
Lower Sand Creek Lake 135
Lower Sandbar Lake 47
Lower Twin Lake 50
Lower Twin Mandall
        Lakes 235
Luna Lake 245
Lyle Creek 228

Lyle Lake 228
Lynx Creek 258
Lynx Pass Lake 238

M

Macey Creek 134
Macey Lakes 134
Machin Lake 169
Mack Mesa Lakes 264
Mackinaw Lake 193
Mad Creek 243
Mahan Lake 205
Main Elk Creek 274
Major Creek 168
Mammoth Reservoir 111
Mancos River 324, 326
Mandall Creek 235
Mandall Lakes 235
Manitou Lake 94
Manville State Wildlife
        Area 35, 41
Manzanares Lake 43
Maroon Creek 230
Maroon Lake 230
Marshall Creek 297
Marten Creek 228
Martha Lake 40
Martin Creek 205
Martin Lake 148
Martinez Heflin Creek 314
Marvine Creek 254, 255
Marvine Lakes 254
Mary Loch Lake 255
Mary's Lake 117
May Creek 64
Mayhem Pond 146
McChivis Reservoir 236
McGinnis Lake 258
McIntyre Creek 49
McIntyre Lake 49

McJunkin Creek 328
McKee Pond 221
McMahon Reservoir 192
McMillan Lake 193
McPhee Reservoir 333
McQueary Lake 190
Meadow Creek 192, 274, 329
Meadow Creek Lake 274
Meadow Creek Reservoir 186
Medano Creek 174
Medano Lake 174
Meredith Reservoir 141
Meridan Lake 307
Merit Reservoir 144
Mesa Creek 160, 265
Mesa Lake 266
Mesa Lakes 266
Michigan Creek 82
Michigan Lakes 82
Michigan River, 35
    North Fork 33
    South Fork 33
Middle Boulder Creek 112
Middle Brush Creek 304
Middle Cottonwood Creek 126
Middle Creek 161, 171, 187, 190
Middle Fork Derby Creek 193
Middle Fork Fish Creek 239
Middle Fork Marvine Creek 254
Middle Fork Rabbit Creek 56
Middle Fork South Platte River 25, 85
Middle Griffith Lake 266
Middle Lake 211
Middle Quartz Creek 298
Middle Sandbar Lake 47
Middle St. Vrain Creek 116
Middle Taylor Creek 134
Middle Taylor Creek State Wildlife Area 134
Middle Thompson Creek 221
Middle Willow Creek 302
Mike Higbee State Wildlife Area 145
Military Park Reservoir 270
Mill Creek 108, 292, 294, 311, 322
Mill Creek Ponds 293
Mill Lake 298
Miller Creek 253
Millions Reservoir 164
Mills Lake 70
Milton Reservoir 75
Mineral Creek 321, 322
Miners Creek 163, 172, 201
Miramonte Reservoir 332
Mirror Creek 255
Mirror Lake 64, 205, 245, 255, 302
Mishak Lakes 172
Missouri Lakes 217
Mitchell Creek 273
Mitchell Lakes 116
Mix Lake 179
Mohawk Lakes 199
Molas Lakes 322
Monarch Lake 185
Monroe and Barnes Reservoirs 266
Montgomery Reservoir 83
Monument Creek Reservoir 271
Monument Lake 149, 197
Moody Creek 236
Moon Lake 229, 317
Moraine Lake 115
Mormon Creek 226
Mormon Lake 226

Morris Reservoir 268
Morrow Point Reservoir 283
Morton Lake 120
Mosquito Creek 83
Mosquito Lake 235
Mount Elbert Foresbay 123
Mountain Home Reservoir 174
Muckie's Lake 209
Mud Lake 193
Mud Mandall Lake 235
Muddy Creek 191, 279
Muddy Creek Reservoir 144
Muddy Pass Lake 39
Muir's Spring Ponds 77
Mulhall Lakes 217
Murphy State Wildlife
    Areas 34
Murray Lake 109
Muskrat Lake 193
Mysterious Lake 299
Mystery Lake 319
Mystic Island Lake 210

N

Narraguinnep Reservoir 333
Native Lake 122
Navajo Lake 329
Navajo Reservoir 313
Navajo River 313
Naylor Lake 109
Nee Gronda reservoir 145
Nee Noshe Reservoir 145
Nee Skah Reservoir 145
Nee So Pah Reservoir 145
Needle Creek 296, 323
Needle Creek Reservoir 296
Neva Lakes 113
Neversweat Reservoir 272
New York Lake 211

Newcomb Creek 40
Nicholls Reservoir 136
Nicholson Lake 306
Nickelson Creek 229
No Name Lake 178
Nolan Creek 210
Nolan Lake 210
Noname Creek 322
Norris Creek 41, 42
North Boulder Creek 114
North Catamount
    Reservoir 137
North Clear Creek 106
North Colony Creek 135
North Colony Lakes 135
North Cottonwood Creek 128
North Delaney Butte
    Lake 22, 38
North Fork Big Thompson
    River 70, 117
North Fork Cache la
    Poudre River 56
North Fork Colorado
    River 71
North Fork Derby Creek 193
North Fork Michigan River 33
North Fork Middle Boulder
    Creek 112
North Fork North Platte
    River 35
North Fork Reservoir 130
North Fork South Platte 95
North Halfmoon Creek 123
North Halfmoon Lakes 123
North Horn Lake 134
North Inlet Creek 66, 71
North Lake 149, 242
North Michigan Creek
    Reservoir 33
North Platte River 22, 25, 32,

37, 40, 41
North Fork 35
North Quartz Creek 298
North Shields Pond 75
North St. Vrain Creek 25,
        67, 116
North Sterling Reservoir 77
North Taylor Creek 134
North Tenmile Creek 201
North Thompson Creek 221
Notch Lake 122
Nunn Creek 49

O

Oak Creek 236, 268
Oak Lake 236
Odd Fellows State Wildlife
        Area 41
Odessa Lake 68
Officer's Gulch Pond 201
Oh Be Joyful Creek 306
O'Haver Lake 131
Ohio Creek 293
Oliver Twist Lake 83
Olney Reservoir 141
Olsen Lake 215
Onahu Creek 71
Opal Lake 313
Ophir Creek 137
Ordway Reservoir 141
Ordway Water Supply
        Pond 141
Osier Creek 25, 177
Otter Creek 205
Ouray Creek 131
Ouzel Creek 67
Ouzel Lake 67
Overland Reservoir 279
Owl Mountain State Wildlife

Area 35

P

Pagoda Lake 255
Palmer Lake 136, 197
Panhandle Creek 56
Panhandle Reservoir 57
Paonia Reservoir 280
Parachute Creek 275
Parachute Pond 264
Paradise Creek 72
Paradise Lakes 218
Parika Lake 182
Park Creek 166
Park Reservoir 270
Parvin Lake 57
Pass Creek 130, 166, 186,
        294, 302
Pass Creek Lake 130, 166
Pastorius Reservoir 324
Pasture Creek 324
Patterson Creek 261
Pauline Creek 296
Pawnee Lake 185
Peacock Pool 67
Pear Reservoir 67
Pearl Lake 157, 243, 323
Pedro Reservoir 269
Peeler Creek 307
Peeler Lake 307
Peggy Lake 37
Peltier Lake 261
Pennock Creek 61
Pennsylvania Creek 85
Percy Lake 40
Peru Creek 202
Peterson Lake 63
Peterson State Wildlife
        Area 35, 40

Petroleum Lake 231
Phillips Creek 235
Piceance Creek 253
Piedra River 314
Pierre Lakes 230
Pika Lake 116
Pine Creek 94, 106, 124,
    230, 246, 303
Pine Isle Lake 255
Piney Lake 192
Piney River 192
Pinkham Creek 33
Pinos Creek 167
Pitcairn Reservoir 268
Pitkin Lake 214
Plateau Creek 264
Platoro Reservoir 179
Platte Spring Creek 91
Plum Creek 94
Plumtaw Creeks 316
Poage Lake 165
Pole Creek 51, 155
Pole Mountain Reservoir 40
Pomeroy Lakes 129
Poncha Creek 131
Poose Creek 248
Porphyry Creek 297
Possum Creek 274
Pot Hole Lakes 303
Potato Lake 323
Poudre Lake 64, 71
Poudre Pass Creek 63
Powderhorn Creek 293
Powderhorn Lake 293
Prewitt Reservoir 77
Priest Gulch Creek 328
Prince Creek 220
Pristine Lake 242
Prospect Lake 136
Prospect Lakes 104

Prospect Ponds 75
Ptarmigan Creek 66, 72, 128
Ptarmigan Lake 128, 242, 303
Pueblo Reservoir 139
Puett Reservoir 333
Pumphouse Lake 187
Purdy Mesa Reservoir 276
Purgatorie River 138, 149

Q

Quail Lake 136
Quartz Creek 297, 310
Quartz Lake 310
Quartzite Creek 155
Queens Reservoirs 145
Quincy Reservoir 103

R

Rabbit Creek 56
Race Creek 165
Ragged Lake 209
Rainbow Falls 94
Rainbow Lake 120, 122,
    124, 126, 132, 201,
    235, 255, 288
Rainbow Lakes 42, 114
Ralph Price Reservoir 116
Ralph White Lake 246
Ramah Reservoir 136
Rampart Reservoir 136
Rams Horn Lake 235
Ranger Lakes 34
Raspberry Creek 41
Rat Creek 163
Rawah Creek 47
Rawah Lakes 47
Razor Creek 296
Red Creek 209, 287
Red Deer Lake 116

Red Dirt Reservoir 192
Red Feather Lakes 57
Red Lake 177, 209
Red Lion Management
    Pond 78
Red Mountain Creek 161, 303
Red Rock Lake 115
Red Sandstone Creek 214
Reed Reservoir 269
Regan Lake 156
Resolution Creek 218
Reynolds Lake 108, 201
Rich Creek 85
Richards State Wildlife
    Area 35
Ridgway Reservoir 277
Rifle Creek 275
Rifle Gap Reservoir 275
Rim Lake 196, 209
Rimrock Lake 268
Rincon La Osa Creek 316
Rincon La Vaca Creek 316
Rio Blanco River 313
Rio Blanco Lake 253
Rio de Los Pinos River 177
Rio Grande Reservoir 153
Rio Grande River 122, 151,
    153, 164, 167
    South Fork 164
Rio Lado Creek 328
Ripple Creek 255
Rito Alto Creek 168
Rito Alto Lake 168
Rito Blanco Creek 313
Rito Hondo Reservoir 157
Riverbend Ponds 75
Riverside Reservoir 75
Road Canyon Reservoir 157
Roan Creek 275

Roaring Fork Creek 35, 62,
    328
Roaring Fork River 23, 25,
    41, 219, 231
Roaring River 70
Rock Creek 122, 319
Rock Hole Lake 45
Rock Lake 68, 177, 179,
    319
Rocky Brook Creek 299
Rocky Ford Ponds 142
Rogers Pass Lake 111
Rolling Creek 96
Roosevelt Lakes 110
Rosa Lake 245
Rosedale Lake 129
Rosemont Reservoir 136
Rough and Tumbling Creek 85
Round Lake 39, 40, 247
Round Mountain Lake 41
Roxy Ann Lake 41
Ruby Anthracite Creek 280
Ruby Creek 157, 323
Ruby Jewel Lake 33
Ruby Lake 85, 160, 323
Ruby Lakes 231
Ruedi Reservoir 225
Runyon/Fountain Lake 140
Russell Lakes 172
Ruybalid Lake 178
Ryan Ponds 142
Ryman Creek 328

S

Sable Lake 258
Sacramento Creek 85
Saddle Creek 179
Saguache Creek 169, 171
Salmon Lake 203

Salt Creek 85
Saltada Creek 332
Same Reservoir 314
San Francisco Creek 167
San Francisco Lakes 167
San Isabel Creek 168
San Isabel Lake 168
San Juan River 310
San Luis Creek 169
San Miguel River 329, 332
       Howard Fork 331
       Lake Fork 331
Sanchez Creek 242
Sanchez Lakes 242
Sanchez Reservoir 172
Sand Creek 51, 135, 168,
      310
Sand Creek Lakes 135
Sandbar Lakes 47
Sandbeach Lake 67
Santa Marie Reservoir 161
Savage Lakes 226
Sawmill Creek 40
Sawmill Lake 40
Sawmill Ponds 105
Sawyer Lake 228
Scotch Creek 328
Scott Gomer Creek 97
Scott Lake 231
Scott Run Creek 242
Seaman Reservoir 56
Seeley Lake 75
Seepage Creek 161
Seepage Lake 161
Sellar Lake 226
Sellers-Cromwell
      Reservoir 247
Service Creek 239
Setchfield Lake 144
Seven Lakes 43

Seven Lakes Reservoir 144
Seven Sisters Lakes 216, 217
Sevenmile Creek 126
Seventh Lake 254
Severy Creek 137
Seymour Lake 39
Shadow Lake 254, 261
Shadow Mountain Lake 182
Shafer Creek 37
Shaffer Reservoir 247
Shagwa Lake 60
Shallow Lake 255
Shamrock Lake 258
Shaw Reservoir 166
Sheep Creek 57, 62, 171
Sheep Lake 280
Sheephorn Creek 192
Shelf Lake 70, 101
Shepherd Lake 196
Sheriff Reservoir 236
Sherman Lake 167
Sherry Lake 226
Sherwin Lake 108
Shingle Lake 209
Shoestring Lake 40
Short Creek 168
Sierra Vandera Creek 316
Silver Creek 107, 131
Silver Creek Lakes 131
Silver Dollar Lake 109
Silver Jack Reservoir 284
Silver King Lake 124
Silver Lake 115, 132, 272,
      321
Simpson Ponds 75
Skaguay Reservoir 136
Skillet Lake 235
Skinny Fish Creek 258
Skinny Fish Lakes 258

Sky Pond 68
Skyscraper Reservoir 114
Slack Weiss Reservoir 39
Slate Creek 203, 246
Slate Lakes 204
Slate River 306
Slater Creek 248
Slater Lake 108
Slaughterhouse Creek 169
Sleepy Cat Ponds State
        Wildlife Area 254
Slide Lake 42, 120, 255
Slide Mandall Lake 235
Sloan Lake 291
Smith Creek 234, 248
Smith Fork Creek 280
Smith Lake 234
Smith Reservoir 174
Snake Lake 60
Snake River 201
Snare Lakes 291
Snell Creek 255
Snow Lake 34
Snowball Creek 311
Snowfield Lake 224
Snowmass Creek 228
Snowmass Lake 229
Snowmass-Maroon Bells
        Wilderness Area 228
Snowslide Creek 316
Snowstorm Lake 245
Snyder Creek 82
Soap Creek 287, 288
Soda Creek 201, 240
Soldier Creek 285
Solitary Lake 193
Sopris Creek 217, 224
Sopris Lake 217
Sourdough Lakes 209
South Arkansas River 130

South Beaver Creek 288
South Boulder Creek 110
South Branch Creek 133
South Catamount Reservoir 137
South Clear Creek 160
South Colony Creek 135
South Delaney Butte Lake 38
South Fork Cache la Poudre
        River 60
South Fork Clear Creek 109
South Fork Colorado
        River 185
South Fork Derby Creek 193
South Fork Eagle River 218
South Fork Elk River 242
South Fork Michigan River 33
South Fork Middle Boulder
        Creek 113
South Fork South Platte
        River 85
South Fork White River 261
South Horn Lake 134
South Leviathan Lake 319
South Mesa Lake 266
South Platte River 23, 25, 81
        Middle Fork 83
        North Fork 95
        South Fork 85
South Platte River Canyon 94
South St. Vrain Creek 115
Spanish Creek 171
Spectacle Lake 178
Spencer Lake 305
Spike Lake 41
Spinney Mountain
        Reservoir 23, 86
Spirit Lake 72
Sprague Lake 70
Spring Creek 94, 169, 240,
        293, 299

Spring Creek Reservoir 299
Spruce Creek 68, 205
Spruce Lake 68
Square Tops Lakes 97
Squaw Creek 156
Squaw Lake 156
St. Charles Reservoir 140
St. Charles River 138
St. Louis Creek 187
St. Louis Lake 189
St. Mary's Lake 107
St Vrain Creek 114
        Middle Fork 116
        South Fork 115
Stagecoach Reservoir 238
Stagecoach State Recreation
        Area 238
Stalker Lake 78
Stambaugh Reservoir 40
Standley Lake 103
Stapp Lakes 116
Starvation Creek 131
Steamboat Lake 243
Steelman Creek 190
Steuart Lake 108
Stillwater Creek 182
Stillwater Reservoir 234
Stone Lake 185
Stoner Creek 328
Storm King Lake 319
Storm Lake 114
Strawberry Creek 146, 187
Strawberry Lake 185
Strawberry Lakes 226
Strontia Springs Reservoir 95
Stuck Creek 51
Stump Lakes 319
Sugar Bowl Lake 49
Sugarloaf Lake 209
Sullenburger Reservoir 314

Summit Creek 248, 333
Summit Lake 40, 110
Summit Reservoir 326
Sunlight Creek 319
Sunlight Lakes 319
Sunnyside Lakes 193
Sunset Lake 266
Supply Basin Lake 196
Supply Creek 182
Surprise Lake 205, 259
Swamp Lakes 122
Swan River 199
Swede Lake 261
Sweetwater Creek 196
Sweetwater Lake 196
Sweitzer Lake 277
Swift Creek 134
Sylvan Lake 210
Sylvan Lakes 120

T

Tabor Creek 231
Tabor Lake 231
Talamantes Creek 252
Tarryall Creek 25, 83
Tarryall Reservoir 83
Taylor Creek 328
Taylor Lake 303
Taylor Reservoir 302
Taylor River 298
Teal Lake 40
Tellerium Creek 303
Tellerium Lake 226, 303
Tenmile Creek 200, 322
Tennessee Creek 120
Terrace Reservoir 172
Teter State Wildlife Area 81
Texas Creek 160, 302
Texas Creek Lakes 302

The Loch 68
Thomas Lakes 220
Thompson Creek 221
Thompson Lake 289
Three Forks 179
Three Island Creek 242
Three Island Lake 242
Three Lakes 122
Threemile Creek 97
Thunder Lake 67
Thurston Reservoir 145
Tiago Lake 40
Timber Creek 71
Timber Lake 45, 71, 142, 178
Timberline Lake 62, 120
Timpas Creek 142
Tipperary Lake 205
Tobacco Lake 179
Tomahawk State Wildlife Area 25
Tomichi Creek 296
Tonahutu Creek 71
Torsido Creek 174
Totten Reservoir 333
Trail Creek 187, 242
Trail Lake 178
Trap Creek 44, 63
Trap Lake 63
Trappers Lake 25, 258
Treasure Vault Lake 215
Triangle Creek 210
Trinchera Creek 174
Trinidad Reservoir 149
Trinity Lake 319
Trio Reservoir 270
Triple Lakes 115
Troublesome Creek 191
Trout Creek 85, 92, 125, 160, 245

Trout Lake 161, 331
Trujillo Meadows Reservoir 177
Truro Creek 231
Truro Lake 231
Tucker Ponds 166
Tuhare Lakes 216
Tunnel Lake 129
Turkey Creek 311
Turkey Creek Lake 311
Turks Pond State Wildlife Area 146
Turquoise Lake 120
Turquoise Lakes 211, 215
Turret Creek 196
Turtle Creek 171
Twelvemile Creek 85
Twelvemile Lakes 86
Twilight Creek 323
Twilight Peaks Lakes 323
Twin Crater Lakes 45
Twin Lake 37
Twin Lake East 45
Twin Lake West 45
Twin Lakes 178, 270, 305
Twin Lakes Reservoir 123
Twin Ute Lakes 156
Two Buttes Reservoir 145
Two Ledge Reservoir 39

U

Uncompahgre River 276
Uneva Lake 201
Union Creek 123
Upper Big Creek Lake 43
Upper Camp Lake 48
Upper Cataract Lake 205
Upper Chicago Lake 107
Upper Coney Lake 116

Upper Cottonwood Lake 168
Upper Crystal 198
Upper Diamond Lake 112
Upper Eagle River 218
Upper Eaglesmere 205
Upper Eggleston Lake 269
Upper Fourmile Lake 311
Upper Geneva Lake 224
Upper Hotel Lake 269
Upper Island Lake 193
Upper La Jara Creek 174
Upper Lake 185
Upper Lake Agnes 34
Upper Lamphier Lake 297
Upper Mandall Lake 235
Upper Marvine Lake 254
Upper Mitchell Lake 116
Upper Sand Creek Lake 135
Upper Sandbar Lake 47
Upper Slide Lake 41
Upper Stillwater Reservoir 234
Upper Twin Lake 50
Urad Reservoir 109
Ute Creek 155, 254
Ute Lake 37, 155, 156

V

Vallecito Creek 317
Vallecito Lake 319
Vallecito Reservoir 317
Valmont Reservoir 112
Vance Creek 110
Vasquez Creek 187
Vaughn Lake 248
Vega Reservoir 264
Vela Reservoir 270
Venable Creek 134
Venable Lakes 134
Ventero Creek 172

Verde Lakes 321
Verner State Wildlife Area 37
Victoria Lake 41
Virginia Gulch Creek 319
Virginia Lake 122

W

Walden Ponds 105
Wall Lake 261
Walters Lake 192
Walton Creek 239
Wannamaker Creek 171
Ward Creek 269
Ward Creek Reservoir 268
Ward Road Pond 105
Washington Gulch Creek 307
Watanga Creek 183
Watanga Lake 183
Water Dog Lake 266
Waterdog Lake 289
Waterdog Lakes 130
Waterton Canyon 94
Watson Creek 235
Watson Lake 55, 75
Webb Lake 323
Weir and Johnson
        Reservoir 270
Weller Lake 231
Wellington Lake 96
Wellington Reservoir 75
Weminuche Creek 156, 316
West (Twin) Lake 60
West Beaver Creek 288
West Branch Creek 45
West Brush Creek 210, 304
West Creek 67, 70, 92
West Cross Creek 215
West Cross Creek Lakes 215
West Elk Creek 287

West Fork Lake 43
West Fork Marvine Creek 254
West Fork San Juan River 310
West Griffith Lake 266
West Indian Creek 174
West Lost Lakes 247
West Maroon Creek 230
West Muddy Creek 279
West Snowmass Creek 229
West Sopris Creek 224
West Tenmile Creek 201
West Tennessee Creek 120
West Tennessee Lakes 120
Whale Creek 40
Wheeler Lakes 83, 201
Whiskey Creek 248
White Creek 313
White Owl Lake 196
White River 252, 253
        South Fork 261
Whitney Lakes 216
Wigwam Creek 91
Wild Cherry Creek 168
Wildcat Creek 307
Williams Creek 316
Williams Creek Reservoir 316
Williams Fork Lake 316
Williams Fork Reservoir 189
Williams Fork River 190, 246
Williams Lake 224
Willis Lake 123
Willow Creek 35, 71, 163,
        167, 186, 203,
        230, 242, 302
Willow Creek Lake 168
Willow Creek Reservoir 186
Willow Lake 39, 156, 230
Willow Lakes 203
Windsor Lake 75, 122
Wolf Lake 148

Wolford Mountain Reservoir 191
Wolverine Basin 242
Wolverine Creek 242
Wolverine Lake 242
Wood Lakes 226
Woodland Lake 114
Woods Lake 109, 332
Woody Creek 230

Y

Yamcolo Reservoir 235
Yampa Reservoir 235
Yampa River 233, 248
Yank Creek 221
Yankee Doodle Lake 110
Yellow Lake 273
Youngs Creek Reservoirs 269
Youngs Lake 271
Ypsilon Lake 70
Yule Creek 221
Yule Lakes 221

Z

Zimmerman Lake 63
Zinn Ponds 94